COLLINS
DICTIONARY
OF
LITERARY
QUOTATIONS

COLLINS
DICTIONARY
OF
LITERARY
QUOTATIONS

COMPILED BY MEIC STEPHENS

HarperCollins*Publishers*

HarperCollins Publishers
P.O. Box, Glasgow G4 0NB

First published in this edition 1991
First published in hardback by Routledge as *A Dictionary of Literary Quotations*

© Meic Stephens 1990

Reprint 10 9 8 7 6 5 4 3 2 1 0

ISBN 0 00 434378 6

A catalogue record for this book is available from the British Library.

Printed in Great Britain by HarperCollins Manufacturing, Glasgow

CONTENTS

PREFACE

This dictionary was begun more than twenty years ago when I fell into the habit of jotting down, in a desk-diary, extracts from whatever I happened to be reading from day to day. Thereafter it grew, casually but steadily, until I had so many quotations that to publish them in book form seemed the most sensible way of putting my compendium to some practical use.

It is inevitable that such a work must reflect the compiler's own reading, which in my case I readily admit to have been unsystematic and, it might even be thought, quite idiosyncratic. Nevertheless, I have been able to draw on several literatures, both ancient and modern, and on books famous and obscure, so that although readers may not find here all the quotations they might have expected, if they discover something entertaining or informative with which they were previously unfamiliar, then my purpose will have been served.

The quotations gathered in this book, some 3250 in all, are 'literary' in the sense that they refer to literature, writers, writing, books and reading, defined in a fairly broad way and taking in a number of contiguous areas such as journalism and the book-trade. This is an enormous field and I have had to restrict my choice in several ways. For example, I have not included quotations about specific authors, however memorable, for the reason that they are easily found elsewhere. Many others were discarded because, in the time available for the book's compilation, I could no longer put my hand on the exact sources.

A list of the headings under which the material has been arranged appears on page v. They are presented in a single, alphabetical sequence, with cross-references to other headings where related quotations may be found. Sometimes the principle of allocation may appear to be somewhat arbitrary, and especially so when the quotation refers to more than one subject, but the reader in search of a particular item will be helped by the Author and Subject Indexes which form the latter part of the dictionary. As for the arrangement of the quotations under each heading, it has been done with the browser in mind: the juxtaposition of contrasting opinions, or in some instances the cumulative effect of similar ones, has an elegant simplicity that makes for stimulating reading.

In this last detail, as in the distribution of the quotations under the various headings, I have relied on the expertise of Betty Palmer.

For their response to my appeal for suitable material I should like to thank the following: Brian Aldiss, John Barnie, Freddie Baveystock, Duncan Bush, Tony Curtis, Walford Davies, Dorothy Eagle, Raymond Garlick, David Gunston, David Hughes, Glyn Tegai Hughes, Bobi Jones, Richard Joseph, Suzanne Kalweit, H.R.F. Keating, Alan Llwyd, Gerda Mayer, the late D. Parry Michael, Derek Parker, Margaret Payne, Alun Rees, Trevor Royle, Morris Venables and Irving Wallace.

I am also grateful to Mark Barragry of Routledge for his genial interest in the work's progress, to my secretary Angela Howells, and as always to my wife Ruth for her encouragement and practical assistance.

The book is inscribed with my son's name, in the hope that he will grow up to share his father's love of books and reading.

Meic Stephens
Cardiff

Cyflwynir y llyfr hwn i

HUW MEREDYDD STEPHENS

fy mab

1 ACADEME

1 And seek for truth in the groves of
Academe.
Horace, *Epistles*

2 The whole business [academic criticism] is a
subsidiary undertaking, like extracting
useful chemicals from smoke.
John Cheever, in interview in *Writers at
Work* (5th series, 1981)

3 The colleges, whilst they provide us with
libraries, furnish no professor of books; and,
I think, no chair is so much wanted.
Ralph Waldo Emerson, 'Books'

4 A mere scholar, who knows nothing but
books, must be ignorant even of them.
William Hazlitt, *The Ignorance of the
Learned* (1821)

5 There is more ado to interpret
interpretations than to interpret things, and
more books upon books than upon any
other subject; we do nothing but comment
upon one another.
Michel de Montaigne, 'Of Experience',
Essays (1580–88)

6 Every place swarms with commentaries; of
authors there is great scarcity.
Michel de Montaigne, 'Of Experience',
Essays (1580–88)

7 Gentlemen who use MSS as drunkards use
lamp-posts — not to light them on their way
but to dissimulate their instability.
A.E. Housman, in introduction to his
edition of the poems of Manilius (1903)

8   Follow'd then
A classic lecture, rich in sentiment,
With scraps of thunderous Epic lilted out
By violet-hooded Doctors, elegies
And quoted odes, and jewels five-words
        long,
That on the stretch'd forefinger of all Time
Sparkle for ever.
Alfred, Lord Tennyson, *The Princess* (1847)

9 Bald heads forgetful of their sins,
Old, learned, respectable bald heads
Edit and annotate the lines
That young men, tossing on their beds,
Rhymed out in love's despair
To flatter beauty's ignorant ear.
W.B. Yeats, 'The Scholars'

10 I cannot see that lectures can do so much
good as reading the books from which the
lectures are taken.
Samuel Johnson, quoted in James Boswell,
Life of Samuel Johnson (1791)

11 It depends on what we read, after all manner
of Professors have done their best for us.
Thomas Carlyle, *On Heroes, Hero-Worship
and the Heroic in History* (1840)

12 I think that one possible definition of our
modern culture is that it is one in which
nine-tenths of our intellectuals can't read
any poetry.
Randall Jarrell, remark to friends

13 It is bad that English is taught in
universities. It's bad over here, where it's
sometimes not badly taught, but over there
(in the United States), where it's horribly
badly taught, it simply stops the thing in its
traces . . . It's an absurd error to put modern
English literature in the curriculum. You
should read contemporary literature for
pleasure or not read it at all. You shouldn't
be taught to monkey with it.
Rebecca West, in interview in *Writers at
Work* (8th series, 1984)

14 Our American professors like their literature
clear and cold and pure and very dead.
Sinclair Lewis, in speech on receiving the
Nobel Prize for Literature (12 Dec. 1930)

15 You cannot lecture on really pure poetry any
more than you can talk about the
ingredients of pure water — it is
adulterated, methylated, sanded poetry that
makes the best lectures.
Virginia Woolf, *The Second Common
Reader* (1932)

16 I think that journalism is a healthier
occupation for a writer than teaching,
especially if he teaches literature. By
teaching literature the writer gets
accustomed to analyzing literature all the
time.
Isaac Bashevis Singer, in interview in
Writers at Work (5th series, 1981)

17 The primary object of a student of literature
is to be delighted. His duty is to enjoy
himself, his efforts should be directed to
developing his faculty of appreciation.
David Cecil, *The Fine Art of Reading* (1957)

18 Gentlemen of the universities, you should
most of you, on poetry, be silent, outside

your tutorials or your lecture-rooms, remembering that in the last four hundred years few persons — and those poets — have written helpfully about poems.
Geoffrey Grigson, *The Private Art* (1982)

19 Poetic diction. What a forbidding, dry biscuit of a term that sounds! And what hungry generations of scholastic weevils have battened upon it!
C. Day-Lewis, 'The Colloquial Element in English Poetry'

20 There is a type of student . . . who has a curious subconscious itch in the presence of poetry; an itch for explaining it, in the hope of explaining it away.
G.K. Chesterton, *Chaucer* (1932)

21 A blonde girl is bent over a poem. With a pencil sharp as a lancet she transfers the words to a blank page and changes them into strokes, accents, caesuras. The lament of a fallen poet now looks like a salamander eaten away by ants.
Zbigniew Herbert, 'Episode in a Library'

22 To underline a poem word by word is the work of a misguided schoolmaster.
Peter Warlock, in *The New Age* (1917)

23 Find me one good poet who thinks that the academic concern for literature isn't toxic and depressant.
Geoffrey Grigson, *The Private Art* (1982)

24 One performs autopsies only on corpses. The idea of lecturing on a living poet is all wrong.
Robert Graves, in *Esquire* (1970)

25 The world is full of young men coming down from the universities with the world's greatest novel that no one wants to read.
Desmond Bagley, in *The Guardian* (1972)

26 Any man who becomes a novelist forfeits all the rights to scholarship.
Anthony Powell, remark on BBC Radio 3 (6 Oct. 1980)

27 I never went to college. But I have lectured on campuses for a quarter-century, and it is my impression that after taking a course in The Novel, it is an unusual student who would ever want to read a novel again.
Gore Vidal, in interview in *Writers at Work* (5th series, 1981)

28 Eventually the novel will simply be an academic exercise, written by academics to be used in classrooms in order to test the ingenuity of students.
Gore Vidal, in interview in *Writers at Work* (5th series, 1981)

29 A writer who lives long enough becomes an academic subject and almost qualified to teach it himself.
Harold Rosenberg, *Discovering the Present* (1973)

30 Vladimir Nabokov is surely the most preposterous Transylvanian monster ever to be created by American Academe. He is not a writer at all but a looming beast that stalks the Old Dark House of Campus Literature.
John Osborne, 'Grievous Bodily Harm', in *The Anti-Booklist* (ed. Brian Redhead and Kenneth McLeish, 1981)

31 My method of teaching precluded genuine contact with my students. At best they regurgitated a few bits of my brain during examination.
Vladimir Nabokov, in interview in *Writers at Work* (4th series, 1977)

32 Fourteen years in the professor dodge has taught me that one can argue ingeniously on behalf of any theory, applied to any piece of literature.
Robert B. Parker, in *Murder Ink* (ed. Dilys Winn, 1977)

33 And why does Gratt teach English? Why,
     because
A law school felt he could not learn the
     laws.
Donald Hall, 'Professor Gratt'

34 Mosher came out into the reception room, looking like a professor of English literature who has not approved of the writings of anybody since Sir Thomas Browne.
James Thurber, *The Years with Ross* (1959)

35 College professors in one-building universities on the prairie, still hoping, at the age of sixty, to get their whimsical essays into the *Atlantic Monthly*.
H.L. Mencken, in *Smart Set* (Nov. 1921)

36 Now that I am Oxford Professor of Poetry,
     Stephen Spender,
I would just like to say Tough Luck, Baby
But that's the way the cookie crumbles;
     Someone has to lose.
Clive James, parody of poem by John Wain, 'Unsolicited Letters to Five Artists'

37 Finally I was given the Chair of comparative
       Ambiguity
    At Armpit University, Java.
    It didn't keep me busy,
    But it kept me quiet.
    It seemed like poetry had been safely tucked
       up for the night.
    Adrian Mitchell, 'The Oxford Hysteria of
    English Poetry'

38 Words never let you conquer them by force,
    But certain possibilities remain.
    I'll make a new anthology. And of course
    I'll have to take up lecturing again.
    Colin Falck, 'Keeping up with Kingsley', in
    Taking Off (ed. Tim Dooley, 1984)

39 Once I went to the University of Tennessee
    in Knoxville with a prepared lecture. When I
    got there I discovered I'd left the lecture at
    home. So I had to get up on stage and
    improvise, which infuriated the professors.
    They were outraged.
    Tennessee Williams, in interview in *Writers
    at Work* (6th series, 1984)

40 I find people call it research nowadays if
    they ever have to look anything up in a
    book.
    Margaret Lane, *A Night at Sea* (1964)

41 Commit no thesis.
    John Knoppswood, 'Inscription for a poet's
    tomb'

42 The average PhD thesis is nothing but the
    transference of bones from one graveyard to
    another.
    J. Frank Dobie, *A Texan in England* (1945)

43 It is not for nothing that the scholar
    invented the PhD thesis as his principal
    contribution to literary form. The PhD
    thesis is the perfect image of his world. It is
    work done for the sake of doing work —
    perfectly concientious, perfectly laborious,
    perfectly irresponsible.
    Archibald MacLeish, *The Irresponsibles*
    (1940)

44 The avocation of assessing the failures of
    better men can be turned into a comfortable
    livelihood, providing you back it up with
    PhD.
    Nelson Algren, in interview in *Writers at
    Work* (1st series, 1958)

45 'Pushing up theses', that is the euphemism
    which men of letters use for being dead; a
    long littleness of dons lies ahead of us,

unless we have been afflicted with the curse
of lucidity.
Cyril Connolly, *Previous Convictions*
(1963)

46 Who Killed James Joyce?
    I, said the commentator,
    I killed James Joyce
    For my graduation.

    What weapon was used
    To slay mighty Ulysses?
    The weapon that was used
    Was a Harvard thesis . . .
    Patrick Kavanagh, 'Who killed James
    Joyce?'

47 Dankwerts, scholarship boy from the slums,
    One of many, studied three years for the
       Tripos,
    Honours, English; grew a beard, imitated
       the gesture
    And the insistent deliberate (but not
       dogmatic)
    'There!' of his supervisor. For a time
    The mimesis was startling. Dankwerts knew
    Uncannily what was good, what bad.
    Life and earning a living, extra muros, for a
       time afterwards,
    Left him hard up: people in their ambiguity
    Nuisances.
    David Holbrook, 'Living? Our Supervisors
    Will Do That For Us!'

2 AGENTS

1 The world is a peculiar place, but it has
   nothing on the world of books. This is
   largely a fantasy world in which the pecking
   order goes as follows: if you can't cope with
   life, write about it; if you can't write,
   publish; if you can't get a job in publishing,
   become a literary agent; if you are a failed
   literary agent — God help you!
   Colin Haycraft, in *The Sunday Telegraph*
   (20 July 1986)

2 The relation of the agent to the publisher is
   the same as that of the knife to the throat.
   Anonymous

3 Pimps who . . . don't do anything, don't
   make anything — they just stand there and
   take their cut.
   Jean Giraudoux, *The Madwoman of
   Chaillot* (1945)

4 When asked whether I believe in literary agents, I always feel inclined to reply as I should were I asked if I 'believed' in spectacles: 'Yes, if you need them and can be quite sure of getting the right kind.'
Stanley Unwin, *The Truth about Publishing* (1926)

5 If you're a writer there will come at least one morning in your life when you wake up and want to kill your agent.
Bernice Rubens, quoted in Anthony Blond, *The Book Book* (1985)

6 Economically, the agent is the only figure behind whom the apparently fierce but actually timid and incompetent individualism of authors can really unite without having to admit it.
V.S. Pritchett, in *The Author* (1940)

7 As far as I'm concerned, Giles takes 10% of my income; as far as he's concerned, I take 90% of his.
Fay Weldon, of her agent Giles Gordon, quoted by Giles Gordon, 'I can't get an agent!' in *The Author* (Spring 1987)

8 Let every eye negotiate for itself, and trust no agent.
William Shakespeare, *Much Ado About Nothing*

ALLEGORY
See FIGURES OF SPEECH

3 ALPHABET

1 The invention of the alphabet will produce forgetfulness in the minds of those who learn it through the neglect of memory, for through trusting to writing, they will remember outwardly by means of foreign marks, and not inwardly by means of their own faculties.
Socrates

2 I struggled through the alphabet as if it had been a bramble-bush; getting considerably worried and scratched by every letter.
Charles Dickens, *Great Expectations* (1860)

3 God have mercy on the sinner
Who must write with no dinner,

No gravy and no grub,
No pewter and no pub,

No belly and no bowels,
Only consonants and vowels.
John Crowe Ransom, 'Survey of Literature'

4 AMBITION

1 To commence author is to claim praise, and no man can justly aspire to honour, but at the hazard of disgrace.
Samuel Johnson, *The Rambler* (1750–2)

2 Oh, to be a *writer*, a real writer given up to it and to it alone!
Katherine Mansfield, *Diary* (29 Feb. 1920)

3 I am earnest, terribly earnest. Carlyle bending over the history of Frederick called the Great was a mere trifle, a volatile butterfly, in comparison.
Joseph Conrad, in letter to Edward Garnett

4 A poet's hope: to be,
like some valley cheese,
local, but prized elsewhere.
W.H. Auden, 'Shorts'

5 I'd like to be the poet my father reads!
Tony Harrison, 'The Rhubarbarians'

5 AMERICA

1 An interviewer asked me what book I thought best represented the modern American Woman. All I could think of to answer was: Madame Bovary.
Mary McCarthy, 'Characters in Fiction'

2 Our fundamental want today in the United States is of a class, and the clear idea of a class, of native authors, literatures, far different, far higher in grade, than any yet known, sacerdotal, modern, fit to cope with our occasions, lands, permeating the whole mass of American mentality, taste, belief, breathing into it a new breath of life, giving it decision.
Walt Whitman, *Democratic Vistas* (1870)

3 Let us await the great American novel!
   Archibald MacLeish, 'Critical Observations'

4 Alas! for the South, her books have grown
         fewer —
   She never was much given to literature.
   J. Gordon Coogler, 'Alas! for the South!'

5 Only one out of five in America, it is said,
   are readers of 'books'. But even this small
   number read far too much.
   Henry Miller, *The Books in my Life* (1952)

6 All modern American literature comes from
   one book by Mark Twain called
   Huckleberry Finn.
   Ernest Hemingway, *The Green Hills of
   Africa* (1935)

7 God bless the U.S.A., so large,
   So friendly, and so rich.
   W.H. Auden, 'On the Circuit'

8 All right, if I go to America, I'll settle down
   to a book; and if I don't go to America I
   will, too.
   Malcolm Muggeridge, *The Diaries of
   Malcolm Muggeridge* (ed. John
   Bright-Holmes, 1981)

9 In America, the majority raises formidable
   barriers around the liberty of opinion:
   within these barriers, an author may write
   what he pleases; but woe to him if he goes
   beyond them.
   Alexis de Tocqueville, *Democracy in
   America* (1835–9)

10 In America the race goes to the loud, the
    solemn, the hustler. If you think you're a
    great writer, you must say that you are.
    Gore Vidal, in interview in *Writers at Work*
    (5th series, 1981)

11 In America they make too much fuss of
    poets; in London they make too little.
    Caitlin Thomas, widow of Dylan Thomas,
    Caitlin: a Warring Absence (1986)

12 In the Soviet Union a writer who is critical,
    as we know, is taken to a lunatic asylum. In
    the United States, he's taken to a talk show.
    Carlos Fuentes, in interview in *Writers at
    Work* (6th series, 1984)

13 In other countries, art and literature are left
    to a lot of shabby bums living in attics and
    feeding on booze and spaghetti, but in
    America the successful writer or
    picture-painter is indistinguishable from any
    other decent business man.
    Sinclair Lewis, *Babbitt* (1922)

14 You talk like an American novel.
    Henry James, *The Tragic Muse* (1890)

6 ANTHOLOGY

1 All these things heer collected, are not mine,
   But diverse grapes make but one sort of
         wine;
   So I, from many learned authors took
   The various matters printed in this book.
   What's not mine own by me shall not be
         father'd,
   The most part I in fifty years have gather'd,
   Some things are very good, pick out the
         best,
   Good wits compiled them, and I wrote the
         rest.
   If thou dost buy it, it will quit thy cost,
   Read it, and all thy labour is not lost.
   John Taylor, 'An Arrant Thief' (1652)

2 I have gathered a posie of other men's
   flowers and nothing but the thread that
   binds them is my own.
   Michel de Montaigne, *Essays* (1580–88)

3 Miscellanists are the most popular writers
   among every people; for it is they who form
   a communication between the learned and
   the unlearned, and, as it were, throw a
   bridge between those two great divisions of
   the public.
   Isaac D'Israeli, 'Miscellanists', *Literary
   Character of Men of Genius* (1795)

4 I am not against anthologies, as long as they
   are not attempts to enforce a poor idea of
   poetry, as long as they discover, and as long
   as they are born of excitement and
   generosity.
   Geoffrey Grigson, *The Private Art* (1982)

5 A well-chosen anthology is a complete
   dispensary of medicine for the more
   common mental disorders, and may be used
   as much for prevention as cure.
   Robert Graves, *On English Poetry* (1962)

6 The anthology . . . tears the soul out and
   labels its squirming parts.
   Frank Jennings, *This is Reading* (1965)

7 The more honest the private anthology,
   particularly when the author is a
   well-known poet, the more dangerous is it
   when put on the market: its publication

makes it appear an act of criticism instead of a mere expression of taste.
Robert Graves, 'True Anthologies and Popular Anthologies', *Anthologies* (1927)

8 To my dear sons Michael and Nicholas without whose school bills this anthology would not have been made.
Dwight Macdonald, dedication in *Parodies* (1960)

7 ANTI-BOOK

1 Books do not teach the use of books.
Anonymous

2 Another damned thick, square book! Always scribble, scribble! Eh! Mr Gibbon?
Duke of Gloucester, upon accepting the second volume of *A History of the Decline and Fall of the Roman Empire* from its author (1781)

3 Big book, big bore.
Callimachus, *The Deipnosophists*

4 Get thee gone then, thou cursed book, which hath seduced so many precious soules; get thee gone, thou corrupt, rotten book, earth to earth, and dust to dust; get thee gone into the place of rottenness, that thou mayest rot with thy author, and see corruption.
Francis Cheynell, *The Sickness, Heresy, Death and Burial of William Chillingworth . . . and a Short Oration at the Burial of His Heretical Book* (1644)

5 A book displeases you? Who forces you to read it?
Nicolas Boileau-Despréaux, *Satires* (1666)

6 Weak men are the worse for the good sense they read in books because it furnisheth them only with more matter to mistake.
Marquess of Halifax, *Moral Thoughts and Reflections* (late 17th cent.)

7 Books, books. One reads so many, and one sees so few people and so little of the world. Great thick books about the universe and the mind and ethics. You've no idea how many there are. I must have read twenty or thirty tons of them in the last five years. Twenty tons of ratiocination, weighted with that, one's pushed out into the world.
Aldous Huxley, *Crome Yellow* (1921)

8 I hate books, for they only teach people to talk about what they do not understand.
Jean-Jacques Rousseau, *Emile* (1762)

9 There can hardly be a stranger commodity in the world than books. Printed by people who don't understand them; sold by people who don't understand them; bound, criticized and read by people who don't understand them; and now even written by people who don't understand them.
Georg Christoph Lichtenberg, *Aphorisms* (1764–99)

10 And to feed on books, for a philosopher or a poet, is still to starve. Books can help him to acquire form, or to avoid pitfalls; they cannot supply him with substance, if he is to have any.
George Santayana, 'The Genteel Tradition in American Philosophy', *The Genteel Tradition: Nine Essays* (1967)

11 Books tell me so much that they inform me of nothing.
St John de Crevecoeur, *Letters from an American Farmer* (1782)

12 People in general do not willingly read, if they can have anything else to amuse them.
Samuel Johnson, quoted in James Boswell, *Life of Samuel Johnson* (1791)

13 Most of today's books have an air of having been written in one day from books read the night before.
Nicolas-Sebastien Chamfort, *Maximes et pensées* (1805)

14 Some books seem to have been written, not to teach us anything, but to let us know that the author has known something.
J.W. Goethe, *Maxims and Reflections* (early 19th cent.)

15 Beware you be not swallowed up in books! An ounce of love is worth a pound of knowledge.
John Wesley, quoted in R. Southey, *Life of Wesley* (1820)

16 Books are less often made use of as spectacles to look at nature with than as blinds to keep out its strong light and shifting scenery from weak eyes and indolent dispositions.
William Hazlitt, *The Ignorance of the Learned* (1821)

17 Have you any right to read, especially novels, until you have exhausted the best

part of the day in some employment that is called practical?
Charles Dudley Warner, 'First Study', *Backlog Studies* (1873)

18 Books are a world in themselves, it is true; but they are not the only world. The world itself is a volume larger than all the libraries in it.
William Hazlitt, 'The Plain Speaker', *On the Conversation of Authors* (1846)

19 The enormous multiplication of books in every branch of knowledge is one of the greatest evils of this age; since it presents one of the most serious obstacles to the acquisition of correct information, by throwing in the reader's way piles of lumber in which he must painfully grope for the scraps of useful matter, peradventure interspersed.
Edgar Allan Poe, *Marginalia* (1844–9)

20 We are too civil to books. For a few golden sentences we will turn over and actually read a volume of four or five hundred pages.
Ralph Waldo Emerson, *Journals* (1841)

21 Books are made not like children but like pyramids . . . and they're just as useless! and they stay in the desert! . . . Jackals piss at their foot and the bourgeois climb up on them.
Gustave Flaubert, in letter to Ernest Feydeau (November 1857)

22 Burn the libraries, for all their value is in the Koran.
Caliph Omar, on the fall of Alexandria (641)

23 If books do not assist to make us better and more substantial men, they are only providing fuel for a fire larger, and more utterly destructive, than that which consumed the Library of the Ptolemies.
Revd F.D. Maurice, 'On Books', *The Friendship of Books* (1893)

24 In old days books were written by men of letters and read by the public. Nowadays books are written by the public and read by nobody.
Oscar Wilde, in *The Saturday Review* (1894)

25 Thank God, Achilles and Don Quixote are well enough known so that we can dispense with reading Homer and Cervantes.
Jules Renard, *Journal* (1895)

26 Books, I don't know what you see in them . . . I can understand a person reading them, but I can't for the life of me see why people have to write them.
Peter Ustinov, *Photo-Finish* (1962)

27 How our life has been warped by books! We are not contented with realities: we crave conclusions.
David Grayson, *Adventures in Contentment* (1907)

28 In the main there are two sorts of books; those that no one reads, and those that no one ought to read.
H.L. Mencken, *Prejudices* (1919)

29 I never was much on this book reading, for it takes 'em too long to describe the color of the eyes of all the characters.
Will Rogers, *Autobiography* (1949)

30 A book is not harmless merely because no one is consciously offended by it.
T.S. Eliot, *Religion and Literature* (1935)

31 I have only read one book in my life, and that is *White Fang*. It's so frightfully good I've never bothered to read another.
Nancy Mitford, *The Pursuit of Love* (1945)

32 Very few books of any nationality are worth reading. People read to kill time; consequently it is no more objection to a book that it is not worth reading than it is to a pack of cards that it does not pile up treasures in heaven.
George Bernard Shaw, remark

33 It was a book to kill time for those who like it better dead.
Rose Macaulay, attr.

34 Tom came to Dick to get advice:
'What present should I give my son?'
Dick thought a book might be quite nice,
'A book? Oh no — you know, he's got one!
Erich Kästner, 'Woche des Buches', in *Die kleine Freiheit* (1976)

35 Gee, dat day ah read a book — some day ah'm gonna do it again!
Jimmy Durante, remark, *c.* 1956

36 Few books today are forgivable.
R.D. Laing, in introduction to *The Politics of Experience* (1967)

37 Don't read much now: the dude
Who lets the girl down before
The hero arrives, the chap
Who's yellow and keeps the store,

Seem far too familiar. Get stewed:
Books are a load of crap.
Philip Larkin, 'A Study of Reading Habits'

38 The most delightful books are the ones
which aren't really books.
Kurt Tucholsky, *Gesammelte Werke*
(1960–62)

39 I hate all Boets and Bainters.
George I, quoted in Lord Campbell, *Lives of
the Chief Justices* (1857)

8 APHORISM

1 What is an Epigram? a dwarfish whole,
Its body brevity, and wit its soul.
Samuel Taylor Coleridge, 'Epigram'

2 'Tis easy to write epigrams nicely, but to
write a book is hard.
Martial, *Epigrams*

3 Our live experiences, fixed in aphorisms,
        stiffen into cold epigram,
Our heart's blood, as we write with it, turns
        to mere dull ink.
F.H. Bradley, *Aphorisms* (1930)

4 I don't see how an epigram, being a bolt
from the blue, with no introduction or cue,
ever gets itself writ.
William James, *Letters* (1920)

5 An aphorism is never exactly truthful. It is
either a half-truth or a truth and a half.
Karl Kraus, *Aphorisms and More Aphorisms*
(1909)

6 There are no sentences, no maxims, no
aphorisms, of which the opposite cannot be
written.
Paul Léautaud, *Propos d'un jour* (1969)

7 Aphorisms are salted, not sugared, almonds
at Reason's feast.
Logan Pearsall Smith, *Afterthoughts* (1931)

8 Epigram: a platitude with vine-leaves in its
hair.
H.L. Mencken, *A Book of Burlesques*
(1916)

9 It's the danger of the aphorism that it states
too much in trying to be small.
George Douglas, *The House with the Green
Shutters* (1901)

10 In lapidary inscriptions a man is not upon
oath.
Samuel Johnson, quoted in James Boswell,
Life of Samuel Johnson (1791)

11 He liked those literary cooks
Who skim the cream of others' books;
And ruin half an author's graces
By plucking bon-mots from their places.
Hannah More, 'Florio'

12 The great writers of aphorisms read as if
they had all known each other well.
Elias Canetti, *The Human Province* (1978)

13 If, with the literate, I am
Impelled to try an epigram,
I never seek to take the credit;
We all assume that Oscar said it.
Dorothy Parker, 'Oscar Wilde', in *Sunset
Gun* (1928)

9 AUDIENCE

1 He who does not expect a million readers
should not write a line.
J.W. Goethe, quoted in Johann Peter
Eckermann, *Conversations with Goethe* (12
May 1825)

2 I never wrote one single Line of Poetry with
the least Shadow of public thought.
John Keats, in a letter to John Hamilton
Reynolds (9 April 1818)

3 The truly great book does not find its
readers, it creates them.
Dagobert D. Runes, *Treasury of Thought*
(1966)

4 To have great poets, there must be great
audiences, too.
Walt Whitman, 'Ventures, on an Old
Theme', *Notes Left Over* (1899)

5 A book, like a landscape, is a state of
consciousness varying with readers.
Ernest Dimnet, *The Art of Thinking* (1928)

6 The spirit of the poet craves spectators —
even if only buffaloes.
Friedrich Nietzsche, 'On Poets', *Thus Spake
Zarathustra* (1883–92)

7 What is responsible for the success of many
works is the rapport between the mediocrity

of the author's ideas and the mediocrity of the public's.
Nicolas-Sebastien-Chamfort, *Maximes et pensées* (1805)

8 Of all artificial relations formed between mankind, the most capricious and variable is that of author and reader.
Earl of Shaftesbury, *Characteristics of Men, Manners, Opinion and Times* (c. 1713)

9 The ideal audience the poet imagines consists of the beautiful who go to bed with him, the powerful who invite him to dinner and tell him secrets of state, and his fellow-poets. The actual audience he gets consists of myopic schoolteachers, pimply young men who eat in cafeterias, and his fellow-poets. This means, in fact, he writes for his fellow-poets.
W.H. Auden, 'Squares and Oblongs', *Poets at Work* (1948)

10 We are all poets when we read a poem well.
Thomas Carlyle, *On Heroes, Hero-Worship and the Heroic in History* (1840)

11 We do not know more than a handful of our readers.
Geoffrey Grigson, *The Private Art* (1982)

12 A book is a bottle thrown into the sea on which this motto must be stuck: catch me who can.
Alfred de Vigny, *Journal d'un poète* (1867)

13 A writer doesn't write for his readers, does he? Yet he has to take elementary precautions all the same to keep them comfortable.
Graham Greene, *A Burnt-out Case* (1961)

14 He that writes to himself writes to an eternal public.
Ralph Waldo Emerson, 'Spiritual Laws', *Essays* (1841)

15 Writing is one of the few professions left where you take all the responsibility for what you do. It's really dangerous and ultimately destroys you as a writer if you start thinking about responses to your work or what your audience needs.
Erica Jong, *The Craft of Poetry* (ed. William Packard)

16 I don't have an audience in mind when I write. I'm writing mainly for myself. After a long devotion to playwriting I have a good inner ear. I know pretty well how a thing is going to sound on the stage, and how it will

play. I write to satisfy this inner ear and its perception. That's the audience I write for.
Tennessee Williams, in interview in *Writers at Work* (6th series, 1984)

17 The play was a great success. But the audience was a failure.
Oscar Wilde, remark on the reception of one of his least successful plays

18 Fit audience find, though few.
John Milton, *Paradise Lost* (Bk. VII, 1667)

19 Leaving great verse unto a little clan.
John Keats, 'Ode to Maia'

20   After all, it's rather a privilege amid
        the affluent traffic
to serve this unpopular art which cannot be
        turned into
    background noise for study
or hung as a status trophy by rising
        executives,
        cannot be 'done' like Venice
or abridged like Tolstoy, but stubbornly still
        insists upon
    being read or ignored: our handful
of clients at least can rune.
W.H. Auden, 'Thanksgiving for a Habitat'

21 A man really writes for an audience of about ten persons. Of course if others like it, that is clear gain. But if those ten are satisfied, he is content.
Alfred North Whitehead, *Dialogues* (1956)

22 Ideally, the writer needs no audience other than the few who understand. It is immodest and greedy to want more.
Gore Vidal, 'French Letters: Theories of the New Novel', in *Encounter* (Dec. 1967)

23 It is not the novel that is declining, but the audience for it.
Gore Vidal, in interview in *Writers at Work* (5th series, 1981)

24 Readers may be divided into four classes: 1. Sponges, who absorb all they read and return it nearly in the same state, only a little dirtied. 2. Sand-glasses, who retain nothing and are content to get through a book for the sake of getting through the time. 3. Strain-bags, who retain merely the dregs of what they read. 4. Mogul diamonds, equally rare and valuable, who profit by what they read, and enable others to profit by it also.
Samuel Taylor Coleridge, *Notebooks* (1794–1819)

25 You were praised, my books,
      because I had just come from the
         country;
  I was twenty years behind the times
      so you found an audience ready.
Ezra Pound, 'Salutation the Second'

---

10 AUTOBIOGRAPHY

---

1 And because I found I had nothing else to
write about, I presented myself as a subject.
Michel de Montaigne, *Essays* (1580–88)

2 I could inform the dullest author how he
might write an interesting book. Let him
relate the events of his own life with
honesty, not disguising the feelings that
accompanied them.
Samuel Taylor Coleridge, in letter to
Thomas Poole (Feb. 1797)

3 If the dullest person in the world would
only put down sincerely what he or she
thought about his or her life, about work
and love, religion and emotion, it would be
a fascinating document.
A.C. Benson, *From a College Window*
(1906)

4 You'll want to know . . . all that David
Copperfield type of crap. But I don't feel like
going into it.
J.D. Salinger, *The Catcher in the Rye* (1951)

5 Twenty-five seems to me the latest age at
which anybody should write an
autobiography. It has an air of finality about
it, as though one had clambered to the
summit of a great hill, and were waving
goodbye to some distant country which can
never be revisited.
Beverley Nichols, *Twenty-five* (1925)

6 All the world may know me by my book,
and my book by me.
Michel de Montaigne, *Essays* (1580–88)

7 Every man's work, whether it be literature
or music or pictures or architecture or
anything else, is always a portrait of himself,
and the more he tries to conceal himself the
more clearly will his character appear in
spite of him.
Samuel Butler, *The Way of all Flesh* (1903)

8 The writer of his own life has, at least, the
first qualification of an historian, the
knowledge of the truth; and though it may
be plausibly objected that his temptations to
disguise it are equal to his opportunities of
knowing it, yet I cannot but think that
impartiality may be expected with equal
confidence from him that relates the passage
of his own life as from him that delivers the
transactions of another.
Samuel Johnson, in *The Idler* (1758–60)

9 Just as there is nothing between the
admirable omelette and the intolerable, so
with autobiography.
Hilaire Belloc, *A Conversation with a Cat*
(1931)

10 All good books are autobiographies; but
bad autobiographies are the worst of all
books.
Theodor Lessing, *Europe and Asia* (1924)

11 I am able to declare that thus far my
autobiography has no more pure fiction in it
than my fiction has pure autobiography.
A.E. Coppard, *It's Me, O Lord*! (1957)

12 Next to the writer of real estate
advertisements, the autobiographer is the
most suspect of prose artists.
Donal Henahan, in *The New York Times*
(1977)

13 When you put down the good things you
ought to have done, and leave out the bad
ones you did do — well, that's Memoirs.
Will Rogers, *Autobiography* (1949)

14 When writing of oneself one should show no
mercy. Yet why at the first attempt to
discover one's own truth does all inner
strength seem to melt away in floods of
self-pity and tenderness and rising tears?
Georges Bernanos, *The Diary of a Country
Priest* (1936)

15 It is a hard and nice thing for a man to write
of himself. It grates his own heart to say
anything of disparagement, and the reader's
ears to hear anything of praise from him.
Abraham Cowley, *Of Myself* (1661)

16 A modest or inhibited autobiography is
written without entertainment to the writer
and read with distrust by the reader.
Neville Cardus, introduction to his
autobiography (1947)

17 Autobiography is an unrivalled vehicle for
telling the truth about other people.
Philip Guedalla, *Supers and Supermen*
(1920)

18 To write one's memoirs is to speak ill of
everybody except oneself.
Henri-Philippe Pétain, remark

19 There ain't nothing that breaks up homes,
country, and nations like somebody
publishing their memoirs.
Will Rogers, *Autobiography* (1949)

20 To start writing about your life is, from one
standpoint, to stop living it. You must avoid
adventures today so as to make time for
registering those of yesterday.
Ned Rorem, 'Random Notes from a Diary',
Music from Inside Out (1967)

21 I have a certain hesitation in starting my
biography too soon for fear of something
important having not yet happened.
Suppose I should end my days as President
of Mexico; the biography would seem
incomplete if it did not mention this fact.
Bertrand Russell, letter to Stanley Unwin
(Nov. 1930)

22 An autobiography is an obituary in serial
form with the last instalment missing.
Quentin Crisp, *The Naked Civil Servant*
(1968)

23 Only when one has lost all curiosity about
the future has one reached the age to write
an autobiography.
Evelyn Waugh, attr.

24 Autobiographies ought to begin with
Chapter Two.
Ellery Sedgwick, *The Happy Profession*
(1948)

11 AVANT-GARDE

1 All poetry is experimental poetry.
Wallace Stevens, *Opus Posthumous* (1942)

2 I am either a sound poet
or a bowl of Rice Crispies
Adrian Mitchell, 'Loose Leaf Poem'

3 Professors of literature, our present masters,
are always more ridiculous when they take
up today's or yesterday's avant-garde.
Geoffrey Grigson, *The Private Art* (1982)

4 Every poetic revolution is necessary, every
poetic revolution becomes ludicrous.
Geoffrey Grigson, *The Private Art* (1982)

5 Yesterday's avant-garde experience is
today's chic and tomorrow's cliché.
Richard Hofstadter, *Anti-Intellectualism in
American Life* (1963)

6 Excessive modernity, excessive revolution in
verse, excessive 'modernity', is a versifier's
way of concealing his ineptitude and his
lying to himself and others. Excessive
obedience to familiar norms is another
method of lying and deceiving yourself and
others.
Geoffrey Grigson, *The Private Art* (1982)

7 It's hard
Keeping up with the avant-garde.
Phyllis McGinley, 'On the Prevalence of
Literary Revivals'

12 BAD WRITING

1 Life being short and the quiet hours of it
few, we ought to waste none of them in
reading valueless books.
John Ruskin, in preface of *Sesame and Lilies*
(1865)

2 Let blockheads read what blockheads write.
Lord Chesterfield, in letter to his son (1
Nov. 1750)

3 People do not deserve to have good writing,
they are so pleased with bad.
Ralph Waldo Emerson, *Journals* (1841)

4 And bad literature of the sort called amusing
is spiritual gin.
George Eliot, 'Leaves from a Notebook:
Authorship', *The Impressions of
Theophrastus Such* (1879)

5 One of the conditions for reading what is
good is that we must not read what is bad;
for life is short and time and energy are
limited.
Arthur Schopenhauer, 'On Reading and
Books', *Parerga and Paralipomena* (1851)

6 The bad journalist seldom, if ever, gets into
print, but the bad novelist — oh, my lord!
Michael Joseph, remark (1926)

7 Some write, confin'd by physic; some, by
      debt;
Some, for 'tis Sunday; some, because 'tis
      wet, . . .

Another writes because his father writ,
And proves himself a bastard by his wit.
Edward Young, *Epistles to Mr Pope* (1730)

8 I have decided that there is no excuse for
poetry. Poetry gives no adequate return in
money, is expensive to print by reason of the
waste of space occasioned by its form, and
nearly always promulgates illusory concepts
of life. But a better case for the banning of
all poetry is the simple fact that most of it is
bad. Nobody is going to manufacture a
thousand tons of jam in the expectation that
five tons may be eatable.
Myles na Gopaleen, *The Best of Myles*
(1968)

9 Poets, like painters, thus unskill'd to trace
The naked nature and the living grace,
With gold and jewels cover ev'ry part,
And hide with ornaments their want of art.
Alexander Pope, *An Essay on Criticism*
(1711)

10 Anyone may be an honourable man, and yet
write verse badly.
Molière, *Le Misanthrope* (1666)

11 But he (his musical finesse was such,
So nice his ear, so delicate his touch)
Made poetry a mere mechanic art;
And ev'ry warbler has his tune by heart.
William Cowper, on Pope, *Table-Talk*
(1782)

12 The only people who can be excused for
letting a bad book loose on the world are the
poor devils who have to write for a living!
Molière, *Le Misanthrope* (1666)

13 There's no book so bad that something
good may not be found in it.
Miguel de Cervantes, *Don Quixote* (1615)

14 We can never know that a piece of writing is
bad unless we have begun by trying to read
it as if it was very good and ended by
discovering that we were paying the author
an undeserved compliment.
C.S. Lewis, *An Experiment in Criticism*
(1961)

15 Bad writing is in fact a rank feverish
unnecessary slough. Good writing is a dyke,
in which there is a leak for every one of our
weary hands.
Glenway Wescott, *F. Scott Fitzgerald: The
Man and his Work* (ed. Alfred Kazin, 1962)

16 But since the world with writing is possest,
I'll versify in spite; and do my best

To make as much waste-paper as the rest.
Juvenal, *Satires*

17 It is easier to write a mediocre poem than to
understand a good one.
Michel de Montaigne, *Essays* (1580–88)

18 Indeed there are few better ways of spending
a hilarious evening than in recalling the
worst lines in English poetry.
W.H. Auden, 'Squares and Oblongs', *Poets
at Work* (1948)

19 Many a fervid man
Writes books as cold and flat as graveyard
stones.
Elizabeth Barrett Browning, *Aurora Leigh*
(1856)

20 The art of writing things that shall sound
right and yet be wrong has made so many
reputations and afforded comfort to such a
large number of readers that I could not
venture to neglect it.
Samuel Butler, *Erewhon* (1872)

21 I am persuaded that foolish writers and
readers are created for each other; and that
Fortune provides readers as she does mates
for ugly women.
Horace Walpole, letter, 17 Aug. 1773

22 Men will forgive a man anything except bad
prose.
Winston Churchill, in election speech at
Manchester (1906)

23 It is a sobering experience for any poet to
read the last page of the Book Section of the
Sunday Times where correspondents seek to
identify poems which have meant much to
them. He is forced to realize that it is not his
work, not even the work of Dante or
Shakespeare, that most people treasure as
magic talismans in times of trouble, but
grotesquely bad verses written by maiden
ladies in local newspapers; that millions in
their bereavements, heartbreaks, agonies,
depressions, have been comforted and
perhaps saved from despair by appalling
trash while poetry stood helplessly and
incompetently by.
W.H. Auden, 'Squares and Oblongs', *Poets
at Work* (1948)

24 It is with noble sentiments that bad literature
gets written.
André Gide, *Journal* (2 Sept. 1940)

25 That's not writing, that's typing.
Truman Capote, on Jack Kerouac, attr.

26 Even bad books are books and therefore
   sacred.
   Günter Grass, *The Tin Drum* (1962)

13 BEAUTY

1 I would define, in brief, the Poetry of words
  as the Rhythmical Creation of Beauty. Its
  sole arbiter is Taste.
  Edgar Allan Poe, *The Poetic Principle*
  (1850)

2 The poet is a man who, seeing something
  ineffable behind the things of this world,
  and seeing it as beauty, makes an effort to
  express it in words: in words that, even as
  they come, make the vision itself a little
  clearer to himself and to others.
  Victor Gollancz, *More for Timothy* (1953)

3 Poetry lifts the veil from the hidden beauty
  of the world, and makes familiar objects be
  as if they were not familiar.
  Percy Bysshe Shelley, *A Defence of Poetry*
  (1821)

4 To be a poet is to apprehend the true and
  the beautiful; in a word, the good which
  exists in the relation subsisting, first
  between existence and perception, and
  secondly between perception and
  expression.
  Percy Bysshe Shelley, *A Defence of Poetry*
  (1821)

5 We mean all sorts of things, I know, by
  Beauty. But the essential advantage for a
  poet is not to have a beautiful world with
  which to deal. It is to be able to see beneath
  both beauty and ugliness; to see the
  boredom, and the horror, and the glory.
  T.S. Eliot, *The Use of Poetry and the Use of
  Criticism* (1933)

6 The poet produces the beautiful by fixing his
  attention on something real.
  Simone Weil, *Gravity and Grace* (1947)

7 The impulse to create beauty is rather rare in
  literary men . . . Far ahead of it comes the
  yearning to make money. And after the
  yearning to make money comes the yearning
  to make a noise.
  H.L. Mencken, *Prejudices* (1919)

14 BEGINNING AND ENDING

1 Writing is just having a sheet of paper, a pen
  and not a shadow of an idea of what you are
  going to say.
  Françoise Sagan, in the *Sunday Express*
  (1957)

2 The last thing one settles in writing a book is
  what one should put in first.
  Blaise Pascal, *Pensées* (1670)

3 How many good books suffer neglect
  through the inefficiency of their beginnings!
  Edgar Allan Poe, *Marginalia* (1844–9)

4 One of the most difficult things is the first
  paragraph. I have spent many months on a
  first paragraph, and once I get it, the rest
  just comes out very easily. In the first
  paragraph you solve most of the problems
  with your book. The theme is defined, the
  style, the tone.
  Gabriel García Márquez, in interview in
  Writers at Work (6th series, 1984)

5 I always make the first verse well, but I have
  trouble making the others.
  Molière, *Les Précieuses Ridicules* (1659)

6 All you have to do is close your eyes and
  wait for the symbols.
  Tennessee Williams, in *Esquire* (1969)

7 A man knows what style of book he wants
  to write when he knows nothing else about
  it.
  G.K. Chesterton, in preface to Charles
  Dickens, *Pickwick Papers*

8 In my experience one never sits down and
  says I will now write a poem about this or
  that, in the abstract.
  Philip Larkin, in interview in *The Observer*
  (1979)

9 I'm always in a dither when starting a novel
  — that's the worst time. It's like going to the
  dentist, because you do make a kind of
  appointment with yourself.
  Kingsley Amis, in interview in *Writers at
  Work* (5th series, 1981)

10 There are two things which I am confident I
   can do very well: one is an introduction to
   any literary work, stating what it is to
   contain, and how it should be executed in
   the most perfect manner; the other is a
   conclusion, shewing from various causes

why the execution has not been equal to what the author promised to himself and to the public.
Samuel Johnson, quoted in James Boswell, *Life of Samuel Johnson* (1791)

11 In general, I begin a book only when it is written.
Alexandre Dumas (père), *Propos d'art et de cuisine* (1877)

12 The important thing is not what the author, or any artist, had in mind to begin with but at what point he decided to stop.
D.W. Harding, *Experience into Words* (1963)

13 Nothing so difficult as a beginning
In Poesy, unless perhaps the end.
Lord Byron, *Don Juan* (1819–24)

14 I have never started a poem yet whose end I knew. Writing a poem is discovering.
Robert Frost, in *The New York Times* (7 Nov. 1955)

15 I can't start writing until I have a closing line.
Joseph Heller, in interview in *Writers at Work* (5th series, 1981)

16 Finishing a book is just like you took a child out in the yard and shot it.
Truman Capote, in *Loose Talk* (ed. Linda Botts, 1980)

17 Every book is like a purge; at the end of it one is empty . . . like a dry shell on the beach, waiting for the tide to come in again.
Daphne Du Maurier, in *Ladies' Home Journal* (Nov. 1956)

18 To finish is both a relief and a release from an extraordinarily pleasant prison.
Robert Burchfield, on completing *The Oxford English Dictionary*, quoted in 'Sayings of the Week' in *The Observer* (11 May 1986)

19 Only a little more
I have to write,
Then I'll give o'er
And bid the world good-night.
Robert Herrick, 'His Poetry his Pillar'

20 If it be true that 'good wine needs no bush', 'tis true that a good play needs no epilogue.
William Shakespeare, *As You Like It*

21 By hook or by crook
I'll be last in this book.
Traditional

15 BEST-SELLER

1 God is the Celebrity-Author of the World's Best-Seller.
Daniel J. Boorstin, *The Image* (1962)

2 A best-seller was a book which somehow sold well simply because it was selling well.
Daniel J. Boorstin, *The Image* (1962)

3 Once a book has been declared a bestseller, its sales accelerate — like the freshwater polyp, the best seller breeds from itself — and the book-buyer can happily accept the judgement of the great majority.
Frank Muir, *The Frank Muir Book* (1976)

4 A best seller is the gilded tomb of a mediocre talent.
Logan Pearsall Smith, 'All Trivia', *Afterthoughts* (1931)

5 The bestseller . . . gives an idea of what is read on the periphery of literacy, the reading matter of those who have graduated from the literature of the lavatory wall to the printed word.
Arthur Calder-Marshall, in *The Author* (Summer 1951)

6 The principle of procrastinated rape is said to be the ruling one in all the great bestsellers.
V.S. Pritchett, 'Clarissa', *The Living Novel & Later Appreciations* (1964)

7 If we should ever inaugurate a hall of fame, it would be reserved exclusively and hopefully for authors who, having written four best-sellers, *still refrained* from starting out on a lecture tour.
E.B. White, *Every Day Is Saturday* (1934)

16 BIBLE AND PRAYER-BOOK

1 Lo, here a little volume, but a great book!
Richard Crashaw, 'Prayer . . . prefixed to a little prayer-book'

2 Read, mark, learn, and inwardly digest.
Book of Common Prayer, (Collect, 2nd Sunday in Advent)

3 The aggregation of large libraries tends to divert men's thoughts from the one great

book, the Bible, which ought, day and night, to be in every one's hand. My object, my hope, in translating the Scriptures, was to check the so prevalent production of new works.
Martin Luther, *Table Talk* (1569)

4 He [the translator] will find one English book and one only, where, as in the *Iliad* itself, perfect plainness of speech is allied with perfect nobleness; and that book is the Bible.
Matthew Arnold, *On Translating Homer* (1861)

5 The number one book of the ages was written by a committee, and it was called the Bible.
Louis B. Mayer, attr.

6 Holy Bible, Writ Divine,
Bound in leather, one-and-nine,
Satan trembles when he sees
Bibles sold as cheap as these.
Advertisement by William Collins (early 20th cent.)

7 Whenever we read the obscene stories, the voluptuous debaucheries, the cruel and torturous executions, the unrelenting vindictiveness, with which more than half the Bible is filled, it would be more consistent that we called it the word of a demon than the word of God. It is a history of wickedness that has served to corrupt and brutalize mankind.
Thomas Paine, *The Age of Reason* (1793)

8 I read the book of Job last night — I don't think God comes well out of it.
Virginia Woolf, *The Letters of Virginia Woolf* (vol. 2, 1975)

9 Both read the Bible day and night,
But thou read'st black where I read white.
William Blake, *The Everlasting Gospel* (1818)

10 The Scripture was his jest-book.
William Cowper, of Voltaire, 'Truth'

11 King David and King Solomon
Led merry, merry lives,
With many, many lady friends
And many, many wives;
But when old age crept over them,
With many, many qualms,
King Solomon wrote the Proverbs
And King David wrote the Psalms.
James Ball Naylor, 'David & Solomon'

12 The English Bible, a book which, if everything else in our language should perish, would alone suffice to show the whole extent of its beauty and power.
Thomas Babington Macaulay, 'On John Dryden', in *The Edinburgh Review* (Jan. 1828)

13 Those who talk of the Bible as a 'monument of English prose' are merely admiring it as a monument over the grave of Christianity.
T.S. Eliot, *Religion and Literature* (1935)

14 Ye never heard of the Twelfth? Away home, man, and read your Bible.
Anonymous Orangeman, when asked by a foreigner about the Orange Celebrations of 12 July, recorded in diary of Lady Spender (12 July 1921)

17 BIBLIOPHILIA

1 Books, books again, and books once more!
Austin Dobson, *Poetical Works* (1907)

2 He deserves to die in dishonour
who does not love books and believe in them.
Anonymous, *Roman de Renart* (late 12th cent.)

3 The Love of Books, the Golden Key
That opens the Enchanted Door.
Andrew Lang, 'Ballade of the Bookworm'

4 The love of books is a love which requires neither justification, apology, nor defense.
J.A. Langford, *The Praise of Books* (1880)

5 I love everything that's old: old friends, old times, old manners, old books, old wine.
Oliver Goldsmith, *She Stoops to Conquer* (1773)

6 First editions, those immortal fledgelings of authorship, first editions of first books, still warm from the creative nest; first-fruits with the bloom of the author's love still upon them; first flights with the adorable clumsiness of all young things; copies which reflect the author's first hot, flushed stare of rapture when he looked upon what he had made and saw that it was good; such books will ever entrance the bookworm.
Holbrook Jackson, *The Anatomy of Bibliomania* (1950)

7 For him was lever have at his beddes heed
   Twenty bokes, clad in blak or reed,
   Of Aristotle and his philosophye,
   Than robes rich, or fithele, or gay sautrye.
   Geoffrey Chaucer, prologue to *The
   Canterbury Tales* (*c.* 1387)

8 Books are becoming everything to me. If I
   had at this moment my choice of life, I would
   bury myself in one of those immense libraries
   that we saw together at the universities, and
   never pass a waking hour without a book
   before me.
   Thomas Babington Macaulay, in G.O.
   Trevelyan, *Life and Letters* (1876)

9 There is no mistaking a real book when one
   meets it. It is like falling in love, and like
   that colossal adventure it is an experience of
   great social import. Even as the tranced
   swain, the booklover yearns to tell others of
   his bliss. He writes letters about it, adds it to
   the postscript of all manner of communi-
   cations, intrudes it into telephone
   messages, and insists on his friends writing
   down the title of the find. Like the
   simple-hearted betrothed, once certain of his
   conquest, 'I want you to love her, too!'
   Christopher Morley, 'On Visiting
   Bookshops', *Safety Pins and Other Essays*
   (1925)

10 . . . we behold another advantage which the
   lover of books has over the lover of women.
   If he be a genuine lover he can and should
   love any number of books, and this
   polybibliophily is not to the disparagement
   of any one of that number.
   Eugene Field, *The Love Affairs of a
   Bibliomaniac* (1896)

11 The true bibliophile loves the existence of a
   book more than its form and content; under
   no circumstances must he read it (is not
   something similar true of every great love?).
   Franz Werfel, *Die 40 Tage des Musa Dagh*
   (1947)

12 The possession of a book becomes a
   substitute for reading it.
   Anthony Burgess, in *The New York Times
   Book Review* (4 Dec. 1966)

13 Of splendid books I own no end,
   But few that I can comprehend.
   Sebastian Brant, *The Ship of Fools* (1494)

14 The Book-Fool is the man, not who wasted
   good money on worthless books, but who
   could not, or would not, read the good
   books he bought.
   Sebastian Brant, as paraphrased in A.W.
   Pollard, *Books in the House* (1907)

15 It is those books which a man possesses but
   does not read which constitute the most
   suspicious evidence against him.
   Victor Hugo, *Toilers of the Sea* (1866)

16 I should never call myself a book lover, any
   more than a people lover: it all depends
   what's inside them.
   Philip Larkin, programme of the
   Antiquarian Book Fair, London (1972)

17 I cannot live without books.
   Thomas Jefferson, in letter to John Adams
   (1815)

18 Bibliophiles are gastronomes, gourmets,
   gourmandes, epicures.
   Holbrook Jackson, *The Anatomy of
   Bibliomania* (1950)

19 Dreams, books, are each a world; and
                     books, we know,
   Are a substantial world, both pure and
                     good:
   Round these, with tendrils strong as flesh
                     and blood,
   Our pastime and our happiness will grow.
   William Wordsworth, 'Personal Talk'

20 Do your duty to yourself immediately; love
   Nature and Books; seek these, and you will
   be happy; for virtuous friendship, and love,
   and knowledge of mankind must mentally
   accompany these, all things thus ripening in
   their due season.
   William Wordsworth, in letter to Thomas
   De Quincey, 6 March 1804

21 You can't get a cup of tea large enough or a
   book long enough to suit me.
   C.S. Lewis, *Of Other Worlds* (1966)

22 It's too bad that the love of books brings you
   into contact with the people who write them.
   Louis Simpson, *Air with Armed Men* (1972)

23 No hobby so old, so enduring, or
   respectable.
   Percy Fitzgerald, of book-hunting, *The
   Book-Fancier* (1886)

24 It [book-hunting] is a sweet game which few
   bookmen can resist, even when they feel
   that they are too much engaged in it.
   Holbrook Jackson, *The Anatomy of
   Bibliomania* (1950)

25 Book collectors . . . may be grouped in three classes, viz: Those who collect from vanity; those who collect for the benefits of learning; those who collect through a veneration and love for books. It is not unfrequent that men who begin to collect books merely to gratify their personal vanity find themselves presently so much in love with the pursuit that they become collectors in the better sense.
Eugene Field, *The Love Affairs of a Bibliomaniac* (1896)

26 What wild desires, what restless torments seize
The hapless man who feels the book-disease!
John Ferriar, *The Bibliomania* (1809)

27 No place like London for the lover of books.
Thomas Dibdin, *Reminiscences of a Literary Life* (1836)

28 Home is where the books are.
Richard Burton, quoted by his wife Sally, in *The Observer* (13 April 1986)

18 BIOGRAPHY

1 The art of Biography
Is different from Geography.
Geography is about maps,
But Biography is about chaps.
Edmund Clerihew Bentley, in introduction to *Biography for Beginners* (1905)

2 It is very pleasant to be written up, even by a writer.
Joyce Cary, *The Horse's Mouth* (1944)

3 Biography should be written by an acute enemy.
A.J. Balfour, quoted by S.K. Ratcliffe in *The Observer* (20 Jan. 1927)

4 To the biographer, all lives bar one are dramatic constructions.
Katherine Anthony, *Writing Biography* (1950)

5 There is so little information about Marshal Louis Nicolas Davout, one of the leaders of Napoleon's army, that a Huddersfield man is writing his biography.
Article in *The Yorkshire Post,* quoted in *Punch* (23 Feb. 1972)

6 There is properly no history; only biography.
Ralph Waldo Emerson, *Journals* (1830)

7 Read no history: nothing but biography, for that is life without theory.
Benjamin Disraeli, *Contarini Fleming* (1844)

8 No great man lives in vain. The history of the world is but the biography of great men.
Thomas Carlyle, *On Heroes, Hero-Worship and the Heroic in History* (1840)

9 Lives of great men all remind us
We can make our lives sublime,
And, departing, leave behind us
Footprints on the sand of time.
Henry Wadsworth Longfellow, 'A Psalm of Life'

10 I enjoy reading biographies because I want to know about the people who messed up the world.
Marie Dressler, *Passing Show* (1934)

11 Great geniuses have the shortest biographies.
Ralph Waldo Emerson, 'Plato', *Representative Men* (1850)

12 Biographies are but the clothes and buttons of the man — the biography of the man himself cannot be written.
Mark Twain, *Autobiography* (1924)

13 After you have traced a man down to the last munched bath bun you are still left with the whole mystery of 'the madness of art'.
Tony Tanner, in review of Leon Edel, *Henry James, The Master* in *The Times* (3 Aug. 1972)

14 I can find my biography in every fable that I read.
Ralph Waldo Emerson, *Journals* (1866)

15 Nobody can write the life of a man but those who have eaten and drunk and lived in social intercourse with him.
Samuel Johnson, quoted in James Boswell, *Life of Samuel Johnson* (1791)

16 Just how difficult it is to write biography can be reckoned by anybody who sits down and considers just how many people know the real truth about his or her love affairs.
Rebecca West, 'The Art of Skepticism', in *Vogue* (Nov. 1952)

17 The primary duty of a serious biographer is

to illuminate his subject's life work, not to play the spy in his bedroom.
Philip Toynbee, in review of Vincent Broome, *Havelock Ellis, Philosopher of Sex*, in *The Observer* (18 Mar. 1979)

18 A well-written Life is almost as rare as a well-spent one.
Thomas Carlyle, 'Richter', in *The Edinburgh Review* (1827)

19 With my usual watchful eye on posterity, I can only suggest to any wretched future biographer that he gets my daily engagement book and from that fills in anything he can find and good luck to him, poor bugger.
Noël Coward, *The Noël Coward Diaries* (ed. Graham Payne and Sheridan Morley, 1982)

20 The best sort of book to start with is biography. If you want to make a success of it, choose as a subject someone very famous who has had plenty of books written about him quite recently. Many young writers make the mistake of choosing some forgotten Caroline clergyman or eighteenth-century traveller.
Evelyn Waugh, 'Passing Show', *The Way to Fame* (2 Feb. 1929)

21 Biography, like big-game hunting, is one of the recognised forms of sport, and it is as unfair as only sport can be.
Philip Guedalla, *Supers and Supermen* (1920)

22 In writing biography, fact and fiction shouldn't be mixed. And if they are, the fiction parts should be printed in red ink, the fact parts in black ink.
Catherine Drinker Bowen, in *Publishers' Weekly* (24 March 1958)

23 Biography, if it is to enhance understanding, add to history or interpret character, must be constructive and not destructive.
Harold Nicolson, in *The Times* (20 Mar. 1949)

24 Biography is by nature the most universally profitable, universally pleasant of all things: especially biography of distinguished individuals.
Thomas Carlyle, *Sartor Resartus* (1833)

25 Biography broadens the vision and allows us to live a thousand lives in one.
Elbert Hubbard, *The Note Book* (1927)

26 Biography is, of the various kinds of narrative writing, that which is most eagerly read and most easily applied to the purposes of life.
Samuel Johnson, in *The Idler* (1758–60)

27 I find biographies of writers riveting, though they tend to end sadly.
Godfrey Smith, in *The Sunday Times* (12 July 1987)

28 An author's works are his esoteric biography.
Sir Arthur Helps, *Thoughts in the Cloister and the Crowd* (1835)

29 Reader, pass on, nor idly waste your time
In bad biography, or bitter rhyme;
For what I am, this cumbrous clay ensures,
And what I was is no affair of yours.
Anonymous, epitaph in Peterborough churchyard

---

19 BOOKS AS MIRRORS

---

1 A book is a mirror; if a monkey peers into it, then it will not be an apostle that looks out.
Georg Christoph Lichtenberg, *Notebooks* (July–Sept. 1775)

2 Everyone, in fact, merely reads himself out of a book; and, if he is a forceful personality, he reads himself into it.
J.W. Goethe, 'Erste Epistel'

3 Isn't everyone who bends over a book constantly discovering himself?
Karl Krolow, in *Die Welt* (23 Dec. 1950)

4 What's a book? Everything or nothing. The eye that sees it is all.
Ralph Waldo Emerson, *Journals* (1834)

5 If a book and a head knock against each other and there is a hollow sound, is it always the book?
Georg Christoph Lichtenberg, *Notebooks* (August 1773–May 1775)

6 What can we see, read, acquire, but ourselves. Take the book, my friend, and read your eyes out, you will never find there what I find.
Ralph Waldo Emerson, *Journals* (1832)

7 When a man says he sees nothing in a book, he very often means that he does not see

himself in it; which, if it is not a comedy or a satire, is likely enough.
Julius Charles Hare and Augustus William Hare, *Guesses at Truth* (1827)

8 Books are like people: one man's revelation is to the other a meaningless bore.
Dagobert D. Runes, *Treasury of Thought* (1966)

9 A book is a friend whose face is constantly changing. If you read it when you are recovering from an illness, and return to it years after, it is changed surely, with the change in yourself.
Andrew Lang, *The Library* (1881)

10 We find little in a book but what we put there. But in great books, the mind finds room to put many things.
Joseph Joubert, *Pensées* (1842)

11 When you read a classic you do not see in the book more than you did before. You see more in *you* than there was before.
Clifton Fadiman, *Any Number Can Play* (1957)

bought, passed from hand to hand, but it cannot be treated like an ordinary commercial property, because it is, at once, multiple and unique, in ample supply yet precious.
Robert Escarpit, *The Book Revolution* (1956)

4 But when the skies of shorter days
    Are dark and all the ways are mine,
How bright upon your books the blaze
    Gleams from the cheerful study fire.
Andrew Lang, 'To F.L.'

5 Books do furnish a room.
Anthony Powell, title of novel (1971)

6 A room without books is a body without a soul.
Cicero, quoted in John Lubbock, *Pleasures of Life*

7 No furniture as charming as books, even if you never open them or read a single word.
Sydney Smith, in Lady Holland's *Memoir* (1855)

20 BOOKS AS OBJECTS

1 Books, like men, are subject to manners, behaviour; they are well or ill bred; well dressed or badly dressed.
Holbrook Jackson, *The Anatomy of Bibliomania* (1950)

2 The important thing about a paperback — and I think printing might have been invented for the paperback — is that it's portable, disposable, and cheap. Essentially not valuable. No morality is involved in taking care of it.
Patrick Wright, in *The Financial Times* (31 Aug. 1985)

3 Like anything that lives, the book is not to be defined. At least, no one had yet been able to provide a complete and final definition of it, because a book is not a thing like other things. When we hold it in our hands, all we hold is the paper: the *book* is elsewhere. And yet it is in the pages as well, and the thought alone without the support of the printed words could not make a book. A book is a reading-machine, but it can never be used mechanically. A book is sold,

BOOKSELLING
See SELLING BOOKS

21 BORROWING BOOKS

1 Who folds a leafe downe
Ye divel toaste browne;
Who makes marke or blotte
Ye divel roaste hot;
Who stealeth this boke
Ye divel shall cooke.
Anonymous

2 Steal not this Book my honest Friend
For fear the Galows should be your hend,
And when you die the Lord will say
And wares the Book you stole away?
Anonymous, inscribed in the Revd Richard Hooper's unique copy of the second edition of Hannah Glasse's *The Art of Cookery made Plain and Easy* (1747)

3 Great collections of books are subject to certain accidents besides the damp, the worms, and the rats; one not less common is

that of the borrowers, not to say a word of
the purloiners.
Isaac D'Israeli, 'The Bibliomania',
Curiosities of Literature (1791–1834)

4 Hard-covered books break up friendships.
You loan a hard-covered book to a friend
and when he doesn't return it you get mad
at him. It makes you mean and petty. But
twenty-five-cent books are different.
John Steinbeck, news summaries (25 April
1954)

5 A friend who borrows a pound or a
handkerchief will punctiliously return it to
you; but he will borrow a book worth five
times as much, and possibly irreplaceable,
with no thought that he holds any of your
property. He will lose the book, deface it,
give it away, or take it from your house
without notice, honestly unconcerned
whether it is his or yours. Indeed, if he
cared, he might find on the flyleaf the name
of a third party from whom you had
purloined it on the same terms.
Jacques Barzun, *The House of Intellect*
(1959)

6 Please return this book; I find that though
many of my friends are poor arithmeticians,
they are nearly all good book-keepers.
Sir Walter Scott, inscription in one of his
books

7 To lend Bysshe [the poet Shelley] a book
was to bid it a long farewell, to take leave of
it forever.
T.J. Hogg, *Life of Shelley* (1858)

8 A friend thinks no more of borrowing a
book now-a-days, than a Roman did of
borrowing a man's wife; and what is worse,
we are so far gone in our immoral notions
on this subject, that we even lend it as easily
as Cato did his spouse.
Leigh Hunt, 'Wedded to Books', *Men,
Women and Books* (1847)

9 Friends,
To borrow my books and set wet glasses on
   them.
Edward Arlington Robinson, 'Captain
Craig'

10 Never lend books, for no one ever returns
them; the only books I have in my library
are books that other folk have lent me.
Anatole France, *La Vie Littéraire* (1888–92)

11 The owner of a country house was showing
some visitors over a superb library. 'Do you
ever lend books?' he was asked. 'No,' he
replied promptly, 'only fools lend books.'
Then, waving his hand to a many-shelved
section filled with handsomely bound
volumes, he added: 'All those books once
belonged to fools'.
Letter in *The Times* (7 March 1928)

12 A fool and his books are soon parted.
Holbrook Jackson, *The Anatomy of
Bibliomania* (1950)

13 I visit them from time to time just to look
over my library.
William Hazlitt, of his book-borrowing
friends

14 No gentleman can be without three copies
of a book, one for show, one for use, and
one for borrowers.
Richard Heber, quoted by F.B. Adams in
The Uses of Provenance (1966)

15 They borrow books they will not buy,
They have no ethics or religions;
I wish some kind Burbankian guy
Could cross my books with homing pigeons.
Carolyn Wells, 'Book-borrowers'

16 I mean your borrower of books — those
mutilators of collections, spoilers of the
symmetry of shelves, and creators of odd
volumes.
Charles Lamb, 'The Two Races of Men',
Essays of Elia (1823)

17 When I get hold of a book I particularly
admire, I am so enthusiastic that I loan it to
some one who never brings it back.
Edgar Watson Howe, *Country Town
Sayings* (1911)

22 BREVITY

1 I struggle to be brief and become obscure.
Horace, *Ars Poetica*

2 Few were his words, but wonderfully clear.
Homer, *The Iliad*

3 What is the use of brevity if it constitutes a
book?
Martial, *Epigrams*

4 No one who cannot limit himself has ever
been able to write.
Nicolas Boileau-Despréaux, *L'Art Poétique*
(1674)

5 Were all books reduced thus to their quintessence, many a bulky author would make his appearance in a pennypaper. There would be scarce such a thing in nature as a folio; the works of an age would be contained on a few shelves: not to mention millions of volumes that would be utterly annihilated.
Joseph Addison, in *The Spectator* (no. 124, 1711)

6 He that uses many words for the explaining any subject, doth, like the cuttle fish, hide himself for the most part in his own ink.
John Ray, *On the Creation* (1691)

7 The writer's first courtesy, is it not to be brief?
Anatole France, *La Vie Littéraire* (1888–92)

8 Whatever you teach, be brief, that your readers' minds may readily comprehend and faithfully retain your words. Everything superfluous slips from the full heart.
Horace, *Ars Poetica*

9 It is my ambition to say in ten sentences what other men say in whole books — what other men do not say in whole books.
Friedrich Nietzsche, *Twilight of the Idols* (1888)

10 One merit of poetry few persons will deny: it says more and in fewer words than prose.
Voltaire, 'Poets', *Philosophical Dictionary* (1764)

11 Poetry teaches the enormous force of a few words, and, in proportion to the inspiration, checks loquacity.
Ralph Waldo Emerson, preface to *Parnassus* (1875)

BROADCASTING
See TELEVISION AND RADIO

---

23 BROWSING

---

1 A man ought to read just as inclination leads him, for what he reads as a task will do him little good.
Samuel Johnson, quoted in James Boswell, *Life of Samuel Johnson* (1791)

2 Read at whim! Read at whim!
Randall Jarrell, *A Sad Heart at the Supermarket* (1965)

3 I try to leave out the parts that people skip.
Elmore Leonard, quoted in *Publishers' Weekly* (8 March 1985)

4 One of the amusements of idleness is reading without the fatigue of close attention; and the world, therefore, swarms with writers whose wish is not to be studied, but to be read.
Samuel Johnson, in *The Idler* (11 Nov. 1758)

5 It is one of the oddest things in the world that you can read a page or more and think of something utterly different.
Christian Morgenstern, *Aphorisms* (1918)

6 In reading some books we occupy ourselves chiefly with the thoughts of the author; in perusing others, exclusively with our own.
Edgar Allan Poe, *Marginalia* (1844–9)

7 It is impossible to read properly without using all one's engine power. If we are not tired after reading, commonsense is not in us.
Arnold Bennett, *Things That Have Interested Me* (1906)

8 One ought to have a supply of good books on newsprint, to be read in the bath or thrown away on a journey.
Ernst Jünger, *Wartime Diary* (14 July 1942)

9 The test of a first-rate work, and a test of your sincerity in calling it a first-rate work, is that you finish it.
Arnold Bennett, *Things That Have Interested Me* (1906)

10 The art of reading is to skip judiciously. Whole libraries may be skipped these days, when we have the results of them in our modern culture without going over the ground again. And even of the books we decide to read, there are almost always large portions which do not concern us, and which we are sure to forget the day after we have read them. The art is to skip all that does not concern us, while missing nothing that we really need. No external guidance can teach us this; for nobody but ourselves can guess what the needs of our intellect may be.
P.G. Hamerton, *The Intellectual Life* (1882)

11 Busy readers are seldom good readers. He

who would read with pleasure and profit
should have nothing else to do or to think
of.
C.M. Wieland, *Die Abderiten* (1774)

12 Some books are to be tasted, others to be
swallowed, and some few to be chewed and
digested.
Francis Bacon, 'Of Studies', *Essays* (1597)

13 I read part of the book right the way
through.
Samuel Goldwyn, attr.

24 BUYING BOOKS

1 Buy good books and read them; the best
books are the commonest and the last
editions are always the best, if the editors
are not blockheads, for they may profit of
the former.
Lord Chesterfield, *Letters* (1750)

2 Though I am continually asking myself the
question, I have never yet come to discover
why you have shown so much zeal in the
purchase of books. Nobody who knows you
in the least would think that you do it on
account of their helpfulness or use, any
more than a bald man would buy a comb, or
a blind man a mirror, or a deaf-mute a
flute-player, or a eunuch a concubine, or a
landsman an oar, or a seaman a plough.
Lucian, 'The Ignorant Book Collector'

3 Many a time I have stood before a stall, or a
bookseller's window, torn by conflict of
intellectual desire and bodily need.
George Gissing, *The Private Papers of
Henry Ryecroft* (1903)

4 To go without a meal rather than a book is a
common experience.
Holbrook Jackson, *The Anatomy of
Bibliomania* (1950)

5 If you can stand their dirty looks,
Talk to your neighbours about your books;
But if you want to make them really stroppy,
Ask them to buy a copy.
T.J. Thomas (Sarnicol), 'Y Ffordd i'w
Dychrynu'

6 If I were back in a school as an English
teacher and there was a choice between a

word-processor and 500 paperbacks of my
own choosing, I would have no qualms
about buying the books.
Daniel Chander, in *The Times Educational
Supplement* (24 Oct. 1986)

7 Buying books and more books, although I
can hardly afford them — yet. I mean to get
on.
Sydney Moseley, in his *Diary* (4 July
1905)

8 To buy books would be a good thing if we
could also buy the time to read them; as it
is, the mere act of purchasing them is often
mistaken for the assimilation and mastering
of their contents.
Arthur Schopenhauer, 'On Reading and
Books', *Parerga and Paralipomena* (1851)

9 I suppose there never was a man who had
had so much to do with books as I have,
who owned so few. I never have purchased a
book which I could do without, or which I
did not mean to read through.
Thomas Carlyle, *Letters* (1913)

10 Many and sundry are the means by which
people will come by books other than by
purchase.
Holbrook Jackson, *The Anatomy of
Bibliomania* (1950)

11 Whoever owns two pairs of trousers ought
to sell one and buy this book instead.
Georg Christoph Lichtenberg, about an
unknown book

12 Wear the old coat and buy the new book.
Austin Phelps, *Theory of Preaching* (1882)

13 When Providence throws a good book in my
way I bow to its decree and purchase it as an
act of Piety, so long as it is reasonably or
unreasonably cheap.
Oliver Wendell Holmes, *The Poet at the
Breakfast Table* (1872)

14 The very cheapness of literature is making
even wise people forget that if a book is
worth reading, it is worth buying. No book
is worth anything which is not worth much;
nor is it serviceable, until it has been read,
and re-read, and loved, and loved again;
and marked, so that you can refer to the
passages you want in it.
John Ruskin, *Sesame and Lilies* (1865)

15 The sums laid out on books one should, at
first sight, think an indication of

encouragement to letters; but booksellers only are encouraged, not books.
Horace Walpole, in letter to Henry Zonch (3 Jan. 1761)

16 When you give someone a book you're giving them the most imaginative of gifts, because you're taking a personal interest in what interests them.
W.H. Smith advertisement in *The Observer* (24 Nov. 1985)

17 For every £3 of consumer spending in Britain, only 1p goes on books — 12 times as much goes on beer.
Editorial in *The Economist* (27 April 1985)

18 Shortly before his death, George Orwell — a bookman if ever there was one — calculated that he spent annually less on books than on the Woodbines that were killing him — around £11 a year.
John Sutherland, *A Pragmatic Popular Educator*

19 There is as much trickery required to grow rich by a stupid book as there is folly in buying it.
La Bruyère, *Characters* (1688)

20 Booksellers' returns and the computer have freed the modern bookbuyer from the agonies of decision making.
Frank Muir, *The Frank Muir Book* (1976)

---

25 CENSORSHIP

1 If we think we regulate printing, thereby to rectify manners, we must regulate all recreations and pastimes, all that is delightful to man.
John Milton, *Areopagitica* (1644)

2 No poem was ever suppressed — if it was a poem. Belayed, yes. Muffled. Ignored for a generation or a century. But not suppressed.
Archibald MacLeish, in interview in *Writers at Work* (5th series, 1981)

3 We all know that books burn — yet we have the greater knowledge that books cannot be killed by fire. People die, but books never die.
Franklin D. Roosevelt, to American Booksellers Association (23 April 1942)

4 Wherever they burn books they will also, in the end, burn human beings.
Heinrich Heine, *Almansor: A Tragedy* (1823)

5 Books are not good fuel . . . In the days when heretical books were burned, it was necessary to place them on large wooden stages, and after all the pains taken to demolish them, considerable readable masses were sometimes found in the embers; whence it was supposed that the devil, conversant in fire and its effects, gave them his special protection. In the end it was found easier and cheaper to burn the heretics themselves than their books.
W.G. Clifford, *Books in Bottles* (1926)

6 As good almost kill a man as kill a good book . . . who kills a man kills a reasonable creature, God's image; but he who destroys a good book, kills reason itself, kills the image of God, as it were, in the eye . . . slays an immortality rather than a life.
John Milton, *Areopagitica* (1644)

7 Give me six lines written by the most honourable of men, and I will find an excuse in them to hang him.
Cardinal Richelieu, *Mirame* (*c.* 1625)

8 We are willing enough to praise freedom when she is safely tucked away in the past and cannot be a nuisance. In the present, amidst dangers whose outcome we cannot foresee, we get nervous about her, and admit censorship.
E.M. Forster, 'The Tercentenary of the "Areopagitica"', *Two Cheers for Democracy* (1951)

9 Censorship is the tool of those who have the need to hide actualities from themselves and others. Their fear is only their inability to face what is real. Somewhere in their upbringing they were shielded against the total facts of our experience. They were only taught to look one way when many ways exist.
Charles Bukowski, in a letter to *Groene Amsterdamer* (1986)

10 If the book be false in its facts, disprove them; if false in its reasoning, refute it. But for God's sake, let us hear freely from both sides.
Thomas Jefferson, quoted in *A Bookman's Weekly* (25 Jan. 1971)

11 As we see censorship it is a stupid giant traffic policeman answering 'Yes' to 'Am I my brother's copper?' He guards a one-way street and his semaphore has four signs, all marked 'STOP'.
Franklin P. Adams, *Nods and Becks* (1944)

12 My considered opinion, after long reflection, is that whilst in many places the effect of *Ulysses* on the reader undoubtedly is somewhat emetic, nowhere does it tend to be an aphrodisiac . . . *Ulysses* may therefore be admitted into the United States.
Judge John Woolsey, giving judgement in the case U.S. v. *Ulysses* and Random House Inc. (1933)

13 You may think one of the ways in which you can test this book is to ask yourself the question: would you approve of your own son and daughter, because girls can read as well as boys, reading this book? Is it a book you could have lying in your house? Is it a book you would wish your wife or your servant to read?
Mervyn Griffiths-Jones, at the *Lady Chatterley's Lover* trial (1960)

14 The Smile of the Goat has a meaning that
                  few
      Will mistake, and explains in a measure
The Censor attending a risqué Revue
      And combining Stern Duty with
                  pleasure.
Oliver Herford, 'The Smile of the Goat'

15 Censorship may be useful for the preservation of morality, but can never be so for its restoration.
Jean-Jacques Rousseau, *The Social Contract* (1762)

16 No government ought to be without censors; and where the press is free, no one ever will.
Thomas Jefferson, in letter to George Washington (9 Sept. 1792)

17 A free press stands as one of the great interpreters between the government and the people. To allow it to be fettered is to be fettered ourselves.
Justice George Sutherland, Grosjean v. American Press Co. (1935)

18 A free press can, of course, be good or bad, but, most certainly, without freedom it will never be anything but bad.
Albert Camus, *Resistance, Rebellion and Death* (1961)

19 The freedom of the press is one of the great bulwarks of liberty, and can never be restrained but by despotic government.
George Mason, Virginia Bill of Rights (12 June 1776)

20 Freedom of the press is not an end in itself but a means to the end of a free society.
Felix Frankfurter, in *The New York Times* (28 Nov. 1954)

21 The liberty of the press is most generally approved when it takes liberties with the other fellow, and leaves us alone.
Edgar Watson Howe, *Country Town Sayings* (1911)

22 Particularly against books the Home Secretary is. If we can't stamp out literature in the country, we can at least stop it being brought in from outside.
Evelyn Waugh, *Vile Bodies* (1930)

23 I never heard of anyone who was really literate or who ever really loved books who wanted to suppress any of them. Censors only read a book with great difficulty, moving their lips as they puzzle out each syllable, when somebody tells them that the book is unfit to read.
Robertson Davies, *The Table Talk of Samuel Marchbanks* (1985)

24 The Censor's task is unique and impossible.
Benn W. Levy, in *The Author* (Summer 1938)

25 Censors are paid to have dirty minds.
John Trevelyan, British film censor (1970)

26 A respectable minority is useful as censors.
Thomas Jefferson, in letter to Joel Barlow (3 May 1802)

27 It is not difficult to censor foreign news, What is hard today is to censor one's own thoughts.
Arthur Waley, 'Censorship'

28 Assassination is the extreme form of censorship.
George Bernard Shaw, *The Rejected Statement* (1916)

29 Censorship is a trouble with which, apart from wartime, British publishers are fortunately not afflicted; but the very absence of a censorship throws grave responsibilities upon the publishers themselves.
Stanley Unwin, *The Truth about Publishing* (1926)

30 The men who died to buy us liberty knew
    that it was better to let in a thousand bad
    books than shut out one good one. We
    cannot, then, silence evil books, but we can
    turn away our eyes from them; we can take
    care that what we read, and what we let
    others read, should be good and
    wholesome.
    Charles Kingsley, 'Of Books' (1881)

31 Where there is official censorship it is a sign
    that speech is serious. Where there is none,
    it is pretty certain that the official
    spokesmen have all the loud-speakers.
    Paul Goodman, *Growing up Absurd* (1960)

32 Every South African cannot go out and buy
    every new book and read it to decide if he
    will like it. Now we have a body that can do
    it for him. We study the book and tell him if
    he will like it or not.
    J.H. Snyman, Chief Censor in South Africa
    (1978)

33 Literature is one of the few areas left where
    black and white feel some identity of
    purpose; we all struggle under censorship.
    Nadine Gordimer, speaking of South
    Africa, in interview in *Writers at Work* (6th
    series, 1984)

34 The real fight to be fought is not against
    writings about sexual intercourse or the use
    of four-letter words, but against obscenities
    like calling a black man 'nigger' or labelling
    a person you disagree with 'commie'.
    Irving Wallace, *The Seven Minutes* (1969)

35 Obscenity today, in the fevered suspicions of
    library censors, is the obscurity of racism or
    sexism located in books like *Huckleberry
    Finn*, *Dr Dolittle* and *Biggles*.
    Editorial in *The Times* (24 Nov. 1986)

36 Ordinarily, the only reason for which I
    should countenance banning books is that
    they bore me.
    Paul Levy, 'Cooking: The Books' in *The
    Anti-Booklist* (ed. Brian Redhead and
    Kenneth McLeish, 1981)

26 CHILDREN'S BOOKS

1 Child! Do not throw this book about;
   Refrain from the unholy pleasure
   Of cutting all the pictures out!
   Preserve it as your chiefest treasure.
   Hilaire Belloc, dedication to *The Bad
   Child's Book of Beasts* (1896)

2 The books one reads in childhood, and
   perhaps most of all the bad and good bad
   books, create in one's mind a sort of false
   map of the world, a series of fabulous
   countries into which one can retreat at odd
   moments throughout the rest of life, and
   which in some cases can even survive a visit
   to the real countries which they are
   supposed to represent.
   George Orwell, 'Riding Down from Bangor'
   (1946)

3 You know how it is in the kid's book world:
   it's just bunny eat bunny.
   Anonymous

4 I don't believe in children's books. I think
   after you've read *Kidnapped*, *Treasure
   Island* and *Huckleberry Finn*, you're ready
   for anything.
   John Mortimer, in *Books and Bookmen*
   (May 1986)

5 The key battle which must be won, and
   which would settle the future of the book-
   trade, is the battle for the children's market.
   Ian Chapman, Chairman of Collins, quoted
   in *The Times* (7 April 1986)

6 Forty thousand children's books printed in
   Britain a year, thousands of bloody awful
   ones, most pulped and never reprinted.
   Roald Dahl, in interview in *The Observer*
   (23 Dec. 1985)

7 Fighting fantasies, pop-up books and
   novelizations of television programmes, may
   have kept the wolf from the children's
   publisher's door, but they must not be
   allowed to become the norm.
   E.J. Craddock, quoted in *The Times* (7 April
   1986)

8 Before a child of our time finds his way clear
   to opening a book, his eyes have been
   exposed to such a blizzard of changing,
   colourful, conflicting letters that his chances
   of penetrating the archaic stillness of the
   book are slight.
   Walter Benjamin, *One-Way Street*
   (1925–6)

9 *Peter Pan* is a charming play for children. It
   is not a rule of conduct for a great nation.
   Edith Shackleton, quoted by James Agate,
   Ego 3 (4 Dec. 1936)

27 CLASS

1 While you converse with lords and dukes,
I have their betters here — my books.
Thomas Sheridan, 'A Bookworm's Content'

2 Lords too are bards, such things at times
       befall,
And 'tis some praise in peers to write at all.
Lord Byron, *English Bards and Scotch Reviewers* (1809)

3 No writer before the middle of the 19th century wrote about the working classes other than as grotesques or as pastoral decoration. Then when they were given the vote certain writers began to suck up to them.
Evelyn Waugh, in *The Paris Review* (1963)

4 There must be something of the peasant in every poet.
Wallace Stevens, *Opus Posthumous* (1957)

5 If a poet meets an illiterate peasant, they may not be able to say much to each other, but if they both meet a public official, they share the same feeling of suspicion; neither will trust one further than he can throw a grand piano.
W.H. Auden, 'The Poet and the City', *The Dyer's Hand* (1962)

6 If any writer thinks the world is full of middle-class people of nice sensibilities, then he is out of his mind.
Tom Sharpe, quoted in 'Sayings of the Week' in *The Observer* (3 Feb. 1985)

28 CLASSICAL LITERATURE

1 A young poet should be bound apprentice to *Pindar* for three years, whether his business be the ode or anything else. He will find nothing in the workshop which he expected to find, but quite enough of highly-wrought tools and well-seasoned materials.
Walter Savage Landor, to John Forster, *Life* (1876)

2 When English poetry goes Classical it goes French, and when it goes French it goes wrong.
Robert Graves, 'Hélas, c'est Victor Hugo', *Observations on Poetry* (1922–5)

3 I knew a gentleman, who was so good a manager of his time, that he would not even lose that small portion of it, which the calls of nature obliged him to pass in the necessary-house; but gradually went through all the Latin poets, in those moments.
Lord Chesterfield, writing to his son (11 Dec. 1747)

4 Yes, always keep the Classics at hand to prevent flop.
Virginia Woolf, *Diary* (23 June 1937)

5 We cannot improve on the classics.
Jean de la Fontaine, 'La Mort et le malheureux'

6 Modern writers are the moons of literature; they shine with reflected light, with light borrowed from the ancients.
Samuel Johnson, quoted in James Boswell, *Life of Samuel Johnson* (1791)

7 Speak of the moderns without contempt and of the ancients without idolatry; judge them all by their merits, but not by their age.
Lord Chesterfield, writing to his son (22 Feb. 1748)

8 The classics are only primitive literature. They belong to the same class as primitive machinery and primitive music and primitive medicine.
Stephen Butler Leacock, *Behind the Beyond: Homer and Humbug* (1913)

9 A strange superstition survives among Classicists that some flowers are poetical and others are not.
Robert Graves, 'Ariphrades', *Observations on Poetry* (1922–5)

10 The girls today in society
Go for classical poetry,
So to win their hearts one must quote with
       ease
Aeschylus and Euripides.
One must know Homer and, b'lieve me, bo,
Sophocles, also Sappho-ho.
Cole Porter, 'Brush up your Shakespeare'

29 CLASSICS

1 A classic is something that everybody wants to have read and nobody wants to read.
Mark Twain, speech 'The Disappearance of Literature', New York (20 Nov. 1900)

2 I do not think altogether the worse of a
   book for having survived the author a
   generation or two. I have more confidence
   in the dead than the living . . . If you want
   to know what any of the authors were who
   lived before our time, you have only to look
   into their works. But the dust and smoke
   and noise of modern literature have nothing
   in common with the pure, silent air of
   immortality.
   William Hazlitt, 'On Reading Old Books',
   The Plain Speaker (1852)

3 Books that have become classics — books
   that have had their day and now get more
   praise than perusal — always remind me of
   retired colonels and majors and captains
   who, having reached the age limit, find
   themselves retired on half-pay.
   Thomas Bailey Aldrich, 'Leaves from a
   Notebook', *Ponkapog Papers* (1903)

4 For what are the classics but the noblest
   recorded thoughts of man? They are the
   only oracles which are not decayed.
   Henry David Thoreau, 'Reading', *Walden*
   (1854)

5 Some will read old books, as if there were no
   valuable truths to be discovered in modern
   publications.
   Isaac D'Israeli, *Literary Miscellanies* (1840)

6 I visit occasionally the Cambridge Library,
   and I can seldom go there without renewing
   the conviction that the best of it all is
   already within the four walls of my study at
   home. The inspection of the catalogue
   brings me continually back to the few
   standard writers who are on every private
   shelf; and to these it can afford only the
   most slight and casual additions. The
   crowds and centuries of books are only
   commentary and elucidation, echoes and
   weakeners of those few great voices of time.
   Ralph Waldo Emerson, 'Books', *Society and
   Solitude* (1870)

7 The worst thing about new books is that
   they keep us from reading the old ones.
   Joseph Joubert, *Pensées* (1842)

8 In Art, the public accept what has been,
   because they cannot alter it, not because
   they appreciate it. They swallow their
   classics whole, and never taste them.
   Oscar Wilde, *The Soul of Man Under
   Socialism* (1891)

9 There is but one way left to save a classic: to
   give up revering him and use him for our
   own salvation.
   José Ortega y Gasset, 'In Search of Goethe
   from Within, Letter to a German', in *The
   Partisan Review* (Dec. 1949)

10 Classics which at home are drowsily read
   have a strange charm in a country inn, or in
   the transom of a merchant brig.
   Ralph Waldo Emerson, *English Traits*
   (1856)

11 Normally, I read my Classics in strip form.
   Tommy Steele, quoted in 'Sayings of the
   Week' in *The Observer* (5 June 1960)

12 Reading the classics is one thing — writing's
          a different story.
   Glyn Jones, 'The Dream of Jake Hopkins'

13 A man with his belly full of the classics is an
   enemy of the human race.
   Henry Miller, *Tropic of Cancer* (1930)

30 COMEDY
See also HUMOUR

1 All that Russian gloom and doom, and
   people shooting themselves from loneliness
   and depression and that sort of thing. But
   then, mother says I don't understand
   comedy. I expect she's right.
   Simon Gray, *Quartermaine's Terms* (1981)

2 Comedy, I imagine, is harder to do
   consistently than tragedy, but I like it spiced
   in the wine of sadness.
   Bernard Malamud, in interview in *Writers
   at Work* (6th series, 1984)

3 In tragedy every moment is eternity; in
   comedy, eternity is a moment.
   Christopher Fry, in *Time* (20 Nov. 1950)

31 CONTEMPORARY LITERATURE

1 The experience of each new age requires a
   new confession, and the world seems always
   waiting for its poet.
   Ralph Waldo Emerson, 'The Poet', *Essays*
   (1844)

2 The poet is a prophet only in so far as he has
   an audience in his own time. To wait for the

future with which he is already abreast is to deliver his message too late. The poet should point out what is happening *while* it is happening: he is not there to deliver funeral orations. This, if it is true, places a terrible burden of responsibility on the poet. His antennae must be moving, his feelers waving with a feverish intensity.
J. Isaacs, *The Background to Modern Poetry* (1951)

3 It is the role of the poet to look at what is happening in the world and to know that quite other things are happening.
V.S. Pritchett, *The Myth Makers* (1979)

4 The gold of the poet must be refined, moulded, stamped with the image and superscription of his time, but with a beauty of design and finish that are of no time. The work must surpass the material.
James Russell Lowell, 'Carlyle', *My Study Window* (1871)

5 I do distrust the poet who discerns
No character or glory in his times.
Elizabeth Barrett Browning, *Aurora Leigh* (1857)

6 There are two classes of authors: the one write the history of their times, the other their biography.
Henry David Thoreau, *Journal* (22 April 1841)

7 Poets who leave their own time out of their work cannot be surprised if their time fails to find them interesting. The life and thought about us must be the foundation of our life and thought. Those poets who shrink from the life about them, however skilfully they may invent or imagine, will appeal, in the main, not to the world but to those few who, like themselves, cannot or will not face the world.
John Masefield, *With the Living Voice* (1925)

8 It is enough for the poet to be the bad conscience of his time.
Saint-John Perse, in letter to Archibald MacLeish (23 Dec. 1941) and in address to the Swedish Academy (10 Dec. 1960)

9 Poetry can communicate the actual quality of experience with a subtlety and precision unapproachable by any other means. But if the poetry and the intelligence of the age lose touch with each other, poetry will cease to matter much and the age will be lacking in finer awareness.
F.R. Leavis, *New Bearings in English Poetry* (1932)

10 No good poetry is written in a manner twenty years old, for to write in such a manner shows conclusively that the writer thinks from books, convention and cliché; and not from life.
Ezra Pound, 'Prolegomena', in *The Poetry Review* (Feb. 1913)

11 The volumes of antiquity, like medals, may very well serve to amuse the curious, but the works of the moderns, like the current coin of a kingdom, are much better for immediate use.
Oliver Goldsmith, *A Citizen of the World* (1760)

12 Good poetry of any age is good forever: the point is that in order to be good poetry, it must be the expression of actual and immediate experience at first hand, the vision of the eternal through what is, here and now — not through what was, yesterday . . . Somehow or other, poetry has always to come to terms with the modern contemporary consciousness.
Aubrey de Selincourt, *On Reading Poetry* (1952)

13 It has to be living, to learn the speech of the place,
It has to face the man of the time.
Wallace Stevens, 'Of Modern Poetry'

32 CRAFT
See also TRADE

1 The lyf so short, the craft so long to lerne.
Geoffrey Chaucer, *The Parlement of Foules* (c. 1372–86), quoting Hippocrates; the Latin version, 'Ars longa, vita brevis', is from Seneca, *De Brevitate Vitae*

2 Writing prose is like laying a mosaic.
Kurt Tucholsky, *Briefe aus dem Schweigen* (1977)

3 Doctors undertake a doctor's work; carpenters handle carpenter's tools: but, skilled, or unskilled, we scribble poetry, all alike.
Horace, *Epistles*

4 What is written without effort is in general
   read without pleasure.
   Samuel Johnson, quoted in Birkbeck Hill's
   Johnsonian Miscellanies (1897)

5 A man may be born a poet, but he has to
   make himself an artist as well. He must
   master the instrument . . . Without clarified
   construction and technical control, no
   poetical communication can be effective.
   Siegfried Sassoon, *On Poetry* (1939)

6 The literary beauty of my work has no other
   significance for me than that found by a
   workman who is aware of having performed
   his task well; I simply did my best; but, had
   I been a carpenter, I should have been just as
   conscientious in planing a plank properly as
   I have been in writing properly.
   Paul Claudel, quoted in *The Journals of
   André Gide* (vol. 1)

7 Writing has laws of perspective, of light and
   shade, just as painting does, or music. If you
   are born knowing them, fine. If not, learn
   them. Then rearrange the rules to suit
   yourself.
   Truman Capote, in interview in *Writers at
   Work* (1st series, 1958)

8 As with many English novelists, he had not
   taken the trouble to learn his job.
   Arnold Bennett, of Thomas Love Peacock,
   Journal (4 Jan. 1929)

9 There is no royal path to good writing; and
   such paths as exist do not lead through neat
   critical gardens, various as they are, but
   through the jungles of self, the world, and of
   craft.
   Jessamyn West in *The Saturday Review* (21
   Sept. 1957)

10 There can be no doubt that the best method
   of writing is to lay our literary compositions
   aside for a while, that we may after a
   reasonable period return to them, and find
   them, as it were, altogether new to us.
   Quintilian, *De Institutione Oratoria*

11 Most people won't realize that writing is a
   craft. You have to take your apprenticeship
   in it like anything else.
   Katherine Ann Porter, in *The Saturday
   Review* (31 March 1962)

12 If a book come from the heart, it will
   contrive to reach other hearts; all art and
   authorcraft are of small amount to that.
   Thomas Carlyle, *On Heroes, Hero-Worship
   and the Heroic in History* (1840)

13 You praise the firm restraint with which
                    they write,
   I'm with you there, of course:
   They use the snaffle and the curb all right,
   But where's the bloody horse?
   Roy Campbell, 'On Some South African
   Novelists'

33 CRITICISM
See also SELF-CRITICISM

General

1 The patter of tiny criticism.
   Christopher Fry, attr.

2 There is one gratification an old author can
   afford a certain class of critics: that, namely,
   of comparing him as he is with what he was.
   It is a pleasure to mediocrity to have its
   superiors brought within range.
   Oliver Wendell Holmes, *Over the Teacups*
   (1891)

3 Criticism is easy, art is difficult.
   Philippe Destouches, *Le Glorieux* (1732)

4 Literary criticism should arise out of a debt
   of love.
   George Steiner, 'Tolstoy or Dostoevsky'
   (1959)

5 Scarcely any literature is entirely
   unprofitable as the so-called criticism that
   overlays a pithy text with a windy sermon.
   John Morley, 'Emerson', *Critical
   Miscellanies* (1871–1908)

6 I am bound by my own definition of
   criticism: a disinterested endeavour to learn
   and propagate the best that is known and
   thought in the world.
   Matthew Arnold, 'Functions of Criticism at
   the Present Time', *Essays in Criticism*
   (1865)

7 A textual critic engaged upon his business is
   not at all like Newton investigating the
   motions of the planets; he is much more like
   a dog hunting for fleas. If a dog hunted for
   fleas on mathematical principles, basing his
   researches on statistics of area and density
   of population, he would never catch a flea,
   except by accident. They require to be
   treated as individuals, and every problem

which presents itself to the textual critic must be regarded as possibly unique.
A.E. Housman, paper read to the Classical Association (1921)

8 One of the commonest but most uncritical faults of criticism — the refusal to consider what it is that the author intended to give us.
George Saintsbury, in preface to Henry Fielding, *Tom Jones*

9 Criticism, I take it, is the formal discourse of an amateur.
R.P. Blackmur, *Language as Gesture* (1952)

10 Literary criticism is constantly attempting a very absurd thing — the explanation of passionate utterance by utterance that is unimpassioned: it is like trying to paint a sunset in lamp-black.
John Davidson, *Sentences and Paragraphs* (1893)

11 True judgement in Poetry takes a view of the whole together; 'tis a sign that malice is hard driven, when 'tis forced to lay hold on a word or syllable.
John Dryden, preface to *Sylvae* (1685)

12 To substitute judgments of fact for judgments of value, is a sign of pedantic and borrowed criticism.
George Santayana, *The Sense of Beauty* (1896)

13 The work of criticism is rooted in the unconscious of the critic just as the poem is rooted in the unconscious of the poet.
Randall Jarrell, *A Sad Heart at the Supermarket* (1965)

14 While there is a great mass of valuable criticism done by critics, the most valuable criticism of all, the only quite essential criticism, has been done by creative writers, for the most part poets.
Arthur Symons, in introduction to S.T. Coleridge, *Biographia Literaria* (1817)

15 When the critics are themselves poets, it may be suspected that they have formed their critical statements with a view to justifying their poetic practice.
T.S. Eliot, introduction to *The Use of Poetry* (1933)

16 Every nation, every race, has not only its own creative, but its own critical turn of mind; and is even more oblivious of the shortcomings and limitations of its critical habits than of those of its creative genius.
T.S. Eliot, 'Tradition and the Individual Talent' (1919)

17 Of all the cants which are canted in this canting world, — though the cant of hypocrites may be the worst, — the cant of criticism is the most tormenting!
Laurence Sterne, *Tristram Shandy* (1760–7)

18 For poets, if they bother to think of it, it is pleasant to reflect that all the speculations and involutions and conclusions of criticism and poetics are derivative — from their poems.
Geoffrey Grigson, *The Private Art* (1982)

19 Criticism is necessary, I suppose; I know. Yet criticism to the poet is no necessity, but a luxury he can ill afford.
Randall Jarrell, *A Sad Heart at the Supermarket* (1965)

20 Criticism is the tenth Muse and Beauty the fourth Grace.
Gustave Flaubert, *Carnets*

21 Criticism is like champagne: nothing more execrable if bad, nothing more excellent if good.
Charles Caleb Colton, *Lacon* (1825)

22 I read a good deal of criticism, but only as a vice, not so good as reading science fiction, rather better than reading mystery stories.
Gore Vidal, *Behind the Scenes*

23 I never read anything concerning my work. I feel that criticism is a letter to the public which the author, since it is not directed to him, does not have to open and read.
Rainer Maria Rilke, *Letters* (1936–9)

24 Instant criticism is a contradiction in terms. Criticism should be considered; reviewing must be done at once.
John Bowen, in *The Author* (Spring 1972)

25 Boredom, after all, is a form of criticism.
William Phillips, *A Sense of the Present* (1967)

26 People ask you for criticism, but they only want praise.
Somerset Maugham, *Of Human Bondage* (1915)

27 Most writers in the course of their careers become thick-skinned and learn to accept vituperation, which in any other profession

would be unimaginably offensive, as a healthy counterpoise to unintelligent praise.
Evelyn Waugh, in *The New York Times Magazine* (30 Nov. 1952)

Adverse

28 What is a modern poet's fate?
To write his thoughts upon a slate;
The critic spits on what is done,
Gives it a wipe — and all is gone.
Thomas Hood, quoted in Hallam Tennyson, *Alfred Lord Tennyson, A Memoir* (1897)

29 I cannot feel happy about that school of modern criticism which treats literature as a mine-field, to be approached in a suspicious attitude, with infinite caution and detectors held out in front of one; nor do I believe the chief task of the critic to be the exploding of reputations, however scientific the instruments employed, however reassuring may seem the fashionable code-word for the process.
C. Day-Lewis, *The Poet's Task* (1951)

30 The slanders of the pen pierce to the heart; they rankle longest in the noblest spirits; they dwell ever present in the mind and render it morbidly sensitive to the most trifling collision.
Washington Irving, 'English Writers on America', *The Sketch Book of Geoffrey Crayon, Gent.* (1819–20)

31 Literature is strewn with the wreckage of men who have minded beyond reason the opinion of others.
Virginia Woolf, *A Room of One's Own* (1929)

32 If the men of wit and genius would resolve never to complain in their works of critics and detractors, the next age would not know that they ever had any.
Jonathan Swift, *Thoughts on Various Subjects* (1706)

33 The crying sin of modern criticism is that it is overloaded with personality. If an author commit an error, there is no wish to set him right for the sake of truth, but for the sake of triumph.
Samuel Taylor Coleridge, *First Lecture on Shakespeare* (1811–12)

34 Criticism hurt me when I had failures. I thought: I'll never write another play: But I'm an alligator. Only the alligators remain.

The others get out of the water.
Arthur Miller, quoted in 'Sayings of the Week' in *The Observer* (5 April 1987)

35 I would rather be attacked than unnoticed. For the worst thing you can do to an author is to be silent as to his works.
Samuel Johnson, quoted in James Boswell, *Life of Samuel Johnson* (1791)

36 The Stones that Critics hurl with Harsh Intent
A Man may use to build his Monument.
Arthur Guiterman, *A Poet's Proverbs* (1924)

Constructive

37 Get your enemies to read your works in order to mend them, for your friend is so much your second self that he will judge too like you.
Alexander Pope, *An Essay on Criticism* (1711)

38 Criticism should not be querulous and wasting, all knife and root-puller, but guiding, instructive, inspiring, a south wind, not an east wind.
Ralph Waldo Emerson, *Journals* (1847)

39 The critic's first duty is neither to condemn nor to praise, but to elucidate technique and meaning.
Michael Roberts, *A Critique of Poetry* (1934)

40 The critic, one would suppose, if he is to justify his existence, should endeavour to discipline his personal prejudices and cranks — tares to which we are all subject — and compose his differences with as many of his fellows as possible, in the common pursuit of true judgement.
T.S. Eliot, *The Function of Criticism* (1923)

41 The critic has one pre-eminent task — the task of easing or widening or deepening our response to poetry. There are, of course, many ways of performing this task. But no critical method will satisfactorily perform it, if there is not respect both for the poem and for the reader.
C. Day-Lewis, *The Poetic Image* (1947)

42 It is only through the vigilant, the militant use of our critical faculties that we can confer any real benefit on the authors whom we love.
Robert Martin Adams, quoted in Elmer Borklund, *Contemporary Literary Critics* (1977)

43 A true critic ought to dwell rather upon excellencies than imperfections, to discover the concealed beauties of a writer, and communicate to the world such things as are worth their observation.
Joseph Addison, in *The Spectator* (no. 291, 1712)

44 The aim of criticism is to distinguish what is essential in the work of a writer. It is the delight of a critic to praise; but praise is scarcely part of his duty . . . What we ask of him is that he should find out for us more than we can find out for ourselves.
Arthur Symons, introduction to S.T. Coleridge, *Biographia Literaria* (1817)

45 A man's mind is hidden in his writings; criticism brings it to light.
Solomon ibn Gabirol, *The Choice of Pearls* (*c.* 1050)

46 Criticism is the windows and chandeliers of art: it illuminates the enveloping darkness in which art might otherwise rest only vaguely discernible, and perhaps altogether unseen.
George Jean Nathan, *The Critic and the Drama* (1922)

47 A perfect judge will read each work of wit With the same spirit that its author writ.
Alexander Pope, *An Essay on Criticism* (1711)

48 I sit with sad civility, I read With honest anguish, and an aching head; And drop at last, but in unwilling ears, This saving counsel, 'Keep your piece nine years'.
Alexander Pope, *Epistle to Dr Arbuthnot* (1735)

Favourable

49 Criticism is the art of praise.
Richard Le Gallienne, *Retrospective Reviews* (1896)

50 There is no reward so delightful, no pleasure so exquisite, as having one's work known and acclaimed by those whose applause confers honour.
Molière, *Le Bourgeois Gentilhomme* (1670)

51 He who first praises a book becomingly is next in merit to the author.
Walter Savage Landor, 'Alfieri and Salomon', *Imaginary Conversations* (1824–9)

52 Sometimes an admirer spends more talent

extolling a work than the author did in creating it.
Jean Rostand, *De la Vanité* (1925)

53 Few men in any age have second sight But never doubt *your* gift. You are right! You are right!
John Ciardi, 'To a Reviewer who Admired my Book'

54 Not unworthy the perusal.
Review of Isaac Walton, *The Compleat Angler* in a London newspaper (10 Oct. 1653)

34 CRITICS

1 A good critic is one who narrates the adventures of his mind among masterpieces.
Anatole France, in preface to *La Vie Littéraire* (1888–92)

2 A wise scepticism is the first attribute of a good critic.
James Russell Lowell, *Among my Books* (1870)

3 I will try to account for the degree of my aesthetic emotion. That, I conceive, is the function of the critic.
Clive Bell, *Art* (1914)

4 He wreathed the rod of criticism with roses.
Isaac D'Israeli, of Bayle, *The Curiosities of Literature* (1791–1834)

5 There should be a dash of the amateur in criticism. For the amateur is a man of enthusiasm who has not settled down and is not habit-bound.
Brooks Atkinson, 'July 8', *Once Around the Sun* (1951)

6 Great critics, of whom there are piteously few, build a home for the truth.
Raymond Chandler, in letter to Frederick L. Allen (1948)

7 A good critic is the sorcerer who makes some hidden spring gush forth unexpectedly under our feet.
François Mauriac, 'A Critique of Criticism', *Second Thoughts* (1961)

8 The critic, to interpret his artist, even to understand his artist, must be able to get

into the mind of his artist; he must feel and comprehend the vast pressure of the creative passion.
H.L. Mencken, *Prejudices* (1919)

9   Critics are sentinels in the grand army of letters, stationed at the corners of newspapers and reviews, to challenge every new author.
Henry Wadsworth Longfellow, *Kavanagh* (1849)

10   A literary critic's task is to create literature.
Saunders Lewis, in *Y Llenor* (Winter 1922)

11   You puff the poets of other days,
The living you deplore,
Spare me the accolade: your praise
Is not worth dying for.
Martial, *Epigrams*

12   He could gauge the old books by the old set of rules,
And his very old nothings pleased very old fools;
But give him a new book, fresh out of the heart,
And you put him at sea without compass or chart.
James Russell Lowell, *A Fable for Critics* (1848)

13   Let us teach others who themselves excel
And censure freely who have written well,
Authors are partial to their wit 'tis true;
But are not critics to their judgment too?
Alexander Pope, *An Essay on Criticism* (1711)

14   Now, in reality, the world have paid too great a compliment to critics, and have imagined them men of much greater profundity than they really are.
Henry Fielding, *Tom Jones* (1749)

15   Critics are like brushers of noblemen's clothes.
Francis Bacon, *Apophthegms* (1625)

16   Some judge of authors' names, not works, and then
Nor praise nor blame the writings, but the men.
Alexander Pope, *An Essay on Criticism* (1711)

17   You can spot the bad critic when he starts by discussing the poet and not the poem.
Ezra Pound, *The ABC of Reading* (1934)

18   You don't expect me to know what to say

about a play when I don't know who the author is, do you?
George Bernard Shaw, *Fanny's First Play* (1911)

19   Pay no attention to what the critics say; no statue has ever been put up to a critic.
Jean Sibelius, attr.

20   All great poets become critics, naturally and fatally.
Charles Baudelaire, *L'Art Romantique* (1931)

21   They who are to be judges must also be performers.
Aristotle, *Poetics*

22   A critic is a man who knows the way but can't drive the car.
Kenneth Tynan, in *The New York Times Magazine* (9 Jan. 1966)

23   A man must serve his time to every trade
Save censure — critics all are ready made.
Take hackneyed jokes from Miller, got by rote,
With just enough of learning to misquote.
Lord Byron, *English Bards and Scotch Reviewers* (1809)

24   A man is a critic when he cannot be an artist, in the same way that a man becomes an informer when he cannot be a soldier.
Gustave Flaubert, in letter to Louise Colet (Oct. 1846)

25   They who write ill, and they who ne'er durst write,
Turn critics out of mere revenge and spite.
John Dryden, *The Conquest of Granada* (1670)

26   Some have at first for wits, then poets pass'd,
Turn'd critics next, and prov'd plain fools at last.
Alexander Pope, *An Essay on Criticism* (1711)

27   You know who critics are? — the men who have failed in literature and art.
Benjamin Disraeli, *Lothair* (1870)

28   Critics are like eunuchs in a harem: they know how it's done, they've seen it done every day, but they're unable to do it themselves.
Brendan Behan, attr.

29   You do not publish your own verses,

Laelius; you criticise mine. Pray cease to criticise mine, or else publish your own.
Martial, *Epigrams*

30 It is exactly because a man cannot do a thing that he is the proper judge of it.
Oscar Wilde, 'The Critic as Artist', in *Intentions* (1891)

31 A good writer is not per se a good book critic. No more than a good drunk is automatically a good bartender.
Jim Bishop, in *New York Journal-American* (26 Nov. 1957)

32 What a blessed thing it is that Nature, when she invented, manufactured and patented her authors, contrived to make critics out of the chips that were left!
Oliver Wendell Holmes, *The Professor at the Breakfast Table* (1860)

33 God created the Poet, then took a handful of the rubbish that was left and made three critics.
T.J. Thomas (Sarnicol), 'Y Bardd a'r Beirniaid'

34 Asking a working writer what he thinks about critics is like asking a lamp-post what it thinks about dogs.
Christopher Hampton, in *The Sunday Times* (1977)

35 Critics . . . are of two sorts: those who merely relieve themselves against the flower of beauty, and those, less continent, who afterwards scratch it up.
William Empson, *Seven Types of Ambiguity* (rev. edn. 1947)

36 It may be well said that these wretched men know not what they do. They scatter their insults and their slanders without heed as to whether the poisoned shaft lights on a heart made callous by many blows, or one, like Keats', composed of more penetrable stuff.
Percy Bysshe Shelley, in preface to *Adonais* (1821)

37 Sing a song of critics
pockets full of lye
four and twenty critics
hope that you will die
hope that you will peter out
hope that you will fail
so that they can be the first one
be the first to hail.
Ernest Hemingway, 'Valentine'

38 O ye critics, will nothing melt ye?
Sir Walter Scott, *Journal* (1890)

39 Has anybody ever seen a dramatic critic in the daytime? Of course not. They come out after dark, up to no good.
P.G. Wodehouse, in *The New York Mirror* (27 May 1955)

40 My native habitat is the theatre. I toil not, neither do I spin. I am a critic and a commentator. I am essential to the theatre — as ants to a picnic, as the boll weevil to a cotton field.
Joseph L. Mankiewicz, film *All About Eve* (1950, based on Mary Orr, 'The Wisdom of Eve')

41 A dramatic critic is a man who leaves no turn unstoned.
George Bernard Shaw, in *The New York Times* (5 Nov. 1950)

42 A great deal of contemporary criticism reads to me like a man saying: 'Of course I do not like green cheese: I am very fond of brown sherry'.
G.K. Chesterton, 'On Jonathan Swift', *All I Survey* (1933)

43 The critic should describe, and not prescribe.
Eugène Ionesco, *Improvisation* (n.d.)

44 Then up spoke a brisk little somebody,
Critic and whippersnapper, in a rage
    To set things right.
Robert Browning, *Balaustion's Adventure* (1871)

45 Insects sting, not from malice, but because they want to live. It is the same with critics — they desire our blood, not our pain.
Friedrich Nietzsche, *Miscellaneous Maxims and Opinions* (1879)

46 The skin of a man of letters is peculiarly sensitive to the bite of the critical mosquito; and he lives in a climate in which such mosquitoes swarm. He is seldom stabbed to the heart — he is often killed by pin-pricks.
Alexander Smith, 'Men of Letters', *Dreamthorp* (1863)

47 Critics! appall'd I venture on the name,
Those cut-throat bandits in the path of
        fame.
Robert Burns, 'On Critics'

48 Seek roses in December — ice in June,
Hope constancy in wind, or corn in draft;

Believe a woman or an epitaph,
Or any other thing that's false, before
You trust in critics who themselves are
        sore.
Lord Byron, *English Bards and Scotch
Reviewers* (1809)

49 If certain Critics were as clear-sighted as
they are malignant, how great would be the
benefit to be derived from their writings.
Percy Bysshe Shelley, in preface to *The
Revolt of Islam* (1818)

50 Readers, real readers, are almost as wild a
species as writers; most critics are so
domesticated as to seem institutions.
Randall Jarrell, *Poetry and the Age* (1953)

51 The artist is a cut above the critic, for the
artist is writing something which will move
the critic. The critic is writing something
which will move everybody but the artist.
William Faulkner, in interview in *Writers at
Work* (1st series, 1958)

52 It seems to me much better to read a man's
own writing than to read what others say
about him, especially when the man is
first-rate and the 'others' are third-rate.
George Eliot, in letter to Miss Hennell
(1865)

53 There is a certain race of men that either
imagine it their duty, or make it their
amusement, to hinder the reception of every
work of learning or genius, who stand as
sentinels in the avenues of fame, and value
themselves upon giving ignorance and envy
the first notice of a prey.
Samuel Johnson, in *The Rambler* (1750–52)

54 And better had they ne'er been born,
Who read to doubt, or read to scorn.
Sir Walter Scott, *The Monastery* (1820)

55 A critic knows more than the author he
criticizes, or just as much, or at least
somewhat less.
Cardinal Manning, *Pastime Papers* (1892)

56 The opinion of a great body of the reading
public is very materially influenced by the
unsupported assertions of those who assume
a right to criticise.
Thomas Babington Macaulay,
'Montgomery's Poems', *Essays Contributed
to the Edinburgh Review* (1843)

57 Authors must be the only craftsmen in the
world who have to submit to the criticism of
inexperienced or incompetent people.
St John Ervine in *The Author* (Summer 1943)

58 People who would think it impertinent to
question the findings of the Astronomer
Royal . . . and who would listen with
respectful silence to an expert on gardening,
burst into clamour over a book of poems or
a piece of sculpture, though their knowledge
of these things may be no greater than their
knowledge of astronomy or horticulture.
Norman Callan, *Poetry in Practice* (1938)

59 Here lies New Critic who would tax us
With his poetic paradoxes.
Though he lies here rigid and quiet,
If he could speak he would deny it.
J.V. Cunningham, 'Epigrams'

60 Some praise at morning what they blame at
        night,
But always think the last opinion right.
Alexander Pope, *An Essay on Criticism*
(1711)

61 When critics disagree, the artist is in accord
with himself.
Oscar Wilde, in preface to *The Picture of
Dorian Gray* (1891)

62 Unless the bastards [critics] have the
courage to give you unqualified praise, I say
ignore them.
John Steinbeck, quoted in J.K. Galbraith, *A
Life in our Times* (1981)

63 The critic who justly admires all kinds of
things simultaneously cannot love any one
of them.
Max Beerbohm, 'George Moore', *Mainly
on the Air* (1946)

64 He takes the long review of things;
He asks and gives no quarter.
And you can sail with him on wings
Or read the book. It's shorter.
David McCord, 'To a Certain Most
Certainly Certain Critic'

65   I sometimes think
His critical judgement is so exquisite
It leaves us nothing to admire except his
        opinion.
Christopher Fry, *The Dark is Light Enough*
(1954)

66 Crritic!
Samuel Beckett, Estragon's final term of
abuse for Vladimir, *Waiting for Godot*
(1955)

35 DEATH

1 At the Day of Judgment, we shall not be asked what we have read but what we have done.
Thomas à Kempis, *Imitation of Christ* (*c.* 1420)

2 Stirring suddenly from long hibernation,
I knew myself once more a poet
Guarded by timeless principalities
Against the worm of death.
Robert Graves, 'Mid-Winter Waking'

3 I have been half in love with easeful Death,
Call'd him soft names in many a mused
        rhyme.
John Keats, 'Ode to a Nightingale'

4 Suicide *attempts*, and then writing *poems* about your suicide attempts, is just pure bullshit!
James Dickey, in interview in *Writers at Work* (5th series, 1981)

5 The words of a dead man
Are modified in the guts of the living.
W.H. Auden, 'In Memory of W.B. Yeats'

6 The theme of Death is to Poetry what Mistaken Identity is to Drama.
Dannie Abse, *Journals from the Ant-heap* (1986)

7 Who wields a poem huger than the grave?
e e cummings, 'but if a living dance upon dead minds'

8 The poem in the rock and
The poem in the mind
Are not one.
It was in dying
I tried to make them so.
R.S. Thomas, 'Epitaph'

9 When I have Fears that I may cease to be
Before my pen has glean'd my teeming
        brain.
John Keats, 'When I have Fears'

10 Once long ago here was a poet; who died.
See how remorse twitching his mouth
        proclaims
It was no natural death, but suicide.
Robert Graves, 'The Laureate'

11 Mighty poets in their misery dead.
William Wordsworth, *Resolution and Independence* (1807)

12 Death is the great Maecenas, Death is the great angel of writing. You must write because you are not going to live any more.
Carlos Fuentes, in interview in *Writers at Work* (6th series, 1984)

13 I wrote the book because we're all gonna die.
Jack Kerouac, *On the Road* (1957)

14 They buried him, but all through the night of mourning, in the lighted windows, his books arranged three by three kept watch like angels with outspread wings and seemed, for him who was no more, the symbol of his resurrection.
Marcel Proust, *Swann's Way* (1913)

15 Does Little Nell die?
Crowd on New York quay to crew of ship carrying the final instalment of Charles Dickens's *The Old Curiosity Shop* (1841)

16 One must have a heart of stone to read the death of Little Nell without laughing.
Oscar Wilde, attr.

17 All playwrights should be dead for three hundred years.
Joseph L. Mankiewicz, film *All About Eve* (1950, based on Mary Orr, 'The Wisdom of Eve')

18 The mortality of all inanimate things is terrible to me, but that of books most of all.
William Dean Howells, in a letter to Charles Eliot Norton (6 April 1903)

19 No more poetry after Auschwitz.
T.W. Adorno, quoted in Elmer Borklund, *Contemporary Literary Critics* (1977)

36 DESPAIR
See also SUFFERING

1 The flesh, alas, is wearied; and I have read all the books there are.
Stéphane Mallarmé, 'Brise Marin'

2 The Poet, gentle creature as he is,
Hath, like the Lover, his unruly times;
His fits when he is neither sick nor well,
Though no distress be near him but his own
Unmanageable thoughts.
William Wordsworth, *The Prelude* (1850)

3 Dogs with broken legs are shot; men with broken souls write through the night.
Kenneth Patchen, *The Journal of Albion Moonlight* (1961)

4 Do not judge the poet's life to be sad because of his plaintive verses and confessions of despair. Because he was able to cast off his sorrows into these writings, therefore went he onward free and serene to new experiences.
Ralph Waldo Emerson, *Journal* (1911)

5 They say my verse is sad: no wonder;
    Its narrow measure spans
Tears of eternity, and sorrow,
    Not mine, but man's.
A.E. Housman, epigraph to *More Poems* (1936)

6 The lengthy error known as Life
Began in a single cell,
And that is where for luckless lads
It sometimes ends as well.

And so it's down the road I go
With my eternal curse
And that's what comes of reading
Pessimistic verse.
Peter DeVries, 'Beth Appleyard's Verses: Loveliest of Pies' (parody of A.E. Housman)

37 DETECTIVE NOVEL

1 Ever since Sherlock Holmes most Englishmen have been born with a detective novel attached to their umbilical cords.
Tristram Busch, *Secret Service Unmasked*

2 There is a great deal of difference between the eager man who wants to read a book, and the tired man who wants to read a book. A man reading a Le Queux mystery wants to get to the end of it. A man reading the Dickens novel wishes that it might never end. Men read a Dickens story six times because they knew it so well. If a man can read a Le Queux story six times it is only because he can forget it six times.
G.K. Chesterton, *Charles Dickens* (1913)

3 Do you abominate detective stories? I read two a week in bed at night; can't concentrate on much else then. To me they are a great solace, a sort of mental knitting where it doesn't matter much if you drop a stitch.
Rupert Hart-Davis, *The Lyttelton-Hart-Davis Letters* (1978)

4 Almost all of the North American novelists of this school — the detective novel — are perhaps the most severe critics of the crumbling North American capitalist society.
Pablo Neruda, in interview in *Writers at Work* (5th series, 1981)

5 The detective novel is the art-for-art's-sake of yawning Philistinism.
V.S. Pritchett, 'The Roots of Detection', *Books in General* (1953)

6 The thriller is an extension of the fairy tale. It is melodrama so embellished as to create the illusion that the story being told, however unlikely, could be true.
Raymond Chandler, *Raymond Chandler Speaking* (1962)

7 The ideal mystery is one you would read if the end was missing.
Raymond Chandler, quoted in Gavin Lambert, *The Dangerous Edge* (1975)

8 Crime writers tend to be a very benign and generous bunch. I can only think it's the obvious psychology: they put all the evil into their books and, as it were, syphon it off.
Simon Brett, in *Publishers Weekly* (25 Oct. 1985)

9 A writer of crook stories ought never to stop seeking new material.
Edgar Wallace, on standing as a parliamentary candidate, quoted in Robert Graves and Alan Hodge, *The Long Weekend* (1940)

38 DIALOGUE

1 'And what is the use of a book,' thought Alice, 'without pictures or conversations?'
Lewis Carroll, *Alice's Adventures in Wonderland* (1865)

2 Dialogue in fiction should be reserved for the culminating moments and regarded as the spray into which the great wave of

narrative breaks in curving towards the watcher on the shore.
Edith Wharton, *The Writing of Fiction* (1925)

3 The dialogue of this author is often so evidently determined by the incident which produces it, and is pursued with so much ease and simplicity, that it seems scarcely to claim the merit of fiction, but to have been gleaned by diligent selection out of common conversation, and common occurrences.
Samuel Johnson, Preface to the Plays of William Shakespeare (1765)

4 I write plays because dialogue is the most respectable way of contradicting myself.
Tom Stoppard, in *The Guardian* (1973)

---

39 DIARY

1 Diary. A daily record of that part of one's life which he can relate to himself without blushing.
Ambrose Bierce, *The Devil's Dictionary* (1911)

2 Why has my motley diary no jokes? Because it is a soliloquy and every man is grave alone.
Ralph Waldo Emerson, *Journal* (1911)

3 I always say, keep a diary and someday it'll keep you.
Mae West, in *Every Day's a Holiday* (1937)

4 Let diaries, therefore, be brought in use.
Francis Bacon, 'Of Travel', *Essays* (1597)

5 It is a strange thing that in sea voyages where there is nothing to be seen but sky and sea, men should make diaries; but in land travel, whereas so much is to be observed, for the most part they omit it.
Francis Bacon, 'Of Travel', *Essays* (1597)

6 Only good girls keep diaries. Bad girls don't have the time.
Tallulah Bankhead, remark

7 I suppose I must go on here with my diary — as I can't get another book.
Elizabeth Barrett Browning, diary entry for Jan. 1832

8 I never travel without my diary. One should

always have something sensational to read in the train.
Oscar Wilde, *The Importance of Being Earnest* (1895)

9 When all is said and done, leading a good life is more important than keeping a good diary.
Siegfried Sassoon, diary entry for 8 July 1923

10 As I think, this diary writing has greatly helped my style; loosened the ligatures.
Virginia Woolf, diary entry for 1 Nov. 1924

11 I suppose this is the reason why diaries are so rarely kept nowadays — that nothing ever happens to anybody.
A.A. Milne, *Not That it Matters* (1919)

12 Why do I keep this volumnous journal? I can hardly tell. Partly because life appears to me such a curious and wonderful thing that it almost seems a pity that even such a humble and uneventful life as mine should pass altogether away without some such record as this, and partly too because I think the record may amuse and interest some who come after me.
Francis Kilvert, diary entry for 3 Nov. 1874

13 Should you wish to make sure that your birthday will be celebrated three hundred years hence, your best course undoubtedly, is to keep a diary.
Virginia Woolf, *The Common Reader* (1925)

14 If a man has no constant lover who shares his soul as well as his body he must have a diary — a poor substitute, but better than nothing.
James Lees-Milne, diary entry for 6 Jan. 1946

15 After a day of humiliation and stripes, if I can write it down, I am straightway relieved and can sleep well. After a day of joy, the beating heart is calmed again by the diary.
Ralph Waldo Emerson, diary entry for 21 Oct. 1841

16 I do not keep a diary. Never have. To write a diary every day is like returning to one's own vomit.
Enoch Powell, in *The Sunday Times* (6 Nov. 1977)

17 I got out this diary and read, as one always reads one's own writing, with a kind of guilty intensity.
Virginia Woolf, *A Writer's Diary* (1953)

18 I have all my life regretted that I did not
keep a regular journal.
Sir Walter Scott, diary entry for 20 Nov.
1825

19 It is a long time since I made an entry —
partly from failing health and partly from
the absence of anything to record.
Benjamin Armstrong, final entry in his diary
(12 May 1887)

---

40 DICTIONARY

1 Dictionary. A malevolent literary device for
cramping the growth of a language and
making it hard and inelastic.
Ambrose Bierce, *The Enlarged Devil's
Dictionary* (1967)

2 From time to time I find myself terribly
limited by the dictionary.
Marcel Aymé, remark to journalist

3 Literature ought to let you make up your
own mind. Dictionaries lay down the law.
George Macbeth, in *The Anti-Booklist* (ed.
Brian Redhead and Kenneth McLeish,
1981)

4 All dictionaries are made from dictionaries.
Voltaire, *Philosophical Dictionary* (1764)

5 What is the metre of the dictionary?
Dylan Thomas, 'Altarwise by Owl-light'

6 When I feel inclined to read poetry I take
down my Dictionary. The poetry of words is
quite as beautiful as that of sentences. The
author may arrange the gems effectively, but
their shape and lustre have been given by the
attrition of ages.
Oliver Wendell Holmes, 'The Autocrat's
Autobiography', *The Autocrat at the
Breakfast Table* (1858)

7 Here's a book full of words; one can choose
            as he fancies,
    As a painter his tint, as a workman his
            tool;
Just think! all the poems and plays and
            romances
    Were drawn out of this, like the fish from
            the pool!
Oliver Wendell Holmes, 'A Familiar Letter'

8 Words — so innocent and powerless as they
are, as standing in a dictionary, how potent
for good and evil they become, in the hands
of one who knows how to combine them!
Nathaniel Hawthorne, *American
Notebooks* (1841–52)

9 The greatest masterpiece in literature is only
a dictionary out of order.
Jean Cocteau, *Le Potomak* (1919)

10 Neither is a dictionary a bad book to read.
There is no cant in it, no excess of
explanation, and it is full of suggestion, the
raw material of possible poems and
histories.
Ralph Waldo Emerson, 'In Praise of Books',
The Conduct of Life (1860)

11 I am not yet so lost in lexicography, as to
forget that words are the daughters of earth,
and that things are the sons of heaven.
Samuel Johnson, in preface to *A Dictionary
of the English Language* (1775)

12 It is the fate of those who toil at the lower
employments of life . . . to be exposed to
censure, without hope of praise; to be
disgraced by miscarriage, or punished for
neglect . . . Among these unhappy mortals
is the writer of dictionaries . . . Every other
author may aspire to praise, the
lexicographer can only hope to escape
reproach.
Samuel Johnson, in preface to *A Dictionary
of the English Language* (1775)

13 No dictionary of a living tongue can ever be
perfect, since while it is hastening to
publication, some words are budding and
some falling away.
Samuel Johnson, in preface to *A Dictionary
of the English Language* (1755)

14 Dictionaries are like watches; the worst is
better than none, and the best cannot be
expected to go quite true.
Samuel Johnson, quoted in Hester Lynch
Piozzi, *Anecdotes of Samuel Johnson* (1786)

15 Lexicographer: a writer of dictionaries, a
harmless drudge.
Samuel Johnson, quoted in James Boswell,
Life of Samuel Johnson (1791)

16 The responsibility of a dictionary is to
record a language, not set its style.
Philip Grove, editor-in-chief of *Webster's
Third New International Dictionary*, in a
letter to *Life* magazine (17 Nov. 1961)

17 The four-letter words in *Lady Chatterley* are
not likely to be included in the Oxford

Dictionary as a result of the case. 'The legal judgment is irrelevant to our purpose,' said Oxford University Press. 'We don't take into account anything but common usage.'
Michael Bateman, quoted in 'This England', in the *Daily Express*

18 He put words into my mouth which I had to look up in the dictionary.
Graham Greene, of Anthony Burgess interviewing him in *The Observer* (28 Nov. 1982)

DRAMA, DRAMATIST
See THEATRE

41 DREAM

1 I bring you with reverent hands
The books of my numberless dreams.
W.B. Yeats, 'A Poet to his Beloved'

2 The poem is the dream made flesh, in a two-fold sense: as work of art, and as life, which is a work of art.
Henry Miller, 'Creative Death', *The Wisdom of the Heart* (1941)

3 A dreamer is always a bad poet.
Jean Cocteau, *Le Rappel à l'ordre* (1926)

4 The poet dreams being awake. He is not possessed by his subject but has dominion over it.
Charles Lamb, 'Sanity of True Genius', *Essays of Elia* (1820–3)

5 Literature is the total dream of man.
Graham Hough, *Image and Experience* (1964)

6 All books are either dreams or swords.
Amy Lowell, *Sword Blades and Poppy Seeds* (1914)

7 It is as easy to dream a book as it is hard to write one.
Honoré de Balzac, *Les Cabines des antiques* (1836)

42 DRINK

1 The most grave and awful denunciations of obscenity in literature are to be found precisely in those periodicals whose directors are most notoriously alcoholic.
Aldous Huxley, *Those Barren Leaves* (1925)

2 When I am a rich man with my own bicycle and can have beer for breakfast, I shall give up writing poetry altogether.
Dylan Thomas and John Davenport, *Death of the King's Canary* (1976)

3 Here lies a man, who, drinking only water,
Wrote twenty books, with each had son or daughter;
Had he but used the juice of generous vats,
The world would scarce have held his books and brats.
Epitaph on Andrew Toraqueau

4 I love my books as drinkers love their wine;
The more I drink, the more they seem divine.
Francis Bennoch, 'My Books'

5 Stranded by my foes,
Nowadays I write in prose,
Forsaking measure, rhyme, and honeyed diction;

Amphora's my muse:
When I finish off the booze,
I hump the jug and fill her up with fiction.
John Barth, 'The Minstrel's Last Lay'

6 I never drink while I'm working, but after a few glasses, I get ideas that would never have occurred to me dead sober. And some of the ideas turn out to be valuable the next day. Some not.
Irwin Shaw, in interview in *Writers at Work* (5th series, 1981)

7 Away! away! for I will fly to thee,
Not charioted by Bacchus and his pards,
But on the viewless wings of poesy.
John Keats, 'Ode to a Nightingale'

8 When I do come to town, bang go my plans in a horrid alcohol explosion that scatters all my good intentions like bits of limbs and clothes over the doorsteps and into the saloon bars of the tawdriest pubs in London.
Dylan Thomas, letter to a friend (1936)

9   Boozing does not necessarily have to go
    hand in hand with being a writer . . . I
    therefore solemnly declare to all young men
    trying to be writers that they do not actually
    have to become drunkards first.
    James Jones, in interview in *Writers at Work*
    (3rd series, 1967)

10 I've been drunk for about a week now and I
    thought it might sober me up to sit in a
    library.
    F. Scott Fitzgerald, *The Great Gatsby*
    (1925)

11 I have left off wine and writing; for I really
    think that a man must be a bold writer who
    trusts to wit without it.
    John Gay, to Dean Swift, *Life and Letters*
    (1921)

12 With punch you never know when you've
    had enough. It's different with authors —
    with them you know only too well.
    Curt Goetz, *Dreimal Täglich* (1965)

13 Souls of poets dead and gone,
    What Elysium have ye known,
    Happy field or mossy cavern,
    Choicer than the Mermaid Tavern?
    Have ye tippled drink more fine
    Than mine host's canary wine?
    John Keats, 'Lines on the Mermaid Tavern'

14 But that which most doth take my Muse
            and me,
    Is a pure cup of rich Canary wine,
    Which is the Mermaid's now, but shall be
            mine:
    Of which, had Horace or Anacreon tasted,
    Their lives, as do their lines, till now had
            lasted.
    Ben Jonson, 'Inviting a Friend to Supper'

15 Oh many a peer of England brews
    Livelier liquor than the Muse,
    And malt does more than Milton can
    To justify God's way to man.
    A.E. Housman, *A Shropshire Lad* (1896)

16 Let schoolmasters puzzle their brain
            With grammar, and nonsense, and
            learning,
    Good liquor, I stoutly maintain,
            Gives genius a better discerning.
    Oliver Goldsmith, *She Stoops to Conquer*
    (1773)

17 The University which once saw Wordsworth
    drunk and once saw Porson sober will see a
    better scholar than Wordsworth, and a

better poet than Porson, betwixt and
between.
A.E. Housman, in speech at farewell dinner,
University College London, on leaving for
Cambridge as Kennedy Professor of Latin
(1911)

18 It's hard to say why writing verse
    Should terminate in drink or worse.
    A.P. Herbert, 'Lines For a Worldly Person'

19 As we read in the first chapter of
    Guinness'es.
    James Joyce, *Ulysses* (1922)

20 Booze, of course, and then, curtains.
    Kingsley Amis, on being asked how he
    would spend the Booker Prize (22 Oct.
    1986)

---

43 DURABILITY OF BOOKS
See also CLASSICS, POSTERITY

---

1   A good book is the precious life-blood of a
    master spirit, embalmed and treasured up
    on purpose to a life beyond life.
    John Milton, *Areopagitica* (1644)

2   Books, like proverbs, receive their chief
    value from the stamp and esteem of ages
    through which they have passed.
    Sir William Temple, 'Of Ancient and
    Modern Learning', *Miscellanea* (1692)

3   The images of men's wits and knowledge
    remain in books, exempted from the wrong
    of time, and capable of perpetual
    renovation.
    Francis Bacon, *The Advancement of
    Learning* (1605)

4   All that mankind has done, thought, gained
    or been: it is lying as in magic preservation
    in the pages of books.
    Thomas Carlyle, 'The Hero as Man of
    Letters', *On Heroes, Hero-Worship and the
    Heroic in History* (1840)

5   Books have an infinite life: they have the
    unique distinction of not being disposed of
    after initial 'consumption'; they are
    susceptible to repeat consumption by
    different people.
    The Book Trade Year Book (1985)

6   For all books are divisible into two classes,
    the books of the hour, and the books of all

time. Make this distinction — it is not one of quality only. It is not merely the bad book that does not last, and the good one that does. It is a distinction of species. There are good books for the hour, and bad ones for all time.
John Ruskin, *Sesame and Lilies* (1865)

7 There is no test of literary merit except survival, which is itself, an index to majority opinion.
George Orwell, *Selected Essays* (1968)

8 We all hope in due course to write an antiquarian book.
John Mortimer, remark on opening the London Antiquarian Book Fair (1987)

9 Some books are undeservedly forgotten; none are undeservedly remembered.
W.H. Auden, *The Dyer's Hand* (1962)

10 In books I find the dead as if they were alive; in books I foresee things to come; in books warlike affairs are set forth; from books come forth the laws of peace. All things are corrupted and decay in time . . . All the glory of the world would be buried in oblivion, unless God had not provided mortals with the remedy of books.
Richard de Bury, *Philobiblon* (1473)

11 Laws die, books never.
Edward Bulwer-Lytton, *Richelieu* (1839)

12 For books are more than books, they are the
    life
The very heart and core of ages past,
The reason why men lived and worked and
    died,
The essence and quintessence of their lives.
Amy Lowell, 'The Boston Athenaeum'

13 The book is still the master of 'quietness and slow time'. It does not quarter the hour to the huckster's rant. It sells nothing but ideas and feelings, remembrances and hopes. The book will wait a minute, a year, a lifetime. It will say again, tirelessly, what it has said well once.
Frank G. Jennings, *This is Reading* (1964)

14 It is a wonderful quality of poems — of some poems — that they outlive everything which moulded and made the writer. There are now more perfect Greek poems than perfect Greek temples.
Geoffrey Grigson, *The Private Art* (1982)

15 Books constitute capital. A library book lasts as long as a house, for hundreds of

years. It is not, then, an article of mere consumption but fairly of capital, and often in the case of professional men, setting out in life, it is their only capital.
Thomas Jefferson, in letter to James Madison (Sept. 1821)

16 Books are the treasured wealth of the world, the fit inheritance of generations and nations.
Henry David Thoreau, 'Reading', *Walden* (1854)

17 Books are the great treasure guardians of the human race. They preserve from one century to another the best that has been imagined or discovered, they proclaim what was once alive on earth. From the time of their invention, almost all that we know and call culture lies within them. Between their covers they in truth contain the spirit of man. Thus the content of all books constructs a great spirit realm on earth, from which departed souls live on and draw near to all those now writing.
Gustav Freytag, *Die verlorene Handschrift* (1864)

18 At the time when the stone-cutter alone handled writing, literature existed, but not books; for the written record still lacked one essential quality: mobility . . . Writing enabled the word to conquer time, but the book enabled it to conquer space.
Robert Escarpit, *The Book Revolution* (1956)

19 Books cannot change. A thousand years hence they are what you find them to-day, speaking the same words, holding forth the same cheer, the same promise, the same comfort; always constant, laughing with those who laugh and weeping with those who weep.
Eugene Field, *The Love Affairs of a Bibliomaniac* (1896)

20 Much is written of the power of the Press, a power which may last but a day; by comparison little is heard of the power of books, which may endure for generations.
Sir Stanley Unwin, *The Truth About Publishing* (1926)

21 The book that he has made renders its author this service in return, that so long as the book survives, its author remains immortal and cannot die.
Richard de Bury, *Philobiblon* (1473)

22 If you would not be forgotten, as soon as you are dead and rotten, either write things worth reading, or do things worth the writing.
Benjamin Franklin, *Poor Richard's Almanac* (1738)

23 What a sense of security in an old book which Time has criticized for us!
James Russell Lowell, 'Library of Old Authors', *Literary Essays* (1864–90)

24 He, with his copy-rights and copy-wrongs, in his squalid garret, in his rusty coat; ruling (for this is what he does), from his grave, after death, whole nations and generations who would, or would not, give him bread while living, — is a rather curious spectacle!
Thomas Carlyle, 'The Hero as Man of Letters', *On Heroes, Hero-Worship and the Heroic in History* (1840)

25 Today the name of Nahum Tate is all but forgotten — except in learned footnotes. Yet every winter, when grown-ups sing or children parody the Christmas hymn 'While shepherds watched their flocks by night', he lives again.
Nick Russel, *Poets by Appointment* (1981)

44 EDITOR

1 Prostitutes have clients, wives have
        husbands,
Poets, you will understand, have editors.
Elizabeth Bartlett, 'My Five Gentlemen'

2 Just get it down on paper, and then we'll see what to do with it.
Maxwell Perkins, advice to Marcia Davenport

3 My definition of a good editor is a man I think charming, who sends me large checks, praises my work, my physical beauty, my sexual prowess, and who has a stranglehold on the publisher and the bank.
John Cheever, in interview in *Writers at Work* (5th series, 1981)

4 Having lunch or dinner with your editor won't gain you much more than a few calories.
Bill Adler, *Inside Publishing* (1982)

5 His wife not only edited his works but edited him.
Van Wyck Brooks, *The Ordeal of Mark Twain* (1920)

6 An editor is a man who takes a French poodle, and clips him into the shape of a lion.
Emery Kelen, quoted in *News Review* (27 May 1948)

7 You're always a little disappointing in person because you can't be the edited essence of yourself.
Mel Brooks, interview in *New York Post* (1975)

8 Editing is the same thing as quarrelling with writers — same thing exactly.
Harold Ross, in *Time* magazine (6 March 1950)

9 Editing is the most companionable form of education.
Edward Weeks, *In Friendly Candor* (1959)

10 An editor is one who separates the wheat from the chaff and prints the chaff.
Adlai Stevenson, *The Stevenson Wit* (1966)

11 Every abridgement of a good book is a stupid abridgement.
Michel de Montaigne, 'Of the Art of Conference', *Essays* (1580–8)

12 Yes, I suppose some editors are failed writers — but so are most writers.
T.S. Eliot, remark to Robert Giroux

13 Everyone needs an editor.
Tim Foote, commenting in *Time* magazine upon the fact that Hitler's original title for *Mein Kampf* was *Four-and-a-Half Years of Struggle against Lies, Stupidity, and Cowardice*

45 EDUCATION
See also LITERACY

1 The poet is the unsatisfied child who dares to ask the difficult question which arises from the schoolmaster's answer to his simple question, and then the still more difficult question which arises from that.
Robert Graves, *The White Goddess* (1948)

2 Poets were the first teachers of mankind.
Horace, *Ars Poetica*

3 Would you be a poet
    Before you've been to school?
Ah, well! I hardly thought you
    So absolute a fool.
Lewis Carroll, 'Poeta Fit, Non Nascitur'

4 Our principal writers have nearly all been
fortunate in escaping regular education.
Hugh MacDiarmid, quoted in 'Sayings of
the Week', *The Observer* (29 March 1953)

5 The true literary mind is likely to develop
slowly; it needs a more comprehensive and
more varied diet, a more miscellaneous
knowledge of facts, a greater experience of
men and of ideas, than the kind required for
the practice of the other arts. It therefore
presents a more baffling educational problem.
T.S. Eliot, 'The Classics and the Man of
Letters' (1942)

6 We insist in the face of a hostile majority
that reading, writing, and ciphering does not
complete the education of a poet.
T.S. Eliot, 'Contemporanea', in *The Egoist*
(June–July 1918)

7 The true university of these days is a
collection of books.
Thomas Carlyle, *On Heroes, Hero-Worship
and the Heroic in History* (1840)

8 Education has produced a vast population
able to read but unable to distinguish what
is worth reading.
G.M. Trevelyan, *English Social History*
(1944)

9 I saw a boy with eager eye
Open a book upon a stall,
And read, as he'd devour it all;
Which, when the stall man did espy,
Soon to the boy I heard him call,
'You, sir, you never buy a book,
Therefore in one you should not look.'
The boy passed slowly on, and with a sigh
He wished he never had been taught to read,
Then of the old churl's books he should
        have no need.
Mary Lamb, 'The Two Boys'

10 There is nothing on earth intended for
innocent people so honourable as a school.
To begin with, it is a prison. But it is in some
respects more cruel than a prison. In a
prison, for instance, you are not forced to
read books written by the warders and the
Governor.
George Bernard Shaw, 'Parents and
Children'

11 I am always for getting a boy forward in his
learning; for that is a sure good. I would let
him at first read *any* English book which
happens to engage his attention; because
you have done a great deal when you have
brought him to have entertainment from
a book. He'll get better books
afterwards.
Samuel Johnson, quoted in James Boswell,
Life of Samuel Johnson (1791)

12 The Tories have an education system in
which the most important book is the
cheque-book.
Neil Kinnock, in General Election speech
(30 May 1986)

---

46 EMOTION

1 Our passions shape our books, repose writes
them in the intervals.
Marcel Proust, *Time Regained* (1927)

2 The emotion of art is impersonal. And the
poet cannot reach this impersonality
without surrendering himself wholly to the
work to be done.
T.S. Eliot, 'Tradition and the Individual
Talent' (1919)

3 The poet is neither an intellectual nor an
emotional being alone; he feels his thoughts
and thinks his sensations.
Elizabeth Drew, *Discovering Poetry* (1933)

4 It is my heart that makes my songs, not I.
Sara Teasdale, 'What do I Care?' *Flame and
Shadow* (1920)

5   Each venture
Is a new beginning, a raid on the inarticulate
With shabby equipment always
            deteriorating
In the general mess of imprecision of feeling.
T.S. Eliot, *Four Quartets* (1943)

6 Poetry is not a turning loose of emotion, but
an escape from emotion; it is not the
expression of personality, but an escape
from personality. But, of course, only those
who have personality and emotion know
what it means to want to escape from these
things.
T.S. Eliot, 'Tradition and the Individual
Talent' (1919)

7 The nucleus of every poem worthy of the name is rhythmically formed in the poet's mind, during a trance-like suspension of his normal habits of thought, by the supra-logical reconciliation of conflicting emotional ideas. The poet learns to induce the trance in self-protection whenever he feels unable to resolve an emotional conflict by simple logic.
Robert Graves, 'The Poetic Trance', *Observations on Poetry* (1922–5)

8 Poetry is the spontaneous overflow of powerful feelings: it takes its origin from emotion recollected in tranquility.
William Wordsworth, preface to second edition of *Lyrical Ballads* (1800)

9 Poetry is a form of speech for the better expression of emotional ideas.
Herbert Spencer, 'Origin and Function of Music'

10 Some writers appear to believe that emotions gain in intensity through being inarticulate. Perhaps the emotions are not significant enough to endure full daylight.
T.S. Eliot, 'Rhetoric and Poetic Drama', *The Sacred Wood* (1920)

11 No tears in the writer, no tears in the reader.
Robert Frost, in preface to *Collected Poems* (1939)

12 A writer's eyes, to be clear, must be dry.
Georges Darien, *L'En-dehors*

13 Maturing as a poet means maturing as the whole man, experiencing new emotions appropriate to one's age, and with the same intensity as the emotions of youth.
T.S. Eliot, 'Yeats' (1940)

14 Let an author so tell his tale as to touch his reader's heart and draw his tears and he has, so far, done his work well.
Anthony Trollope, *Autobiography* (1883)

15 Many readers judge of the power of a book by the shock it gives their feelings.
Henry Wadsworth Longfellow, *Kavanagh* (1849)

16 We read fine things but never feel them to the full until we have gone the same steps as the author.
John Keats, in letter to John Hamilton Reynolds (3 May 1818)

ENDING
See BEGINNING

47 ENGLAND AND THE ENGLISH

1 I hold that no man can have any just conception of the history of England who has not often read, and meditated, and learnt to love the great poets of England.
Sir James Stephen, 'Desultory and Systematic Reading'

2 I think . . . that some of the best English poets, particularly Philip Larkin, are making a virtue of the unexcitingness of England, insisting on the quietness of England.
Stephen Spender, in interview in *Writers at Work* (6th series, 1984)

3 I am ashamed to live in England today. What a country of illiterate creatures it has become.
Nirad C. Chaudhuri, in *The Observer* (29 Nov. 1987)

4 In this country it is rare for anyone, let alone a publisher, to take writers seriously.
Anthony Powell, in *The Daily Telegraph* (8 Feb. 1979)

5 Of all the peoples in the world the English have the least sense of literature.
Oscar Wilde, *The Picture of Dorian Gray* (1890)

6 Barbara Cartland's cheque is a reflection of, and on, the taste of England.
Anthony Blond, *The Book Book* (1985)

7 Curse the blasted, jelly-boned swines, the slimy, the belly-wriggling invertebrates, the miserable sodding rutters, the flaming sods, the snivelling, dribbling, dithering, palsied, pulse-less lot that make up England today. They've got white of egg in their veins and their spunk is that watery it's a marvel they can breed.
D.H. Lawrence, to Edward Garnett on Heinemann's rejection of *Sons and Lovers* (1913)

8 Viewed in the national context, English literary life is unusually metropolitan: viewed in a world context, it is unusually provincial.
Francis King, in *The Author* (Spring 1977)

48 THE ENGLISH LANGUAGE

1 Our fathers have, in process of centuries, provided this realm, its colonies and wide dependencies, with a speech as malleable and pliant as Attic, dignified as Latin, masculine, yet free of Teutonic guttural, capable of being precise as French, dulcet as Italian, sonorous as Spanish, and captaining all these excellences to its service.
Arthur Quiller-Couch, introduction to *The Oxford Book of English Prose* (1900)

2 English. A language so haughty and reserved that few writers succeed in getting on terms of familiarity with it.
Amrbose Bierce, *The Enlarged Devil's Dictionary* (1967)

3 Ours is a precarious language, as every writer knows, in which the merest shadow line often separates affirmation from negation, sense from nonsense, and one sex from another.
James Thurber, 'Such a Phrase as Drifts Through Dreams', *Lanterns and Lances* (1961)

4 By its very looseness, by its way of evoking rather than defining, suggesting rather than saying, English is a magnificent vehicle for emotional poetry.
Max Beerbohm, 'On Speaking French', *And Even Now* (1920)

5 Out of us all
That make rhymes,
Will you choose
Sometimes —
As the winds use
A crack in a wall
Or a drain,
Their joy or their pain
To whistle through —
Choose me,
You English words?
Edward Thomas, 'Words'

6 Remember that you are a human being with the divine gift of articulate speech; that your native language is the language of Shakespeare and Milton and the Bible; and don't sit there crooning like a bilious pigeon.
George Bernard Shaw, *Pygmalion* (1913)

7 English is a fine language; a little of it goes a long way.
Pierre-Augustin Caron de Beaumarchais, *The Marriage of Figaro* (1784)

8 The masculine pronouns are he, his, and him,
But imagine the feminine she, shis and shim!
So our English, I think you will all agree,
Is the trickiest language you ever did see.
Anonymous, 'Why English is so Hard'

ENVY
See JEALOUSY

EPIGRAM
See APHORISM

49 ESSAY

1 An essayist is a lucky person who has found a way to discourse without being interrupted.
Charles Poore, in *The New York Times* (31 May 1962)

2 A good essay must have this peculiar quality about it: it must draw its curtain round us, but it must be a curtain that shuts us in, not out.
Virginia Woolf, *The Common Reader* (1925)

3 Meanwhile, you will write an essay on 'self-indulgence'. There will be a prize of half a crown for the longest essay, irrespective of any possible merit.
Evelyn Waugh, *Decline and Fall* (1928)

50 FAME

1 The universal object and idol of men of letters is reputation.
John Adams, *Discourses on Davila* (1791)

2 Literature is an avenue to glory, ever open
for those ingenious men who are deprived of
honours or of wealth.
Isaac D'Israeli, *Literary Character of Men of
Genius* (1818)

3 Pray consider what a figure a man would
make in the republic of letters.
Joseph Addison, *Dialogues upon the
Usefulness of Ancient Medals* (1726)

4 There is no surer way to make oneself a
name than by writing about things which
have a semblance of importance but which a
reasonable man is not likely to take the time
to investigate for himself.
Georg Christoph Lichtenberg, *Aphorisms*
(1764–99)

5 He that cometh in print because he would
be known, is like the fool that cometh into
the Market because he would be seen.
John Lyly, 'To the Gentlemen Readers',
Euphues (1580)

6 Make him (the reader) laugh and he will
think you a trivial fellow, but bore him in
the right way and your reputation is
assured.
Somerset Maugham, *The Gentleman in the
Parlour* (1930)

7 It took me fifteen years to discover I had no
talent for writing, but I couldn't give it up
because by that time I was too famous.
Robert Benchley, *On Himself*

8 Literary fame is the only fame of which a
wise man ought to be ambitious, because it
is the only lasting and living fame.
Robert Southey, quoted in Forster's *Life of
Landor* (1876)

9 Fame is a powerful aphrodisiac.
Graham Greene, quoted in *Radio Times* (10
Sept. 1964)

10 Unfortunately many young writers are more
concerned with fame than with their own
work . . . It's much more important to write
than to be written about.
Gabriel García Márquez, in interview in
Writers at Work (6th series, 1984)

11 Enduring fame is promised only to those
writers who can offer to successive
generations a substance constantly renewed;
for every generation arrives upon the scene
with its own particular hunger.
André Gide, 'Baudelaire and M. Faguet',
Pretexts (1903)

12 There is no luck in literary reputation. They
who make up the final verdict upon every
book are not the partial and noisy readers of
the hour when it appears; but a court as of
angels, a public not to be bribed, not to be
entreated, and not to be overawed, decides
upon every man's title to fame.
Ralph Waldo Emerson, 'Spiritual Laws',
Essays (1841)

13 Between the reputation of the author living
and the reputation of the same author dead
there is ever a wide discrepancy.
Thomas Bailey Aldrich, 'Leaves from a
Notebook', *Ponkapog Papers* (1903)

14 While an author is yet living, we estimate his
powers by his worst performance; and when
he is dead, we rate them by his best.
Samuel Johnson, *Works* (1792)

15 A man may write himself out of reputation
when nobody else can do it.
Thomas Paine, *The Rights of Man* (1791)

16 No one, not even a pretty woman who wakes
up to find a pimple on her nose, feels so
vexed as an author who threatens to survive
his own reputation.
Denis Diderot, *Rameau's Nephew* (1762)

17 Celebrity does not often come to poets, but
it is as hard for them to bear as for anyone
else . . . For poets it is better — in a way —
if celebrity comes after death.
Geoffrey Grigson, *The Private Art* (1982)

18 Mere wealth, I am above it,
It is the reputation wide,
The playwright's pomp, the poet's pride
That eagerly I covet.
Phyllis McGinley, 'A Ballad of Anthologies'

19 Personally, I have
Not found the
Time to get round
To reading the books
That have made you
A household name.
E.J. Thribb, 'Lines on the Hundredth
Anniversary of the Birth of W. Somerset
Maugham'

20 The only happy author in this world is he
who is below the care of reputation.
Washington Irving, 'Poor-Devil Author',
Tales of a Traveller (1824)

21 A famous writer who wants to continue

writing has to be constantly defending himself against fame.
Gabriel García Márquez, in interview in *Writers at Work* (6th series, 1984)

22 He [Robert Frost] worked very hard at his own reputation even when he had no need to.
Archibald MacLeish, in interview in *Writers at Work* (5th series, 1981)

23 To have the deep poetic heart
Is more than all poetic fame.
Alfred, Lord Tennyson, *The New Timon and the Poets* (1846)

24 I am more famed in heaven for my work than I could well conceive.
William Blake, in letter to John Flaxman (21 Sept. 1800)

25 Mark how my fame rings out from zone to zone;
A thousand critics shouting, 'He's unknown!'
Ambrose Bierce, 'Couplet'

26 In America only the successful writer is important, in France all writers are important, in England no writer is important, and in Australia you have to explain what a writer is.
Geoffrey Cotterell, in the *New York Journal-American* (22 Sept. 1961)

27 A lone letter from a young man: that is fame.
John Berryman, no. 342, *Dream Songs* (1964, 1968)

28 Lunching with poets, dining late with peers,
I felt that I had come into my own.
John Betjeman, 'Oxford Ode'

29 I should like one of these days to be so well known, so popular, so celebrated, so famous, that it would permit me to break wind in society, and society would think it a most natural thing.
Honoré de Balzac, remark in conversation with friends

30 I awoke one morning and found myself famous.
Lord Byron, entry in memoranda after publication of *Childe Harold* (1812)

31 I don't give a damn for the world, for the future, for what people say, for any settled establishment whatever, even for literary fame — which once upon a time made me

spend so many sleepless nights imagining it.
Gustave Flaubert, in a letter to his mother (15 Dec. 1850)

32 Whatever may be the success of my stories, I shall be resolute in preserving my incognito, having observed that a nom de plume secures all the advantages without the disagreeables of reputation.
George Eliot, in letter to John Blackwood (1857)

33 Let such as have not got a passport from nature be content with happiness, and leave to the poet the unrivalled possession of his misery, his garret, and his fame.
Oliver Goldsmith, 'The Poet', in *Critical Review* (1759)

34 It is a good lesson — though it may often be a hard one — for a man who has dreamed of literary fame . . . to step aside out of the narrow circle in which his claims are recognized, and to find how utterly devoid of significance, beyond that circle, is all that he achieves, and all he aims at.
Nathaniel Hawthorne, 'The Custom House', *The Scarlet Letter* (1850)

35 And coming to my own century
with its critics' compulsive hurry

to place a poet, I must smile
at the congestion at the turnstile

of fame, the faceless, formless amoeba
with the secretion of its *vers libre*.
R.S. Thomas, 'Taste'

36 Why stir the wasps that rim Fame's luscious pot?
Love costs us nothing, satire costs a lot!
Edgell Rickword, 'The Contemporary Muse'

37 I consider an author's literary reputation to be alive only while his name will insure a good price for his copy from the booksellers.
Oliver Goldsmith, quoted in James Boswell, *Life of Samuel Johnson* (1791)

38 Fame is rot; daughters are the thing.
J.M. Barrie, *Dear Brutus* (1917)

51 FASHION

1 Of all odd crazes, the craze to be forever reading new books is one of the oddest.
Augustine Birrell, 'Books Old and New', *Essays* (1922)

2 If you would know what nobody knows,
   read what everybody reads, just one year
   afterwards.
   Ralph Waldo Emerson, *Journals* (1834)

3 The choice of books, like the toilet of
   gentility, is governed by fashion, whose laws
   admit of no appeal.
   Gustave Brunet, *Bibliomania in the Present
   Day in France and England* (1880)

4 The three practical rules, then, which I have
   to offer, are (1) Never read any book that is
   not a year old. (2) Never read any but famed
   books. (3) Never read any but what you
   like.
   Ralph Waldo Emerson, 'Books', *Society and
   Solitude* (1870)

5 I am the kind of writer that people think
   other people are reading.
   V.S. Naipaul, in *Radio Times* (24 March
   1979)

6 Considering the multitude of mortals that
   handle the pen in these days, and can mostly
   spell, and write without glaring violations of
   grammar, the question naturally arises:
   How is it, then, that no work proceeds from
   them, bearing any stamp of authenticity and
   permanence, of worth for more than one
   day?
   Thomas Carlyle, 'Biography' (1832)

7 I shall not be satisfied unless I produce
   something which shall for a few days
   supersede the last fashionable novel on the
   tables of young ladies.
   Thomas Babington Macaulay, quoted in
   G.O. Trevelyan, *Life and Letters* (1876)

8 For years a secret shame destroyed my
                   peace —
   I'd not read Eliot, Auden, or MacNeice,
   But now I think a thought that brings me
                   hope:
   Neither had Chaucer, Shakespeare, Milton,
                   Pope.
   Justin Richardson, 'Take Heart, Illiterates'

FEELING
See EMOTION

52 FICTION
See also NOVEL

1 Truth must necessarily be stranger than
   fiction; for fiction is the creation of the
   human mind and therefore congenial to it.
   G.K. Chesterton, *The Club of Queer Trades*
   (1905)

2 Truth may be stranger than fiction, but
   fiction is truer.
   Frederic Raphael, in *Contemporary
   Novelists* (1976)

3 I have seen so little of the world that I have
   nothing but thin air to concoct my stories of,
   and it is not easy to give a life-like
   semblance to such shadowy stuff.
   Nathaniel Hawthorne, in letter to Henry
   Wadsworth Longfellow (1838)

4 Fiction is not a dream. Nor is it guess work.
   It is imagining based on facts, and the facts
   must be accurate or the work of imagining
   will not stand up.
   Margaret Culkin Banning, in *The Writer*
   (March 1960)

5 In journalism just one fact that is false
   prejudices the entire work. In contrast, in
   fiction one single fact that is true gives
   legitimacy to the entire work.
   Gabriel García Márquez, in interview in
   Writers at Work (6th series, 1984)

6 Journalism allows its readers to witness
   history; fiction gives its readers an
   opportunity to live it.
   John Hersey, in *Time* magazine (13 March
   1950)

7 Fiction, imaginative work that is, is not
   dropped like a pebble upon the ground, as
   science may be; fiction is like a spider's web,
   attached ever so lightly perhaps, but still
   attached to life at all four corners.
   Virginia Woolf, *A Room of One's Own*
   (1929)

8 The ancient historians gave us delightful
   fiction in the form of fact; the modern
   novelist presents us with dull facts under the
   guise of fiction.
   Oscar Wilde, 'The Decay of Lying',
   Intentions (1891)

9 Fiction carries a greater amount of truth in
   solution than the volume which purports to
   be all true.
   William Makepeace Thackeray, 'Steele',
   The English Humorists (1851)

10 The pedantic decisions and definable
   readjustments of man may be found in
   scrolls and statute books and scriptures: but
   men's basic assumptions and everlasting
   energies are to be found in penny dreadfuls
   and halfpenny novelettes.
   G.K. Chesterton, *Heretics* (1905)

11 What is fictitious in a novel is not so much
   the story but the method by which thought
   develops into action, a method which never
   occurs in daily life.
   Alain (E.A. Chartier), quoted in E.M.
   Forster, *Aspects of the Novel* (1927)

12 Nothing I have said is factual except the bits
   that sound like fiction.
   Clive James, *Unreliable Memoirs* (1980)

13 You should study the Peerage, Gerald . . .
   It is the best thing in fiction the English have
   ever done.
   Oscar Wilde, *A Woman of No Importance*
   (1893)

14 The librarian gave Geordie 'Mother Goose's
   Nursery Rhymes'. Georgie read it from
   cover to cover, and when I asked him how he
   liked it he said 'It's nowt but a pack of lies.'
   Gerald Kersh, *The Nine Lives of Bill Nelson*
   (1941)

15 All fiction is for me a kind of magic and
   trickery — a confidence trick, trying to
   make people believe something is true that
   isn't.
   Angus Wilson, in interview in *Writers at
   Work* (1st series, 1958)

16 Character in decay is the theme of the great
   bulk of superior fiction.
   H.L. Mencken, *Prejudices* (1919)

17 The reader turns away from a book where
   all the characters are good without shades
   or weakness; he knows very well that this
   isn't human.
   George Sand, letter to Gustave Flaubert (12
   Jan. 1876)

18 Nobody can tell a writer what can or ought
   to be done, or not done, in his fiction. A
   living death if you fall for it.
   Bernard Malamud, in interview in *Writers
   at Work* (6th series, 1984)

19 Poetry is the supreme fiction, madame.
   Wallace Stevens, 'A High-toned Old
   Christian Woman'

20 The real, if unavowed, purpose of fiction is
   to give pleasure by gratifying the love of the
   uncommon in human experience, mental or
   corporal.
   Thomas Hardy, entry in notebook (July
   1881)

21 Fiction is to the grown man what play is to
   the child; it is there that he changes the
   atmosphere and tenor of his life.
   Robert Louis Stevenson, 'A Gossip on
   Romance' (1882)

22 The good ended happily, the bad unhappily.
   That is what fiction means.
   Oscar Wilde, *The Importance of Being
   Earnest* (1895)

23 All tragedies are finish'd by a death,
   All comedies are ended by a marriage;
   The future states of both are left to faith.
   Lord Byron, *Don Juan* (1819–24)

24 Literature is a luxury; fiction is a necessity.
   G.K. Chesterton, *The Defendant* (1901)

---

53 FIGURES OF SPEECH

1 Figures of speech, which poets think so fine.
   (Art's needless varnish to make Nature
            shine)
   All are but paint upon a beauteous face.
   John Sheffield, 1st Duke of Buckingham and
   Normanby, *Essay on Poetry* (1682)

2 The greatest thing in style is to have a
   command of metaphor.
   Aristotle, *Poetics*

3 I hate to hunt down a tired metaphor.
   Lord Byron, *Don Juan* (1819–24)

4 The coldest word was once a glowing new
   metaphor.
   Thomas Carlyle, *Past and Present* (1843)

5 One thing that literature would be greatly
            the better for
   Would be a more restricted employment by
            authors of simile and metaphor.
   Authors of all races, be they Greeks,
                Romans, Teutons or Celts,
   Can't see guilt to say that anything is the
            thing it

is but theve to go out of their way to say that
it is something else.
Ogden Nash, 'Very like a Whale'

6 Yesterday's daring metaphors are today's
clichés.
Arthur Koestler, *The Heel of Achilles* (1974)

7 The metaphor is probably the most fertile
power possessed by man.
José Ortega y Gasset, *The Dehumanisation
of Art* (1925)

8 Farewell sweet phrases, lovely metaphors.
George Herbert, 'The Forerunners'

9 I love metaphor the way some people love
junk food.
William Gass, in interview in *Writers at
Work* (5th series, 1981)

10 I love metaphor. It provides two loaves
where there seems to be one. Sometimes it
throws in a load of fish.
Bernard Malamud, in interview in *Writers
at Work* (6th series, 1984)

11 Most of our expressions are metaphorical —
the philosophy of our forefathers lies hidden
in them.
Georg Christoph Lichtenberg, *Aphorisms*
(1764–99)

12 Man be my metaphor.
Dylan Thomas, 'If I were tickled by the rub
of love'

13 Similes should be sparingly used in prose,
for they are at bottom poetical.
Aristotle, *Rhetoric*

14 A simile committing suicide is always a
depressing spectacle.
Oscar Wilde, 'Sententiae', *A Critic in Pall
Mall* (1919)

15 We've had a big best-seller . . . I haven't got
round to it yet. I suspect the presence of
allegory, which is always a slight deterrent.
Alan Bennett, *The Old Country* (1978)

16 Any euphemism ceases to be euphemistic
after a time and the true meaning begins to
show through. It's a losing game, but we
keep on trying.
Joseph Wood Krutch, *If You don't Mind My
Saying So* (1964)

54 FILM

1 Film is not the art of scholars but of
illiterates.
Werner Herzog, quoted in *The Guardian*
(1978)

2 One written sentence is worth 800 hours of
film.
Elie Wiesel, remark

3 The film is the freest of all media, you can
do marvels with it. In fact I would welcome
the day when the film would displace
literature, when there'd be no more need to
read. You remember faces in films, and
gestures, as you never do when you read a
book.
Henry Miller, in interview in *Writers at
Work* (2nd series, 1963)

4 Writers love the theme of other writers,
erotically, selling their virtue to the wicked
film producer — it gives them a *frisson*.
Hilary Bailey, in review of Malcolm
Bradbury, *Cuts* (1987) in *The Guardian* (27
April 1987)

5 I can't think of any one film that improved
on a good novel, but I can think of many
good films that came from very bad novels.
Gabriel García Márquez, in interview in
Writers at Work (6th series, 1984)

6 The chances of your book being made into a
motion picture are about as good as your
chances of becoming the president of the
United States.
Bill Adler, *Inside Publishing* (1982)

7 I have recently been amused and taken by
surprise several times at my poetry readings
. . . And on another occasion, a man asked,
'How many movies have been made of your
poems?' Alas, there've been none, none at
all.
Stephen Spender, in interview in *Writers at
Work* (6th series, 1984)

8 So Beckett stammers into silence, and the
rest is cinema.
Gore Vidal, in interview in *Writers at Work*
(5th series, 1981)

55 FINE EDITIONS

1 Books are like women: to strike they must
be well-dressed.
Samuel Foote, *The Author* (1757)

2 You can't tell a book by its cover.
English proverb

3 There are books of which the backs and
covers are by far the best parts.
Charles Dickens, *Oliver Twist* (1837–8)

4 A well-bound book is a hymn of praise, a
song of love.
Holbrook Jackson, *The Anatomy of
Bibliomania* (1950)

5 One of the silliest questions you can ask a
book collector is, 'Have you read all these?'
Of course he hasn't. Some books are bought
to look at, not to read.
John Betjeman, quoted in *The Daily Herald
News Review* (28 Nov. 1946)

6 Decoration, rich trappings, or other
ornamentation, may be added for delight or
homage, or even vanity . . . but they are
tolerable only insofar as they hold no check
upon the purpose of a book, which is to be
read.
Holbrook Jackson, *The Anatomy of
Bibliomania* (1950)

7 Those are the books they don't read — they
keep them in their bookcases, handsomely
bound.
Kurt Tucholsky, *Briefe aus dem Schweigen*
(1977)

8 Through and through th' inspired leaves,
Ye maggots, make your windings;
But O, respect his lordship's taste,
And spare his golden bindings!
Robert Burns, 'The Book Worms'

9 Was ever book containing such vile matter
So fairly bound? O, that deceit should dwell
In such a gorgeous palace!
William Shakespeare, *Romeo and Juliet*

10 In some respects the better a book is, the less
it demands from binding.
Charles Lamb, 'Detached Thoughts on
Books and Reading', *Last Essays of Elia*
(1833)

11 A book on cheap paper does not convince. It
is not prized, it is like a wheezy doctor with
pigtail tobacco breath, who needs a
manicure.
Elbert Hubbard, *The Philistine*
(1895–1915)

12 Machine-made poetry on hand-made paper.
T. Marchant Williams, of John Morris
Jones's *Caniadau* (1907)

13 There is nothing more fit to be looked at
than the outside of a book.
Thomas Love Peacock, *Crotchet Castle*
(1831)

14 If you give Jack and Jill Public really
beautiful books you are going to get a new
awareness that will have a knock-on effect
for bookshops.
Sebastian Walker, in *The Bookseller* (23
March 1985)

56 FOOD

1 There is more reason for saying grace before
a new book than before dinner.
Charles Lamb, 'Grace before Meat', *Essays
of Elia* (1820–3)

2 Many people believe that it is enough to
supply the body, insatiable as it is, with
victuals. Far from it — the spirit requires
nourishment just as much as the body, but it
receives it from the printer rather than from
the cook. In short: what a little cake is for
the stomach, a little book is for the soul.
Abraham a Santa Clara, *Etwas für Alle*
(1699)

3 Sir, he hath never fed of the dainties that are
bred in a book. He hath not eat paper, as it
were; he hath not drunk ink: his intellect is
not replenished; he is only an animal, only
sensible in the duller parts.
William Shakespeare, *Love's Labour's Lost*

4 The readers and the hearers like my books,
But yet some writers cannot them digest;
But what care I? for when I make a feast
I would my guests should praise it, not the
    cooks.
Sir John Harington, 'Against Writers who
Carp at other Men's Books', *Epigrams*
(1618)

5 Books take their place according to their
specific gravity as surely as potatoes in a tub.
Ralph Waldo Emerson, *Journals* (1834)

6 Never write on a subject without having first
read yourself full on it; and never read on a
subject 'till you have thought yourself
hungry on it.
Jean Paul (J.P.F. Richter), *Hesperus* (1795)

7 To expect a man to retain everything that he
has ever read is like expecting him to carry
about in his body everything that he has ever
eaten.
Arthur Schopenhauer, 'On Reading and
Books', *Parerga and Paralipomena* (1851)

8 It is no more necessary that a man should
remember the different dinners and suppers
which have made him healthy, than the
different books which have made him wise.
Let us see the result of good food in a strong
body, and the result of great reading in a full
and powerful mind.
Sydney Smith, *Elementary Sketches of
Moral Philosophy* (1806)

9 The man who reads everything is like the
man who eats everything: He can digest
nothing; and the penalty for cramming one's
mind with other men's thoughts is to have
no thoughts of one's own.
Woodrow Wilson, in letter to Ellen Axson
(1884)

10 To read without reflecting, is like eating
without digesting.
Edmund Burke, *Letters*

11 Books cannot always please, however good;
Minds are not ever craving for their food.
George Crabbe, *The Borough* (1810)

12 What the mulberry leaf is to the silkworm,
the author's book, treatise, essay, poem, is
to the critical larvae that feed upon it. It
furnishes them with food and clothing.
Oliver Wendell Holmes, *Over the Teacups*
(1891)

13 Howard Nolan, 20, an undergraduate at
Brasenose College, Oxford, yesterday
finished eating the 566 pages of a copy of
the University Examination Statues, which
he began six days earlier.
News item in *The Daily Telegraph* (8 June
1966)

57 FORM

1 Technique is inseparable from its matter and
. . . a poet must take care to choose a form

which enables him to say exactly what he
means in all its range and its subtlety.
Maurice Bowra, *The Creative Experiment*
(1949)

2 To attend to form in poetry is always to
attend to a most important aspect of the
meaning of poetry.
Lascelles Abercrombie, *Poetry: Its Music
and Meaning* (1932)

3 There are two kinds of writers, those who
are and those who aren't. With the first,
content and form belong together like soul
and body; with the second, they match each
other like body and clothes.
Karl Kraus, *Spruche und Widerspruche*
(1955)

FREE VERSE
See VERS LIBRE

58 GENIUS

1 In literature, there are only oxen. The
biggest ones are the geniuses — the ones
who toil eighteen hours a day without tiring.
Jules Renard, *Journal* (1887)

2 Genius is one per cent inspiration and
ninety-nine per cent perspiration.
Thomas A. Edison, interview in *Life* (1932)

3 No author is a man of genius to his
publisher.
Heinrich Heine, attr.

4 The Genius of Poetry must work out its own
salvation in a man: it cannot be matured by
law and precept, but by watchfulness in
itself. That which is creative must create
itself.
John Keats, in letter (1818)

5 Oh! many are the Poets that are sown
By Nature; men endowed with highest gifts,
The vision and the faculty divine;
Yet wanting the accomplishment of verse.
William Wordsworth, *The Excursion*
(1814)

6 Feeble verses are those which sin not against
rules, but against genius.
Voltaire, 'Style', *Philosophical Dictionary*
(1764)

7 Good sense is the body of poetic genius, fancy its drapery, motion its life, and imagination the soul.
Samuel Taylor Coleridge, *Biographia Literaria* (1817)

8 Never have I read such tosh . . . Of course, genius may blaze out on page 652 but I have my doubts.
Virginia Woolf, in letter to Lytton Strachey on reading first six chapters of James Joyce's *Ulysses* (1922)

9 Good God! what a genius I had when I wrote that book.
Jonathan Swift, *A Tale of a Tub* (1704)

10 I have nothing to declare except my genius.
Oscar Wilde, remark at New York Custom House

11 I have put my genius into my life; I have put only my talent into my work.
Oscar Wilde, remark to André Gide

12 Talent alone cannot make a writer. There must be a man behind the book.
Ralph Waldo Emerson 'Goethe', *Representative Men* (1850)

13 No one can tell me who has talent, if any — Only one thing is certain. We are too many.
W.B. Yeats, remark in the Cheshire Cheese, quoted in Anthony Thwaite, 'On Consulting *Contemporary Poets of the English Language*'

14 In our age if a boy or girl is untalented, the odds are in favour of their thinking they want to write.
W.H. Auden, 'Squares and Oblongs', *Poets at Work* (1948)

15 Talent is a question of quantity. Talent does not write one page: it writes three hundred.
Jules Renard, *Journal* (1887)

---

59 GOD

1 The word is the Verb, and the Verb is God.
Victor Hugo, *Contemplations* (1856)

2 Hear the voice of the Bard!
Who present, past, and future sees;
Whose ears have heard
The Holy Word

That walked among the ancient trees.
William Blake, in introduction to *Songs of Experience* (1795)

3 My desire is that the Almighty would answer me, and that mine adversary had written a book.
Job 31:35

4 Make us, O Lord, a people fit for poetry.
Idris Davies, 'Psalm'

5 If God were a poet or took poetry seriously (or science for that matter), he would never have given man free will.
W.H. Auden, 'Squares and Oblongs', *Poets at Work* (1948)

6 An Apology for the Devil: It must be remembered that we have only heard one side of the case. God has written all the books.
Samuel Butler, *Note Books* (ed. H. Festing Jones, 1912)

7 God is a writer and we are both the heroes and the readers.
Isaac Bashevis Singer, in *Esquire* (1974)

8 It was subtle of God to learn Greek when he wished to become an author — and not to learn it better.
Friedrich Nietzsche, *Beyond Good and Evil* (1886)

9 These poems, with all their crudities, doubts, and confusions, are written for the love of Man, and in praise of God, and I'd be a damn' fool if they weren't.
Dylan Thomas, note to *Collected Poems* (1952)

10 If God exists, why write literature?
And if He doesn't, why write literature?
Eugène Ionesco, *Non* (1934)

11 God is the perfect poet,
Who in his person acts his own creations.
Robert Browning, *Paracelsus* (1835)

12 What is the prose for God?
H. Granville-Barker, *Waste* (1907)

13 The joy and function of poetry is, and was, the celebration of man, which is also the celebration of God.
Dylan Thomas, letter to student (1951)

14 Poets are dangerous men to have in chapel.
Idris Davies, 'The Lay Preacher Ponders'

60 GRAFFITI

1 The words of the prophet are written
On the subway halls and tenement walls.
Paul Simon, song, 'Sound of Silence' (1970)

2 If God had not meant us to write on walls he
would never have set us an example.
Graffito, quoted by Nigel Rees, *Graffiti 2*
(1980)

3 Popular education was bringing the graffito
lower on the walls.
Oliver St John Gogarty, *As I was Going
Down Sackville Street* (1937)

61 GRAMMAR
See also PARTS OF SPEECH

1 Grammere, that grounde is of alle.
William Langland, *The Vision of William
concerning Piers the Plowman* (*c.* 1370)

2 Once the grammar has been learnt writing is
simply talking on paper and in time learning
what not to say.
Beryl Bainbridge, in *Contemporary
Novelists* (1976)

3 Why care for grammar as long as we are
good?
Artemus Ward (Charles Farrar Browne),
'Pyrotechny'

4 Where shall we look for standard English,
but to the words of a standard man?
Henry David Thoreau, 'Sunday', *A Week
on the Concord and Merrimack Rivers*
(1849)

5 The grammar has a rule absurd
Which I would call an outworn myth:
A preposition is a word
You mustn't end a sentence with!
Berton Braley, 'No Rule to be Afraid Of'

6 Those upon whom the fear of infinitive
splitting sits heavy, should remember that to
give conclusive evidence, by distortions, of
misconceiving the nature of the split
infinitive, is far more damaging to their
literary pretensions than an actual lapse
could be.
H.W. Fowler, *Modern English Usage* (1965)

7 I have laboured to refine our language to
grammatical purity, and to clear it from
colloquial barbarisms, licentious idioms,
and irregular combinations.
Samuel Johnson, in *The Rambler* (14 March
1752)

8 When I read some of the rules for speaking
and writing the English language correctly
. . . I think —
Any fool can make a rule
And every fool will mind it.
Henry David Thoreau, *Journal* (1860)

9 I am the king of the Romans and above
grammar.
Emperor Sigismund 1, at the Council of
Constance (1414)

10 I never made a mistake in grammar but one
in my life and as soon as I done it I seen it.
Carl Sandburg, 'The People, Yes'

11 Sad study, grammar! Its whole content's
one long string of accidents!
Tony Harrison, 'Palladas: Poems'

12 Grammar is the grave of letters.
Elbert Hubbard, *A Thousand and One
Epigrams* (1923)

62 GREAT WRITING
See also GENIUS

1 The 'greatness' of literature cannot be
determined solely by literary standards
though we must remember that whether it is
literature or not can be determined only by
literary standards.
T.S. Eliot, 'Religion and Literature' (1935)

2 If the works of the great poets teach
anything, it is to hold mere invention
somewhat cheap. It is not the finding of a
thing, but the making something out of it
after it is found, that is of consequence.
James Russell Lowell, 'Chaucer', *My Study
Window* (1871)

3 The works of the great poets have never yet
been read by mankind, for only the great
poets can read them . . . Most men have
learned to read to serve a paltry convenience
. . . but of reading as a noble intellectual
exercise they know little or nothing.
Henry David Thoreau, 'Reading', *Walden*
(1854)

4 A great man's book is a compromise
   between the reader and himself.
   Eugène Delacroix, *Lettre à Balzac* (1832)

5 A great writer creates a world of his own
   and his readers are proud to live in it. A
   lesser writer may entice them in for a
   moment, but soon he will watch them filing
   out.
   Cyril Connolly, *Enemies of Promise* (1938)

6 Poetry should be vital — either stirring our
   blood by its divine movements, or snatching
   our breath by its divine perfection. To do
   both is supreme glory, to do either is
   enduring fame.
   Augustine Birrell, 'Browning's Poetry',
   Obiter Dicta (1884)

7 Of course you want to be admired. Any poet
   wants to be admired — to be a great poet.
   But who is a great poet? Maybe a handful in
   the world's history. So that's irrelevant.
   What's really going to come out of your
   work is something else. If you have
   succeeded at all you have become part —
   however small a part — of the consciousness
   of your time. Which is enough. No?
   Archibald MacLeish, in interview in *Writers
   at Work* (5th series, 1981)

8 What is so wonderful about great literature
   is that it transforms the man who reads it
   towards the condition of the man who
   wrote, and brings to birth in us also the
   creative impulse.
   E.M. Forster, 'Anonymity: An Enquiry',
   Two Cheers for Democracy (1951)

9 A great book should leave you with many
   experiences, and slightly exhausted at the
   end. You live several lives while reading it.
   William Styron, in interview in *Writers at
   Work* (1st series, 1958)

10 Every great writer is a writer of history, let
   him treat on almost what subject he may.
   He carries with him for thousands of years a
   portion of his times.
   Walter Savage Landor, 'Diogenes and
   Plato', *Imaginary Conversations* (1853)

11 Read *A Town Like Alice* by Nevil Shute, it is
   dead brill. I wish I had an intellectual friend
   whom I could discuss great literature with.
   Sue Townsend, *The Secret Diary of Adrian
   Mole* (1982)

63 HAPPINESS

1 And I dream of the days when work was
        scrappy,
      And rare in our pockets the mark of
        the mint,
   And we were angry and poor and happy,
      And proud of seeing our names in
        print.
   G.K. Chesterton, 'A Song of Defeat'

2 A poet could not but be gay
   In such jocund company.
   William Wordsworth, 'Daffodils'

3 Poetry is the record of the best and happiest
   moments of the happiest and best minds.
   Percy Bysshe Shelley, *A Defence of Poetry*
   (1820)

4 The poet camouflages, in the expression of
   joy, his despair at not having found its
   reality.
   Max Jacob, *La Défense de Tartuffe* (1919)

5 If artists and poets are unhappy, it is after all
   because happiness does not interest them.
   George Santayana, *The Sense of Beauty*
   (1896)

6 Why does my Muse only speak when she is
        unhappy?
   She does not, I only listen when I am
        unhappy
   When I am happy I live and despise writing
   For my Muse this cannot but be dispiriting.
   Stevie Smith, 'My Muse'

7 It's very difficult to write about being happy.
   Very easy to write about being miserable.
   Philip Larkin, in interview in *The Observer*
   (1979)

8 Writing is not a profession but a vocation of
   unhappiness.
   Georges Simenon, in interview in *Writers at
   Work* (1st series, 1958)

9 Why, after all, should readers never be
   harrowed? Surely there is enough happiness
   in life without having to go to books for it.
   Dorothy Parker, attr.

64 HELL

1 Ugly hell, gape not! come not, Lucifer!
   I'll burn my books!
   Christopher Marlow, *Dr Faustus* (1604)

2 The reason Milton wrote in fetters when he
   wrote of Angels and God, and at liberty
   when of Devils and Hell, is because he was a
   true Poet, and of the Devil's party without
   knowing it.
   William Blake, *The Marriage of Heaven and
   Hell* (c. 1790)

3 When the poet depicts Hell, he depicts his
   own life.
   Victor Hugo, 'Après une Lecture de Dante',
   Les Voix Intérieures

4 I am increasingly convinced that the *Church
   Times* is now edited by the Devil in person.
   Bishop Gore, quoted in C.A. Alington,
   Things Ancient and Modern (1936)

65 HERO

1 This book is not about heroes. English
   poetry is not yet fit to speak of them.
   Wilfred Owen, in draft preface to a volume
   of his poems (1920)

2 Why are epics
   always about
   the anti-life
   of a noble lout?
   Raymond Garlick, 'Note on the Iliad'

3 Poets are not often heroes. They watch what
   goes on, half concealed by the corner of the
   haystack, or the petrol pumps.
   Geoffrey Grigson, *The Private Art* (1982)

66 HISTORY

1 History, with all her volumes vast,
   Hath but one page.
   Lord Byron, *Childe Harold's Pilgrimage*
   (1812–18)

2 History is the essence of innumerable
   biographies.
   Thomas Carlyle, *Essay on History* (1830)

3 Great nations write their autobiographies in
   three manuscripts: the book of their deeds,
   the book of their words, and the book of
   their art. No one of these books can be
   understood unless we read the two others;
   but of the three, the only quite trustworthy
   one is the last.
   John Ruskin, preface to *St Mark's Rest*
   (1884)

4 To be ignorant of what occurred before you
   were born is to remain always a child. For
   what is the worth of human life, unless it is
   woven into the life of our ancestors by the
   records of history?
   Cicero, *Orator*

5 It is always curious to read as 'history' what
   one has experienced oneself.
   Max Beloff, in *The Daily Telegraph* (5 April
   1979)

6 It is impossible to write ancient history
   because we lack source materials, and
   impossible to write modern history because
   we have far too many.
   Charles Péguy, *Clio* (1917)

7 Writers are supposed to create history.
   Kate Roberts, *Tywyll Heno* (1962)

8 The writing of history may be as creative as
   the making of it. Both are interpretations of
   life.
   Philip Hope-Wallace, quoted in obituary in
   The Times (17 Dec. 1979)

9 The talent of historians lies in their creating
   a true ensemble out of facts which are but
   half-true.
   Ernest Renan, preface to 18th edition of *The
   Life of Jesus* (1863)

10 Great abilities are not requisite for an
   historian, for in historical composition all
   the greatest powers of the human mind are
   quiescent.
   Samuel Johnson, quoted in James Boswell,
   Life of Samuel Johnson (1791)

11 The middle sort of historians, of which the
   most part are, they spoil all; they will chew
   our meat for us.
   Michel de Montaigne, 'Of Books', *Essays*
   (1580–8)

12 These gentle historians, on the contrary, dip
   their pens in nothing but the milk of human
   kindness.
   Edmund Burke, *A Letter to a Noble Lord*
   (1796)

13 History does not repeat itself. Historians repeat each other.
A.J. Balfour, quoted by his biographer Kenneth Young

14 What makes a good writer of history is a guy who is suspicious. Suspicion marks the real difference between the man who wants to write honest history and the one who'd rather write a good story.
Jim Bishop, in *The New York Times* (5 Feb. 1955)

15 History, n. An account mostly false, of events mostly unimportant, which are brought about by rulers mostly knaves, and soldiers mostly fools.
Ambrose Bierce, *The Devil's Dictionary* (1911)

16 What is history after all? History is facts which become lies in the end; legends and lies which become history in the end.
Jean Cocteau, in *The Observer* (22 Sept. 1957)

17 As soon as histories are properly told there is no more need of romances.
Walt Whitman, in preface to *Leaves of Grass* (1855–92)

18 Poetry is more philosophical and of higher value than history.
Aristotle, *Poetics*

19 It takes a great deal of history to produce a little literature.
Henry James, *Life of Nathaniel Hawthorne* (1879)

20 History is not a department of *belles lettres*, not just an elegant, instructive, amusing narrative, but a brand of science.
York Powell, quoted by A.L. Rowse in *The Use of History* (1946)

21 History must not be written with bias, and both sides must be given, even if there is only one side.
John Betjeman, *First and Last Loves* (1952)

22 A man without a bias cannot write interesting history — if indeed such a man exists.
Bertrand Russell, *Autobiography* (vol. 2, 1967)

23 The very ink with which all history is written is merely fluid prejudice.
Mark Twain, 'Pudd'nhead Wilson's New Calendar', *Following the Equator* (1897)

24 The one duty we have to history is to rewrite it.
Oscar Wilde, 'The Critic as Artist', *Intentions* (1891)

25 History can be well written only in a free country.
Voltaire, in letter to Frederick the Great (27 May 1737)

26 Historians have a responsibility to make some sense of the past and not simply to chronicle it.
Michael Howard, review of Herbert Butterfield's *The Origin of History* in *The Times Literary Supplement* (7 Aug. 1981)

27 The frontiers between history and imagination are very little more than Chinese screens, removable at will.
Richard Cobb, in *The Listener* (1978)

28 History is the recital of facts represented as true. Fable, on the other hand, is the recital of facts represented as fiction.
Voltaire, 'History', *Philosophical Dictionary* (1764)

67 HUMOUR
See also COMEDY

1 Among all kinds of writing, there is none in which authors are more apt to miscarry than in works of humour, as there is none in which they are more ambitious to excel.
Joseph Addison, in *The Spectator* (1711–12)

2 There are several kinds of stories, but only one difficult — the humorous.
Mark Twain, 'How to Tell a Story' (1895)

3 They [humorists] lead, as a matter of fact, an existence of jumpiness and apprehension. They sit on the edge of the chair of Literature. In the house of Life they have the feeling that they have never taken off their overcoats.
James Thurber, in preface to *My Life and Hard Times* (1933)

4 Authors hear at length one general cry, Tickle and entertain us, or we die!
William Cowper, 'Retirement'

5 From the moment I picked your book up until I laid it down I was convulsed with

laughter. Someday I intend reading it.
Groucho Marx, on S.J. Perelman's first
book

6 I did not intend to write a funny book, at
first. I did not know I was a humorist. I have
never been sure about it.
Jerome K. Jerome, *My Life and Times*
(1926)

7 *The Times*, in an editorial, referred to me as
a 'humorist'. I feel the writer meant to be
complimentary; but by later critics the term
has generally been hurled at me as a
reproach.
Jerome K. Jerome, *My Life and Times*
(1926)

8 If a playwright is funny, the English look for
the serious message, and if he is serious they
look for the joke.
Sacha Guitry, quoted in 'Sayings of the
Week' in *The Observer* (19 April 1957)

9 The phrase 'unconscious humour' is the one
contribution I have made to the current
literature of the day.
Samuel Butler, *Note Books* (ed. H. Festing
Jones, 1912)

ILLITERACY
See LITERACY

---

68 IMAGE

---

1 It is better to present one Image in a lifetime
than to produce voluminous works.
Ezra Pound, *Pavannes and Divisions* (1918)

2 I make only one image — though 'make' is
not the word; I let, perhaps, one image be
'made' emotionally in me and then apply it
to what intellectual and critical forces I
possess — let it breed another, let that image
contradict the first, make, of the third image
bred out of the other two together, a fourth
contradictory image, and let them all, within
my imposed formal limits, conflict.
Dylan Thomas, in a letter to Henry Treece
(23 March 1938)

3 The poet, then, must feel in images: he must
grasp the connections between things — but

grasp them emotionally, rather than
logically, and he must be capable of seeing
one thing in terms of another. Now if we
consider those three abilities, we realize that
there is a certain innocence, a child-like
nature common to all of them. Imagination
demands — and not only from the poet — a
quality of innocence.
C. Day-Lewis, 'The Nurture of the
Imagination' (1936)

---

69 IMAGINATION

---

1 What is poetry? The suggestion, by the
imagination, of noble grounds for the noble
emotions.
John Ruskin, *Modern Painters* (1888)

2 The poet's eye, in a fine frenzy rolling,
Doth glance from heaven to earth, from
                    earth to heaven;
And, as imagination bodies forth
The forms of things unknown, the poet's
                    pen
Turns them to shapes, and gives to airy
                    nothing
A local habitation and a name.
William Shakespeare, *A Midsummer
Night's Dream*

3 The lunatic, the lover, and the poet,
Are of imagination all compact.
William Shakespeare, *A Midsummer
Night's Dream*

4 One Power alone makes a Poet:
Imagination, the Divine Vision.
William Blake, annotations to
Wordsworth's poems

5 A poet soaring in the high region of his
fancies with his garland and singing robes
about him.
John Milton, introduction to *The Reason of
Church Government* (1642)

6 The art of the poem is to rouse the inward
vision . . . That is why the poets, who spring
imagination with a word or a phrase, paint
lasting pictures.
George Meredith, *Diana of the Crossways*
(1885)

7 . . . and they say, 'Hah-hah? My goodness,
Mr Hall, but you certainly do have an

imagination, huh!' 'Thank you, indeed,' I say; 'it brings in the bacon'.
Donald Hall, 'To a Waterfowl'

8 All poets adore explosions, thunderstorms, tornadoes, conflagrations, ruins, scenes of spectacular carnage. The poetic imagination is not at all a desirable quality in a statesman.
W.H. Auden, 'The Poet and the City', in *The Dyer's Hand* (1962)

9 Having imagination, it takes you an hour to write a paragraph that, if you were unimaginative, would take only a minute. Or you might not write the paragraph at all.
Franklin P. Adams, *Half a Loaf* (1927)

10 Liberty of the imagination should be the most precious possession of a novelist.
Joseph Conrad, 'Books' (1905)

11 A long poem is a test of invention which I take to be the Polar star of poetry, as fancy is the sails, and imagination the rudder.
John Keats, in letter to Benjamin Bailey (1817)

70 INDEX

1 'The English,' Herr Heinrich had said, 'do not understand indexing. It is the root of all good organisation.'
H.G. Wells, *Mr Britling Sees it Through* (1916)

2 So essential did I consider an Index to be to every book, that I proposed to bring a Bill into parliament to deprive an author who publishes a book without an Index of the privilege of copyright; and, moreover, to subject him, for his offence, to a pecuniary penalty.
Lord Campbell, in preface to *Lives of the Chief Justices* (1857)

3 The Reason why there is no table or Index added hereafter, is, that every Page in this Work is so full of Signal Remarks, that were they couched in an Index, it would make a volume as big as the Book, and so make the Postern Gate to bear no proportion with the building.
John Howell, *Proedria Basilike* (1664)

4 One may recollect generally that certain thoughts or facts are to be found in a certain book; but without a good index such a recollection may already be no more available than that of the cabin-boy who knew where the ship's tea-kettle was because he saw it fall overboard, and unless he has good indexes he will never find it again.
Horace Binney, in a letter to Samuel Austin Allibone (20 Feb. 1866)

5 The most accomplished way of using books at present is two-fold: either, first, to serve them as some men do lords, learn their titles exactly, and then brag of their acquaintance. Or, secondly, which is indeed the choicer, the profounder, and politer method, to get a thorough insight into the index, by which the whole book is governed and turned, like fishes by the tail.
Jonathan Swift, *A Tale of a Tub* (1704)

6 There are the men who pretend to understand a book by scouting through the index: as if a traveler should go about to describe a palace when he had seen nothing but the privy.
Jonathan Swift, 'On the Mechanical Operation of the Spirit'

7 One writer, for instance, excels at a plan or a title page, another works away at the body of the book, and a third is a dab at an index.
Oliver Goldsmith, in *The Bee* (no. 1, 6 Oct. 1759)

8 Must the book end, as you would end it, With testamentary appendices And graveyard indices?
Robert Graves, 'Leaving the Rest Unsaid'

INSPIRATION
See MUSE

71 IRELAND AND THE IRISH

1 Ireland never was contented.
Say you so? You are demented.
Ireland was contented when
All could use the sword and pen.
Walter Savage Landor, 'Ireland Never was Contented'

2 Know, that I would accounted be
  True brother of a company
  That sang, to sweeten Ireland's wrong,
  Ballad and story, rann and song.
  W.B. Yeats, 'To Ireland in the Coming
  Times'

3 Mad Ireland hurt you into poetry.
  W.H. Auden, 'In Memory of W.B. Yeats'

4 Did that play of mine send out
  Certain men the English shot?
  W.B. Yeats, 'The Man and the Echo'

5 Think of the evacuation of Ireland by
  foreign troops. Why, it seems like a fairy
  vision. All the old Gaelic poets sang of the
  going of the foreign hosts out of Ireland as
  an unreal dream of far-off happiness. They
  did not sing of a Republic.
  Piaras Béaslaí, in speech in Irish Parliament
  (3 Jan. 1922)

6 Everywhere in Irish prose there twinkles and
  peers the merry eye and laugh of a people
  who had little to laugh about in real life.
  Diarmuid Russell, in *The Portable Irish
  Reader*

7 Irish poets, learn your trade,
  Sing whatever is well made,
  Scorn the sort now growing up
  All out of shape from toe to top.
  W.B. Yeats, 'Under Ben Bulben'

8 We Irish are too poetical to be poets.
  Oscar Wilde, quoted in W.B. Yeats,
  Autobiography (1936)

9 The English Language has an unbroken
  tradition of excellence and when it goes to
  sleep there is always an Irishman who
  appears and wakes it up.
  Carlos Fuentes, in interview in *Writers at
  Work* (6th series, 1984)

---

72 ITCH TO WRITE
  See also URGE TO WRITE

---

1 An inveterate and incurable itch for writing
  besets many and grows old with their sick
  hearts.
  Juvenal, *Satires*

2 Why did I write? What sin to me unknown
  Dipt me in ink, my parents', or my own?
  Alexander Pope, *Epistle to Dr Arbuthnot*
  (1735)

3 *Scratch, scratch* his pen goes
      Day and night,
  And much inflames his
      Itch to write.
  William Plomer, 'Making Things Worse'

4 When once the itch of literature comes over
  man, nothing can cure it but the scratching
  of a pen.
  Samuel Lover, *Handy Andy* (1842)

5 Once writing has become your major vice
  and greatest pleasure only death can stop it.
  Ernest Hemingway, in interview in *Writers
  at Work* (2nd series, 1963)

6 Women will write novels to while away their
  pregnancies; bored noblemen, axed officers,
  retired civil servants fly to the pen as one
  might fly to the bottle. There is an
  impression abroad that everyone has it in
  him to write a book; but if by this is implied
  a good book the impression is false.
  Somerset Maugham, *The Summing Up*
  (1938)

7 Most of my recent plays were written in the
  railway train between Hatfield and King's
  Cross. I write anywhere, on the top of
  omnibuses or wherever I may be; it is all the
  same to me.
  George Bernard Shaw, in *The Daily Mail*
  (23 May 1928)

8 And always this piece of staring, white
  paper in front of me with the few and feeble
  words strung across it . . . Nothing could be
  more stubborn than my devotion, nothing
  more stupid than my persistence. After all, I
  have written nothing — I will write nothing.
  Twenty years have not been enough to
  convince me of my lack of talent.
  Charles Ritchie, *The Siren Years:
  Undiplomatic Diaries 1937–1945*

9 If you would be a reader, read; if a writer,
  write.
  Epictetus, *Discourses*

10 The more a man writes, the more he can
  write.
  William Hazlitt, *Lectures on Dramatic
  Literature* (1820)

11 The fondness for writing grows with
  writing.
  Erasmus, *Adagia* (1508)

12 This before all: ask yourself in the quietest
  hour of your night: *must* I write? Dig down
  into yourself for a deep answer. And if this

should be in the affirmative, if you may meet this solemn question with a strong and simple, *I must*, then build your life according to this necessity.
Rainer Maria Rilke, *Letters to a Young Poet* (1903–8)

13 All writers are vain, selfish and lazy, and at the very bottom of their motives lies a mystery. Writing a book is a long, exhausting struggle, like a long bout of some painful illness. One would never undertake such a thing if one were not driven by some demon whom one can neither resist nor understand.
George Orwell, 'Why I Write', *England, Your England* (1953)

14 Write your heart out.
Bernard Malamud, advice to young writers, in interview in *Writers at Work* (6th series, 1984)

73 JEALOUSY AND ENVY

1 So, naturalists observe, a flea
Hath smaller fleas that on him prey;
And these have smaller fleas to bite 'em,
And so proceed ad infinitum.
Thus every poet, in his kind,
Is bit by him that comes behind.
Jonathan Swift, 'On Poetry'

2 Authors are like cattle going to a fair: those of the same field can never move on without butting one another.
Walter Savage Landor, 'Archdeacon Hare and Walter Landor', *Imaginary Conversations* (1824–9)

3 As there are none more ambitious of fame than those who are conversant in poetry, it is very natural for such as have not succeeded in it to depreciate the works of those who have.
Joseph Addison, 'Against Detraction'

4 Poets arguing about modern poetry: jackals snarling over a dried-up well.
Cyril Connolly, *The Unquiet Grave* (1945)

5 The literary world is made up of little confederacies, each looking upon its own members as the lights of the universe; and considering all others as mere transient meteors, doomed soon to fall and be forgotten, while its own luminaries are to shine steadily on to immortality.
Washington Irving, 'Literary Life', *Tales of a Traveller* (1824)

6 Authors are sometimes like tomcats: they distrust all the other toms, but they are kind to kittens.
Malcolm Cowley, introduction to *Writers at Work* (1st series, 1958)

7 The only reward to be expected from the cultivation of literature is contempt if one fails and hatred if one succeeds.
Voltaire, in letter to Mlle Quinault

8 Indignation at literary wrongs I leave to men born under happier stars. I cannot afford it.
Samuel Taylor Coleridge, *Biographia Literaria* (1817)

9 Though by whim, envy, or resentment led,
They damn those authors whom they never read.
Charles Churchill, *The Candidate* (1764)

10 No author ever spar'd a brother;
Wits are gamecocks to one another.
John Gay, 'The Elephant and the Bookseller'

11 Poets are sultans, if they had their will;
For every author would his brother kill.
Roger Boyle, *Prologues* (17th cent.)

12 The praise of ancient authors proceeds not from the reverence of the dead, but from the competition and mutual envy of the living.
Thomas Hobbes, 'A Review and Conclusion', *Leviathan* (1651)

13 Just so much as I am humbled by the genius above my grasp am I exalted and look with hate and contempt upon the literary world.
John Keats, in letter to John Taylor (23 Aug. 1819)

14 How odious all authors are, and how doubly so to each other!
Henry Edward Fox, 4th Lord Holland, *Journal* (3 Jan. 1821)

15 What poet would not grieve to see
His brother write as well as he?
But rather than they should excel,
Would wish his rivals all in Hell?
Jonathan Swift, 'On the Death of Dr Swift'

16 I think none but Pikes and Poets prey upon their kind.
William Warburton, to David Garrick (22 April 1762)

17 In Pope I cannot read a line,
But with a sigh I wish it mine;
Jonathan Swift, 'On the Death of Dr Swift'

18 *War and Peace* maddens me because I didn't
write it myself, and worse, I couldn't.
Jeffrey Archer, 'The Spell of Words', in *The
Anti-Booklist* (ed. Brian Redhead and
Kenneth McLeish, 1981)

JOURNAL
See DIARY

---

74 JOURNALISM
See also THE PRESS

---

1 You cannot hope
To bribe or twist
Thank God! the British journalist,
But seeing what
That man will do
Unbribed, there's no occasion to.
Humbert Wolfe, *The Uncelestial City*
(1930)

2 The only qualities essential for real success
in journalism are rat-like cunning, a
plausible manner, and a little literary ability.
Nicholas Tomalin, in *The Sunday Times
Magazine* (26 Oct. 1969)

3 One of the most valuable philosophical
features of journalism is that it realizes that
truth is not a solid but a fluid.
Christopher Morley, *Inward Ho!* (1923)

4 Good taste is, of course, an utterly
dispensable part of any journalist's
equipment.
Michael Hogg, in *The Daily Telegraph* (2
Dec. 1978)

5 It is the gossip columnist's business to write
about what is none of his business.
Louis Kronenberger, 'Fashions in
Vulgarity', *The Cart and the Horse* (1964)

6 Journalism — an ability to meet the
challenge of filling the space.
Rebecca West, in *The New York Herald
Tribune* (22 April 1956)

7 Media is a word that has come to mean bad
journalism.
Graham Greene, *Ways of Escape* (1980)

8 The fault I find with our journalism is that it
forces us to take an interest in some fresh
triviality or other every day, whereas only
three or four books in a lifetime give us
anything that is of real importance.
Marcel Proust, *Swann's Way* (1913)

9 Literature is the art of writing something
that will be read twice; journalism what will
be grasped at once.
Cyril Connolly, *Enemies of Promise* (1938)

10 Surely the glory of journalism is its
transience.
Malcolm Muggeridge, introduction to *The
Most of Malcolm Muggeridge* (1966)

11 There is much to be said in favour of
modern journalism. By giving us the
opinions of the uneducated, it keeps us in
touch with the ignorance of the community.
Oscar Wilde, 'The Critic as Artist',
Intentions (1891)

12 Most interlectuals reckon that us
sportswriters is too busy falling over in bars
to have ever herd of Albert Hemingway and
that.
Ian Wooldridge, 'Slant-Eyed Oriental' in
The Anti-Booklist (ed. Brian Redhead and
Kenneth McLeish, 1981)

13 The distinction between literature and
journalism is becoming blurred; but
journalism gains as much as literature loses.
William Ralph Inge, 'England'

14 The life of the journalist is poor, nasty,
brutish and short. So is his style.
Stella Gibbons, in foreword to *Cold
Comfort Farm* (1932)

15 Journalism is popular, but it is popular
mainly as fiction. Life is one world, and life
seen in the newspapers another.
G.K. Chesterton, 'On the Cryptic and the
Elliptic', *All Things Considered* (1908)

16 Journalism largely consists in saying 'Lord
Jones Dead' to people who never knew Lord
Jones was alive.
G.K. Chesterton, *The Wisdom of Father
Brown* (1914)

17 Every journalist has a great novel within
him. Every journalist has an excellent reason
why it never got out.
John Timpson, 'Why It Never Got Out' in
The Anti-Booklist (ed. Brian Redhead and
Kenneth McLeish, 1981)

18 In America journalism is apt to be regarded
as an extension of history: in Britain, as an
extension of conversation.
Anthony Sampson, *Anatomy of Britain*
(1962)

19 Journalism is the only job that requires no
degrees, no diplomas and no specialised
knowledge of any kind.
Patrick Campbell, *My Life and Easy Times*
(1967)

20 The trouble with daily journalism is that you
get so involved with 'Who hit John?' that
you never really know why John had his
chin out in the first place.
Chalmers Roberts, *Newsweek* (6 Jan. 1958)

21 One reads the papers as one wants to with a
bandage over one's eyes without trying to
understand the facts, listening to the
soothing words of the editor as to the words
of one's mistress.
Marcel Proust, *Time Regained* (1927)

22 *The Times* is speechless, and takes three
columns to express its speechlessness.
Winston Churchill, in speech on Irish Home
Rule, Dundee (14 May 1908)

23 If an editor can only make people angry
enough, they will write half his newspaper
for him for nothing.
G.K. Chesterton, *Heretics* (1905)

24 Rock journalism is people who can't write
interviewing people who can't talk for
people who can't read.
Frank Zappa, attr.

25 With regard to modern journalists, they
always apologise to one in private for what
they have written against one in public.
Oscar Wilde, *The Soul of Man under
Socialism* (1891)

---

75 JOYS OF READING
See also READING, SOLACE OF BOOKS, USES
OF BOOKS

---

1 Books are a part of man's prerogative;
In formal ink they thought and voices hold,
That we to them our solitude may give,
And make time present travel that of old.
Sir Thomas Overbury, 'A Wife'

2 I would rather be a poor man in a garret
with plenty of books, than a king who did
not love reading.
Thomas Babington Macaulay, in G.O.
Trevelyan, *Life and Letters* (1876)

3 Give a man a book he can read;
And his home is bright with a calm delight,
Though the room be poor indeed.
James Thomson, 'Gifts'

4 I wish I lived in a small provincial town and
spent the evenings reading aloud the
Victorian novelists to my wife and my
daughters.
Charles Ritchie, *The Siren Years:
Undiplomatic Diaries 1937–1945*

5 The pleasure of all reading is doubled when
one lives with another who shares the same
books.
Katherine Mansfield, *Letters* (1928)

6 Give me a bed and a book and I am happy.
Logan Pearsall Smith, *All Trivia* (1931)

7 All good and true book-lovers practise the
pleasing and improving avocation of reading
in bed. Indeed . . . no book can be
appreciated until it has been slept with and
dreamed over.
Eugene Field, *The Love Affairs of a
Bibliomaniac* (1896)

8 Then I thought of reading — the nice and
subtle happiness of reading . . . this joy not
to be dulled by Age, this polite and
unpunishable vice, this selfish, serene,
life-long intoxication.
Logan Pearsall Smith, 'Consolation', *Trivia*
(1902)

9 What a convenient and delightful world is
this world of books! — if you bring to it not
the obligations of the student, or look upon
it as an opiate for idleness, but enter it rather
with the enthusiasm of the adventurer!
David Grayson, *Adventures in Contentment*
(1907)

10 I seek in the reading of books, only to please
myself, by an honest diversion.
Michel de Montaigne, 'Of books', *Essays*
(1580–8)

11 A book reads the better, which is our own,
and has been so long known to us, that we
know the topography of its blots, and
dog's-ears, and can trace the dirt in it to
having read it at tea with buttered muffins,

or over a pipe, which I think is the
maximum.
Charles Lamb, in letter to S.T. Coleridge
(11 Oct. 1802)

12 O for a Booke and a shadie nooke,
      (eyther in-a-doore or out);
With the grene leaves wisp'ring overhede,
      or the Street cries all about.
Where I maie Reade all at my ease,
      both of the Newe and Olde;
For a jollie goode Booke whereon to looke,
      is better to me than Golde.
John Wilson, 'O for a Booke'

13 The love of learning, the sequestered nooks,
And all the sweet serenity of books.
Henry Wadsworth Longfellow, 'Morituri
Salutamus'

14 In the highest civilization the book is still the
highest delight.
Ralph Waldo Emerson, 'Quotations and
Originality', *Letters and Social Aims* (1876)

15   I never knew
More sweet and happy hours than I
            employ'd
Upon my books.
James Shirley, *The Lady of Pleasure* (1635)

16 I have always come to life after coming to
books.
Jorge Luis Borges, quoted in *The New York
Review of Books* (1971)

17 A good book is the best of friends, the same
today and for ever.
Martin Tupper, *Proverbial Philosophy*
(series 1, 1838)

18 The first time I read an excellent book, it is
to me just as if I had gained a new friend:
when I read over a book I have perused
before, it resembles the meeting with an old
one.
Oliver Goldsmith, *The Citizen of the World*
(1762)

19 To read a writer is for me not merely to get
an idea of what he says, but to go off with
him, and travel in his company.
André Gide, 'Third Imaginary Interview',
Pretexts (1903)

20 How many a man has dated a new era in his
life from the reading of a book!
Henry David Thoreau, 'Reading', *Walden*
(1854)

21 I love to lose myself in other men's minds.
When I am not walking, I am reading; I
cannot sit and think. Books think for me.
Charles Lamb, 'Detached Thoughts on
Books and Reading', *Last Essays of Elia*
(1833)

22 It is chiefly through books that we enjoy
intercourse with superior minds . . . In the
best books, great men talk to us, give us
their most precious thoughts, and pour their
souls into ours. God be thanked for books.
They are the voices of the distant and the
dead, and make us heirs of the spiritual like
of past ages.
William Ellery Channing, *Self-Culture*
(1838)

23 I have no pleasure from books which equals
that of reading over the hundredth time
great productions which I almost know by
heart.
Thomas Babington Macaulay, in G.O.
Trevelyan, *Life and Letters* (1876)

24 When I take up a work that I have read
before (the oftener the better) I know what I
have to expect. The satisfaction is not
lessened by being anticipated.
William Hazlitt, 'On Reading Old Books',
The Plain Speaker (1852)

25 When I read a good book . . . I wish that life
were three thousand years long.
Ralph Waldo Emerson, *Journal* (1911)

26 It is the pleasures and not the profits,
spiritual or temporal, of literature which
most require to be preached in the ear of the
ordinary reader.
Arthur J. Balfour, 'The Pleasures of
Reading', *Essays and Addresses* (1889)

27 In anything fit to be called by the name of
reading, the process itself should be
absorbing and voluptuous; we should gloat
over a book, be rapt clean out of ourselves.
Robert Louis Stevenson, 'A Gossip on
Romance' (1882)

28 When one can read, can penetrate the
enchanting world of books, why write?
Colette, *Earthly Paradise* (1966)

29 Of all that has been written, I love only that
which was written in blood.
Friedrich Nietzsche, *Thus Spake
Zarathustra* (1885)

76 KNOWLEDGE

1 The proper study of mankind is books.
   Aldous Huxley, *Crome Yellow* (1921)

2 I have rather studied books than men.
   Francis Bacon, 'Advice to Sir George
   Villiers', *Letters* (ed. James Spedding, 1872)

3 What delightful teaching there is in books.
   How easily, how secretly, how safely in
   books do we make bare without shame the
   poverty of human ignorance! These are the
   masters that instruct us without rod and
   ferrule, without words of anger, without
   payment of money or clothing. Should ye
   approach them, they are not asleep; if ye
   seek to answer them, they do not hide
   themselves; should ye err, they do not chide;
   and should ye show ignorance, they know
   not how to laugh. O Books! ye alone are free
   and liberal. Ye give to all that seek, and set
   free all that serve you zealously.
   Richard de Bury, *Philobiblon* (1473)

4 For without books God is silent, justice
   dormant, natural science at a stand,
   philosophy lame, letters dumb, and all
   things involved in Cimmerian darkness.
   Thomas Bartholin, *Dissertations* (1672)

5 Whence is thy learning? Hath thy toil
   O'er books consum'd the midnight oil?
   John Gay, introduction to *Fables* (1738)

6 At learning's fountain it is sweet to drink,
   But 't is a nobler privilege to think;
   And oft from books apart, the thirsting
        mind
   May make the nectar which it cannot find,
   'T is well to borrow from the good and
        great;
   'T is wise to learn; 't is godlike to create!
   John Godfrey Saxe, 'The Library'

7 Knowledge is the foundation and source of
   good writing.
   Horace, *Ars Poetica*

8 There are many virtues in books, but the
   essential value is the adding of knowledge to
   our stock by the record of new facts, and,
   better, by the record of intuitions which
   distribute facts, and are the formulas which
   supersede all histories.
   Ralph Waldo Emerson, *Letters and Social
   Aims* (1876)

9 The expansion of knowledge implies that
   each book . . . contains a progressively
   smaller fraction of all that is known.
   Alvin Toffler, *Future Shock* (1970)

10 This book tells more about penguins than I
   am interested in knowing.
   Anonymous schoolboy

11 How much there is in books that one does
   not want to know, that it would be a mere
   weariness and burden to the spirit to know.
   John Burroughs, *Indoor Studies* (1889)

12 That writer does the most, who gives his
   reader the most knowledge, and takes from
   him the least time.
   Charles Caleb Colton, preface to *Lacon*
   (1825)

13 Until you understand a writer's ignorance,
   presume yourself ignorant of his
   understanding.
   Samuel Taylor Coleridge, *Biographia
   Literaria* (1817)

14 Poetry is the identity of all other
   knowledges, the blossom and fragrance of
   all human knowledge, human thoughts,
   human passions, emotions, language.
   Samuel Taylor Coleridge, *Biographia
   Literaria* (1817)

15 The reason why so few good books are
   written is that so few people that can write
   know anything.
   Walter Bagehot, 'Shakespeare', *Literary
   Studies* (1879–95)

16 The writer is more concerned to know than
   to judge.
   Somerset Maugham, *The Moon and
   Sixpence* (1919)

17 Book-learning. The dunce's derisive term for
   all knowledge that transcends his own
   impertinent ignorance.
   Ambrose Bierce, *The Enlarged Devil's
   Dictionary* (1967)

18 Reading furnishes the mind only with
   materials of knowledge; it is thinking makes
   what we read ours.
   John Locke, *Of the Conduct of the
   Understanding* (1706)

19 Here stand my books, line upon line,
   They reach the roof, and row by row,
   They speak of faded tastes of mine,
   And things I did, but do not, know.
   Andrew Lang, 'Ballade of his Books'

20 If you wouldst profit by thy reading, read humbly, simply, honestly, and not desiring to win a character for learning.
Thomas à Kempis, *The Imitation of Christ* (*c.* 1420)

21 The bookful blockhead, ignorantly read, With loads of learned lumber in his head, With his own tongue still edifies his ears, And always list'ning to himself appears.
Alexander Pope, *An Essay on Criticism* (1711)

22 A reading-machine, always wound up and going,
He mastered whatever was not worth the knowing.
James Russell Lowell, *A Fable for Critics* (1848)

23 Books give not wisdom where was none before,
But where some is, there reading makes it more.
Sir John Harington, *Epigrams* (1615)

24 Two theories of poetry. Poetry as a magical means for inducing desirable emotions and repelling undesirable emotions in oneself and others, or Poetry as a game of knowledge, a bringing to consciousness, by naming them, of emotions and their hidden relationships. The first view was held by the Greeks, and is now held by MGM, Agit-Prop, and the collective public of the world. They are wrong.
W.H. Auden, 'Squares and Oblongs', *Poets at Work* (1948)

25 Woe be to him that reads but one book.
George Herbert, *Jacula Prudentum* (1651)

26 If you understood everything you have read in your life, you would already know what you are looking for now.
P.D. Ouspensky, *In Search of the Miraculous* (1950)

27 What you don't know would make a great book.
Sydney Smith, in Lady Holland's *Memoir* (1855)

77 LABOUR OF WRITING

1 Of making many books there is no end; and much study is a weariness of the flesh.
Ecclesiastes 12:12

2 Workers of the word, unite!
Slogan of the Welsh Union of Writers

3 Who casts to write a living line, must sweat.
Ben Jonson, 'To the Memory of . . . William Shakespeare'

4 All good poetry is forged slowly and patiently, link by link, with sweat and blood and tears.
Lord Alfred Douglas, introduction to *Collected Poems* (1919)

5 While pensive poets painful vigils keep Sleepless themselves to give their readers sleep.
Alexander Pope, *The Dunciad* (1728)

6 When I write in a Hurry I always feel to be not worth reading, and what I try to take Pains with, I am sure never to finish.
Richard Brinsley Sheridan, in letter to David Garrick (10 Jan. 1778)

7 Composition is, for the most part, an effort of slow diligence and steady perseverance, to which the mind is dragged by necessity or resolution.
Samuel Johnson, in *The Adventurer* (no. 138, 1752–4)

8 A line will take us hours may be;
Yet if it does not seem a moment's thought, Our stitching and unstitching has been naught.
W.B. Yeats, 'Adam's Curse'

9 I and Pangur Ban, my cat,
'Tis a like task we are at:
Hunting mice is his delight,
Hunting words I am all night.

Practice every day has made
Pangur perfect in his trade;
I get wisdom day and night
Turning darkness into light.
Anonymous Irish poet, translated by Robin Flower

10 I know nothing in the world but poetry that is not acquired by application and care.
Lord Chesterfield, *Letters* (1750)

11 Contrary to what many of you might imagine, a career in letters is not without its drawbacks — chief among them the unpleasant fact that one is frequently called upon to sit down and write.
Fran Lebowitz, *Metropolitan Life* (1978)

12 For forty-odd years in this noble profession I've harboured a guilt and my conscience is smitten,

So here is my slightly embarrassed
    confession —
I don't like to write, but I love to have
    written.
Michael Kanin, 'My Sin', quoted in *The
Author* (Autumn 1979)

13 I was once told that the surest aid to the
writing of a book was a piece of cobbler's
wax on my chair. I certainly believe in the
cobbler's wax much more than the
inspiration.
Anthony Trollope, *Autobiography* (1883)

14 I have discovered that I cannot burn the
candle at one end and write a book with the
other.
Katherine Mansfield, *Journal* (10 June 1919)

15 Experience has shown me that there are no
miracles in writing. The only thing that
produces good writing is hard work. It's
impossible to write a good story by carrying
a rabbit's foot in your pocket.
Isaac Bashevis Singer, in interview in
Writers at Work (5th series, 1981)

16 A man may write at any time, if he will set
himself doggedly to it.
Samuel Johnson, in James Boswell, *Journal
of a Tour of the Hebrides with Samuel
Johnson* (16 Aug. 1773)

17 All desire to practise the art of a writer has
completely left me . . . It's not the writing
but the architecting that strains. If I write
this paragraph, then there is the next and
then the next.
Virginia Woolf, diary entry for 27 April
1935

18 True ease in writing comes from art, not
    chance,
As those move easiest who have learned to
    dance.
Alexander Pope, *An Essay On Criticism*
(1711)

19 When our friend is delivered of a couplet,
with infinite labour and pain, he takes to his
bed, has straw laid down, the knocker tied
up, and expects his friends to call and make
inquiries.
Sydney Smith, in Lady Holland's *Memoir*
(1855)

20 A bad book is as much of a labour to write
as a good one; it comes as sincerely from the
author's soul.
Aldous Huxley, *Point Counter Point* (1928)

21 Eight hours a day, seven days a week, 365
days a year, that's the only way I know how
to do it.
Philip Roth, quoted in *The Observer* (8
March 1987)

22 Three hours a day will produce as much as a
man ought to write.
Anthony Trollope, *Autobiography* (1883)

23 Little do such men know the toil, the pains,
The daily, nightly racking of the brains,
To range the thoughts, the matter to digest,
To cull fit phrases, and reject the rest.
Charles Churchill, *Gotham* (1764)

24 Writing poetry is the only form of literary
labour which gives me entire satisfaction.
Peter Porter, in *The Author* (Spring 1977)

25 writing poems
(keeping rabbits)
each day the shite
to be cleared
fresh straw to be laid.
Tom Pickard, 'The Work'

26 There is a pleasure in poetic pains
Which only poets know.
William Cowper, 'The Timepiece', *The
Task* (1785)

27 A page takes me quite a long time. Two
pages a day is good. Three pages is splendid.
Kingsley Amis, in interview in *Writers at
Work* (5th series, 1981)

28 The writer, like the priest, must be
exempted from secular labor. His work
needs a frolic health; he must be at the top
of his condition.
Ralph Waldo Emerson, 'Poetry and
Imagination'

29 There ain't nothing more to write about and
I'm rotten glad of it, because if I'd knowd
what a trouble it was to make a book, I
wouldn't a tackled it.
Mark Twain, *The Adventures of
Huckleberry Finn* (1885)

---

78 LANGUAGE

---

1 Happy is the poet who has the heritage of a
great language to work with, even as the
architect is fortunate who has stone quarries

and not brickfields at his command.
S.R. Lysaght, *A Reading of Poetry* (1934)

2 The poet is the father who begets the poem
which the language bears.
W.H. Auden, 'Squares and Oblongs', *Poets
at Work* (1948)

3 To grasp the meaning of the world of today
we use a language created to express the
world of yesterday. The life of the past
seems to us nearer our true natures, but only
for the reason that it is nearer our language.
Antoine de Saint-Exupéry, *Wind, Sand, and
Stars* (1939)

4 The language of the age is never the
language of poetry, except among the
French, whose verse, where the thought or
image does not support it, differs in nothing
from prose.
Thomas Gray, *Letters* (1742)

5 A poet is, before anything else, a person
who is passionately in love with language.
Whether this love is a sign of his poetic gift
or the gift itself — for falling in love is given
not chosen — I don't know, but it is
certainly the sign by which one recognizes
whether a young man is potentially a poet or
not.
W.H. Auden, 'Squares and Oblongs', *Poets
at Work* (1948)

6 I live on good soup and not fine language.
Molière, *Les Femmes Savantes* (1672)

7 If language be not in accordance with the
truth of things, affairs cannot be carried on
to success.
Confucius, *Analects*

8 Language is by its very nature a communal
thing; that is, it expresses never the exact
thing but a compromise — that which is
common to you, me, and everybody.
T.E. Hulme, *Speculations* (1924)

9 As men abound in copiousness of language,
so they become more wise, or more mad
than ordinary.
Thomas Hobbes, *Leviathan* (1651)

10 I work with language. I love the flowers of
afterthought.
Bernard Malamud, in interview in *Writers
at Work* (6th series, 1984)

11 The poet's essential task is to possess his
own language.
Saunders Lewis, 'Diwylliant yng Nghymru'

12 Poetry should help, not only to refine the
language of the time, but to prevent it from
changing too rapidly.
T.S. Eliot, 'Milton' (1947)

13 As a poet there is only one political duty —
and that is to defend one's language from
corruption. When it is corrupted people lose
faith in what they hear and this leads to
violence.
W.H. Auden, in *The Observer* (1971)

14 Every age has a language of its own; and the
difference in the words is often far greater
than in the thoughts. The main employment
of authors, in their collective capacity, is to
translate the thoughts of other ages into the
language of their own.
Julius Charles Hare and Augustus Hare,
Guesses at Truth (1827)

15 Great literature is simply language charged
with meaning to the utmost possible degree.
Ezra Pound, *How to Read* (1931)

16 I don't know of any case in which a man
wrote great or even fine poems equally well
in two languages.
T.S. Eliot, in interview in *Writers at Work*
(2nd series, 1963)

17 A writer can have only one language, if
language is going to mean anything to him.
Philip Larkin, in interview in *The Paris
Review* (1982)

18 Languages happily restrict the mind to what
is of its own native growth and fitted for it,
as rivers and mountains bound countries; or
the empire of learning, as well as states,
would become unwieldy and overgrown.
William Hazlitt, 'On Old English Writers
and Speakers' (1825)

19 The sum of human wisdom is not contained
in any one language, and no single language
is capable of expressing all forms and
degrees of human comprehension.
Ezra Pound, *The ABC of Reading* (1934)

20 Writers who pontificate about their own use
of language drive me right up the wall.
S.J. Perelman, in interview in *Writers at
Work* (2nd series, 1963)

21 Language, if it throws a veil over our ideas,
adds a softness and refinement to them, like
that which the atmosphere gives to naked
objects.
William Hazlitt, 'On Classical Education',
The Round Table (1817)

22 Mere elegance of language can produce at
best but an empty renown.
Petrarch, *Letter to Posterity* (1367–72)

23   Among the forests
Of metal the one human
Sound was the lament of
The poets for deciduous language.
R.S. Thomas, 'Postscript'

24 Language, — human language, — after all is
but little better than the croak and crackle of
fowls, and other utterances of brute nature,
— sometimes not so adequate.
Nathaniel Hawthorne, *American
Note-Books* (14 July 1850)

25 Every work of enduring literature is not so
much a triumph of language as a victory
over language; a sudden injection of
life-giving perceptions into a vocabulary
that is, but for the energy of the creative
writer, perpetually on the verge of
exhaustion.
J. Middleton Murry, *The Problem of Style*
(1922)

26 Language is the archives of history.
Ralph Waldo Emerson, 'The Poet', *Essays*
(1844)

27 'Language, man!' roared Parsons; 'why, it's
LITERATURE!'
H.G. Wells, *The History of Mr Polly* (1910)

LEARNING
See KNOWLEDGE

---

79 LETTERS

---

1 I am afraid that we small fry of the press are
about the worst letter-writers in the world.
We always smell of the shop so
confoundedly, and will be scribbling about
literature or politics, or mayhap
metaphysics, to the people who would
rather hear news of their friends or
economics of the wardrobe.
Hartley Coleridge, to his mother (16 May
1835)

2 I don't believe I ever wrote a literary letter
— ever got discussing books or literary men

or writers or artists of any sort in letters: the
very idea of it makes me sick. I like letters to
be personal — very personal — and then
stop.
Walt Whitman, Horace Traubel, *With Walt
Whitman in Camden* (1908)

3 A letter which is not mainly about the writer
of it lacks the prime flavour. The wine must
smack a little of the cask.
James Russell Lowell, to Charles Eliot
Norton, 5 September 1871

4 I have now attained the true art of
letter-writing, which we are always told is to
express on paper exactly what one would
say to the same person by word of mouth. I
have been talking to you almost as fast as I
could the whole of this letter.
Jane Austen, to her sister Cassandra, 3
January 1801

5 Sir, more than kisses, letters mingle souls;
For, thus friends absent speak.
John Donne, 'To Sir Henry Wotton' (1633)

6 Thank you for your letter; it was as pleasant
as a quiet chat, as welcome as spring
showers, as reviving as a friend's visit, in
short, it was very like a page of *Cranford*.
Charlotte Brontë, to Mrs Gaskell, 5 July
1853

7 The true use of a letter is to let one know
that one is remembered and valued.
James Russell Lowell, to Mrs Leslie
Stephen, 11 September 1889

8 Methinks I am grown an uninteresting
correspondent. Yet I know not how to help
it. I never could compose letters; they were
forced to write themselves, and live upon
their daily bread.
Horace Walpole, to Sir Horace Mann, 7
May 1775

9 Correspondences are like small-clothes
before the invention of suspenders: it is
impossible to keep them up.
Sydney Smith, to Mrs Crowe, 31 Jan. 1841

10 An intention to write never turns into a
letter.
Rainer Maria Rilke, *Letters* (1936–9)

11 Partly from some constitutional infirmities,
and partly from certain habits of mind, I do
not write any letters unless upon business,
not even to my dearest friends. Except
during absence from my own family I have

not written five letters of friendship during the last five years.
William Wordsworth, *Early Letters of William and Dorothy Wordsworth* (1935)

12 Oh! that I had a letter from William!
Dorothy Wordsworth, *Journals* (14 May 1800)

13 Why it should be such an effort to write to the people one loves I can't imagine. It's none at all to write to those who don't really count.
Katherine Mansfield, *Journals* (1954)

14 I have made this letter longer than usual, only because I have not had the time to make it shorter.
Blaise Pascal, *Lettres Provinciales* (1657)

15 We lay aside letters never to read them again, and at last we destroy them out of discretion, and so disappears the most beautiful, the most immediate breath of life, irrecoverably for ourselves and for others.
J.W. Goethe, *Elective Affinities* (1809)

16 *Millamant*: O ay, letters — I had letters — I am persecuted with letters — I hate letters — no body knows how to write letters; and yet one has 'em, one does not know why — They serve one to pin up one's hair.
Witwoud: . . . Pray, Madam, do you pin up your hair with all your letters: I find I must keep copies.
Millamant: Only with those in verse, Mr Witwoud. I never pin up my hair with prose.
William Congreve, *The Way of the World* (1700)

17 I knew one, that when he wrote a letter, he would put that which was most material, in the Post-script, as if it had been a by-matter.
Francis Bacon, 'Of Cunning', *Essays* (1597)

18 A woman seldom writes her mind but in her postscript.
Richard Steele, *The Spectator* (no. 79, 1711)

19 'That's rather a sudden pull up, ain't it, Sammy?' inquired Mr Weller.
'Not a bit on it,' said Sam; 'she'll vish there wos more, and that's the great art o' letter writin.'
Charles Dickens, *Pickwick Papers* (1837)

20 A man who publishes his letters becomes a nudist — nothing shields him from the world's gaze except his bare skin. A writer, writing away, can always fix himself up to make himself more presentable, but a man who has written a letter is stuck with it for all time.
E.B. White, to Corona Macheiner, 11 June 1975

80 LIBRARY

Private

1 Books that stand thinne on the shelves, yet so as the owner of them can bring forth every one of them into use, are better than farre greater libraries.
Thomas Fuller, 'Of Books', *The Holy State* (1642)

2 A library implies an act of faith.
Victor Hugo, *L'Année Terrible* (1871)

3 A man should keep his little brain attic stocked with all the furniture that he is likely to use, and the rest he can put away in the lumber room of his library, where he can get it if he wants it.
Sir Arthur Conan Doyle, 'Five Orange Pips', *The Adventures of Sherlock Holmes* (1892)

4 The first thing to have in a libry is a shelf. Fr'm time to time this can be decorated with lithrachure. But th' shelf is th' main thing.
Finley Peter Dunne, 'Books', *Mr Dooley Says* (1910)

5 Good as it is to inherit a library, it is better to collect one.
Augustine Birrell, 'Book-Buying', **Obiter Dicta** (1884)

6 Far more seemly to have thy Studie full of Bookes, than thy Purse full of money.
John Lyly, *Euphues* (1579)

7   My library
Was dukedom large enough.
William Shakespeare, *The Tempest*

8 Consider what you have in the smallest chosen library. A company of the wisest and wittiest men that could be picked out of all civil countries in a thousand years have set in best order the results of their learning and wisdom. The men themselves were hid and inaccessible, solitary, impatient of interruption, fenced by etiquette; but the thought which they did not uncover to their bosom friend is here written out in

transparent words to us, the strangers of another age.
Ralph Waldo Emerson, 'Books', *Society and Solitude* (1870)

9 Come, and take choice of all my library,
And so beguile thy sorrow.
William Shakespeare, *Titus Andronicus*

10 When evening has arrived, I return home, and go into my study . . . I pass into the antique courts of ancient men, where, welcomed lovingly by them, I feed upon the food which is my own, and for which I was born. Here, I can speak with them without show, and they respond to me by virtue of their humanity. For hours together, the miseries of life no longer annoy me; I forget every vexation; I do not fear poverty; altogether transferred myself to those with whom I hold converse.
Niccolò Machiavelli, *Opere*

11 I go into my library, and all history rolls before me. I breathe the morning air of the world while the scent of Eden's roses yet lingered in it . . . I see the pyramids building; I hear the shoutings of the armies of Alexander . . . I sit as in a theatre — the stage is time, the play is the play of the world.
Alexander Smith, 'Books and Gardens', *Dreamthorp* (1863)

12 Meek young men grow up in libraries, believing it is their duty to accept the views which Cicero, which Locke, which Bacon, have given; forgetful that Cicero, Locke, and Bacon were only young men in libraries when they wrote these books.
Ralph Waldo Emerson, *The American Scholar* (1837)

13 I have now a library of nearly nine hundred volumes, over seven hundred of which I wrote myself.
Henry David Thoreau, on taking unsold copies of his book from the publisher

14 To arrange a library is to practise in a quiet and modest way the art of criticism.
Jorge Luis Borges, 'June 1968'

15 A home library cannot be brought under the direction of an interior decorator. The only interior to be decorated is your own mind.
Frank G. Jennings, *This is Reading* (1964)

16 It is a vanity to persuade the world one hath much learning, by getting a great library. As soon shall I believe every one is valiant that hath a well-furnished armoury.
Thomas Fuller, 'Of Books', *The Holy State* (1642)

17 Affect not as some do that bookish ambition to be stored with books and have well-furnished libraries, yet keep their heads empty of knowledge; to desire to have many books, and never to use them, is like a child that will have a candle burning by him all the while he is sleeping.
Henry Peacham, *The Compleat Gentleman* (1622)

18 The Bibliomania, or the collecting of an enormous heap of books without intelligent curiosity, has, since libraries have existed, infected weak minds, who imagine that they themselves acquire knowledge when they keep it on their shelves.
Isaac D'Israeli, *Curiosities of Literature* (1791–1834)

19 We cannot bring ourselves to admit that the library we have collected is in great part closed to us simply by want of time. A dear friend of mine indulged in wonderful illusions about reading, and collected several thousand volumes, all fine editions, but he died without having cut their leaves.
P.G. Hamerton, *The Intellectual Life* (1882)

20 A man's library is a sort of harem.
Ralph Waldo Emerson, 'In Praise of Books', *The Conduct of Life* (1860)

21 Unlearned men of books assume the care,
As eunuchs are the guardians of the fair.
Edward Young, *The Love of Fame* (c. 1727)

22 Twenty-two acknowledged concubines, and a library of sixty-two thousand volumes attested the variety of his inclinations; and from the productions which he left behind him, it appears that both the one and the other were designed for use rather than for ostentation.
Edward Gibbon, of the Emperor Gordian the Younger, *The Decline and Fall of the Roman Empire* (1776–88)

23 He that revels in a well-chosen library, has innumerable dishes, and all of admirable flavour.
William Godwin, 'Early Taste for Reading', *The Enquirer* (1797)

24 Keep the modern magazine and novel out of

your girl's way: turn her loose into the old
library every wet day, and let her alone.
John Ruskin, *Sesame and Lilies* (1865)

25 The first thing naturally when one enters a
scholar's study or library, is to look at his
books. One gets a notion very speedily of his
tastes and the range of his pursuits, by a
glance round the book-shelves.
Oliver Wendell Holmes, *The Poet at the
Breakfast Table* (1872)

26 There is no mood in which a man may not
administer the appropriate medicine at the
cost of reaching down a volume from his
bookshelf.
A.J. Balfour, *Essays and Addresses* (1893)

27 I feel I want to be wise with white hair in a
tall library in a deep chair by a fireplace.
Gregory Corso, 'Writ on the Eve of my
32nd Birthday', *Long Live Man* (1963)

28 A library is but the soul's burying ground. It
is a land of shadows.
Henry Ward Beecher, *Star Papers* (1855)

29 I have a wife, a son, a home, six good
hunters and a library of Romance literature.
I mean to enjoy them. If I am wanted, I can
be found.
George Wyndham, in letter to Charles Boyd
(23 Feb. 1908)

30 Anyone who has experienced the burning of
a capital city or the invasion of eastern
armies will never lose a lively mistrust of
everything one may possess. That is an
advantage, as he may count himself one of
those able to turn their back on farm, or
house or library without overmuch regret, if
this proves necessary. And he will find that
an act of freedom is associated with it.
Ernst Jünger, *Der Waldgang* (1951)

Public

31 Shut not your doors to me proud libraries,
For that which was lacking on all your
        well-fill'd shelves,
        yet needed most, I bring
Forth from the war emerging, a book I have
        made.
Walt Whitman, 'Shut not your doors'

32 A great library contains the diary of the
human race.
George Dawson, in address on opening of
the Birmingham Free Library (26 Oct. 1866)

33 Let every man, if possible, gather some good

books under his roof, and obtain access for
himself and family to some social library.
Almost any luxury should be sacrificed to
this.
William Ellery Channing, preface to
Self-Culture (1838)

34 What a place to be in is an old library! It
seems as though all the souls of all the
writers, that have bequeathed their labours
to those Bodleians, were reposing here, as in
some dormitory, or middle state. I do not
want to handle, to profane the leaves, their
winding-sheets. I could as soon dislodge a
shade. I seem to inhale learning, walking
amid their foliage; and the odour of their
old moth-scented coverings is fragrant as the
first bloom of those sciential apples which
grew amid the happy orchard.
Charles Lamb, 'Oxford in the Vacation',
Essays of Elia (1823)

35 You ask me where I spend my evenings.
Where do you suppose, with a free prentice
library containing more than four thousand
volumes within a quarter of a mile of me
and nobody at home to talk to?
Mark Twain, letter to his sister Emma from
New York at age 18 (1853)

36 The diffusion of these silent teachers, books,
through the whole community, is to work
greater effects than artillery, machinery, and
legislation. Its peaceful agency is to
supersede stormy revolutions. The culture,
which is to spread, whilst an unspeakable
good to the individual, is also to become the
stability of nations.
William Ellery Channing, *Self-Culture*
(1838)

37 (Our) libraries have improved the general
conversation of the Americans, made the
common tradesmen and farmers as
intelligent as most gentlemen from other
countries, and perhaps have contributed in
some degree to the stand so generally made
throughout the colonies in defence of their
privileges.
Benjamin Franklin, *Autobiography* (1793)

38 My alma mater was books, a good library
. . . I could spend the rest of my life reading,
just satisfying my curiosity.
Malcolm X, *Autobiography* (1964)

39 What a sad want I am in of libraries, of
books to gather facts from! Why is there not
a Majesty's library in every country town?

There is a Majesty's gaol and gallows in every one.
Thomas Carlyle, quoted by R. Irwin and R. Staveley, *The Libraries of London* (1961)

40 What do we, as a nation, care about books? How much do you think we spend altogether on our libraries, public or private, as compared with what we spend on our horses?
John Ruskin, *Sesame and Lilies* (1865)

41 Library borrowing is on the decline. Public libraries are not what they were and the book-borrowing habit has not really taken root in the younger generation.
Brian Appleyard, in *The Times* (26 April 1986)

42 Invoking the great names of education and enlightenment, it has become a system which largely supplies free pulp fiction to those who could well afford to buy it.
Adam Smith Institute, in report 'Ex Libris' on public libraries, quoted in *The Times* (23 June 1986)

43 Public libraries are among Britain's most enlightened achievements. We have grown, rightly, to take them for granted as part of our birthright. They are the bedrock of a culture whose greatest pride is its literature . . . Closing a library would have been unthinkable ten years ago. Now a richer society can't support it. Something is seriously wrong.
Joan Bakewell, in *The Sunday Times* (29 Nov. 1987)

44 In a society where individuals are treated as economic units, and hope for the future lies in the latest Treasury statistics, the value of a free library service should not be underestimated.
Shirley Anderson, in letter to *The Financial Times* (28 June 1986)

45 My experience with public libraries is that the first volume of the book I inquire for is out, unless I happen to want the second, when that is out.
Oliver Wendell Holmes, *The Poet at the Breakfast Table* (1872)

46 One of the great offices of a Reference Library is to keep at the service of everybody what everybody cannot keep at home for his own service.
George Dawson, in address at the opening of the Birmingham Free Reference Library (1866)

47 Every library should try to be complete on something, if it were only on the history of pin-heads.
Oliver Wendell Holmes, *The Poet at the Breakfast-Table* (1872)

48 Keepers of books, keepers of print and paper on the shelves, librarians are keepers also of the records of the human spirit — the records of men's watch upon the world and on themselves. In such a time as ours, when wars are made against the spirit and its works, the keeping of these records is itself a kind of warfare. The keepers, whether they so wish or not, cannot be neutral.
Archibald MacLeish, 'Of the Librarian's Profession', *A Time to Speak* (1941)

49 There can be few more unrewarding tasks for the educated man of curiosity than the routine duties of librarianship.
Angus Wilson, *The Wild Garden* (1963)

50 No place affords a more striking conviction of the vanity of human hopes, than a public library.
Samuel Johnson, in *The Rambler* (23 March 1751)

51 Under the hive-like dome the stooping haunted readers
Go up and down the alleys, tap the cells of knowledge —
Honey and wax, the accumulation of years —
Some on commission, some for the love of learning,
Some because they have nothing better to do
Or because they hope these walls of books will deaden
The drumming of the demon in their ears.
Louis MacNeice, 'The British Museum Reading Room'

52 Our libraries are getting bigger, which makes it more difficult to find a good book. The shelves are groaning under the pressure of clothbound nothingness.
Dagobert D. Runes, *Treasury of Thought* (1966)

53 Of the forty miles of shelves in the Museum, forty feet would contain all the real literature of the world.
Coventry Patmore, *Memoirs* (1901)

54 A library is not worth anything without a catalogue — it is a Polyphemus without any eye in his head.
Thomas Carlyle, testimony before the

Commissioners appointed to inquire into the constitution and government of the British Museum (1849)

55 As to the devotees of the circulating libraries, I dare not compliment their *pass-time*, or rather *kill-time*, with the name of *reading*.
Samuel Taylor Coleridge, *Biographia Literaria* (1817)

56 I keep my books at the British Museum and at Mudie's.
Samuel Butler, 'Ramblings in Cheapside', *The Humour of Homer* (1892)

57 We call ourselves a rich nation, and we are filthy and foolish enough to thumb each other's books out of circulating libraries!
John Ruskin, *Sesame and Lilies* (1865)

58 A circulating library in a town is an ever-green tree of diabolical knowledge! It blossoms through the year.
Richard Brinsley Sheridan, *The Rivals* (1775)

59 One day there will be no libraries. Only a global bookshelf.
Brian Redhead, 'To Have or Have Not' in *The Anti-Booklist* (ed. Brian Redhead and Kenneth McLeish, 1981)

---

81 LIFE

1 No man understands a deep book until he has seen and lived at least part of its contents.
Ezra Pound, *The ABC of Reading* (1934)

2 To take Measures wholly from Books, without looking into Men and Business, is like Travelling in a Map, where though Countries and Cities are well enough distinguished, yet Villages and private Seats are either Overlooked, or too generally Marked for a Stranger to find. And therefore he that would be a Master, must Draw from Life, as well as Copy from Originals, and join Theory and Experience together.
Jeremy Collier, *Essays upon Several Moral Subjects* (1698)

3 The globe we inhabit is divided into two worlds: the common geographical world, and the world of books . . . in habit and perception between real and unreal, we may say that we more frequently wake out of common life to them, than out of them to common life.
Leigh Hunt, farewell address in *Monthly Repository* (1828)

4 Literature always anticipates life. It does not copy it, but moulds it to its purpose.
Oscar Wilde, 'The Decay of Lying', *Intentions* (1891)

5 Life is the reflection of literature.
Wallace Stevens, *Opus Posthumous* (1957)

6 The Iliad is only great because all life is a battle, the Odyssey because all life is a journey, the Book of Job because all life is a riddle.
G.K. Chesterton, quoted in Burton Rascoe, *The Joys of Reading* (1937)

7 The main difference between living people and fictitious characters is that the writer takes great pains to give the characters coherence and inner unity, whereas the living people may go to extremes of incoherence because their physical existence holds them together.
Hugo von Hofmannsthal, *The Book of Friends* (1922)

8 That was the chief difference between literature and life. In books, the proportion of exceptional to commonplace people is high; in reality, very low.
Aldous Huxley, *Eyeless in Gaza* (1936)

9 In my plays I want to look at life — at the commonplace of existence — as if we had just turned a corner and run into it for the first time.
Christopher Fry, in *Time* (20 Nov. 1952)

10 Of all the inanimate objects, of all men's creations, books are the nearest to us, for they contain our very thoughts, our ambitions, our indignations, our illusions, our fidelity to truth, and our persistent leaning towards error. But most of all they resemble us in their precarious hold on life.
Joseph Conrad, *Notes on Life and Letters* (1921)

11 Neither Christ nor Buddha nor Socrates wrote a book, for to do that is to exchange life for a logical process.
W.B. Yeats, 'Estrangement', *Autobiography* (1936)

12 In truth, writers live alongside, on the

margin of life and of humanity. That's why they're very great or very small.
Blaise Cendrars, in interview in *Writers at Work* (3rd series, 1967)

13 No man would set a word down on paper if he had the courage to live out what he believed in.
Henry Miller, *Sunday after the War* (1944)

14 The illusion of art is to make one believe that great literature is very close to life, but the exact opposite is true. Life is amorphous, literature is formal.
Françoise Sagan, in interview in *Writers at Work* (1st series, 1958)

15 Literature is based not on life but on propositions about life, of which this is one.
Wallace Stevens, 'Adagia', *Opus Posthumous* (1957)

16 Writing's an important way of living.
William S. Burroughs, in *The Sunday Telegraph* (1964)

17 The great writer does not really come to conclusions about life; he discerns a quality in it.
J. Middleton Murry, *The Problem of Style* (1922)

18 It is the function of literature — indeed, of all the arts — to make us more aware of the life we live and see about us.
Burton Rascoe, *The Joys of Reading* (1937)

19 While thought exists, words are alive and literature becomes an escape, not from, but into living.
Cyril Connolly, *The Unquiet Grave* (1945)

20 My writing is a hollow and failing substitute for real life, real feeling.
Sylvia Plath, journal

21 The poet who sets up a principle or ideal or policy which prevents him from accepting life as it is, limits himself and creates a false picture of life.
Stephen Spender, *Life and the Poet* (1942)

22 The world is so great and rich, and life so full of variety, that you can never lack occasions for poems.
J.W. Goethe, quoted in Johann Peter Eckermann, *Conversations with Goethe* (18 Sept. 1823)

23 Literature's function is to explain the great mystery underlying life, and not to deal with the small questions which happen to be important at the time.
W.J. Gruffydd, quoted in R.M. Jones, *Llenyddiaeth Gymraeg 1902–1936* (1987)

24 Consonance and assonance and inner

rhyme won't make up for the fact that I can't figure out how to get

down on paper the real or the true which we call life.
William Wantling, 'Poetry'

25 Books succeed,
And lives fail.
Elizabeth Barrett Browning, *Aurora Leigh* (1856)

26 I armed her against the censure of the world, showed her that books were sweet unreproaching companions to the miserable, and that if they could not bring us to enjoy life, they would at least teach us to endure it.
Oliver Goldsmith, *The Vicar of Wakefield* (1764)

27 Do not read, as children do, to amuse yourself, or like the ambitious, for the purpose of instruction. No, read in order to live.
Gustave Flaubert, in letter to Mlle de Chantepie (June 1857)

28 Poetry cannot cure cancer, nor put an end to fire, famine, and flood. But it can provide a fusion of relaxation and excitement without the penalties attaching to either. To a greater degree than the other arts, it can reveal the conditions of living. This should help us to amend them.
Babette Deutsch, *Poetry in Our Time* (1956)

29 Poetry is a way of taking life by the throat.
Robert Frost, in *Vogue* (1963)

30 All great poetry gives the illusion of a view of life.
T.S. Eliot, 'Shakespeare and the Stoicism of Seneca' (1927)

31 Books are good enough in their own way, but they are a mighty bloodless substitute for life.
Robert Louis Stevenson, 'An Apology for Idlers', *Virginibus Puerisque* (1881)

32 People say that life is the thing, but I prefer reading.
Logan Pearsall Smith, *Afterthoughts* (1931)

33 I want a normal life, with wallpaper and
    bookends.
    Damon Runyon, Adelaide in *Guys and
    Dolls* (1932)

---

82 LITERACY
   See also EDUCATION

---

1 To be a well-favoured man is the gift of
   fortune; but to write and read comes by
   nature.
   William Shakespeare, *Much Ado about
   Nothing*

2 Editors have to be able to spell: publishers
   can be illiterate.
   Anthony Blond, *The Book Book* (1985)

3 It is frightening to speculate about the next
   generation that is being educated to know
   nothing of our history and culture and can
   be expected to resemble the robots they are
   learning to manipulate . . . Who will still be
   able to read, let alone read anything that
   requires intelligence and concentration?
   Centuries of reforming effort to increase
   literacy and produce and educate the
   electorate, the only possible basis for a
   democracy, is being destroyed in less than
   one generation.
   John Calder, in a letter to *The Guardian* (17
   April 1987)

4 There is a sense in which the daily tabloids
   like *The Sun* and *The Mirror* have become
   standard-bearers of illiteracy.
   Emyr Humphreys, 'Fickle Fact and Sober
   Fiction' (1986)

5 The ratio of literacy to illiteracy is constant,
   but nowadays the illiterates can read and
   write.
   Alberto Moravia, quoted by Mary
   McCarthy in *The Observer*, 'A World Out
   of Joint' (14 Oct. 1979)

6 One thing is certain today — the illiterates
   are definitely not the least intelligent among
   us.
   Henry Miller, *The Books in my Life* (1952)

7 I'm quite illiterate, but I read a lot.
   J.D. Salinger, *The Catcher in the Rye* (1951)

8 It is better to be able neither to read nor
   write than to be able to do nothing else.
   William Hazlitt, *The Ignorance of the
   Learned* (1821)

9 If there's one major cause for the spread of
   mass illiteracy, it's the fact that everybody
   can read and write.
   Peter de Vries, *The Tents of Wickedness*
   (1959)

10 Violence is the repartee of the illiterate.
    Alan Brien, in *Punch* (7 Feb. 1973)

11 The gaping goldfish in his bowl
    I'm sure is happy, on the whole:
    He has that silly vacant look
    Because he's never read a book.
    A.G. Prys-Jones, 'The Goldfish'

---

83 LITERATI

---

1 Writers, like teeth, are divided into incisors
   and grinders.
   Walter Bagehot, 'The First Edinburgh
   Reviewers', *Literary Studies* (1879–95)

2 An author! 'tis a venerable name!
   How few deserve it, and what numbers
            claim!
   Edward Young, *Epistles to Mr Pope* (1730)

3 Well, great authors are great people — but I
   believe that they are best seen at a distance.
   Mrs Mitford, in letter to Mrs Hofland (28
   March 1819)

4 The London literati appear to me to be very
   much like little potatoes, that is . . . a
   compost of nullity and dullity.
   Samuel Taylor Coleridge, in letter to Robert
   Southey (1797)

5 God, how stupid literary men are!
   Napoleon I, letter to Cambarcérès (24 Jan.
   1806)

6 I hate the whole race . . . There is no
   believing a word they say — your
   professional poets, I mean — there never
   existed a more worthless set than Byron and
   his friends for example.
   Duke of Wellington, noted in Lady
   Salisbury's diary (26 Oct. 1833)

7 One hates an author that's all author —
            fellows
   In foolscap uniforms turned up with ink,
   So very anxious, clever, fine, and jealous,
   One don't know what to say to them, or
            think,
   Unless to puff them with a pair of bellows.
   Lord Byron, *Beppo* (1818)

8 They're so damned polite to each other they swallow the worst kind of piddling nonsense from each other as though it was sugar candy.
Irwin Shaw, in interview in *Writers at Work* (5th series, 1981)

9 I met Sir Bulwer Lytton. He is anxious about some scheme for some association of literary men. I detest all such associations. I hate the notion of gregarious authors. The less we have to do with each other the better.
Thomas Babington Macaulay, in G.O. Trevelyan, *Life and Letters* (1876)

10 There's nothing more despicable than literati calling literati literati.
Kurt Tucholsky, *Gesammelte Werke* (1960–2)

11 It is dangerous to have any intercourse or dealing with small authors. They are as troublesome to handle, as easy to discourage, as difficult to pacify, and leave as unpleasant marks on you, as small children.
Walter Savage Landor, *Imaginary Conversations* (1853)

12 Authors are easy enough to get on with — if you are fond of children.
Michael Joseph, quoted in *The Observer* (29 May 1949)

13 I am quite disgusted with literary men.
John Keats, in letter to Benjamin Bailey (8 Oct. 1817)

14 Writers are interesting people, but often mean and petty . . . Writers can be the stinkers of all time, can't they?
Lillian Hellman, in interview in *Writers at Work* (3rd series, 1967)

15 I have put up with a lot, to please the sensitive race of poets.
Horace, *Epistles*

16 Avoid the company of poets: human beings are much more interesting.
R. Williams Parry, 'Deg Gorchymyn i Feirdd'

17 The llama is a woolly sort of fleecy hairy
    goat
With an indolent expression and an
    undulating throat,
Like an unsuccessful literary man.
Hilaire Belloc, 'The Llama'

18 He's a distinguished man of letters. He works for the Post Office.
Max Kauffmann, attr.

84 LITERATURE

1 In the civilization of today it is undeniable that, over all the arts, literature dominates, serves beyond all.
Walt Whitman, *Democratic Vistas* (1871)

2 There is first the literature of knowledge, and secondly, the literature of power. The function of the first is — to teach; the function of the second is — to move; the first is a rudder, the second an oar or a sail. The first speaks to the mere discursive understanding; the second speaks ultimately, it may happen, to the higher understanding of reason.
Thomas De Quincey, 'Pope', *Essay on the Poets* (1853)

3 Literature, like nobility, runs in the blood.
William Hazlitt, *Table Talk* (1821)

4 It is in literature that the concrete outlook of humanity receives its expression.
Alfred North Whitehead, *Science and the Modern World* (1925)

5 A great literature is chiefly the product of inquiring minds in revolt against the immovable certainties of the nation.
H.L. Mencken, *Prejudices* (1919)

6 The function of literature through all its mutations, has been to make us aware of the particularity of selves, and the high authority of the self in its quarrel with its society and its culture. Literature is in that sense subversive.
Lionel Trilling, *Beyond Culture* (1966)

7 Literature by its very nature is committed to questioning yesterday's assumptions and today's commonplaces.
Robert Martin Adams, quoted in Elmer Borklund, *Contemporary Literary Critics* (1977)

8 Literature has the right and the duty to give to the public the ideas of the time.
Bertolt Brecht, testimony to the House Committee on UnAmerican Activities (1947)

9 No wonder the really powerful men in our society, whether politicians or scientists, hold writers and poets in contempt. They do it because they get no evidence from modern literature that anybody is thinking about any significant question.
Saul Bellow, in interview in *Writers at Work* (3rd series, 1967)

10 Literature is a state of culture, poetry a state of grace, before and after culture.
Juan Ramón Jiménez, 'Poetry and Literature', *Selected Writings* (1957)

11 Literature exists to please — to lighten the burden of men's lives; to make them for a short while forget their sorrows and their sins, their silenced hearths, their disappointed hopes, their grim futures — and those men of letters are the best loved who have best performed literature's truest office.
Augustine Birrell, 'Office of Literature', *Obiter Dicta* (1884)

12 The land of literature is a fairy land to those who view it at a distance, but, like all other landscapes, the charm fades on a nearer approach, and the thorns and briars become visible.
Washington Irving, 'Notoriety', *Tales of a Traveller* (1824)

13 Literature has soared up like an eagle to the skies. And has fallen down. Now it is quite clear that literature is not the 'sought-after invisible city'.
V.V. Rozanov, *Solitaria* (1912)

14 The existence of good bad literature — the fact that one can be amused or excited or even moved by a book that one's intellect simply refuses to take seriously — is a reminder that art is not the same thing as cerebration.
George Orwell, 'Good Bad Books', *Shooting an Elephant* (1950)

15 Literature is the human activity that takes the fullest and most precise account of variousness, possibility, complexity, and difficulty.
Lionel Trilling, in preface to *The Liberal Imagination* (1950)

16 He set out seriously to describe the indescribable. That is the whole business of literature and it is a hard row to hoe.
G.K. Chesterton, *All I Survey* (1933)

17 It is clear that 'the ordinary man' cannot understand the extraordinary except in the fullness of time; and the extraordinary is the essence of literature.
Saunders Lewis, in *Y Llenor* (Winter 1922)

18 The unusual is only found in a very small percentage, except in literary creations, and that is exactly what makes literature.
Julio Cortazar, *The Winners* (1960)

19 Literature is not an abstract science, to which exact definitions can be applied. It is an art, the success of which depends on personal persuasiveness, on the author's skill to give as on ours to receive.
Sir Arthur Quiller-Couch, in Inaugural Lecture at Cambridge University (1913)

20 Literature is not about something: it is the thing itself, the quiddity.
Vladimir Nabokov, *Lectures on Literature* (1980)

21 To you literature like painting is an end; to me literature like architecture is a means, it has a use.
H.G. Wells, in letter to Henry James

22 Literature and butterflies are the two sweetest passions known to man.
Vladimir Nabokov, quoted in *Radio Times* (Oct. 1962)

23 Literature: proclaiming in front of everyone what one is careful to conceal from one's immediate circle.
Jean Rostand, *Journal d'un caractère* (1931)

24 Literature is the question minus the answer.
Roland Barthes, in *The New York Times* (1978)

25 The world could get along very well without literature; it could get along even better without man.
Jean-Paul Sartre, *Situations* (1947–9)

26 Persons devoted to mere literature commonly become devoted to mere idleness.
Walter Bagehot, *Literary Studies* (1879)

27 He knew everything about literature except how to enjoy it.
Joseph Heller, *Catch 22* (1961)

28 For me, Literature with a capital L is rubbish.
Georges Simenon, quoted by Fenton Bresler, *The Mystery of Georges Simenon* (1983)

29 Literature is the orchestration of platitudes.
Thornton Wilder, in *Time* magazine (12 Jan. 1953)

30 Literature is news that *stays* news.
Ezra Pound, *The ABC of Reading* (1931)

31 While much that is in print is not literature, all literature is in print.
Nigel Cross, in *The Times Literary Supplement* (27 Sept. 1985)

32 I think that if a third of all the novelists and maybe two thirds of all the poets now writing dropped dead suddenly, the loss to literature would not be great.
Charles Osborne, Literature Director of the Arts Council of Great Britain, quoted in 'Sayings of the Week' in *The Observer* (3 Nov. 1985)

85 LOVE

1 Every man is a poet when he is in love.
Plato, *Symposium*

2 That I make poetry and give pleasure (if I give pleasure) are because of you.
Horace, *Odes*

3 Chameleons feed on light and air:
Poets' food is love and fame.
Percy Bysshe Shelley, 'An Exhortation'

4 A poet without love were a physical and metaphysical impossibility.
Thomas Carlyle, 'Burns', *The Edinburgh Review* (1828)

5 By heaven, I do love, and it hath taught me to rhyme, and to be melancholy.
William Shakespeare, *Love's Labour's Lost*

6 I never wrote anything worth mentioning till I was in love.
Lord Byron, *Conversations* (1824)

7 For a man to become a poet . . . he must be in love, or miserable.
Lord Byron, 'Medwin', *Conversations* (1824)

8 Never durst poet touch a pen to write
Until his ink were temper'd with Love's sighs.
William Shakespeare, *Love's Labour's Lost*

9 Give all to love:
Obey thy heart;

Friends, kindred, days,
Estate, good fame,
Plans, credit, and the Muse, —
Nothing refuse.
Ralph Waldo Emerson, 'Give all to love'

10 I am two fools, I know,
For loving, and for saying so,
In whining Poetry.
John Donne, 'The Triple Fool'

11 I have read this book in your garden; — my love, you were absent, or else I could not have read it.
Lord Byron, to the Marchesa Guiccioli, written in a copy of *Corinne* which he found in her garden at Bologna, 25 Aug. 1819

12 There's many a would-be poet at this hour,
Rhymes of a love that he hath never woo'd,
And o'er his lamp-lit desk in solitude
Deems that he sitteth in the Muses' bower.
Robert Bridges, 'Growth of Love'

13 The girl whose boy-friend starts writing her love poems should be on her guard.
W.H. Auden, 'Squares and Oblongs', *Poets at Work* (1948)

14 I court others in verse: but I love thee in prose:
And they have my whimsies, but thou hast my heart.
Matthew Prior, 'A Better Answer (to Cloe Jealous)'

15 Poets should never marry. The world should thank me for not marrying you.
Maud Gonne, to W.B. Yeats, quoted in Nancy Cardozo, *Maud Gonne* (1978)

16 Hundreds of men love more than one woman, you're always reading about it.
Dylan Thomas, 'Patricia, Edith, and Arnold'

17 Great is the poverty of novelists' inventions. She was beautiful and he fell in love.
Ralph Waldo Emerson, 'Books', *Society and Solitude* (1870)

18 Those perfectly happy in their affections never read novels, because real love is so much more fascinating than that described.
O.S. Fowler, *Sexual Science* (1875)

19 Only connect! That was the whole of her sermon. Only connect the prose and the passion, and both will be exalted, and human love will be seen at its highest.
E.M. Forster, *Howards End* (1910)

20 Writing a poem is like a short love affair,
writing a short story like a long love affair,
writing a novel like a marriage.
Amos Oz, quoted in 'Sayings of the Week'
in *The Observer* (21 July 1985)

---

86 LYRIC

1 The loss of sin is a loss to literature. Without
sin we shall never have anything except
lyrical poetry.
Saunders Lewis, in *Y Llenor* (Summer 1927)

2 A new type of poem has been evolved and
popularized by the demands of the
anthology-reading public. It is called 'The
perfect modern lyric'. Like the best-seller
novel, it is usually achieved in the dark; but
certain critical regulations can be made for
it. It must be fairly regular in form and easily
memorized, it must be a new combination
of absolutely worn-out material, it must
have a certain unhealthy vigour or langour,
and it must start off engagingly with a
simple sentimental statement.
Robert Graves, 'The Perfect Modern Lyric',
Anthologies (1927)

3 All lyrical poetry beats with the heart, tells
not of things coldly and calmly considered,
but of things seen and felt in a sudden
clearness of the senses, and with a flame in
the thought.
Walter De La Mare, *Behold This Dreamer*
(1939)

4 All good lyrics must make sense as a whole
yet in details be a little absurd.
J.W. Goethe, *Sprüche in Prosa* (1819)

5 Lyricism cannot exist without rules, and it is
essential that they should be strict.
Otherwise there is only a faculty for
lyricism, and that exists everywhere.
Charles Albert Cingria, quoted by Igor
Stravinsky, *An Autobiography* (1936)

---

87 MADNESS

1 All poets are mad.
Robert Burton, *The Anatomy of Melancholy*
(1621)

2 We Poets in our youth begin in gladness;
But thereof come in the end despondency
and madness.
William Wordsworth, *Resolution and
Independence* (1807)

3 The poet makes himself a seer by a long,
immense, and reasoned unruliness of the
senses.
Arthur Rimbaud, in letter to Delahaye
(1872)

4 The courage of the poet is to keep ajar the
door that leads into madness.
Christopher Morley, *Inward Ho!* (1923)

5 Poetry is a whim of Nature in her lighter
moods; it requires nothing but its own
madness and, lacking that, it becomes a
soundless cymbal, a belfry without a bell.
Pietro Aretino, in letter to Nicolò Franco
(25 June 1537)

6 Nothing more abnormal than the poet who
approximates to the normal man: Hugo or
Goethe. This is the madman at large. The
madman who does not appear mad.
Jean Cocteau, *Opium* (1930)

7 The most beautiful things are those that
madness prompts and reason writes.
André Gide, *Journals* (1894)

8 The writer is the Faust of modern society,
the only surviving individualist in a mass
age. To his orthodox contemporaries he
seems a semi-madman.
Boris Pasternak, in *The Observer* (20 Dec.
1959)

9 Writers can treat their mental illnesses every
day.
Kurt Vonnegut Jr., in *Playboy* (1973)

10 Those who ever follow the steps of the poets
. . . they rave as bereft of their senses.
The Koran

---

88 MAGAZINES

1 I'm told that when poets complete a work
they appear in some kind of literary
magazine. I am now ready to appear.
Mark Vinz, *Letters to the Poetry Editor*
(1975)

2 That's it, you've finished for now —
just brush your poems down: dead, fluffed

things but your own almost. Get
them mounted in magazines. Or stuffed.
John Davies, 'How to write Anglo-Welsh
Poetry'

3 Lone scholars, sniping from the walls
Of learned periodicals,
              Our facts defend,
Our intellectual marines,
Landing in little magazines
              Capture a trend.
W.H. Auden, 'Under Which Lyre, A
Reactionary Tract for the Times'

4 i do however protest, anent the un
-spontaneous and otherwise scented merde
              which
greets one (Everywhere Why) as divine
              poesy per
that and this radically defunct periodical.
e e cummings, 'Poem, or Beauty Hurts Mr
Vinal'

5 Magazines all too frequently lead to books
and should be regarded as the heavy petting
of literature.
Fran Lebowitz, *Metropolitan Life* (1978)

6 Of all the literary scenes
Saddest this sight to me:
The graves of little magazines
Who died to make verse free.
Keith Preston, 'The Liberators'

89 MANKIND

1 The human race, to which so many of my
readers belong.
G.K. Chesterton, *The Napoleon of Notting
Hill* (1904)

2 No man can write who is not first a
humanitarian.
William Faulkner, in *Time* magazine (25
Feb. 1957)

3 Man is man's A.B.C. There's none that can
Read God aright unless he first spell man.
Francis Quarles, 'Hieroglyphics of the Life
of Man'

4 Poetry . . . is the attempt to imagine, in
terms of the transitory forms of the present
in which a generation lives, the universal
nature of man's being.
Stephen Spender, *Life and the Poet* (1942)

5 Poetry is the universal possession of
mankind, revealing itself everywhere, and at
all times, in hundreds and hundreds of men.
J.W. Goethe, quoted in Johann Peter
Eckermann, *Conversations with Goethe* (31
Jan. 1827)

6 Mankind are the creatures of books.
Leigh Hunt, introduction to *A Book for a
Corner* (1852)

7 Of the things which man can do or make
here below, by far the most momentous,
wonderful, and worthy are the things we
call Books!
Thomas Carlyle, 'The Hero as Man of
Letters', *On Heroes, Hero-Worship and the
Heroic in History* (1840)

8 A good book is the purest essence of a
human soul.
Thomas Carlyle, in speech in support of the
London Library (1840)

9 We must wash literature off ourselves. We
want to be men first of all; to be human.
Antonin Artaud, *Les Oeuvres et les
hommes* (1922)

10 Camarado, this is no book,
Who touches this touches a man.
Walt Whitman, 'So Long!' from 'Songs of
Parting', *Leaves of Grass* (1881)

11 There ought to be some sign in a book about
Man, that the writer knows thoroughly one
man at least.
Frank Moore Colby, 'Simple Simon', *The
Colby Essays* (1926)

12 A vein of poetry exists in the hearts of all
men.
Thomas Carlyle, *On Heroes, Hero-Worship
and the Heroic in History* (1840)

13 How does the poet speak to men with
power, but by being still more a man than
they?
Thomas Carlyle, 'Burns', in *The Edinburgh
Review* (1828)

14 Great writers are significant in terms of the
human awareness they promote.
F.R. Leavis, *The Great Tradition* (1948)

15 All authentic writing comes from an
individual; but a final judgment of it will
depend, not on how much individuality it
contains, but how much of common
humanity.
John Peale Bishop, *Collected Essays* (1948)

16 I'm an American, I'm a Jew, and I write for
    all men. A novelist has to, or he's built
    himself a cage.
    Bernard Malamud, in interview in *Writers
    at Work* (6th series, 1984)

17 Everything mankind does, their hope, fear,
    rage, pleasure, joys, business, are the
    hotch-potch of my little book.
    Juvenal, *Satires*

18 The world is a great Volume, and man the
    Index of that Booke; Even in the body of
    man, you may turne to the whole world;
    This body is an illustration of all Nature.
    John Donne, Sermon 39, 'Imperfection'

90 MANUSCRIPT

1 The long-lived books of tomorrow are
   concealed somewhere amongst the so-far
   unpublished MSS of today.
   Philip Unwin, in epilogue to Stanley Unwin,
   The Truth About Publishing (8th edn.,
   1976)

2 The unpublished manuscript is like an
   unconfessed sin that festers in the soul,
   corrupting and contaminating it.
   Antonio Machado, *Juan de Mairena*
   (1943)

3 Only ambitious nonentities and hearty
   mediocrities exhibit their rough drafts. It is
   like passing around samples of one's
   sputum.
   Vladimir Nabokov, *Strong Opinions*
   (1974)

4 A meeting of British national and university
   librarians to discuss modern literary
   manuscripts resembles an annual
   convention of stable-door lockers.
   Philip Larkin, remark at the Standing
   Conference of National and University
   Libraries (1979)

5 Who deal in early drafts and casual words
   Would starve the horse to death and prize
                            his turds.
   X.J. Kennedy, 'Japanese Beetles: At a Sale
   of Manuscripts'

91 MASTERPIECE

1 Of all the arts in which the wise excel,
   Nature's chief masterpiece is writing well.
   John Sheffield, 1st Duke of Buckingham and
   Normanby, *Essay on Poetry* (1682)

2 When one thinks of the attention that a
   great poem demands there is something
   frivolous about the idea of spending every
   day with one. Masterpieces should be kept
   for High Days of the Spirit.
   W.H. Auden, *The Dyer's Hand* (1963)

3 For the creation of a master-work of
   literature two powers must concur, the
   power of the man and the power of the
   moment.
   Matthew Arnold, *The Function of Criticism*
   (1864)

4 The true function of a writer is to produce a
   masterpiece; no other task is of any
   consequence.
   Cyril Connolly, quoted in Kenneth Tynan,
   Tynan Right and Left (1967)

5 The effect of studying masterpieces is to
   make me admire and do otherwise.
   G.M. Hopkins, in letter to Robert Bridges
   (25 Sept. 1888)

6 A book is never a masterpiece; it becomes
   one.
   Edmond and Jules de Goncourt, *Journal*
   (1851–96)

7 Your book may be a masterpiece but do not
   suggest that to the publisher because many
   of the most hopeless manuscripts that have
   come his way have probably been so
   described by their authors.
   Stanley Unwin, *The Truth about Publishing*
   (1926)

92 MEANING

1 I want the books to speak for themselves.
   You can read? All right, tell me what my
   books mean. Astonish me.
   Bernard Malamud, in interview in *Writers
   at Work* (6th series, 1984)

2 The 'meaning' of a poem is not what it would mean if translated into prose, but what it means to each reader when he translates it into the terms of his own spiritual experience. Poetry is above all a way of using words to say things which could not possibly be said in any other way, things which in a sense do not exist till they are born (or re-born) in poetry. As Mr Middleton Murry has said, great poets are 'men who have uttered a truth so mysterious that it cannot be wrenched apart from the words in which they uttered it'.
C. Day-Lewis, *Enjoying Poetry* (1947)

3 About the best poetry, and not only the best, there floats an atmosphere of infinite suggestion. The poet speaks to us of one thing, but in this one thing there seems to lurk the secret of all. He said what he meant, but his meaning seems to beckon away beyond itself, or rather to expand into something boundless which is only focused in it.
A.C. Bradley, *Oxford Lec. .es on Poetry* (1909)

4 In true poetry it is . . . impossible to express the meaning in any but its own words, or to change the words without changing the meaning.
A.C. Bradley, *Oxford Lectures on Poetry* (1909)

5 A language not thoroughly recorded by poetry would become so discredited and stripped of meaning that a threat would arise to meaning itself.
Lord Kilmarnock, in speech in House of Lords (22 Nov. 1978)

6 Meanings receive their dignity from words instead of giving it to them.
Blaise Pascal, *Pensées* (1670)

7 We do not write in order to be understood; we write in order to understand. But the more successfully a poem has interpreted to its writer the meaning of his own experience, or of others' experience which imagination has enabled him to make his own, the more surely will it in the long run be understood.
C. Day-Lewis, *The Poet's Task* (1951)

8 The only important thing in a book is the meaning it has for you.
Somerset Maugham, *The Summing Up* (1938)

9 Nobody, I think, ought to read poetry, or look at pictures or statues, who cannot find a great deal more in them than the poet or artist has actually expressed.
Nathaniel Hawthorne, *The Marble Faun* (1860)

10 In literature it is our business to give people the thing that will make them say, 'Oh yes, I know what you mean'. It is never to tell them something they don't know, but something they know and hadn't thought of saying. It must be something they recognize.
Robert Frost, in letter to John T. Bartlett

11 Be sure you go to the author to get at his meaning, not to find yours.
John Ruskin, *Sesame and Lilies* (1865)

12 I will go stark: and let my meanings show
Clear as a milk-white feather in a crow
Or a black stallion on a field of snow.
Roy Campbell, 'A Good Resolution'

13 A poem should not mean
But be.
Archibald MacLeish, 'Streets in the Moon', *Ars Poetica*

14 All poetry is difficult to read,
The sense of it is, anyhow.
Robert Browning, *The Ring and the Book* (1868–9)

15 A poet's pleasure is to withold a little of his meaning, to intensify by mystification. He unzips the veil from beauty, but does not remove it.
E.B. White, 'Poetry', *One Man's Meat* (1944)

16 Even when poetry has a meaning, as it usually has, it may be inadvisable to draw it out . . . Perfect understanding will sometimes almost extinguish pleasure.
A.E. Housman, *The Name and Nature of Poetry* (1933)

17 The chief use of the 'meaning' of a poem, in the ordinary sense, may be . . . to satisfy one habit of the reader, to keep his mind diverted and quiet, while the poem does its work upon him; much as the imaginary burglar is always provided with a bit of nice meat for the house-dog.
T.S. Eliot, *The Use of Poetry* (1933)

18 If the poem can be improved by its author's explanations, it never should have been published.
Archibald MacLeish, note in *Poems* (1933)

19 It does seem to me very bad to spend
    months writing a book and then months
    constantly being asked what you meant by
    it.
    Sir John Gielgud, in speech at a Foyles
    Literary Lunch (8 Feb. 1979)

20 It is impossible to say just what I mean!
    But as if a magic lantern threw the nerves in
                    patterns on
    a screen.
    T.S. Eliot, 'The Love Song of J. Alfred
    Prufrock'

21 Everything's been said, no doubt. If words
    hadn't changed meaning, and meaning,
    words.
    Jean Paulhan, *Clef de la poésie* (1944)

MEMOIRS
See AUTOBIOGRAPHY

METAPHOR
See FIGURES OF SPEECH

---

93 METRE

1 There neither is, nor can be, any essential
   difference between the language of prose
   and metrical composition.
   William Wordsworth, preface to the *Lyrical
   Ballads* (1798)

2 Things unattempted yet in prose or rhyme.
   John Milton, *Paradise Lost* (1667)

3 He had written much blank verse, and
   blanker prose.
   Lord Byron, of Southey, in *The Vision of
   Judgement* (1822)

4   The rise
   And long roll of the Hexameter.
   Alfred, Lord Tennyson, 'Lucretius'

5 A needless Alexandrine ends the song
   That, like a wounded snake, draws its slow
              length along.
   Alexander Pope, *Essay on Criticism* (1711)

6 The fatal facility of the octosyllable verse.
   Lord Byron, in preface to *The Corsair*
   (1814)

7 The bitter but wholesome iambic.
   Sir Philip Sidney, *A Defence of Poetry*
   (1580)

8 I am Taliesin, I sing perfect metre,
   Which will last to the end of the world.
   Anonymous (13th-cent. ms.)

9 Here lies the peerless peer Lord Peter
   Who broke the laws of God and man and
              metre.
   John Gibson Lockhart, epitaph for Patrick
   ('Peter'), Lord Robertson, quoted in Sir
   Walter Scott's *Journal* (1890)

10 I hate loose metre even more than loose
    living.
    William Inge, of Robert Bridge's *The
    Testament of Beauty* (1929)

11 I think more of a bird with broad wings
    flying and lapsing through the air, than
    anything when I think of metre.
    D.H. Lawrence, in a letter to Edward Marsh
    (Nov. 1913)

12 There was a young man of Cwmbran
    Who wrote verse that just didn't scan,
            When told this was so,
            He replied, 'Yes, I know',
    It's because I always try to get as many
                words in the last line as I possibly
                can.
    Anonymous

---

94 MONEY

1 Be a successful writer. Make money writing
   and earn while you learn . . . All you supply
   is the ambition to succeed, and then spend
   just a few hours each week in a pleasurable
   occupation that will bring you great
   personal satisfaction, and useful extra
   income.
   Advertisement for The Writing School,
   London (1980s)

2 'Fifty pounds!' He was dumbfounded, and
   looked at me with shrewd eyes, as if I were a
   swindler.
   'Fifty pounds! An' tha's niver done a day's
   hard work in thy life.'
   D.H. Lawrence's father, on being told how

much his son had been paid for *The White Peacock* (1911), quoted in Edward D. McDonald, *Phoenix: The Posthumous Papers* (1936)

3 Poor starving bard, how small thy gains!
   Jonathan Swift, 'On Poetry: A Rhapsody'

4 In the same way that a woman becomes a prostitute. First I did it to please myself, then I did it to please my friends, and finally I did it for money.
   Ferenč Molnár, on being asked how he became a writer

5 Barefaced poverty drove me to writing verses.
   Horace, *Epistles*

6 Almost anyone can be an author; the business is to collect money and fame from this state of being.
   A.A. Milne, *Not That It Matters* (1919)

7 Most authors are as hopeless at business and economics as they are at mathematics.
   George Bernard Shaw, in *The Author* (1940)

8 He is the richest author that ever grazed the common of literature.
   Samuel Johnson, of Dr John Campbell

9 As soon as any art is pursued with a view to money, then farewell, in ninety-nine cases out of a hundred, all hope of genuine good work.
   Samuel Butler, *Note Books* (ed. H. Festing Jones, 1912)

10 A dilettante is a product of where wealth and literature meet.
   Douglas Dunn, in *The Listener* (1977)

11 I find it impossible to work with security staring me in the face.
   Sherwood Anderson, to his publisher, declining a weekly cheque

12 I'm tired of Love: I'm still more tired of Rhyme,
   But Money gives me pleasure all the time.
   Hilaire Belloc, 'Fatigue'

13 Money is a kind of poetry.
   Wallace Stevens, *Opus Posthumous* (1957)

14 There's no money in poetry, but then there's no poetry in money either.
   Robert Graves, remark on BBC TV (1962)

15 It is well known that, when two or three authors meet, they at once start talking about money — like everyone else.
   V.S. Pritchett, in *The Author* (Spring 1978)

16 It is a sad fact about our culture that a poet can earn much more money writing or talking about his art than he can by practising it.
   W.H. Auden, *The Dyer's Hand* (1962)

17 It is not poetry that makes men poor,
   For few do write that were not so before,
   And those that have writ best, had they been rich,
   Had ne'er been clapp'd with a poetic itch.
   Samuel Butler, 'Miscellaneous Thoughts'

18 One of my great surprises when I was in America was about twenty-five years ago in Harvard, hearing Randall Jarrell deliver a bitter attack on the way poets were neglected. Yet there were about two thousand people present, and he was being paid five hundred dollars for delivering this attack.
   Stephen Spender, in interview in *Writers at Work* (6th series, 1984)

19 Writers don't need love: all they require is money.
   John Osborne, quoted in 'Sayings of the Week' in *The Observer* (1980)

20 The only thing I want from my money is to die in comfort.
   Catherine Cookson, quoted in 'Sayings of the Week' in *The Observer* (3 March 1985)

21 I should like to see the custom introduced of readers who are pleased with a book sending the author some small cash token: anything between half-a-crown and a hundred pounds . . . Not more than a hundred pounds — that would be bad for my character — not less than half-a-crown — that would do no good to yours.
   Cyril Connolly, *Enemies of Promise* (1938)

22 I am a freelance writer from Manhattan specialising in children's books and first person articles . . . Send me your payment schedule and I'll consider writing you a poem.
   Mark Vinz, *Letters to the Poetry Editor* (1975)

23 A man who thinks he has got anything to say should always write for money. There is always some air of priggishness in one who 'gives his advice gratis'. Modesty is preserved by the money-motive. Besides, the subtlest truths are like the remoter stars: you cannot see them unless you look a little on one side of them. You are likely to say your

say the better for having your direct gaze fixed upon the five, ten, or twenty pound note which your prophecy is to bring you.
Coventry Patmore, *Memoirs and Correspondence* (1900)

24 No man but a blockhead ever wrote, except for money.
Samuel Johnson, quoted in James Boswell, *Life of Samuel Johnson* (1791)

25 This year I have written 335,340 words, grand total . . . My total earnings were £592 3s 1d, of which sum I have yet to receive £72 10s.
Arnold Bennett, in entry in his *Diary* (31 Dec. 1899)

26 It is a fine world and I wish I knew how to make £200 a year in it.
Edward Thomas, in letter to Gordon Bottomley (16 June 1915)

27 If indeed a man writes his books badly, or paints his pictures badly, because he can make his money faster in that fashion than by doing them well, and at the same time proclaims them to be the best he can do, — if in fact he sells shoddy for broadcloth, — he is dishonest, as is any other fraudulent dealer.
Anthony Trollope, *Autobiography* (1883)

28 Write without pay until somebody offers pay. If nobody offers within three years, the candidate may look upon this circumstance with the most implicit confidence as the sign that sawing wood is what he was intended for.
Mark Twain, 'A General Reply'

29 Being a novelist these days has almost nothing going for it; in fact in terms of money and social status you would probably be far better off as a tea plantation worker in Sri Lanka.
Tom Davies, in *The Sunday Telegraph* (23 Nov. 1986)

30 The profession of letters is, after all, the only one in which one can make no money without being ridiculous.
Jules Renard, *Journal* (1906)

31 Words are like money; there is nothing so useless, unless when in actual use.
Samuel Butler, 'On the Making of Music, Pictures and Books', *Note Books* (ed. H. Festing Jones, 1912)

32 The greatest threat to literature is merchant bankers.
Anonymous publisher, quoted in *The Standard* (25 Jan. 1985)

95 MORALITY

1 Coleridge was a drug addict. Poe was an alcoholic. Marlowe was killed by a man whom he was treacherously trying to stab. Pope took money to keep a woman's name out of a satire then wrote a piece so that she could still be recognised anyhow. Chatterton killed himself. Byron was accused of incest. Do you still want to be a writer — and if so, why?
Bennett Cerf, *Shake Well Before Using* (1948)

2 In books there is something profitable for everybody, provided, be it understood, the reading is done with discrimination and that only is selected which is edifying to faith and morals . . . Accurate reading on a wide range of subjects makes the scholar; careful selection of the better makes the saint.
John of Salisbury, *Polycraticus* (12th cent.)

3 Let the young avoid bad books as they would bad men and bad women.
The Presbyterian (1889), quoted in J.G. Vaughan, *The Gem Encyclopaedia of Illustrations* (1889)

4 Reading is not a virtue, unless the enjoyment be virtuous.
Holbrook Jackson, *The Anatomy of Bibliomania* (1950)

5 We do not so much want books for good people, as books which will make bad ones better.
Hannah More, in letter (10 Sept. 1804)

6 A wicked book is the wickeder because it cannot repent.
Thomas Fuller, *Gnomologia* (1732)

7 People expect from a writer what they once expected from a priest. They want spiritual and moral guidance, some of the greatest needs in modern world.
Alberto Moravia, in *Time* magazine (1978)

8 Books have always a secret influence on the understanding; we cannot at pleasure

obliterate ideas: he that reads books of science, though without any desire fixed of improvement, will grow more knowing; he that entertains himself with moral or religious treatises will imperceptibly advance in goodness.
Samuel Johnson, in *The Adventurer* (26 Feb. 1753)

9 Poetry does not teach us, but it allows us to be taught, as life and the universe permit us, if we will, to learn. The poet's sense of ethical values, if he has it, may communicate itself to us, as Shakespeare's does, implicitly, without the intrusion of a moral sentiment.
J.L. Lowes, *Convention and Revolt in Poetry* (1919)

10 If good books did good, the world would have been converted long ago.
George Moore, *Hail and Farewell* (1914)

11 We must not place in antithesis poetry and human good, for poetry is one kind of human good; and . . . we must not determine the intrinsic value of this kind of good by direct reference to another.
A.C. Bradley, *Oxford Lectures on Poetry* (1909)

12 Poetry is not concerned with telling people what to do, but with extending our knowledge of good and evil, perhaps making the necessity for action more urgent and its nature more clear, but only leading us to the point where it is possible to make a rational and moral choice.
W.H. Auden, in introduction to *The Poet's Tongue* (1935)

13 A poetry of revolt against moral ideas is a poetry of revolt against life; a poetry of indifference towards moral ideas is a poetry of indifference towards life.
Matthew Arnold, 'Wordsworth', *Essays in Criticism* (2nd series, 1888)

14 Ethics are no more a part of poetry than they are of painting.
Wallace Stevens, *Opus Posthumous* (1957)

15 Anon, Idem, Ibid and Trad.
Wrote much that is morally bad:
Some ballads, some chanties,
All poems on panties —
And limericks, too, one must add.
Anonymous

16 The great writer runs before the moral standards of his age and creates the moral standards of a new age.
Bobi Jones, in *Y Llenor* (Autumn 1950)

17 Some kind of moral discovery should be the object of every tale.
Joseph Conrad, *Under Western Eyes* (1911)

18 A story with a moral appended is like the bite of a mosquito. It bores you, and then injects a stinging drop to irritate your conscience.
O. Henry, 'The Gold That Glittered', *Strictly Business* (1910)

19 I do not claim to be a literary critic, but I know dirt when I smell it and here it is in heaps — festering putrid heaps which smell to high heaven.
W. Charles Pilley, review of D.H. Lawrence, *Women in Love* in *John Bull* (17 Sept. 1921)

20 There is no such thing as a moral or an immoral book. Books are well written, or badly written. That is all.
Oscar Wilde, preface to *The Picture of Dorian Gray* (1891)

21 My English text is chaste, and all licentious passages are left in the decent obscurity of a learned language.
Edward Gibbon, *Autobiography* (1827)

96 MOT JUSTE

1 Without accuracy of expression, no poetry.
Théodore de Banville, *Petit Traité de poésie Française* (1872)

2 To use the language of common speech, but to employ always the exact word, not the nearly-exact nor the merely decorative word.
Imagist Manifesto, preface to *Some Imagist Poets* (1915)

3 The difference between the almost-right word and the right word is really a large matter — it's the difference between the lightning-bug and the lightning.
Mark Twain, letter to an unknown clergyman, in *The Mark Twain Journal* collection

4 How many verses have I thrown
Into the fire because the one

Peculiar word, the wanted most,
Was irrecoverably lost.
Walter Savage Landor, 'Verses — Why
Burnt'

5 William tired himself with seeking an
epithet for the cuckoo.
Dorothy Wordsworth, *Journals*

97 MUSE

1 O! for a Muse of fire, that would ascend
The brightest heaven of invention.
William Shakespeare, *King Henry V*

2 All great epic poets compose their fine
poems not from art, but because they are
inspired and possessed.
Plato, *Ion*

3 Not by wisdom do they [poets] make what
they compose, but by a gift of nature and an
inspiration similar to that of the diviners and
the oracles.
Socrates, in Plato's *Apology*

4 Such, poets, is your bride, the Muse! young,
gay,
Radiant, adorn'd outside; a hidden ground
Of thought and of austerity within.
Matthew Arnold, 'The Austerity of Poetry'

5 Instead of whining complaints concerning
the imagined cruelty of their mistresses, if
poets would address the same to their Muse,
they would act more agreeably to nature
and to truth.
William Shenstone, *Essays on Men and
Manners* (1764)

6 But I must say to the Muse of fiction, as the
Earl of Pembroke said to the ejected nun of
Wilton, 'Go spin, you jade, go spin!'
Sir Walter Scott, *Journal* (9 Feb. 1826)

7 Popular poets are the parish priests of the
Muse, retailing her ancient divinations to a
long since converted public.
George Santayana, *The Life of Reason:
Reason in Art* (1905–6)

8 A good poet is someone who manages, in a
lifetime of standing out in thunderstorms, to
be struck by lightning five or six times; a
dozen or two dozen times and he is great.
Randall Jarrell, *Poetry and the Age* (1955)

9 Illustrious acts high raptures do infuse,

And every conqueror creates a Muse.
Edmund Waller, 'Panegyric to my Lord
Protector'

10 'What is the use or function of poetry
nowadays?' is a question not the less
poignant for being defiantly asked by so many
stupid people or apologetically answered by
so many silly people. The function of poetry
is religious invocation of the Muse; its use
is the experience of mixed exaltation and
horror that her presence excites.
Robert Graves, *The White Goddess* (1948)

11 When I say that a poet writes his poems for
the Muse, I mean simply that he treats
poetry with a single-minded devotion which
may be called religion, and that he allows no
other activity in which he takes part,
whether concerned with his livelihood or
with his social duties, to interfere with it.
Robert Graves, 'The Poet and his Public',
The Crowning Privilege (1955)

12 Whatever a poet writes with enthusiasm and
a divine inspiration is very fine.
Democritus, *Fragment*

13 Good poetry could not have been otherwise
written than it is. The first time you hear it,
it sounds rather as if copied out of some
invisible tablet in the Eternal mind, than as
if arbitrarily composed by the poet. The
feeling of all great poets has accorded with
this. They found the verse, not made it. The
muse brought it to them.
Ralph Waldo Emerson, 'Art', *Essays* (1841)

14 If you would hear the Muse you must
prepare silent hours for her and not be
disappointed if she breaks the appointment
you have made with her.
George Moore, quoted in J.M. Hone, *Life*
(1936)

15 It seems that I must bid the Muse go pack.
W.B. Yeats, 'The Tower'

16 Inspiration is the act of drawing up a chair
to the writing desk.
Anonymous (20th cent.)

17 Gin-and-water is the source of all my
inspiration.
Lord Byron, *Conversations* (1824)

18 First coffee. Then a bowel movement. Then
the muse joins me.
Gore Vidal, in interview in *Writers at Work*
(5th series, 1981)

19 Perversity is the muse of modern literature.
Susan Sontag, 'Camus' Notebooks', *Against Interpretation* (1961)

---

98 MUSIC

1 A verbal art like poetry is reflective. It stops to think. Music is immediate: it goes on to become.
W.H. Auden, quoted by Aaron Copland, *Music and Imagination* (1952)

2 Music is the universal language of mankind — poetry their universal pastime and delight.
Henry Wadsworth Longfellow, *Outre-Mer* (1836)

3 Poetry must be read as music and not as oratory.
Ezra Pound, 'Vers Libre and Arnold Dolmetsch' in *The Egoist* (July 1917)

4 Poetry, therefore, we will call musical Thought. The Poet is he who thinks in that manner.
Thomas Carlyle, 'The Hero as Poet', *On Heroes, Hero-Worship and the Heroic in History* (1840)

5 Not philosophy, after all, not humanity, just sheer joyous power of song, is the primal thing in poetry.
Max Beerbohm, 'No. 2, The Pines', *And Even Now* (1920)

6 Poetry withers and dries out when it leaves music, or at least imagined music, too far behind it. Poets who are not interested in music are, or become, bad poets.
Ezra Pound, quoted by J.M. Gibbon in 'Melody and the Lyric'

7 The music of poetry is not something which exists apart from meaning. Otherwise, we could have poetry of great musical beauty which made no sense, and I have never come across such poetry.
T.S. Eliot, *The Music of Poetry* (1942)

---

99 NATURE

1 A book is like a garden carried in the pocket.
Chinese proverb

2 If poetry comes not as naturally as the leaves to a tree, it had better not come at all.
John Keats, in a letter to John Taylor (27 Feb. 1818)

3 The poetry of earth is never dead:
  When all the birds are faint with the hot
    sun,
  And hide in cooling trees, a voice will run
From hedge to hedge about the new-mown
    mead.
John Keats, 'Sonnet, On the Grasshopper and Cricket'

4 A poet, any real poet, is simply an alchemist who transmutes his cynicism regarding human beings into an optimism regarding the moon, the stars, the heavens, and the flowers, to say nothing of Spring, love, and dogs.
George Jean Nathan, 'Poet', *Monks Are Monks* (1929)

5 I think that I shall never see
A poem lovely as a tree,

A tree whose hungry mouth is pressed
Against the earth's sweet flowing breast . . .

Poems are made by fools like me,
But only God can make a tree.
Joyce Kilmer, 'Trees'

6 The best poets, after all, exhibit only a tame and civil side of nature. They have not seen the west side of any mountain.
Henry David Thoreau, *Journal* (18 Aug. 1841)

7 I'm replacing some of the timber used up by my books. Books are just trees with squiggles on them.
Hammond Innes, on growing trees, in interview in *Radio Times* (18 Aug. 1984)

8 I think the great poet, who is going to come, is going to be the poet who can see in a single grass blade — a single surviving grass blade — heaven and earth, or the lost paradise. There are not going to be that many grass blades. The animals are going, the trees are going, the flowers are going, everything is going. So the poet who is going to be the great poet of the future is going to be that poet who can tell us what that last grass blade, popping up through the cement means — really.
James Dickey, in interview in *Writers at Work* (5th series, 1981)

9 Landscape is a passive creature which lends itself to an author's mood.
T.S. Eliot, 'Thomas Hardy'

10 The danger of the English landscape as a poetic ingredient is that its gentleness can tempt those who love it into writing genteely.
W.H. Auden, introduction to *A Choice of de la Mare's Verse* (1963)

11 No human being ever spoke of scenery for above two minutes at a time, which makes me suspect that we hear too much of it in literature.
Robert Louis Stevenson, 'Talk and Talkers', *Familiar Studies of Men and Books* (1882)

12 The English Muse her annual theme rehearses
To tell us birds are singing in the sky . . .
Only the poet slams the door and curses,
And all the little sparrows wonder why!
Roy Campbell, 'Georgian Spring'

13 To speak in literature with the perfect rectitude and insouciance of the movements of animals and the unimpeachableness of the sentiment of trees in the woods and grass by the roadside is the flawless triumph of art.
Walt Whitman, preface to *Leaves of Grass* (1855)

14 The two cardinal points of poetry, the power of exciting the sympathy of the reader by a faithful adherence to the truth of nature, and the power of giving the interest of novelty by the modifying colours of imagination.
Samuel Taylor Coleridge, *Biographia Literaria* (1817)

15 A poet ought not to pick nature's pocket: let him borrow, and so borrow to repay by the very act of borrowing. Examine nature accurately, but write from recollection: and trust more to your imagination than to your memory.
Samuel Taylor Coleridge, 22 Sept. 1830, *Table Talk* (1836)

16 Coleridge came in with a sack full of books and a branch of mountain ash. He had been attacked by a cow.
Dorothy Wordsworth, *Journals,* 10 June 1802

17 There are too many poems
About cats.
Kenneth Rexroth, 'A Bestiary'

NEWSPAPERS
See THE PRESS

100 THE NOVEL

Definitions

1 A novel is a mirror walking along a main road.
Stendhal, *Le Rouge et le noir* (1830)

2 The only reason for the existence of a novel is that it does attempt to represent life.
Henry James, 'The Art of Fiction', *Partial Portraits* (1888)

3 There should be no episodes in a novel.
Anthony Trollope, *Autobiography* (1883)

4 What is a novel if not a conviction of our fellow-men's existence strong enough to take upon itself a form of imagined life clearer than reality and whose accumulated verisimilitude of selected episodes puts to shame the pride of documentary history?
Joseph Conrad, *A Personal Record* (1912)

5 What, in fact, is a novel but a universe in which action is endowed with form, where final words are pronounced, where people possess one another completely, and where life assumes the aspect of destiny?
Albert Camus, 'Rebellion and the Novel', *The Rebel* (1951)

6 The only obligation to which in advance we may hold a novel, without incurring the accusation of being arbitrary, is that it be interesting.
Henry James, 'The Art of Fiction', *Partial Portraits* (1888)

7 A novel is balanced between a few true impressions and the multitude of false ones that make up most of what we call life.
Saul Bellow, in speech accepting the Nobel Prize (1976)

8 A good novel tells us the truth about its hero; but a bad novel tells us the truth about its author.
G.K. Chesterton, *Heretics* (1905)

9 It is clear that a novel cannot be too bad to be worth publishing . . . It certainly is

possible for a novel to be too good to be worth publishing.
George Bernard Shaw, in preface to *Plays Pleasant and Unpleasant* (vol. 1, 1898)

10 Novels seem to me to be richer, broader, deeper, more enjoyable than poems.
Philip Larkin, interview in *The Paris Review* (1982)

11 The novel is practically a Protestant form of art; it is a product of the free mind, of the autonomous individual.
George Orwell, *Inside the Whale* (1940)

12 A novel is a static thing that one moves through: a play is a dynamic thing that moves past one.
Kenneth Tynan, *Curtains* (1967)

·13 One of the things that makes novels less plausible than history, I find, is the way they shrink from coincidence.
Tom Stoppard, *Night and Day* (1978)

14 Ever since I can remember there have been fashionable critics ready to rush into print and announce in banner headlines that 'the novel is dead'. Certainly like most other traditional art forms it is in dire straits. But then so is civilisation in general.
Emyr Humphreys, 'Fickle Fact and Sober Fiction' (1986)

Reading

15 The novel could disappear, but it won't die . . . The human race needs the novel . . . Those who say the novel is dead can't write them.
Bernard Malamud, in interview in *Writers at Work* (6th series, 1984)

16 Novels are sweets. All people with healthy literary appetites love them — almost all women; a vast number of clever, hard-headed men.
William Makepeace Thackeray, 'On a Lazy, Idle Boy', *The Roundabout Papers* (1860–3)

17 Lady Peabury was in the morning room reading a novel; early training gave a guilty spice to this recreation, for she had been brought up to believe that to read a novel before luncheon was one of the gravest sins it was possible for a gentlewoman to commit.
Evelyn Waugh, *Work Suspended* (1942), and *An Englishman's Home* (1939)

18 'And what are you reading, Miss —?'
'Oh! it is only a novel!' replies the young lady: while she lays down her book with affected indifference, or momentary shame. —'It is only Cecilia, or Camilla, or Belinda:' or, in short, only some work in which the most thorough knowledge of human nature, the happiest delineation of its varieties, the liveliest effusions of wit and humour are conveyed to the world in the best chosen language.
Jane Austen, *Northanger Abbey* (1818)

19 Of course, we can Learn even from Novels, Nace Novels that is, but it isn't the same thing as serious reading.
H.G. Wells, *Kipps* (1905)

20 Do your bit to save humanity from lapsing back into barbarity by reading all the novels you can.
Richard Hughes, in speech at Foyle's Literary Luncheon on his 75th birthday (1975)

21 The love of novels is the preference of sentiment to the senses.
Ralph Waldo Emerson, *Journals* (1831)

22 For the most part, our novel-reading is a passion for results.
Ralph Waldo Emerson, 'In Praise of Books', *The Conduct of Life* (1860)

23 Readers of novels are a strange folk, upon whose probable or even possible tastes no wise book-maker would ever venture to bet.
E.V. Lucas, *Reading, Writing, and Remembering* (1932)

24 In my opinion the readers of novels are far more intelligent than unsuccessful authors will believe.
Nevil Shute, in *The Author* (1951)

25 The final test for a novel will be our affection for it, as it is the test of our friends, and of anything else which we cannot define.
E.M. Forster, 'Introductory', *Aspects of the Novel* (1927)

26 Now that few in England go to church, the reading of novels is probably the most effective training for emotional life — and for distinguishing between right and wrong.
Neal Ascherson, in *The Observer* (23 August 1987)

27 Don't let me catch you reading novels: you

remember what happened to Emma Bovary.
Mother's advice, quoted in *The New
Review* (July 1977)

28 Oh Ken, be careful, you know what he's like
after a few novels.
Monty Python's Flying Circus, BBC
Television (1969)

Writing

29 All novels are about certain minorities: the
individual is a minority.
Ralph Ellison, in interview in *Writers at
Work* (2nd series, 1963)

30 Novelists should never allow themselves to
weary of the study of real life.
Charlotte Brontë, *The Professor* (1857)

31 When writing a novel a writer should create
living people; people not characters. A
character is a caricature.
Ernest Hemingway, *Death in the Afternoon*
(1932)

32 I am a man, and alive . . . For this reason I
am a novelist. And being a novelist, I
consider myself superior to the saint, the
scientist, the philosopher, and the poet, who
are all great masters of different bits of man
alive, but never get the whole hog.
D.H. Lawrence, 'Why the Novel Matters'

33 For, to achieve his lightest wish, he must
Become the whole of boredom, subject to
Vulgar complaints like love, among the Just

Be just, among the Filthy filthy too,
And in his own weak person, if he can,
Must suffer dully all the wrongs of Man.
W.H. Auden, 'The Novelist'

34 The poor novelist constructs his characters,
he controls them and makes them speak.
The true novelist listens to them and
watches them function; he eavesdrops on
them even before he knows them.
André Gide, *Les Faux Monnayeurs* (1926)

35 Novelists are not normal human citizens.
George Bernard Shaw, in *The Author*
(Summer 1943)

36 The novelist is, above all, the historian of
conscience.
Frederic Raphael, in *Contemporary
Novelists* (1976)

37 The Novel Writers . . . are the great
instructors of the country. They help the
Church and are better than the Law. They
teach ladies to be women, and they teach
men to be gentlemen.
Anthony Trollope, at Royal Literary Fund
dinner, quoted in *The Author* (Summer,
1983)

38 Novel writing is really a matter of coming to
terms with your own squalor.
Frederic Raphael, in interview in *Books
and Bookmen* (Feb. 1983)

39 Essential characteristic of the really great
novelist: a Christ-like, all-embracing
compassion.
Arnold Bennett, entry in notebook (15 Oct.
1896)

40 But then I'm a battered old novelist and it's
my business to comprehend.
Henry James, in letter to Edward Marsh
(1915)

41 If you try to nail anything down, in the
novel, either it kills the novel, or the novel
gets up and walks away with the nail.
D.H. Lawrence, 'Morality and the Novel'
(1925)

42 The impulse to write a novel comes from a
momentary unified vision of life.
Angus Wilson, *The Wild Garden* (1963)

43 If you caricature friends in your first novel
they will be upset, but if you don't they will
feel betrayed.
Mordecai Richler, *GQ* (1984)

44 There are three rules for writing the novel.
Unfortunately, no one knows what they are.
Somerset Maugham, attr.

OBSCENITY
See PORNOGRAPHY

101 OBSCURITY

1 Real books should be the offspring not of
daylight and casual talk but of darkness and
silence.
Marcel Proust, *Time Regained* (1927)

2 There should always be an enigma in poetry.
Jules Huret, *Enquête sur l'évolution
Littéraire* (1891)

3 Bad authors are those who write with
reference to an inner context which the
reader cannot know.
Albert Camus, *Notebooks* (1935–42)

4 Words, like glass, obscure when they do not
aid vision.
Joseph Joubert, *Pensées* (1842)

5 Unintelligible, the borrowings cheap and the
notes useless.
F.L. Lucas, on T.S. Eliot's *The Waste Land*
in *New Statesman and Nation* (Nov. 1923)

6 Whate'er is well-conceived is clearly said,
And the words to say it flow with ease.
Nicolas Boileau-Despréaux, *L'Art Poétique*
(1674)

7 The easiest books are generally the best; for,
whatever author is obscure and difficult in
his own language, certainly does not think
clearly.
Lord Chesterfield, in letter to his son (1750)

8 For light being the universal mother of
things, wise philosophers hold all writings
to be fruitful in the proportion as they are
dark.
Jonathan Swift, *A Tale of a Tub* (1704)

9 Let the obscure poet persevere in his
obscurity, if he wishes to find the light.
Jean Paulhan, in preface to *Contes de Noël
Devaulx*

10 When I write after dark the shades of
evening scatter their purple through my
prose.
Cyril Connolly, *Enemies of Promise* (1938)

11 I am getting more obscure day by day.
Dylan Thomas, in letter to Pamela
Hansford Johnson (9 May 1934)

12 Clear writers, like fountains, do not seem so
deep as they are; the turbid look the most
profound.
Walter Savage Landor, 'Southey and
Porson', *Imaginary Conversations* (1824–9)

13 My relatives say that they are glad I'm rich,
but that they simply cannot read me.
Kurt Vonnegut Jr, in interview in *Writers at
Work* (6th series, 1984)

14 I'm afraid of losing my obscurity.
Genuineness only thrives in the dark. Like
celery.
Aldous Huxley, *Those Barren Leaves*
(1925)

102 OLD AGE

1 An old author is constantly rediscovering
himself in the more or less fossilized
productions of his earlier years.
Oliver Wendell Holmes, *Over the Teacups*
(1891)

2 Poets are almost always bald when they get
to be about forty.
John Masefield, attr.

3 When one hears of a poet past thirty-five, he
seems somehow unnatural and even a trifle
obscene; it is as if one encountered a greying
man who still played the Chopin waltzes
and believed in elective affinities.
H.L. Mencken, *Prejudices* (1919)

4 The poet is a man who lives at last by
watching his moods. An old poet comes at
last to watch his moods as narrowly as a cat
does a mouse.
Henry David Thoreau, *Journal* (1851)

5 The delight of opening a new pursuit, or a
new course of reading, imparts the vivacity
and novelty of youth, even to old age.
Isaac D'Israeli, *The Literary Character*
(1795)

6 The writer who loses his self-doubt, who
gives way as he grows old to a sudden
euphoria, to prolixity, should stop writing
immediately: the time has come for him to
lay aside his pen.
Colette, 'Lady of Letters', *Earthly Paradise*
(1966)

7 When you are old and grey and full of sleep
And, nodding by the fire, take down this
          book,
And slowly read, and dream of the soft look
Your eyes had once, and of their shadows
          deep.
W.B. Yeats, 'When You are Old'

8 I shall be found by the fire, I suppose,
     O'er a great wise book as beseemeth age,
While the shutters flap as the cross-wind
          blows
     And I turn the page, and I turn the page,
Not verse now, only prose!
Robert Browning, 'By the Fireside'

9 Here I am, an old man in a dry month,
Being read to by a boy.
T.S. Eliot, 'Gerontion'

10 I read, much of the night, and go south in
the winter.
T.S. Eliot, *The Waste Land* (1922)

11 You think it horrible that lust and rage
Should dance attention upon my old age;
They were not such a plague when I was
                            young;
What else have I to spur me into song?
W.B. Yeats, 'The Spur'

12 *Vicar's wife (sympathizingly):* Now that you
can't get about, and are not able to read,
how do you manage to occupy the time?
Old Man: Well, mum, sometimes I sits and
thinks; and then again I just sits.
Gunning-King, caption to cartoon in *Punch*
(24 Oct. 1906)

103 ORIGINALITY

1 The two most engaging powers of an author
are to make new things familiar, and
familiar things new.
Samuel Johnson, 'Pope', *The Lives of the
English Poets* (1779–81)

2 The sign and credentials of the poet are that
he announces that which no man has
foretold.
Ralph Waldo Emerson, 'The Poet', *Essays*
(1844)

3 The poet shares with other artists the faculty
of seeing things as though for the first time.
To a certain extent this faculty is merely
childish wonder extended into maturer life.
But it differs from mere childishness because
it is combined with a vividly imagined
memory of past experiences, so that while
experiences can never be re-experienced as
though they were new, at the same time they
can be related and compared with the past
forms in which they were experienced,
which still remain fresh and distinct.
Stephen Spender, *Life and the Poet* (1942)

4 A poem gives the world back to the maker
of the poem, in all its original strangeness,
the shock of its first surprise.
John Hall Wheelock, 'A True Poem Is a
Way of Knowing', *What Is Poetry?* (1963)

5 The most original authors of modern times
are so, not because they create anything
new, but only because they are able to say

things in a manner as if they had never been
said before.
J.W. Goethe, *Sprüche in Prosa* (1819)

6 It is one test of a fully developed writer that
he reminds us of no one but himself.
Melvin Maddocks, in the *Christian Science
Monitor* (2 May 1963)

7 The original writer is not he who refrains
from imitating others, but he who can be
imitated by none.
François-René de Chateaubriand, *Le Génie
du Christianisme* (1802)

8 Never forget what I believe was observed to
you by Coleridge, that every great and
original writer, in proportion as he is great
and original, must himself create the taste by
which he is to be relished.
William Wordsworth, letter to Lady
Beaumont (21 May 1807)

9 The original writer, if he is not dead, is
always scandalous.
Simone de Beauvoir, *The Second Sex* (1949)

10 Not pickt from the leaves of any author, but
bred amongst the weeds and tares of mine
own brain.
Sir Thomas Browne, *Religio Medici* (1642)

104 PAINTING

1 Poetry is like painting: one piece takes your
fancy if you stand close to it, another if you
keep at some distance.
Horace, *Ars Poetica*

2 Does he paint? he fain would write a poem
    —
Does he write? he fain would paint a
                            picture.
Robert Browning, 'One Word More'

3 One picture is worth ten thousand words.
Frederick R. Barnard, in *Printer's Ink* (8
Dec. 1921)

4 Poetry is the impish attempt to paint the
color of the wind.
Maxwell Bodenheim, quoted in Ben Hecht,
Winkelberg (1958)

5 There are pictures in poems and poems in
pictures.
William Scarborough, *Chinese Proverbs*

6 Poetry is articulate painting, and painting is silent poetry.
Plutarch, 'How to Study Poetry', *Moralia*

7 Painters and poets have leave to lie.
English proverb

8 Just as the painter thinks with his brush and paints, the novelist thinks with his story.
Somerset Maugham, *The Summing Up* (1938)

9 The critic in *The Vicar of Wakefield* lays down that you should always say that the picture would have been better if the painter had taken more pains; but in the case of the practised literary man, you should often say that the writings would have been much better if the writer had taken less pains.
Walter Bagehot, *Literary Studies* (1879–95)

10 Painting's the easiest art to cultivate:
Three months of doodling sees you in the Tate . . .
Poetry is tougher. Over and above
The art of rhyming, poets need to love.
Wynford Vaughan-Thomas, 'An Epistle to R.D. Smith Esq.'

105 PARODY

1 Parodies and caricatures are the most penetrating of criticisms.
Aldous Huxley, *Point Counter Point* (1928)

2 Nobody is going to parody you if you haven't a style.
Geoffrey Grigson, *The Private Art* (1982)

PARTICULAR
See UNIVERSAL

106 PARTS OF SPEECH
See also GRAMMAR

1 Syllables govern the world.
John Selden, *Table Talk* (1689)

2 Who climbs the grammar-tree, distinctly knows
Where Noun, and Verb, and Participle grows.
John Dryden, 'Juvenal's Sixth Satire'

3 A verb has a hard time enough of it in this world when it's all together. It's downright inhuman to split it up. But that's just what those Germans do.
Mark Twain, in address at dinner of the Nineteenth Century Cub, New York (20 Nov. 1900) to the toast 'The Disappearance of Literature'

4 God loveth adverbs.
Bishop Joseph Hall, *Holy Observations* (1607)

5 I'm glad you like adverbs — I adore them.
Henry James, in letter to Miss Edwards (5 Jan. 1912)

6 As to the adjective: when in doubt, strike it out.
Mark Twain, *Pudd'nhead Wilson* (1894)

7 Adjectives are the betrayers of poetry, the poet's chief enemies.
Saunders Lewis, 'Barddoniaeth Fodern'

8 Epithets, like pepper,
Give zest to what you write;
And if you strew them sparely,
They whet the appetite:
But if you lay them on too thick,
You spoil the matter quite!
Lewis Carroll, 'Poeta Fit, Non Nascitur' (1869)

9 I lately lost a preposition:
It hid, I thought, beneath my chair.
And angrily I cried: 'Perdition!'
Up from out of in under there!
Morris Bishop, 'The Naughty Preposition'

10 The English-speaking world may be divided into (1) those who neither know nor care what a split infinitive is; (2) those who do not know, but care very much; (3) those who know and condemn; (4) those who know and approve; and (5) those who know and distinguish. Those who neither know nor care are the vast majority and are a happy folk, to be envied by most of the minority classes.
H.W. Fowler, *Modern English Usage* (1965)

11 When I split an infinitive, god damn it, I split it so it stays split.
Raymond Chandler, in a letter to his publisher

12 Who often, but without success, have pray'd
For apt Alliteration's artificial aid.
Charles Churchill, *The Prophecy of Famine*
(1763)

13 Good poets have a weakness for bad puns.
W.H. Auden, 'The Truest Poetry is the
Most Feigning'

14 Circumlocution, n. A literary trick whereby
the writer who has nothing to say breaks it
gently to the reader.
Ambrose Bierce, *The Devil's Dictionary*
(1911)

15 Higgledy-piggledy
Thomas Stearns Eliot
Wrote dirty limericks
Under the rose,

Using synecdoches,
Paranomasias,
Zeugmas, and rhymes he de-
Plored in his prose.
Anthony Hecht, 'Vice'

107 PATRIOTISM

1 I have a fatherland: the French language.
Albert Camus, *Carnets*

2 To be born in a country and to grow up to
love it, but never fully to possess it, never
completely to belong to it, may create not
just great literature but also unhappy men
and women.
F.S.L. Lyons, 'The Twilight of the Big
House', in *Ariel* (vol. 1, 1970)

3 All that is best in the great poets of all
countries is not what is national in them, but
what is universal.
Henry Wadsworth Longfellow, *Kavanagh*
(1849)

4 All day I'd looked in the face
What I had hoped 'twould be
To write for my own race
And the reality.
W.B. Yeats, 'The Fisherman'

5 The proof of a poet is that his country
absorbs him as affectionately as he has
absorbed it.
Walt Whitman, in preface to *Leaves of
Grass* (1855)

6 An author's first duty is to let down his
country.
Brendan Behan, in *The Guardian* (1960)

108 PATRONAGE

1 I present you to a person who will give you
immortality; but you must give him
something to live on in the meantime.
Nicolas Boileau-Despréaux, introducing a
poet to a prospective patron

2 Found heaps of letters, some of them from
poets and authors, who are the pest of my
life . . . Another begging to know whether I
was acquainted with 'any man or woman to
whom money was for a time useless', who
would venture £100 upon a literary
speculation he had in hand.
Thomas Moore, Diary (24 Aug. 1818)

3 Patron — commonly a wretch who supports
with insolence, and is paid with flattery.
Samuel Johnson, *Dictionary of the English
Language* (1755)

4 Catullus, the worst of all poets, gives you his
warmest thanks; he being as much the worst
of all poets as you are the best of all patrons.
Catullus, *Carmina*

5 Today the State must act as the patron of
literature as it does for other 'minority' arts.
Literature has never suffered as a result of
generous patronage: the enemy has always
been meanness.
Nigel Cross, in *The Times Literary
Supplement* (21 August 1981)

6 The only permanent solution to the poet's
dilemma would seem to lie in the extension
of official patronage beyond the £97 a year
at present allowed to the Laureate.
John Hayward, in introduction to *Poems
1951* (1951)

7 If we are prepared to pay more than
lip-service to the art in which our nation has
always excelled, we have to do something
about the writer's situation today.
Cecil Day-Lewis, Chairman of the Arts
Council of Great Britain Literature Panel
(1966)

8 Whatever the drawbacks of public as
compared with private patronage, it is the

only possible solution in a socialist state, and better than nothing at all.
Kathleen Raine, in *The Author* (Autumn 1949)

9 Any small publisher relying on state subsidy for more than 20% of its revenue is on dangerous ground.
Michael Schmidt, quoted in *The Economist* (18 May 1985)

10 What I don't like about subsidies and official support is that they destroy the essential nexus between the writer and the reader. If the writer is being paid to write and the reader is being paid to read, the element of compulsive contact vanishes.
Philip Larkin, *Required Writing* (1983)

11 Something's got to be done, now that free enterprise has made it impossible for them to support themselves through free enterprise.
Kurt Vonnegut Jr, when asked whether young writers should be subsidised, in interview in *Writers at Work* (6th series, 1984)

12 I think there is in the public mind a wrong idea that if you leave things to private enterprise you in fact encourage freedom, enterprise, variety and non-conformity, which I think is exactly opposite of the truth. And I think it is very important work to try and convince people that if you leave literature, or indeed drama or music or painting, to the operations of the market, what you get is conformity. And that in order to support enterprise and experiment, you need intervention by the Government.
Stuart Hampshire, remark on BBC Radio (Jan. 1978)

13 It is wrong for the state or one of its agencies to decide which poets should be encouraged, and which should not.
Charles Osborne, former Literature Director of the Arts Council of Great Britain, *Giving it Away* (1986)

14 None of us, writers or others, are owed a living. We have no pre-emptive right to State support.
Richard Hoggart, in conference on 'The State v. Literature', National Book League (1985)

15 If those who, over the years, have been crying out simply for more public money for literature had been able to produce sound

reasons for spending more, then literature would no doubt have featured in the Arts Council's development plans, and we could now be contemplating perhaps a doubling rather than a halving of its spending on literature.
Charles Osborne, former Literature Director of the Arts Council of Great Britain, *Giving it Away* (1986)

16 The hardship and worry over money in writers as they get older is a social horror; grants given to writers should be *sufficient*, so that they are able to live with amplitude, and, yes, some dignity.
William Goyen, in interview in *Writers at Work* (6th series, 1984)

17 We cultivate literature on a little oatmeal.
Sydney Smith, proposed motto for *The Edinburgh Review*, in preface to *Works* (vol. 1, 1859)

109 THE PEOPLE

1 If one has no heart, one cannot write for the masses.
Heinrich Heine, *Letter to Julius Campe* (1840)

2 The poets of the people will judge who are the men of courage.
Aneirin (6th cent.)

3 The chief glory of every people arises from its authors.
Samuel Johnson, in preface to his *Dictionary of the English Language* (1755)

4 Literature exists for the sake of the people — to refresh the weary, to console the sad, to hearten the dull and downcast, to increase man's interest in the world, his joy of living, and his sympathy in all sorts and conditions of man.
Dissenting opinion in the U.S. v. One Book entitled *Ulysses* (1934)

5 The people which ceases to care for its literary inheritance becomes barbaric; the people which ceases to produce literature ceases to move in thought and sensibility. The poetry of a people takes its life from the people's speech and in turn gives life to it; and represents its highest point of

consciousness, its greatest power and its most delicate sensibility.
T.S. Eliot, in introduction to *The Use of Poetry and the Use of Criticism* (1933)

6 Literature, strictly consider'd, has never recognized the people, and, whatever may be said, does not today. Speaking generally, the tendencies of literature as hitherto pursued, have been to make mostly critical and querulous men.
Walt Whitman, *Democratic Vistas* (1871)

7 The People's Theatre, what nonsense! Call it the Aristocrats' Theatre and the people will come.
Jules Renard, *Journal* (1903)

8 The people fancy they hate poetry, and they are all poets and mystics.
Ralph Waldo Emerson, 'The Poet', *Essays* (1844)

9 Are my poems spoken in the factories and
        fields,
     In the streets o' the toon?
   Gin they're no', then I'm failin' to doe
     What I ocht to ha' dune.

   Gin I canna win through to the man in the
        street,
     The wife by the hearth,
   A' the cleverness on earth'll no' mak' up
     For the damnable dearth.
Hugh MacDiarmid, 'Second Hymn to Lenin'

---

110 THE PERFECT READER

1 Hypocrite reader — my likeness — my brother.
Charles Baudelaire, preface to *Les Fleurs du mal* (1857)

2 Poetry, good or bad, depends for its very life on the hospitable reader, as tinder awaits the spark.
Walter De La Mare, 'The Green Room'

3 Every book has a collaborator in its reader.
Maurice Barrès, *Mes Cahiers* (1929–38)

4 'Tis the good reader that makes the good book; in every book he finds passages which seem confidences or asides hidden from all else and unmistakably meant for his ear; the profit of books is according to the sensibility of the reader; the profoundest thought or passion sleeps as in a mine, until it is discovered by an equal mind and heart.
Ralph Waldo Emerson, 'Success', *Society and Solitude* (1870)

5 A book is made better by good readers and clearer by good opponents.
Friedrich Nietzsche, *Miscellaneous Maxims and Opinions* (1879)

6 Next to being a great poet, is the power of understanding one.
Henry Wadsworth Longfellow, *Hyperion* (1839)

7 There is an art of reading, as well as an art of thinking, and an art of writing.
Isaac D'Israeli, *Literary Character of Men of Genius* (1795)

8 Imaginative readers rewrite books to suit their own taste, omitting and mentally altering what they read. And most readers automatically correct obvious errors in sense as well as misprints.
Robert Graves, *The Reader over your Shoulder* (1947)

9 Due attention to the inside of books, and due contempt for the outside, is the proper relation between a man of sense and his books.
Lord Chesterfield, in letter to his son (10 Jan. 1749)

10 For some in ancient books delight;
    Others prefer what moderns write:
    Now I should be extremely loth
    Not to be thought expert in both.
Matthew Prior, 'Alma'

11 Your true lover of literature is never fastidious.
Robert Southey, *The Doctor* (1812)

12 That ideal reader suffering from an ideal insomnia.
James Joyce, *Finnegans Wake* (1939)

13 The Perfect reader . . . broods constantly as to whether he himself, in some happy conjuncture of quick mind and environing silence and the sudden perfect impulse, might have written something like that . . . On every page he is aware of his own mind running with him, tingling him with needle-pricks of conscience for the golden chapters he has never written.
Christopher Morley, 'The Perfect Reader', *Safety Pins* (1925)

14 Persons with manners do not read at table.
Dylan Thomas, Mrs Pugh in *Under Milk Wood* (1954)

111 PLAGIARISM

1 Your comedy I've read, my friend,
And like the half you pilfered best.
Be sure the piece you may yet mend,
Take courage, man, and steal the rest.
Anonymous

2 They lard their lean books with the fat of others' works.
Robert Burton, *The Anatomy of Melancholy* (1621)

3 Next o'er his books his eyes began to roll,
In pleasing memory of all he stole,
How here he sipped, how there he
        plundered snug,
And sucked all o'er, like an industrious bug.
Alexander Pope, *The Dunciad* (1728)

4 Immature poets imitate; mature poets steal; bad poets deface what they take, and good poets make it into something better, or at least something different.
T.S. Eliot, 'Philip Massinger' in *The Times Literary Supplement* (27 May 1920)

5 There is no sixth commandment in art. The poet is entitled to lay his hands on whatever material he finds necessary for his work.
Heinrich Heine, *Letters on the Fench Stage* (1837)

6 To read means to borrow; to create out of one's readings is paying off one's debts.
Georg Christoph Lichtenberg, *Aphorisms* (1764–99)

7 For such kind of borrowing as this, if it be not betterd by the borrower, among good authors is accounted plagiary.
John Milton, *Eikonoclastes* (1649)

8 I have somewhere seen it observed, that we should make the same use of a book that the bee does of a flower: she steals sweets from it, but does not injure it.
Charles Caleb Colton, *Lacon* (1825)

9 If we steal thoughts from the moderns, it will be cried down as plagiarism; if from the ancients, it will be cried up as erudition.
Charles Caleb Colton, *Lacon* (1825)

10 If an author writes better than his contemporaries, they will term him a plagiarist; if as well, a pretender; but if worse, he may stand some chance of commendation as a genius of some promise, from whom much may be expected by a due attention to their good counsel and advice.
Charles Caleb Colton, *Lacon* (1825)

11 Plagiarists are always suspicious of being stolen from, — as pick-pockets are observed commonly to walk with their hands in their breeches' pockets.
Samuel Taylor Coleridge, *Table Talk* (1836)

12 I am taxed with being a plagiarist, when I am least conscious of being one; but I am not very scrupulous, I own, when I have a good idea, how I came into possession of it.
Lord Byron, *Conversations* (1824)

13 The human plagiarism which is most difficult to avoid, for individuals (and even for nations which persevere in their faults and continue to aggravate them) is the plagiarism of oneself.
Marcel Proust, *The Sweet Cheat Gone* (1925)

14 I get real pleasure out of stealing other people's writings . . . I do that at least partly because of a peculiar and unfortunate quality of my mind: I remember things. Word for word.
John Gardner, in interview in *Writers at Work* (6th series, 1984)

15 The little finger of Brecht's hand which pinched 25 lines from Villon is more genuine than the entire Kerr who's found him out.
Karl Kraus, attr.

16 He invades authors like a monarch; and what would be theft in other poets, is only victory to him.
John Dryden, of Ben Jonson, *Essay of Dramatic Poesy* (1668)

17 The only 'ism she believes in is plagiarism.
Dorothy Parker, of a writer

18 Another illusion, seldom entertained by competent authors, is that the publisher's readers and others are waiting to plagiarize their work. I think it may be said that the more worthless the manuscript, the greater the fear of plagiarism.
Sir Stanley Unwin, *The Truth about Publishing* (1926)

112 PLOT

1 You have left your hero and heroine tied up in a cavern for a week, and they are not married.
G.K. Chesterton, quoting in his *Autobiography* (1936) an editor's complaint to his sister-in-law about a serial story.

2 It is not improbabilities of incident but improbabilities of character that matter.
Thomas Hardy, *The Mayor of Casterbridge* (1886)

3 If a writer is true to his characters they will give him his plot.
Phyllis Bottome, quoted in *Who's Who in Spy Fiction* (1977)

4 What the devil does the plot signify, except to bring in fine things?
George Villiers, 2nd Duke of Buckingham, *The Rehearsal* (1671)

5 Plot implies narrative and a lot of crap.
John Cheever, in interview in *Writers at Work* (5th series, 1981)

6 When the plot flags, bring in a man with a gun.
Raymond Chandler, advice to an interviewer, quoted in *Raymond Chandler Speaking* (1962)

7 Ay, now the plot thickens very much upon us.
George Villiers, 2nd Duke of Buckingham, *The Rehearsal* (1671)

8 As regards plots I find real life no help at all. Real life seems to have no plots.
Ivy Compton-Burnett, 'A Conversation between Ivy Compton-Burnett and M. Jourdain', *Orion* (1945)

9 *Finnegans Wake*
Is one long spelling mistake
With not a lot
Of plot
V. Ernest Cox, 'Finnegans Wake'

10 If the audience never understands the plot it can be counted on to be attentive to the very end.
Benedetto Marcello, *Il teatro alla moda* (1720)

11 Persons attempting to find a motive in this narrative will be prosecuted; persons attempting to find a moral in it will be banished; persons attempting to find a plot in it will be shot.
Mark Twain, *The Adventures of Huckleberry Finn* (1884)

12 Cynics have claimed there are only six basic plots. Frankenstein and My Fair Lady are really the same story.
Leslie Halliwell, in *The Filmgoer's Book of Quotes* (1973)

13 Plots are no more exhausted than men are. Every man is a new creation, and combinations are simply endless.
Charles Dudley Warner, 'Sixth Study', *Backlog Studies* (1873)

14 She is the Enid Blyton of economics. Nothing must be allowed to spoil her simple plots.
Richard Holme, of Prime Minister Margaret Thatcher, in speech, UK Liberal Party Conference (10 Sept. 1980)

113 THE POET

1 There exist only three respectable beings: the priest, the warrior, the poet. Knowing, killing, creating.
Charles Baudelaire, *Mon Cœur mis à nu* (1917)

2 What is a Poet? He is a man speaking to men: a man, it is true, endowed with more lively sensibility, more enthusiasm and tenderness, who has a greater knowledge of human nature and a more comprehensive soul, than are supposed to be common among mankind; a man pleased with his own passions and volitions, and who rejoices more than other men in the spirit of life that is in him; delighting to contemplate similar volitions and passions as manifested in the goings-on of the Universe, and habitually impelled to create them where he does not find them.
William Wordsworth, in preface to second edition of *Lyrical Ballads* (1800)

3 There are three requisites to form the poet: 1. Sensibility; 2. Imagination; 3. Power of Association.
Samuel Taylor Coleridge, Lectures on Shakespeare, 4 (1811–12)

4 The poet begins where the man ends. The man's lot is to live his human life, the poet's to invent what is nonexistent.
José Ortega y Gasset, *The Dehumanization of Art* (1925)

5 The poet's mind is in fact a receptacle for seizing and storing up numberless feelings, phrases, images, which remain there until all the particles which can unite to form a new compound are present together.
T.S. Eliot, 'Tradition and the Individual Talent' (1919)

6 A poet is not an author, but — the subject of a lyric, facing the world in the first person.
Boris Pasternak, *Safe Conduct* (1931)

7 The poet is a bird of strange moods. He descends from his lofty domain to tarry among us, singing; if we do not honor him he will unfold his wings and fly back to his dwelling place.
Kahlil Gibran, 'The Poet from Baalbek', *Thoughts and Meditations* (1960)

8 The mass of men are very unpoetic, yet that Adam that names things is always a poet.
Henry David Thoreau, *Journal* (1853)

9 Poets acquire humanity.
Wallace Stevens, 'Adagia', *Opus Posthumous* (1957)

10 The poet should be a professor of hope.
Jean Giono, *L'Eau Vive* (1944)

11 And they shall be accounted poet kings
Who simply tell the most heart-easing
                things.
John Keats, 'Sleep and Poetry'

12 The business of the poet and novelist is to show the sorriness underlying the grandest things, and the grandeur underlying the sorriest things.
Thomas Hardy, entry in notebook (19 April 1885)

13 Poetry comes fine-spun from a mind at peace.
Ovid, *Tristia*

14 Of all mankind the great poet is the equable man. Not in him but off from him things are grotesque or eccentric or fail of their sanity.
Walt Whitman, preface to *Leaves of Grass* (1855)

15 A settled and reposed man doth in vain knock at Poesie's gate.
Michel de Montaigne, *Essays* (1580–8)

16 The business of the poet . . . is to give order and coherence, and so freedom, to a body of experience.
I.A. Richards, *Science and Poetry* (1935)

17 To a poet nothing can be useless.
Samuel Johnson, *Rasselas* (1759)

18 The poet is really engaged in recreating the familiar, he's not committed to introducing the unfamiliar.
Philip Larkin, interview in *The Observer* (1979)

19 The poet makes silk dresses out of worms.
Wallace Stevens, *Opus Posthumous* (1957)

20 Obsession begets poems. But you need to vary your obsessions. One obsession, one poem.
Geoffrey Grigson, *The Private Art* (1982)

21 To be a poet is to have an appetite for a certain anxiety which, when tasted among the swirling sum of things existent or forefelt, causes, as the taste dies, joy.
René Char, *Hypnos Waking* (1956)

22 He who, in an enlightened and literary society, aspires to be a great poet must first become a little child, he must take to pieces the whole web of his mind.
Thomas Babington Macaulay, 'Milton', in *The Edinburgh Review* (1825)

23 Angling is somewhat like poetry, men are to be born so.
Izaac Walton, *The Compleat Angler* (1653)

24 A good poet's made as well as born.
Ben Jonson, *To the Memory of . . . Shakespeare* (1616)

25 There was never poet who had not the heart in the right place.
Ralph Waldo Emerson, 'Success', *Society and Solitude* (1870)

26 The true poet is a friendly man. He takes to his arms even cold and inanimate things, and rejoices in his heart.
Henry Wadsworth Longfellow, 'Twice-Told Tales', *Driftwood* (1857)

27 No bad man can be a good poet.
Boris Pasternak, quoted in Ilya Ehrenburg, *Truce*

28 It is a man's sincerity and depth of vision that makes him a poet.
Thomas Carlyle, *On Heroes, Hero-Worship and the Heroic in History* (1840)

29 Not deep the poet sees, but wide.
    Matthew Arnold, 'Resignation'

30 The void yields up nothing. You have to be
    a great poet to make it ring.
    Jules Renard, *Journal* (Dec. 1906)

31 Most people do not believe in anything very
    much and our greatest poetry is given to us
    by those who do.
    Cyril Connolly, quoted in Stephen Spender,
    The Making of a Poem (1955)

32 A merely great intellect can produce great
    prose, but not poetry, not one line.
    Edward Thomas, in letter to Gordon
    Bottomley (26 Feb. 1908)

33 I can understand you wanting to write
    poems. But I don't know what you mean by
    'being a poet'.
    T.S. Eliot, quoted in Stephen Spender,
    World Within World (1951)

34 Not to be second-rate is the poet's most
    private prayer.
    John Holmes, *The Poet's Work*

35 To poets to be second-rate is a privilege
    which neither men, nor gods, nor bookstalls
    ever allowed.
    Horace, *Ars Poetica*

36 A very good or very bad poet is remarkable;
    but a middling one who can bear?
    Thomas Fuller, *Gnomologia* (1732)

37 A great poet, a really great poet, is the most
    unpoetical of all creatures. But inferior poets
    are absolutely fascinating.
    Oscar Wilde, *The Picture of Dorian Gray*
    (1891)

38 A true poet does not bother to be poetical.
    Nor does a nursery gardener scent his
    roses.
    Jean Cocteau, *Professional Secrets* (1922)

39 A poet in history is divine, but a poet in the
    next room is a joke.
    Max Eastman, attr.

40 Poets are the only poor fellows in the world
    whom anybody will flatter.
    Alexander Pope, *Letter to William
    Trumbull* (1713)

41 Hail, Bard triumphant! and some care
                                    bestow
    On us, the Poets Militant below!
    Abraham Cowley, 'On the Death of Mr
    Crashaw'

42 Had in him those brave translunary things,
    That the first poets had.
    Michael Drayton, of Christopher Marlowe,
    'To Henry Reynolds, of Poets and Poesy'
    (1627)

43 For three years, out of key with his time
    He strove to resuscitate the dead art
    Of poetry; to maintain 'the sublime'
    In the old sense. Wrong from the start.
    Ezra Pound, 'Pour l'élection de son sépulcre'
    Hugh Selwyn Mauberley (1920)

44 Many brave men lived before Agamemnon,
    but all unwept and unknown they sleep in
    endless night, for they had no poets to
    sound their praises.
    Horace, *Carmina*

45 The business of a poet, said Imlac, is to
    examine, not the individual, but the species;
    to remark general properties and large
    appearances: he does not number the
    streaks of the tulip, or describe the different
    shades in the verdure of the forest.
    Samuel Johnson, *Rasselas* (1759)

46 A philosophical poet should be specific
    As well as prolific,
    And I trust I am not being offensive
    If I suggest that he should also be
                                    comprehensive.
    Ogden Nash, 'Lines to a World-Famous
    Poet Who Failed to Complete a
    World-Famous Poem; or, Come Clean, Mr
    Guest!'

47 Poets are the hierophants of an
    unapprehended inspiration; the mirrors of
    the gigantic shadows which futurity casts
    upon the present.
    Percy Bysshe Shelley, *A Defence of Poetry*
    (1821)

48 Poets are the unacknowledged legislators of
    the world.
    Percy Bysshe Shelley, *A Defence of Poetry*
    (1821)

49 It isn't the poets who are the
    unacknowledged legislators of the world,
    it's the secret police.
    W.H. Auden, in discussion with Stephen
    Spender at the ICA (1971)

50 A poet's task is not to criticise life, but to
    explain it. When he turns to criticism, he is
    no longer a poet.
    John Jenkins (Gwili), in *Y Geninen* (April
    1907)

51 The poet is a sensitive instrument, not a leader.
C. Day-Lewis, *A Hope for Poetry* (1936)

52 Poets, like husbands, are good, bad and indifferent. Some are Victorian tyrants who treat language like a doormat, some are dreadfully hen-pecked, some bored, some unfaithful. For all of them, there are periods of tension, brawls, sulky silences, and, for many, divorce after a few passionate years.
W.H. Auden, 'Squares and Oblongs', *Poets at Work* (1948)

53 It is a better and a wiser thing to be a starved apothecary than a starved poet; so back to the shop Mr John, back to 'plasters, pills, and ointment boxes'.
John Gibson Lockhart, in review of John Keats's *Endymion*, in *Blackwood's Magazine* (1818)

54 When you wound a poet you forfeit eternity.
Oscar Venceslas de Lubicz Milosz, *Les Eléments* (1915)

55 A poet today, like a coin of Peter the Great, has become really rare.
Yevgeny Yevtushenko, 'Fuku'

56 O poets, you have always been proud; be more so, become disdainful.
Stéphane Mallarmé, *Proses de jeunesse*

57 Poets don't seem to have fun any more.
Blaise Cendrars, in interview in *Writers at Work* (3rd series, 1967)

58 Alas for our art, scandal
Is rampant about us all!
Siôn Tudur, 'Warning to the Poets' (16th cent.)

59 Oh! blame not the bard.
Thomas Moore, 'Oh! Blame Not', *Irish Melodies* (1834)

60 If you want to get poetry out of me you must be either a relative or a duchess, and you are neither.
A.E. Housman, when asked to contribute to *Georgian Poetry*, quoted in Christopher Hassall, *Edward Marsh* (1959)

114 POET LAUREATE

1 Who would not be
The Laureate bold,
With his butt of sherry
To keep him merry,
And nothing to do but to pocket his gold?
William Aytoun, 'The Laureate'

2 The Muse is mute when public men
Applaud a modern throne:
Those cheers that can be bought or sold,
That office fools have run.
W.B. Yeats, 'A Model for the Laureate'

3 O what indignity and shame
To prostitute the Muse's name,
By flatt'ring kings whom Heav'n designed
The plague and scourges of mankind.
Jonathan Swift, 'On Poetry: A Rhapsody'

4 Then, Poet, if you mean to thrive,
Empty your Muse on kings alive.
Jonathan Swift, 'On Poetry: A Rhapsody'

5 To laureats is no pity due?
William Whitehead, Poet Laureate, 'A Pathetic Apology for all Laureates Past, Present, and to Come' (1788)

6 Thomas Shadwell has had a bad press for 300 years.
Nick Russel, *Poets by Appointment* (1981)

7 In England the Poet Laureate is an officer of the sovereign's court, acting as dancing skeleton at every royal feast and singing-mute at every royal funeral.
Ambrose Bierce, *The Devil's Dictionary* (1911)

8 Not that he had much regard for his official utterances. When he sent a poem to *The Times*, he always included a stamped addressed envelope — just in case.
Nick Russel, of John Masefield, *Poets by Appointment* (1981)

9 As our leading nature poet, he might find some sort of inspiration from the wild life of Balmoral.
David Holloway, greeting the appointment of Ted Hughes as Poet Laureate in *The Daily Telegraph* (1984)

115 POETRY

Definitions

1 'Sir, what is poetry?'
'Why, Sir, it is much easier to say what it is

not. We all know what light is; but it is not easy to tell what it is.'
Laurence Sterne, *Tristram Shandy* (1759–67)

2 To give a sense of the freshness or vividness of life is a valid purpose for poetry.
Wallace Stevens, *Opus Posthumous* (1957)

3 If you want a definition of poetry, say: 'Poetry is what makes me laugh or cry or yawn, what makes my toenails twinkle, what makes me want to do this or that or nothing' and let it go at that.
Dylan Thomas, in letter to student (1951)

4 What's Poetry? Lines without end.
R. Williams Parry, 'Ceiriog — Bardd heb ei Debyg'

5 Poetry is the stuff that poets write.
Anonymous schoolboy

6 I'm a poet. And then I put the poetry in the drama, I put it in short stories, and I put it in the plays. Poetry's poetry. It doesn't have to be called a poem, you know.
Tennessee Williams, in interview in *Writers at Work* (6th series, 1984)

7 Poetry is a comforting piece of fiction set to more or less lascivious music.
H.L. Mencken, *Prejudices* (1919)

8 Poetry's a mere drug, Sir.
George Farquhar, *Love and a Bottle* (1698)

9 It seems to me that all poets' precepts about the nature of poetry are true, even when they seem to contradict each other.
Geoffrey Grigson, *The Private Art* (1982)

10   Mincing poetry.
'Tis like the forc'd gait of a shuffling nag.
William Shakespeare, *Henry IV* (Part 1)

11 Poetry is the Honey of all Flowers, the Quintessence, the Marrow of Art and the very Phrase of Angels.
Thomas Nashe, quoted in Walter De La Mare, *Come Hither* (1923)

12 Poetry is sissy stuff that rhymes.
Geoffrey Williams and Ronald Searle, 'Down with Skool!', *The Complete Molesworth* (1958)

13 Poetry turns all things to loveliness . . . it marries exultation and horror, grief and pleasure, eternity and change; it subdues to

union, under its light yoke, all irreconcilable things.
Percy Bysshe Shelley, *A Defence of Poetry* (1821)

14 Poetry is simply the most beautiful, impressive, and widely effective mode of saying things, and hence its importance.
Matthew Arnold, *Essays in Criticism* (1865)

15 Poetry should be a continuous and controlling mood, the mind should be steeped in poetical associations, and the diction nourished on the purest store of the Attic bee.
James Russell Lowell, *Letters* (1894)

16 I wish our clever young poets would remember my homely definitions of prose and poetry; that is, prose = words in their best order; — poetry = best words in the best order.
Samuel Taylor Coleridge, *Table Talk* (12 July 1827)

17 It is fatal to decide, intellectually, what good poetry is because you are then in honour bound to try to write it, instead of the poems that only you can write.
Philip Larkin, *Poets of the 1950s* (ed. D.J. Enright, 1955)

18 There's no second-rate in poetry.
John Oldham, 'An Ode on St Cecilia's Day'

19 Poetry's unnat'ral; no man ever talked poetry 'cept a beadle on boxin' day.
Charles Dickens, *The Pickwick Papers* (1836–7)

20 The difference between genuine poetry and the poetry of Dryden, Pope, and all their school, is briefly this: their poetry is conceived and composed in their wits, genuine poetry is conceived and composed in the soul.
Matthew Arnold, *Essays in Criticism* (1865)

21 Poetry is the opening and closing of a door, leaving those who look through to guess about what is seen during a moment.
Carl Sandburg, 'Tentative (First Model) Definitions of Poetry', *Complete Poems* (1950)

22 Poetry is a pheasant disappearing in the brush.
Wallace Stevens, 'Adagia', *Opus Posthumous* (1957)

23 Genuine poetry can communicate before it is understood.
T.S. Eliot, *Dante* (1929)

24 The poem — that prolonged hesitation between sound and sense.
Paul Valéry, in *Tel quel* (1943)

25 The best poem is that whose worked-upon unmagical passages come closest, in texture and intensity, to those moments of magical accident.
Dylan Thomas, 'On Poetry', *Quite Early One Morning* (1960)

26 Poetry is a response to the daily necessity of getting the world right.
Wallace Stevens, 'Adagia', *Opus Posthumous* (1957)

27 Poetry has no role to play except beyond philosophy.
André Breton, *Les Pas Perdus* (1924)

28 Poetry makes its own pertinence, and a single stanza outweighs a book of prose.
Ralph Waldo Emerson, *Journals* (1913)

29 The crown of literature is poetry. It is its end and aim. It is the sublimest activity of the human mind. It is the achievement of beauty and delicacy. The writer of prose can only step aside when the poet passes.
Somerset Maugham, in *The Saturday Review* (20 July 1957)

30 It isn't choral, it isn't communal; it has nothing to do with poetry societies or with the busybodies of art (as we know them) appointed by the state; it is resistant — if underneath or out of sight of journalists and Americans and teachers of literature — to vulgarization.
Geoffrey Grigson, *The Private Art* (1982)

31 Poetry is certainly something more than good sense, but it must be good sense at all events; just as a palace is more than a house, but it must be a house, at least.
Samuel Taylor Coleridge, *Table Talk* (9 May 1830)

32 A poetry the quality of which
Is a stand made against intellectual apathy,
Its material founded, like Gray's, on difficult
       knowledge
And its metres those of a poet
Who has studied Pindar and Welsh poetry.
Hugh MacDiarmid, 'The Kind of Poetry I Want'

33 As to Twentieth Century poetry, and the poetry which I expect to see written during the next decade or so, it will, I think, move against poppy-cock, it will be harder and saner . . . 'nearer the bone'. It will be as much like granite as it can be, its force will lie in its truth, its interpretative power . . . We will have fewer pointed adjectives impeding the shock and stroke of it. At least for myself, I want it so, austere, direct, free from emotional slither.
Ezra Pound, *Literary Essays* (1954)

34 Poetry, our poetry, is to be read like a newspaper. The newspaper of the world that is to come.
Louis Aragon, *Blanche ou l'oubli* (1968)

35 Poetry is not a science but an act of faith.
Robert Graves, 'Schools', *Observations on Poetry* (1922–5)

36 I affirm, Sir, that Poetry, that the imagination, generally speaking, delights in power, in strong excitement, as well as in truth, in good, in right, whereas pure reason and the moral sense approve only of the true and good.
John Keats, in letter to George and Georgina Keats (Feb.–May 1819)

37 Poetry must resist the intelligence almost successfully.
Wallace Stevens, 'Adagia', *Opus Posthumous* (1957)

38 Poetic licence. There's no such thing.
Théodore de Banville, *Petit Traité de poésie Française* (1872)

39 It is essential to poetry that it be simple, and appeal to the elements and primary laws of our nature.
Samuel Taylor Coleridge, *Lectures on Poetry* (1818)

40 I hold that a long poem does not exist. I maintain that the phrase, 'a long poem', is simply a flat contradiction in terms.
Edgar Allan Poe, 'The Poetic Principle'

41 Poetry heals the wounds inflicted by reason.
Novalis, *Detached Thoughts* (late 18th cent.)

42 Poetry is a purging of the world's poverty and change and evil and death.
Wallace Stevens, *Opus Posthumous* (1957)

43 Poetry is adolescence fermented and thus preserved.
José Ortega y Gasset, 'In Search of Goethe from Within, Letter to a German', in *The Partisan Review* (Dec. 1949)

44 Poetry is the revelation of a feeling that the poet believes to be interior and personal but which the reader recognizes as his own.
Salvatore Quasimodo, in *The New York Times* (14 May 1960)

45 Poetry is often a mirror to the condition of a nation's culture.
Saunders Lewis, 'Diwylliant yng Nghymru'

46 As civilization advances, poetry almost necessarily declines.
Thomas Babington Macaulay, *Literary Essays contributed to the 'Edinburgh Review'* (Aug. 1825)

47 I have nothing to say and I am saying it and that is poetry.
John Cage, '45 for a Speaker', *Silence* (1961)

48 For poetry makes nothing happen: it
                     survives
In the valley of its saying where executives
Would never want to tamper; it flows south
From ranches of isolation and the busy
                     griefs,
Raw towns that we believe and die in; it
                     survives,
A way of happening, a mouth.
W.H. Auden, 'In Memory of W.B. Yeats'

49 The virtues common to good living and good poetry seem to me not so much matters of what used to be called 'virtue' as, above all, of sane vitality.
F.L. Lucas, *Decline and Fall of the Romantic Ideal* (1936)

50 And certainly poetry is not the inculcation of morals, or the direction of politics; and no more is it religion or an equivalent of religion, except by some monstrous abuse of words.
T.S. Eliot, in preface to *The Sacred Wood* (1920)

51 Poetry should be great and unobtrusive, a thing which enters into one's soul, and does not startle it or amaze it with itself, but with its subject.
John Keats, in letter to J.H. Reynolds (3 Feb. 1818)

52 Journalism is for the public; poetry is a kind of secret vice.
Stephen Spender, in interview in *Writers at Work* (6th series, 1984)

53 I think we got much better poetry when it was all regarded as sinful or subversive, and you had to hide it under the cushion when somebody came in.
Philip Larkin, *Required Writing* (1983)

54 True poetry, the best of it, is but the ashes of a burnt-out passion.
Oliver Wendell Holmes, *Over the Teacups* (1891)

55 Poetry is the language in which man explores his own amazement. It is the language in which he says heaven and earth in one word. It is the language in which he speaks of himself and his predicament as though for the first time.
Christopher Fry, in broadcast talk, 'A Playwright Speaks', *The Listener* (23 Feb. 1950)

56 Poetry is life distilled.
Gwendolyn Brooks, *Augusta Chronicle* (1976)

57 We learn what poetry is — if ever we learn — by reading it.
T.S. Eliot, *The Sacred Wood* (1920)

58 All poetry is mis-representation.
Jeremy Bentham, quoted by John Stuart Mill in *The Westminster Review* (1838)

59 . . . that willing suspension of disbelief for the moment, which constitutes poetic faith.
Samuel Taylor Coleridge, *Biographia Literaria* (1817)

60 Not the poem which we have read, but that to which we return, with the greatest pleasure, possesses the genuine power, and claims the name of essential poetry.
Samuel Taylor Coleridge, *Biographia Literaria* (1817)

Effects

61 When power narrows the areas of man's concern, poetry reminds him of the richness and diversity of his existence. When power corrupts, poetry cleanses.
John F. Kennedy, in speech at dedication of Robert Frost Library, Amherst College, Mass. (Nov. 1962)

62 Poetry has been to me 'its own exceeding
    great reward'; it has soothed my afflictions;
    it has multiplied and refined my enjoyments;
    it has endeared solitude; and it has given me
    the habit of wishing to discover the good
    and the beautiful in all that meets and
    surrounds me.
    Samuel Taylor Coleridge, *Biographia
    Literaria* (1817)

63 It . . . purges from our inward sight the film
    of familiarity which obscures from us the
    wonder of our being. It compels us to feel
    that which we perceive, and to imagine that
    which we know.
    Percy Bysshe Shelley, *A Defence of Poetry*
    (1820)

64 The poet's business is not to describe things
    to us, or to tell us about things, but to create
    in our minds the very things themselves.
    Lascelles Abercrombie, *Poetry: Its Music
    and Meaning* (1932)

65 It is not enough for poems to be fine; they
    must charm, and draw the mind of the
    listener at will.
    Horace, *Ars Poetica*

66 In every volume of poems something good
    may be found.
    Samuel Johnson, quoted in James Boswell,
    Life of Samuel Johnson (1791)

67 I think one of the greatest pleasures is to
    come across a poem that one can honestly
    like; it is like finding a new flower.
    James Russell Lowell, in letter to E.C.
    Stedman (12 Feb. 1866)

68 In poetry, you must love the words, the
    ideas and the images and rhythms with all
    your capacity to love anything at all.
    Wallace Stevens, *Opus Posthumous* (1957)

69 Poetry should surprise by a fine excess, and
    not by singularity; it should strike the reader
    as a wording of his own highest thoughts,
    and appear almost a remembrance. Its
    touches of beauty should never be half-way,
    thereby making the reader breathless,
    instead of content. The rise, the progress,
    the setting of imagery should, like the sun,
    come natural to him.
    John Keats, in letter to John Taylor (27 Feb.
    1818)

70 I do not perceive the poetic and dramatic
    capabilities of an anecdote or story which is
    told me, its significance, till some time

afterwards . . . We do not enjoy poetry
unless we know it to be poetry.
Henry David Thoreau, *Journal* (1 Oct.
1856)

71 Poems very seldom consist of poetry and
    nothing else; and pleasure can be derived
    also from their other ingredients.
    A.E. Housman, 'The Name and Nature
    of Poetry', lecture delivered at Cambridge
    University (9 May 1933)

72 The simple way to arrive at an appreciation
    of poetry is to read it — and then to read it
    again.
    Desmond Flower, *The Pursuit of Poetry*
    (1939)

73 One reads poetry with one's nerves.
    Wallace Stevens, *Opus Posthumous*
    (1957)

74 More often than prose or mathematics,
    poetry is received in a hostile spirit, as if its
    publication were an affront to the reader.
    Michael Roberts, introduction to *The Faber
    Book of Modern Verse* (1936)

75 Quantity of pleasure being equal, push-pin
    is as good as poetry.
    Jeremy Bentham, quoted by John Stuart
    Mill, in *The Westminster Review* (1838)

76 One gets the impression from so many
    readers of poetry that they are embarrassed,
    almost as though they had been asked to
    discuss their love affairs at a public meeting.
    But reading poetry is as natural an activity
    as eating one's breakfast.
    Vicars Bell, *On Learning the English
    Tongue* (1953)

77 I, too, dislike it: there are things that are
         important beyond all this fiddle.
    Reading it, however, with a perfect
         contempt for it, one discovers in
    it after all, a place for the genuine.
    Marianne Moore, 'Poetry'

78 I think poetry should be alive. You should
    be able to dance to it.
    Benjamin Zephaniah, in *The Sunday Times*
    (23 August 1987)

79 This book, which would enflame a heart of
    ice, must set your ardent soul on fire.
    Petrarch, quoted in C. Isaac and M.A.
    Elton, *The Great Book Collectors*
    (1893)

80 We hate poetry that has a palpable design

upon us — and if we do not agree, seems to put a hand in its breeches pocket.
John Keats, in a letter to John Hamilton Reynolds (3 Feb. 1818)

81 Curst be the verse, how well soe'er it flow, That tends to make one worthy man my foe.
Alexander Pope, *Epistle to Dr Arbuthnot* (1735)

82 Nothing I wrote in the thirties saved one Jew from Auschwitz.
W.H. Auden, in discussion with Stephen Spender at the ICA (1971)

83 Poem me no poems.
Rose Macaulay, in *The Poetry Review* (Autumn 1963)

116 POETRY READINGS

1 Poetry is a spoken and not a written art.
Imagist Manifesto (1915)

2 Though the poet ought to write as if his work were intended to be read aloud, in practice the reading aloud of a poem distracts attention from its subtler properties by emphasizing the more obvious ones. The outward ear is easily deceived. A beautiful voice can make magic even with bad or fraudulent poetry which the eye, as the most sophisticated organ of service, would reject at once; for the eye is in close communication with the undeceivable inward ear.
Robert Graves, 'The Outward and Inward Ears', *Observations on Poetry* (1922–5)

3 Poetry readings are for those too indifferent and too lazy to read for themselves.
Geoffrey Grigson, *The Private Art* (1982)

4 When people say, 'I've told you fifty times,' They mean to scold, and very often do; When poets say, 'I've written fifty rhymes,' They make you dread that they'll recite them too.
Lord Byron, *Don Juan* (1819–24)

5 'I can repeat poetry as well as other folk if it comes to that —'
'Oh, it needn't come to that!' Alice hastily said.
Lewis Carroll, *Through the Looking-Glass* (1872)

6 Fire in each eye, and papers in each hand, They rave, recite, and madden round the land.
Alexander Pope, *Epistle to Dr Arbuthnot* (1735)

7 Most of us laugh
because the others are laughing
most of us clap
because the others are clapping
Dannie Abse, 'The Poetry Reading'

8 All poets who, when reading from their own works, experience a choked feeling, are major.
E.B.White, 'How to Tell a Major Poet', *Quo Vadimus?* (1939)

9 Her family are very intellectual and give poetry readings in their drawing-room, which Thetis says are very embarrassing.
Joan Wyndham, *Love Lessons: A Wartime Diary* (1985)

10 Everybody *loved* him; he was screwing all the coeds in America, drinking all the whiskey, and he'd get up there and read his poems, and then he'd go on and read them somewhere else. He got a lot of dough for it.
James Dickey, of Dylan Thomas in interview in *Writers at Work* (5th series, 1981)

11 I thought I'd begin with a sonnet by Shakespeare but then I thought why should I? He never reads any of mine.
Spike Milligan, remark at Poetry and Jazz concert, Hampstead Town Hall (1961)

12 What do you want me to do? Say it over again in worser English?
Robert Frost, on being asked to recite one of his poems a second time

117 POLITICS

1 There is complaint that we have no literature: that is the fault of the Minister of the Interior.
Napoleon I, in letter to Arch-Chancellor Cambacérès (21 Nov. 1806)

2 Perfection, of a kind, was what he was after, And the poetry he invented was easy to understand.
W.H. Auden, 'Epitaph on a Tyrant'

3 Passionately held political convictions are likely to unhinge one who sets himself up as a literary critic, especially if he lacks a sense of humour.
Dannie Abse, *Journals from the Ant-heap* (1986)

4 The history of poets pronouncing on public issues is notoriously dismal.
James Dickey, in interview in *Writers at Work* (5th series, 1981)

5 Poets are, by the nature of their interests and the nature of artistic fabrication, singularly ill-equipped to understand politics or economics.
W.H. Auden, 'The Poet and the City', *The Dyer's Hand* (1962)

6 I wrote 'Leda and the Swan' because the editor of a political review asked me for a poem.
W.B. Yeats, in *The Dial* (June 1924)

7 Political poetry is more profoundly emotional than any other — at least as much as love poetry — and cannot be forced because it then becomes vulgar and unacceptable. It is necessary first to pan through all other poetry in order to become a political poet.
Pablo Neruda, in interview in *Writers at Work* (5th series, 1981)

8 Don't make a novel to establish a principle of political economy. You will spoil both.
Ralph Waldo Emerson, *Journals* (1857)

9 I think it is better that in times like these A poet's mouth be silent, for in truth We have no gift to set a statesman right.
W.B. Yeats, 'On Being Asked for a War Poem'

10 The best thing that governments can do for authors in wartime is to leave them alone.
John Strachey, in *The Author* (1940)

11 If a poet would influence politics he must join a party, and then he is lost as a poet: goodbye to his free spirit and his open mind . . . The poet as a man and a citizen will love his native land, but the native land of his genius lies in the world of goodness, greatness and beauty, a country without frontiers or boundaries, ready for him to seize and shape wherever he finds it.
J.W. Goethe, quoted in Johann Peter Eckermann, *Conversations with Goethe* (1832)

12 He should have been a poet, political parties only chain such spirits.
Michael Foot, *Aneurin Bevan* (1962)

13 Most histories of English Poetry are a record of 'schools', 'political tendencies', and metrical fashions. But poets appear spasmodically, write their best poetry at uncertain intervals, owe nothing to schools and, in so far as they are behaving poetically, steer well clear of politics.
Robert Graves, 'Schools', *Observations on Poetry* (1922–5)

14 The present state of the world is so miserable and degraded that if anyone were to say to the poet: 'for God's sake, stop humming and put the kettle on or fetch bandages. The patient's dying,' I do not know how he could justifiably refuse.
W.H. Auden, 'Squares and Oblongs', *Poets at Work* (1948)

15 I have never thought of my life as divided between poetry and politics.
Pablo Neruda, in acceptance speech as Communist Party candidate for the Presidency of Chile (30 Sept. 1969)

16 Authors don't usually make very good politicians and it is hard to name one who succeeded in gaining public office.
Robert Hendrickson, *The Literary Life and Other Curiosities* (1981)

17 Poets with progress make no peace or pact: the act of poetry is a rebel act.
Michael Hartnett, 'A Farewell to English'

18 The nobility of our calling will always be rooted in two commitments difficult to observe: refusal to lie about what we know, and resistance to oppression.
Albert Camus, in speech accepting the Nobel Prize (1957)

19 Our liberal ideology has produced a large literature of social and political protest, but not, for several decades, a single writer who commands our real literary admiration.
Lionel Trilling, 'The Function of the Little Magazine'

20 Politics in a work of literature are like a pistol-shot in the middle of a concert, something loud and vulgar and yet a thing to which it is not possible to refuse one's attention.
Stendhal, *La Chartreuse de Parme* (1839)

21 The attempt to make poetry serve a cause or interest is likely to deprive it of the freedom without which it cannot arrive at its particular kind of truth. For interests and causes see existence through blinkers; they distort being in order to achieve their ends. Poetry cannot take sides except with life.
Stephen Spender, *Life and the Poet* (1942)

22 Today we should make poems including
        iron and steel
And the poet also should know how to lead
        an attack.
Ho Chi-Minh, on reading *Anthology of a Thousand Poets*

23 Ah, Lenin, you were right. But I'm a poet
(And you cu'd mak allowances for that!)
Aimin' at mair than you aimed at
Tho' yours comes first, I know it.
Hugh MacDiarmid, 'Second Hymn to Lenin'

24 One thing we used to discuss in the 1930s was whether a fascist could be a good writer. We always decided that he couldn't because fascism was stupid and inhuman. So by definition a person who was a good writer might call himself a fascist, but couldn't really be one.
Stephen Spender, in interview in *Writers at Work* (6th series, 1984)

25 Poets who turn to politics nearly always turn to the popular sort and go as far to the left as they dare. When they concern themselves with aristocratic politics, this is largely for the pleasure of moving in refined society, on an island of proud retirement from the populace.
Robert Graves, 'Poetry and Politics', *Epilogue* (1935–7)

26 The poem or the story or the novel must follow a certain line — it is a kind of party line even though what is in question is not a political party, but it *is*, in the true sense of the word, a party line.
Nadine Gordimer, in interview in *Writers at Work* (6th series, 1984)

27 The sentence was seven years' hard labour, to be followed by five in exile. I was not frightened. I was even flattered to get such a long term, which was the first official acknowledgement of my work in the country.
Irina Ratushinskaya, interview in *The Observer* (21 Dec. 1986)

28 Under communism, the State kills or silences poets. Under capitalism, they destroy themselves.
Jeremy Hooker, 'Barbarous Reflections', *The Presence of the Past* (1987)

29 Dictators are as scared of books as they are of cannon.
Henry Golden, *Only in America* (1958)

30 Many who have read Marxist books have become renegades from the revolution, whereas illiterate workers often grasp Marxism very well.
Mao Tse Tung, *Oppose Book Worship* (1966)

31 If ten or twelve Hungarian writers had been shot at the right moment, there would have been no revolution.
Nikita Kruschev, attr.

32 True poets are the guardians of the state.
Wentworth Dillon, *Essay on Translated Verse* (1684)

33 Sometimes I think I would like a spell in
        prison
In a humane country, for a political offence;
Somewhere where the library service is
        efficient,
Or Scandinavia, where wives come in at the
        weekends.
Ned Thomas, 'Supermarket'

34 The aim of a Socialist policy for Literature must be to make more books available to more people, both in quantity and scope, and to encourage people to write.
British Labour Party, *The Arts: A Discussion Document* (1975)

---

118 POPULARITY
See also FASHION

---

1 I equally dislike the favour of the public with the love of a woman. They are both a cloying treacle to the wings of independence.
John Keats, in letter to John Taylor (23 Aug. 1819)

2 Only two classes of books are of universal appeal. The very best and the very worst.
Ford Madox Ford, *Joseph Conrad* (1924)

3 The art of *not* reading is extremely important. It consists in our not taking up

whatever happens to be occupying the larger public at the time.
Arthur Schopenhauer, 'On Reading and Books', *Parerga and Paralipomena* (1851)

4 I neither am, nor ever shall be popular. Such never was my ambition.
Walter Savage Landor, to John Forster (1850)

5 Books for all the world are always foul-smelling books: the smell of small people clings to them.
Friedrich Nietzsche, *Beyond Good and Evil* (1886)

6 I write what I would like to read — what I think other women would like to read. If what I write makes a woman in the Canadian mountains cry and she writes and tells me about it, especially if she says, 'I read it to Tom when he came in from work and he cried too', I feel I have succeeded.
Kathleen Norris, on the publication of her seventy-eighth book

7 Popular, Popular, Unpopular!
'You're no Poet' — the critics cried!
'Why?' said the Poet. 'You're unpopular!'
Then they cried at the turn of the tide —
'You're no Poet!' 'Why?' — 'You're
                    popular!'
Pop-gun, Popular and Unpopular!
Alfred, Lord Tennyson, 'Popular'

---

119 PORNOGRAPHY

1 My scrofulous French novel
    On grey paper with blunt type!
Robert Browning, 'Soliloquy in a Spanish Cloister'

2 At last an unprintable book that is readable.
Ezra Pound, of Henry Miller's *Tropic of Cancer* (1934)

3 The test of obscenity is whether the tendency of the matter charged as obscene is to deprave and corrupt those whose minds are open to such immoral influences and into whose hands a publication of this sort may fall.
Chief Justice Cockburn, in the Hicklin case (1868)

4 Obscenity is whatever happens to shock some elderly and ignorant magistrate.
Bertrand Russell, in *Look* magazine (23 Feb. 1934)

5 Dirty old men are incapable of being corrupted any further, and as long as they make up the majority of regular customers a bookseller does not break the law in selling dirty books to them, two High Court judges decided yesterday.
News item in *The Daily Telegraph*, quoted by Alan Coren in *Punch* (23 Feb. 1972)

6 Lord Longford is against us reading or seeing things that keep our minds below the navel.
William Hardcastle, in *Punch* (1 Dec. 1972)

7 The worst that can be said about pornography is that it leads not to 'anti-social' acts but to the reading of more pornography.
Gore Vidal, *Reflections upon a Sinking Ship* (1969)

8 It's not a dirty book, it's an earthy book, which is a very different thing.
Librarian to borrower, cartoon caption in *The New Yorker*

9 Obscenity is such a tiny kingdom that a single tour covers it completely.
Heyward Brown, quoted by Bennett Cerf, *Shake Well Before Using* (1948)

10 All my good reading, you might say, was done in the toilet.
Henry Miller, *Black Spring* (1936)

11 Nine-tenths of the appeal of pornography is due to the indecent feelings concerning sex which moralists inculcate in the young; the other tenth is physiological, and will occur in one way or another whatever the state of the law may be.
Bertrand Russell, 'The Taboo on Sex Knowledge', *Marriage and Morals* (1929)

12 A taste for dirty stories may be said to be inherent in the human animal.
George Moore, *Confessions of a Young Man* (1888)

13 Obscenity is a cleansing process, whereas pornography only adds to the murk.
Henry Miller, in interview in *Writers at Work* (2nd series, 1963)

14 Pornography is the attempt to insult sex, to do dirt on it.
D.H. Lawrence, *Phoenix* (1936)

15 Inside every pornographer there is an infant screaming for the breast from which it has been torn. Pornography represents an endless and infinitely repeated effort to recapture that breast, and the bliss it offered.
Steven Marcus, *The Other Victorians* (1966)

16 Don't be daft. You don't get pornography on there, not on the telly. You get filth, that's all. The only place you get pornography is in yer Sunday papers.
Johnny Speight, Alf Garnett in *Till Death Us Do Part* (BBC TV, 1973)

17 A woman reading *Playboy* feels a little like a Jew reading a Nazi manual.
Gloria Steinem, attr.

120 POSTERITY
See also DURABILITY OF BOOKS

1 Poetry remembers the future.
Jean Cocteau, *Journal d'un inconnu* (1953)

2 Trying to make your poems lick the arse of posterity is as bad as making them lick the arse of your own time.
Geoffrey Grigson, *The Private Art* (1982)

3 People will not look forward to posterity, who never look backward to their ancestors.
Edmund Burke, *Observations on a Publication*, 'The present state of the nation' (1769)

4 The only test of a work of literature is that it shall please other ages than its own.
Gerald Brenan, *Thoughts in a Dry Season* (1978)

5 Posterity is as likely to be wrong as anybody else.
Heywood Brown, 'The Last Review', *Sitting on the World* (1924)

6 Books are the legacies that a great genius leaves to mankind, which are delivered down from generation to generation, as presents to the posterity of those who are yet unborn.
Joseph Addison, in *The Spectator* (10 Sept. 1711)

7 Literature would be altogether too tense if it were written solely by immortal authors. We must take writers as they are, and not expect them all to last.
Oliver Edwards, in *The Times* (25 April 1965)

8 No slightest golden rhyme he wrote
That held not something men must quote;
Thus by design of chance did he
Drop anchors to posterity.
Thomas Bailey Aldrich, 'A Hint from Herrick'

9 When a man is in doubt about this or that in his writing, it will often guide him if he asks himself how it will tell a hundred years hence.
Samuel Butler, *Note Books* (ed. H. Festing Jones, 1912)

10 There is something touching in the firm trust every author of a flop puts in posterity.
Kurt Tucholsky, *Gesammelte Werke* (1975)

11 You can keep the things of bronze and stone and give me one man to remember me just once a year.
Damon Runyon, last words

12 An author ought to write for the youth of his own generation, the critics of the next, and schoolmasters of ever after.
F. Scott Fitzgerald, quoted in *The Guardian* (13 Nov. 1964)

13 All poets pretend to write for immortality, but the whole tribe have no objection to present pay and present praise.
Charles Caleb Colton, *Lacon* (1825)

14 A writer should have another lifetime to see whether he is appreciated.
Jorge Luis Borges, *Conversations with Jorge Luis Borges* (ed. Richard Burgin, 1973)

15 What I fear is not being forgotten after my death, but, rather, not being enough forgotten. As we were saying, it is not our books that survive, but our poor lives that linger in the histories.
François Mauriac, in interview in *Writers at Work* (1st series, 1958)

16 I think I shall be among the English Poets after my death.
John Keats, in letter to George and Georgiana Keats (Oct. 1818)

17 When I am dead, I hope it may be said:
'His sins were scarlet, but his books were read'.
Hilaire Belloc, 'On His Books'

121 THE PRESS
See also JOURNALISM

1 Have you noticed that life, real
honest-to-goodness life, with murders and
catastrophes and fabulous inheritances,
happens almost exclusively in the
newspapers?
Jean Anouilh, *The Rehearsal* (1950)

2 The man must have a fair recipe for
melancholy, who can be dull in Fleet Street.
Charles Lamb, in letter to Thomas Manning
in *The Londoner* (1802)

3 Top people read *The Times*.
Anonymous, advertisement, 1970s

4 Nothing is news until it has appeared in *The
Times*.
Ralph Deakin, Foreign News Editor of *The
Times*, quoted in Claud Cockburn,
Cockburn Sums Up (1975)

5 Writing letters to *The Times*, according to
Barrie, is — or was in our young days — the
legitimate ambition of every Englishman.
Jerome K. Jerome, *My Life and Times* (1926)

6 A good newspaper, I suppose, is a nation
talking to itself.
Arthur Miller, in *The Observer* (26 Nov.
1961)

7 We like to appear in the newspapers, so long
as we are in the right column.
T.S. Eliot, *The Family Reunion* (1939)

8 There is a lot to be said for not being known
to the readers of *The Daily Mirror*.
Anthony Burgess, *Inside Mr Enderby* (1966)

9 How many beautiful trees gave their lives
that today's scandal should, without delay,
reach a million readers!
Edwin Way Teale, 'March 13', *Circle of the
Seasons* (1953)

10 If you want to make mischief come and
work on my papers.
Lord Beaverbrook, to Anthony Howard,
quoted in *Radio Times* (27 June 1981)

11 A newspaper, not having to act on its
descriptions and reports, but only to sell
them to idly curious people, has nothing but
honor to lose by inaccuracy and unveracity.
George Bernard Shaw, *The Doctor's
Dilemma* (1913)

12 I don't read the Press. I read responsible
literature.
Princess Michael of Kent, quoted in
'Sayings of the Week' in *The Observer* (30
Nov. 1986)

13 News is what a chap who doesn't care much
about anything wants to read. And it is only
news until he has read it. After that it's
dead.
Evelyn Waugh, *Scoop* (1938)

14 People everywhere confuse what they read
in newspapers with news.
A.J. Liebling, 'A Talkative Something or
Other', *The New Yorker* (7 April 1956)

15 News is whatever a good editor chooses to
print.
Arthur MacEwen, quoted in Daniel J.
Boorstin, *The Image* (1962)

16 Once a newspaper touches a story, the facts
are lost forever, even to the protagonists.
Norman Mailer, *The Presidential Papers*
(1964)

17 You should always believe all you read in
newspapers, as this makes them more
interesting.
Rose Macaulay, *A Casual Commentary*
(1925)

18 Newspapers always excite curiosity. No one
ever lays one down without a feeling of
disappointment.
Charles Lamb, 'Detatched Thoughts on
Books and Reading', *Last Essays of Elia*
(1833)

19 Early in life I had noticed that no event is
ever correctly reported in a newspaper.
George Orwell, *Essays* (1968)

20 Were it left to me to decide whether we
should have a government without
newspapers, or newspapers without a
government, I should not hesitate a moment
to prefer the latter.
Thomas Jefferson, in letter to Col. Edward
Carrington (16 Jan. 1787)

21 Madame, we are the press. You know our
power. We fix all values. We set all
standards. Your entire future depends on us.
Jean Giraudoux, *The Madwoman of
Chaillot* (1945)

22 Four hostile newspapers are more to be
feared than a thousand bayonets.
Napoleon 1, *Maxims* (1804–15)

23 We live under a government of men and
morning newspapers.
Wendell Phillips, in speech (28 Jan. 1852)

24 Nowhere else can one find so miscellaneous,
so various, an amount of knowledge as is
contained in a good newspaper.
Henry Ward Beecher, *Proverbs from
Plymouth Pulpit* (1887)

25 The man who never looks into a newspaper
is better informed than he who reads them:
inasmuch as he who knows nothing is
nearer to truth than he whose mind is filled
with falsehood and errors.
Thomas Jefferson, in letter to John Norvell
(11 June 1807)

26 A serious and profitable occupation, reading
the papers. It removes everything abnormal
from your make-up, everything that doesn't
conform to accepted ideas. It teaches you to
reason as well as the next person. It gives
you irrefutable and generally admitted
opinions on all events.
Michel de Ghelderode, *Pantagleize* (1929)

27 I read the newspapers avidly. It is my one
form of continuous fiction.
Aneurin Bevan, quoted in 'Sayings of the
Week', *The Observer* (3 April 1960)

28 The readers of the *Boston Evening
            Transcript*
Sway in the wind like a field of ripe corn.
T.S. Eliot, 'The Boston Evening Transcript'

29 If there is something of interest to you on
every page of the daily paper — foreign
news, home news, sport, the theatre, music,
books, stock exchange — you are very much
alive. Not only does this mean a continually
enlarging curiosity but it is the best form of
insurance against old age.
William Lyon Phelps, *Autobiography with
Letters* (1939)

30 That ephemeral sheet of paper, the
newspaper, is the natural enemy of the
book, as the whore is of the decent woman.
Edmond and Jules de Goncourt, *Journal*
(July 1885)

31 A single sentence will suffice for modern
man: he fornicated and read the papers.
Albert Camus, *The Fall* (1956)

32 You will see me any morning in the park
Reading the comics and the sporting page.
T.S. Eliot, 'Portrait of a Lady'

33 Produced by office boys for office boys.
Marquis of Salisbury, of *The Daily Mail*

34 He had been kicked in the head by a mule
when young and believed everything he read
in the Sunday papers.
George Ade, *The Slim Princess* (1908)

35 They [newspapers] were not so much
published as carried screaming into the
street.
H.G. Wells, *The War in the Air* (1908)

36 The best headlines never fi
Bernard Levin, in *The Times* (5 July 1980)

122 PRINTING

1 He who first shortened the labour of
Copyists by device of Movable Types was
disbanding hired Armies and cashiering
most Kings and Senates, and creating a
whole new Democratic world: he had
invented the art of printing.
Thomas Carlyle, *Sartor Resartus* (1833–4)

2 Gutenberg's invention has served mankind
well ever since, though in former times it
was the books which bore the brunt of the
pressure. Nowadays it's the authors.
Werner Fink, *Finckenschläge* (1976)

3 A second part of the history of the world
and the arts begins with the invention of
printing.
J.W. Goethe, in letter to J.Ch. Lobe (July
1820)

4 Since the discovery of printing, knowledge
has been called to power, and power has
been used to make knowledge a slave.
Napoleon I, *Maxims* (1804–15)

5 Every school boy and school girl who has
arrived at the age of reflection ought to
know something about the history of the art
of printing.
Horace Mann, 'Printing and Paper Making',
in *The Common School Journal* (Feb. 1843)

6 The circumstance which gives authors an
advantage above all these great masters
[painters], is this, that they can multiply
their originals; or rather, can make copies of
their works, to what number they please,

which shall be as valuable as the originals themselves.
Joseph Addison, in *The Spectator* (no. 166, 1711)

7 Printers are educated in the belief that when men differ in opinion both sides ought equally to have the advantage of being heard by the public; and that when truth and error have fair play, the former is always an overmatch for the latter: hence they cheerfully serve all contending writers that pay them well, without regarding on which side they are of the question in dispute
Benjamin Franklin, 'Apology for Printers' (10 June 1731)

8 Learning hath gained most by those books by which the printers have lost.
Thomas Fuller, 'Of Books', *The Holy State and the Profane State* (1642)

9 I thank God there are no free schools nor printing, and I hope we shall not have them these hundred years; for learning has brought disobedience and heresy and sects into the world, and printing has divulged them, and libels against the best government. God keep us from both!
William Berkeley, Governor of Virginia, *Report to the English Committee for the Colonies* (1671)

10 Th' printin'-press isn't wondherful. What's wondherful is that annybody shud want it to go on doin' what it does.
Finley Peter Dunne, 'On the Midway', *Mr Dooley's Opinions* (1901)

11 The printing-press is either the greatest blessing or the greatest curse of modern times, one sometimes forgets which.
J.M. Barrie, *Sentimental Tommy* (1896)

12 Our debt to the printing press is great — so great that it is vain to try to measure it — but it has not all been gain, and one of the losses to the people in general is that they no more hear the voice of poetry.
Alexander Haddow, *On the Teaching of Poetry* (1926)

13 Self-effacement is the etiquette of good printers.
Holbrook Jackson, *The Anatomy of Bibliomania* (1950)

14 I suffered so much from printer's errors That death for me can hold no terrors; I'll bet this stone has been misdated —

I wish to God I'd been cremated.
Anonymous, epitaph

15 Some say the reason for these [misprints] is the increasingly liberal attitude of the Church of England. Not enough parsons are unfrocked these days. The unfortunates of earlier days were often happy to find themselves employment in printing houses, correcting proofs.
David Holloway, in *The Daily Telegraph* (21 April 1979)

16 The Body of Benjamin Franklin, Printer (like the cover of an old book, its contents torn out, and stript of its lettering and gilding), lies food for worms; yet the work itself shall not be lost, for it will (as he believed) appear once more, in a new and more beautiful edition, corrected and amended by the Author.
Benjamin Franklin, inscription on his grave in Philadelphia

---

123 PRIZES

---

1 I think this is the most extraordinary collection of talent, of human knowledge, that has ever been gathered together at the White House — with the possible exception of when Thomas Jefferson dined alone.
John F. Kennedy, remark at a dinner for the American Nobel Prize winners (29 April 1962)

2 I cannot think that Real Poets have any competition. None are the greatest in the Kingdom of Heaven; it is so in Poetry.
William Blake, annotation to Wordsworth's *Poems* (1826)

3 Writing . . . is practically the only activity a person can do that is not competitive.
Paul Theroux, in *Time* magazine (1978)

4 Let all the little poets be gathered together in classes
And let prizes be given to them by the Prize Asses.
Stevie Smith, 'To School!'

5 Not only should you not accept a prize. You should not try to deserve one either.
Jean Cocteau, quoted by Geoffrey Grigson in *The Sunday Times* (23 Jan. 1973)

6 A writer who receives a literary prize is
   dishonoured.
   Paul Léautaud, *Entretiens avec Robert
   Mallet* (1951)

7 I was asked the other day if I would be
   interested in the Nobel Prize, but I think that
   for me it would be an absolute catastrophe. I
   would certainly be interested in deserving it,
   but to receive it would be terrible. It would
   just complicate even more the problems of
   fame.
   Gabriel García Márquez, in interview in
   Writers at Work (6th series, 1984)

8 A writer must refuse to allow himself to be
   transformed into an institution.
   Jean-Paul Sartre, on declining the Nobel
   Prize for Literature (1964)

9 The Nobel Prize, wherever it falls, is always
   an honor to literature.
   Pablo Neruda, in interview in *Writers at
   Work* (5th series, 1981)

10 It really means nothing in this country
   whatsoever — but then being a writer here
   means nothing either.
   William Golding, on winning the Nobel
   Prize, quoted in *The Observer* (31 May
   1987)

11 Well, after all, one doesn't *have* to get it.
   Tennessee Williams, of the Nobel Prize for
   Literature, in interview in *Writers at Work*
   (6th series, 1984)

12 Stop babbling, man! How much?
   W.B. Yeats, attributed, on hearing by
   telephone that he had won the Nobel Prize
   (1923)

13 It is extraordinary, an act of illiterates, to
   give prizes for literature.
   Geoffrey Grigson, *The Private Art* (1982)

14 It is the prize, not the novelist, that grabs the
   attention of the fiction business now.
   Anonymous, editorial in *The Economist* (25
   Oct. 1986)

15 Judging from previous winners the
   archetypal Booker novel would be an epic
   work offering liberal amounts of sex, violent
   incident, history, anguish, the odd
   intimation of apocalypse, and so forth.
   Simon Banner, in interview in *The Guardian*
   (4 Sept. 1985)

16 To be a judge you don't have to know about

books, you have to be skilled at picking
shrapnel out of your head.
Joanna Lumley, on the Booker Prize, quoted
in 'Sayings of the Week' in *The Observer*
(1985)

17 I was on the Booker Prize Committee twice.
   It almost drove me mad.
   Rebecca West, in interview in *Writers at
   Work* (6th series, 1984)

18 One can't help suspecting that the greatest
   boon provided by the Booker Prize is to
   those who suffer a collapse of imagination
   when it comes to Christmas shopping.
   Julian Chancellor, 'Bringing the Glittering
   Prizes to Book' in *The Wordsmith* (Nov/Dec
   1986)

19 Prizes are not a cure-all: they resemble a
   lottery in which the better books get most
   tickets.
   Michael Holroyd, *Guide to Literary Prizes*
   (1979)

20 Ridiculous poets do not cease to be
   ridiculous when eight other poets and
   eighteen critics and three selectors of the
   Poetry Book Society say they are sublime.
   Geoffrey Grigson, *The Private Art* (1982)

21 Every poet looks down on prizes, until he is
   given a prize. Then he recovers from this
   affront to himself and continues to look
   down on prizes.
   Geoffrey Grigson, *The Private Art* (1982)

22 I don't think literature is ever finished in any
   country which has more prizes than it has
   writers.
   Gore Vidal, quoted in 'Sayings of the Week'
   in *The Observer* (27 Sept. 1987)

23 Unlike the Christian, the true poet goes
   from his prize to his work.
   R. Williams Parry, 'Deg Gorchymyn i
   Feirdd'

---

124 PROFESSION
See also TRADE

---

1 When people, women included, hear that
   you are writing, they assume that it is simply
   a hobby to fill in time between doing the
   washing-up and the ironing. It couldn't
   possibly be a profession.
   Rachel Billington, quoted in *The Times* (14
   Jan. 1987)

2 I have worked at poetry — it has not been to me reverie, but art. As the physician and lawyer work at their several professions, so have I, and so do I, apply to mine.
Elizabeth Barrett Browning, *Letters to R.H. Horne* (1877)

3 To be a poet is a condition rather than a profession.
Robert Graves, in answer to a questionnaire in *Horizon* (1946)

4 But if a stranger in the train asks me my occupation I never answer 'writer' for fear that he may go on to ask me what I write, and to answer 'poetry' would embarrass us both, for we both know that nobody can earn a living simply by writing poetry.
W.H. Auden, in *The Dyer's Hand* (1962)

5 I guess that I shall clear between two and three hundred pounds by my authorship; with that sum I intend, so far as I may be said to have any intention, to return to my old acquaintance, the plough, and, if I can meet with a lease by which I can live, to commence Farmer. — I do not intend to give up Poetry . . . while following my plough, or building up my stocks, I shall cast a leisure glance to that dear, that only feature of my character which gave me the notice of Caledonia, and the patronage of a Wallace.
Robert Burns, in letter to Mrs Dunlop (22 March 1787)

6 I'm a popular poet who actually earns a living rather than sitting in a garret feeling sorry for myself.
Attila the Stockbroker, quoted in 'Sayings of the Week' in *The Observer* (27 Sept. 1987)

7 It is not possible for a poet to be a professional. Poetry is essentially an amateur activity.
Viscount Barrington, in speech in the House of Lords (23 Nov. 1978)

8 O God, O Venus, O Mercury, patron of
            thieves,
Lend me a little tobacco-shop,
      or install me in any profession
Save this damn'd profession of writing,
      Where one needs one's brains all the
            time.
Ezra Pound, 'The Lake Isle'

9 Nowadays you *can* live by being a poet. A lot of people do it: it means a blend of giving readings and lecturing and spending a year at a university as poet in residence or something. But I couldn't bear that: it would embarrass me very much. I don't want to go around pretending to be me.
Philip Larkin, in interview in *The Observer* (1979)

10 Poetry is not a career, but a mug's game. No honest poet can ever feel quite sure of the permanent value of what he has written, he may have wasted his time and messed up his life for nothing.
T.S. Eliot, *The Use of Poetry and the Use of Criticism* (1932)

11 The arrogance of the poet is based on his courageous dedication to a thankless profession, the difficulties and humiliation of which he alone fully realizes.
Robert Graves, 'The Arrogance of Poets', *Observations on Poetry* (1922–5)

12 I have decided to be a poet. My father said there isn't a suitable career structure for poets and no pensions and other boring things, but I am quite decided.
Sue Townsend, *The Secret Diary of Adrian Mole* (1982)

13 Literature — the most seductive, the most deceiving, the most dangerous of professions.
John, Viscount Morley, 'Burke', *Critical Miscellanies* (1871–7)

14 Faced with a developing market, printing and bookselling underwent a major change, as nascent capitalist industry took charge of the book. The publisher appeared as the responsible entrepreneur relegating the printer and bookseller to a minor role. As a side effect, the literary profession began to organize; until then literature had been left to the rich amateur or relied upon the support of the art patron, but now the writer began to claim a livelihood from his words.
Robert Escarpit, *The Book Revolution* (1957)

15 The profession of book writing makes horse racing seem like a solid, stable business.
John Steinbeck, in *Newsweek* (24 Dec. 1962)

16 The only reason for being a professional writer is that you just can't help it.
Leo Rosten, in *Contemporary Novelists* (1976)

17 Literature is a noble calling, but only when
the call obeyed by the aspirant issues from a
world to be enlightened and blessed, not
from a void stomach clamoring to be
gratified and filled.
Horace Greeley, in letter to Robert Dale
Owen (5 March 1860)

18 You must not suppose, because I am a man
of letters, that I have never tried to earn an
honest living.
George Bernard Shaw, preface to *The
Irrational Knot* (1968)

19 Innumerable are the men and women now
writing for bread, who have not the least
chance of finding in such work a permanent
livelihood . . . With a lifetime of dread
experience behind me, I say that he who
encourages any young man or woman to
look for his living in 'literature', commits no
less than a crime.
George Gissing, *The Private Papers of
Henry Ryecroft* (1903)

20 I don't want to be a doctor, and live by
men's diseases; nor a minister to live by their
sins; nor a lawyer to live by their quarrels.
So I don't see there's anything left for me
but to be an author.
Nathaniel Hawthorne, remark to his
mother

21 To have lived in vain must be a painful
thought to any man, and especially so to
him who has made literature his profession.
Samuel Taylor Coleridge, *Biographia
Literaria* (1817)

22 There can be no society of authors.
Geoffrey Grigson, *The Private Art* (1982)

23 Your Majesty is head of the literary
profession.
Benjamin Disraeli, remark to Queen
Victoria

125 PROPAGANDA
See also POLITICS

1 I have always had the greatest contempt for
novels written with a purpose.
Ford Madox Ford, *It Was the Nightingale*
(1934)

2 Tedious polemic writers are more severe to
their readers than those they contend with.
Samuel Butler, *Prose Observations*
(1660–80)

3 For God's sake steer clear of verse
Which wants to heal the universe
Anonymous

4 No more movements. No more manifestoes.
Every poet stands alone.
W.H. Auden, 'Squares and Oblongs', *Poets
at Work* (1948)

5 I hate conferences, manifestos, groups,
movements . . . I feel that people write best
when they write independent of groups.
Vernon Watkins, in letter to Pennar Davies
(1939)

6 A manifesto usually intimidates the writer
and is meaningless after a few weeks.
Idris Davies, in letter to Pennar Davies
(1939)

7 There is a halfway house between the
Ministry of Propaganda and the Ivory
Tower and this is the safest address for a
poet.
Clive Sansom, *The World of Poetry* (1959)

8 I run the *Daily Express* purely for
propaganda and for no other purpose.
Lord Beaverbrook, to the Royal
Commission on the Press (1948)

126 PROSE

1 *M. Jourdain*: What? When I say: 'Nicole,
bring me my slippers, and give me my
night-cap' is that prose?
Philosophy Teacher: Yes, Sir.
M. Jourdain: Good heavens! For more than
forty years I have been speaking prose
without knowing it.
Molière, *Le Bourgeois Gentilhomme* (1670)

2 All that is not prose is verse; and all that is
not verse is prose.
Molière, *Le Bourgeois Gentilhomme* (1670)

3 The poet gives us his essence, but prose
takes the mould of the body and mind entire.
Virginia Woolf, 'The Captain's Death Bed'

4 Poetry has done enough when it charms, but
prose must also convince.
H.L. Mencken, *Prejudices* (1919)

5   And this unpolished rugged verse I chose
    As fittest for discourse and nearest prose
    John Dryden, *Religio Laici* (1682)

6   Who both by precept and example, shows
    That prose is verse, and verse is merely
    Prose.
    Lord Byron, *English Bards and Scotch
    Reviewers* (1809)

7   And he, whose fustian's so sublimely bad,
    It is not poetry, but prose run mad.
    Alexander Pope, *Epistle to Dr Arbuthnot*
    (1735)

8   Prose on certain occasions can bear a great
    deal of poetry: on the other hand, poetry
    sinks and swoons under a moderate weight
    of prose.
    Walter Savage Landor, 'Archdeacon Hare
    and Walter Landor', *Imaginary
    Conversations* (1824–9)

9   Poetry has as much to learn from prose as
    from other poetry; and I think that an
    interaction between prose and verse, like the
    interaction between language and language,
    is a condition of vitality in literature.
    T.S. Eliot, *The Use of Poetry* (1933)

10 Hardly any good poet in English has written
    bad prose; and some English poets have
    been among the greatest of English prose
    writers.
    T.S. Eliot, introduction (1930) to Samuel
    Johnson's *London*

11 For to write good prose is an affair of good
    manners. It is, unlike verse, a civil art . . .
    Poetry is baroque.
    Somerset Maugham, *The Summing Up*
    (1938)

12 It has been said that good prose should
    resemble the conversation of a well-bred
    man.
    Somerset Maugham, *The Summing Up*
    (1938)

13 Good prose is like a window pane.
    George Orwell, 'Why I Write', *Collected
    Essays* (1968)

14 'How are you?'
    'Not very well, I can only write prose today.'
    W.B. Yeats, remark

127 PROVERB

1   A proverb is much matter decocted into few
    words.
    Thomas Fuller, *The History of the Worthies
    of England* (1662)

2   Proverbs may be called the literature of the
    illiterate.
    Frederick S. Cozzens, *The Sayings of Dr
    Bushwhacker* (1867)

3   The proverb is something musty.
    William Shakespeare, *Hamlet*

4   Don't quote your proverb until you bring
    your ship into port.
    Gaelic proverb

5   Solomon made a book of proverbs, but a
    book of proverbs never made a Solomon.
    Anonymous

6   Proverbs are always platitudes until you
    have personally experienced the truth of
    them.
    Aldous Huxley, *Jesting Pilate* (1926)

7   Patch grief with proverbs.
    William Shakespeare, *Much Ado about
    Nothing*

128 PUBLISHING

1   Some said, John, print it; others said, not
    so;
    Some said, It might do good; others said,
    No.
    John Bunyan, author's apology for his
    book, *The Pilgrim's Progress* (1678)

2   He that publishes a book runs a very great
    hazard, since nothing can be more
    impossible than to compose one that may
    secure the approbation of every reader.
    Miguel de Cervantes, *Don Quixote* (1605)

3   A person who publishes a book wilfully
    appears before the public with his pants
    down.
    Edna St Vincent Millay, *Letters* (1952)

4 Publishing a volume of poetry is like
   dropping a rose petal down the Grand
   Canyon and waiting for the echo.
   Don Marquis, *Sun Dial Time* (1936)

5 The most important difference between
   poetry and any other department of
   publishing is, that whereas with most
   categories of books you are aiming to make
   as much money as possible, with poetry you
   are aiming to lose as little as possible.
   T.S. Eliot, in speech to the Society of Young
   Publishers (1952)

6 Gentlemen, I agree with you that Napoleon
   is a tyrant, a monster, the sworn foe of our
   nation. But, gentlemen — he once shot a
   publisher.
   Thomas Campbell, in proposing a toast to
   Napoleon

7 Now Barabbas was a publisher.
   Thomas Campbell, attr.

8 As repressed sadists are said to become
   policemen or butchers so those with an
   irrational fear of life become publishers.
   Cyril Connolly, *Enemies of Promise*
   (1938)

9 Take an idiot man from a lunatic asylum
   and marry him to an idiot woman, and the
   fourth generation of this connection should
   be a good publisher from the American
   point of view.
   Mark Twain, related in F.N. Doubleday,
   Memoirs of a Publisher (1972)

10 The more enormous one's output the more
   the publishers get to regard you as a reliable
   milch cow.
   Hilaire Belloc, in letter to Maurice Baring

11 Publishing is a literary mafia.
   Peter Owen, 'Book Lines and Sinkers' in
   The Guardian (13 April 1987)

12 A copy of verses kept in the cabinet, and
   only shown to a few friends, is like a virgin
   much sought after and admired; but when
   printed and published, is like a common
   whore, whom anybody may purchase for
   half-a-crown.
   Jonathan Swift, *Thoughts on Various
   Subjects* (1711)

13 Publishers are neither rogues nor
   philanthropists.
   Stanley Unwin, *The Truth about Publishing*
   (1926)

14 Publishers don't nurse you; they buy and sell
   you.
   P.D. James, quoted in *The London Standard*
   (16 Oct. 1986)

15 The key decision a publisher makes is
   whether or not to publish. If they offload
   that decision onto booksellers, or allow
   booksellers to assume it, their raison d'être
   disappears. Authors and agents might just
   as well send their manuscripts direct to the
   bookselling cabal, and they would then farm
   out the chosen 20% to selected
   manufacturers.
   Michael Pountney, in *Publishing News* (26
   Sept. 1986)

16 Publishing can take you round the world
   and I made it pay for my travels. It's given
   me all I ever wanted from life.
   George Rainbird, quoted in *The Observer*
   (19 May 1985)

17 Those who start with a lot of money and
   think they're God's gift to publishing are the
   ones who go broke.
   George Rainbird, quoted in *The Observer*
   (19 May 1985)

18 He'd rather be seen as a hick publisher and
   run a successful company, than be a
   glamorous trade publisher making a loss.
   David Blunt, of Nigel Farrow, in *Publishing
   News* (31 Jan. 1986)

19 The worst sin of publishers, to my mind . . .
   is their suicidal wish not to sell the books
   they publish.
   Brenda Maddox, in *The Sunday Telegraph*
   (19 Oct. 1986)

20 Publishing is a very mysterious business. It is
   hard to predict what kind of sale or
   reception a book will have, and advertising
   seems to do very little good.
   Thomas Wolfe, in a letter to his mother

21 The good editor or publisher is . . . part
   chameleon, part humming-bird, tasting
   every literary flower, and part warrior ant.
   Cass Canfield, in *Esquire* (1969)

22 Great editors do not discover nor produce
   great authors; great authors create and
   produce great publishers.
   John Farrar, *What Happens in Book
   Publishing* (1957)

23 No publisher should ever express an opinion
   of the value of what he publishes. That is a

matter entirely for the literary critic to decide.
Oscar Wilde, letter in *St James's Gazette* (28 June 1890)

24 Publishers are like farmers. They love saying how bad things are.
Anonymous publisher, quoted in *The Sunday Times* (5 Oct. 1986)

25 Things are so bad that publishers are being honest to each other about how bad things are.
Simon Master, in *The Times* (10 July 1986)

26 Publishers are very un-Kiplingesque about keeping their heads.
Tim Waterstone, in *The Times* (10 July 1986)

27 Publishing pays . . . if you don't charge for your time.
Jonathan Cape, quoted in Michael Turner and Michael Geare, *Gluttony, Pride and Lust* (1984)

28 We really ought to be subsidised by the NHS. We're much more effective than valium.
John Boon, on the books of Mills and Boon in *The Daily Telegraph* (3 Nov. 1986)

29 The publisher is a being slow to move, slow to take in changed conditions, always two generations, at least, behind his authors.
Richard le Gallienne, *Prose Fancies* (1894)

30 When you start, the world of publishing seems like a great cathedral citadel of talent, resisting attempts to let you inside. It isn't like that at all. It may be more difficult now, and take longer than when I started to write, but there's a great, empty warehouse out there looking for simple talent.
Alan Garner in *The Guardian* (17 June 1987)

31 Everything worthwhile gets reissued about every five years.
Anonymous, editorial in *The Daily Telegraph* (13 April 1969)

32 Publishers are usually not very intelligent, or they might be intelligent, but it's usually hard to tell. Publishers don't publish a lot of fine books they should publish.
Leroi Jones, 'Black Writing', *Home* (1966)

33 Publishers are much abused people. It is doubtful whether, in proportion to their numbers, any class in the community comes

in for quite so much criticism, or has so much publicity given to its every shortcoming.
Stanley Unwin, *The Truth about Publishing* (1926)

34 In order to guarantee to all workers real freedom of opinion, the Russian Socialist Federated Soviet Republic abolishes the dependence of the press on capitalism and places at the disposal of the working class and the peasantry all the technical and material means for the publication of newspapers, pamphlets, books, and all other productions of the press, and guarantees free circulation for them throughout the country.
Constitution of the USSR (31 January 1924)

35 Direct state intervention in the shape of a state publishing house with regional branches may become a necessity.
Labour Party, *The Arts: A Discussion Document* (1975)

36 All great publishing houses are participatory dictatorships — it's leadership that's important, not committees.
David Godine, in *Publishers Weekly* (1 Aug. 1986)

37 Publish and be damned.
Duke of Wellington, when Harriette Wilson, his ex-mistress, threatened to recount their affair in *Memoirs of Herself and Others* (1825)

38 My motto is publish and be sued.
Richard Ingrams, editor of *Private Eye*, on BBC Radio (4 May 1977)

129 PUNCTUATION

1 Many writers profess great exactness in punctuation, who never yet made a point.
George Dennison Prentice, *Prenticeana* (1860)

2 Do not be afraid of the semicolon; it can be most useful.
Ernest Gowers, *The Complete Plain Words* (1954)

3 To one who has enjoyed the full life of any scene, of any hour, what thoughts can be

recorded about it seem like the commas and semicolons in the paragraph — mere stops.
Margaret Fuller, *Summer on the Lakes* (1844)

4 If you take hyphens seriously you will surely go mad.
Anonymous, style book of Oxford University Press, New York

5 The use of commas cannot be learned by rule.
Ernest Gowers, *The Complete Plain Words* (1954)

6 Cut out all those exclamation marks. An exclamation mark is like laughing at your own joke.
F. Scott Fitzgerald, quoted in Sheila Graham and Gerold Frank, *Beloved Infidel* (1959)

130 QUOTATION

1 It is a good thing for an uneducated man to read books of quotations.
Winston Churchill, *My Early Life* (1930)

2 It needs no dictionaries of quotations to remind me that the eyes are the windows of the soul.
Max Beerbohm, *Zuleika Dobson* (1911)

3 Quotation brings to many people one of the intensest joys of living.
Bernard Darwin, introduction to *The Oxford Dictionary of Quotations* (2nd edn, 1941)

4 To be amused by what you read — that is the great spring of happy quotations.
C.E. Montague, *A Writer's Notes on His Trade* (1936)

5 One has to secrete a jelly in which to slip quotations down people's throats and one always secretes too much jelly.
Virginia Woolf, *Leave the Letters Till We Are Dead* (1981)

6 A book that furnishes no quotations is, me judice, no book — it is a plaything.
Thomas Love Peacock, *Crotchet Castle* (1831)

7 By necessity, by proclivity — and by delight, we all quote.
Ralph Waldo Emerson, 'Quotation and Originality', *Letters and Social Aims* (1876)

8 Next to the originator of a good sentence is the first quoter of it.
Ralph Waldo Emerson, 'Quotation and Originality', *Letters and Social Aims* (1876)

9 Classical quotation is the parole of literary men all over the world.
Samuel Johnson, quoted in James Boswell, *Life of Samuel Johnson* (1791)

10 In England only uneducated people show off their knowledge; nobody quotes Latin or Greek authors in the course of conversation, unless he has never read them.
George Mikes, *How to be an Alien* (1946)

11 Don't make classical quotations — that's digging up your grandmother in front of your mistress.
Leon-Paul Fargue, *Sous la Lampe* (1929)

12 In the dying world I come from, quotation is a national vice. It used to be the classics, now it's lyric verse.
Evelyn Waugh, *The Loved One* (1948)

13 Every quotation contributes something to the stability or enlargement of the language.
Samuel Johnson, in preface to his *Dictionary of the English Language* (1755)

14 To be occasionally quoted is the only fame I care for.
Alexander Smith, 'Men of Letters', *Dreamthorp* (1863)

15 Nothing gives an author so much pleasure as to find his works respectfully quoted by other learned authors.
Benjamin Franklin, *Poor Richard's Almanac* (1738)

16 Ah, yes! I wrote the 'Purple Cow' —
    I'm sorry, now, I wrote it!
But I can tell you anyhow,
    I'll kill you if you quote it!
Frank Gelett Burgess, 'The Purple Cow', *Burgess Nonsense Book* (1914)

17 It would be nice if sometimes the kind things I say were considered worthy of quotation. It isn't difficult, you know, to be witty or amusing when one has something to say that is destructive, but damned hard to be clever and quotable when you are singing someone's praises.
Noël Coward, quoted by William Marchant, *The Pleasure of His Company* (1981)

18 Famous remarks are seldom quoted
correctly.
Simeon Strunksy, *No Mean City* (1945)

19 In quoting of books, quote such authors as
are usually read; others you may read for
your own satisfaction, but not name them.
John Selden, *Table Talk* (1689)

20 Writers love quotations. They love quoting
someone else's work almost as much as they
enjoy quoting their own.
James Charlton, *The Writer's Quotation
Book* (1980)

21 I often quote myself. It adds spice to my
conversation.
George Bernard Shaw, quoted in *Reader's
Digest* (June 1943)

22 A widely read man never quotes accurately
. . . Misquotation is the pride and privilege
of the learned.
Hesketh Pearson, *Common Misquotations*
(1937)

23 It is gentlemanly to get one's quotations
very slightly wrong. In that way one unprigs
oneself and allows the company to correct
one.
Lord Ribblesdale, reported in Lady Diana
Cooper, *The Light of Common Day* (1959)

24 Everything I've ever said will be credited to
Dorothy Parker.
George S. Kaufman, quoted on BBC Radio
4, *Quote Unquote* (28 June 1979)

25 Some for renown, on scraps of learning
                              dote,
And think they grow immortal as they
                              quote.
Edward Young, *The Universal Passion*
(1725–8)

26 Sometimes it seems the only
accomplishment my education ever
bestowed on me was the ability to think in
quotations.
Margaret Drabble, *A Summer Birdcage*
(1963)

27 Mr Blunden is no more able to resist a
quotation than some people are to refuse a
drink.
George Orwell, of Edmund Blunden in the
Manchester Evening News (20 April 1944)

28 The quotation of two or three lines of a
stanza from Spenser's *Faerie Queen* is

probably as good an all-round silencer as
anything.
Stephen Potter, *Lifemanship* (1950)

29 Every man is a borrower and a mimic, life is
theatrical and literature a quotation.
Ralph Waldo Emerson, 'Success', *Society
and Solitude* (1870)

30 A quotation, a chance word heard in an
unexpected quarter, puts me on the trail of
the book destined to achieve some
intellectual advancement in me.
George Moore, *Confessions of a Young
Man* (1888)

31 One advantage there certainly is in
quotation, that if the authors cited be good,
there is at least so much worth reading in
the book of him who quotes them.
Samuel Johnson, quoted in James Boswell,
Life of Samuel Johnson (1791)

32 Quoting: the act of repeating erroneously
the words of another.
Ambrose Bierce, *The Devil's Dictionary*
(1911)

33 I hate quotations.
Ralph Waldo Emerson, *Journals* (May
1849)

131 READING
See also JOYS OF READING, THE NOVEL,
SOLACE OF BOOKS, USES OF BOOKS

1 Christ, a reader! You come under the
protection of the Endangered Species Act,
you know.
Dennis Potter, *The Singing Detective* (BBC
TV, 1986)

2 There is no distracting element about a
book: leave it alone and it will leave you
alone.
Falconer Madan, *The Ideal Bodleian* (1933)

3 He that I am reading seems always to have
the most force.
Michel de Montaigne, 'Apology for
Raimond de Sebonde', *Essays* (1580–8)

4 Choose an author as you choose a friend.
Wentworth Dillon, *Essay on Translated
Verse* (1684)

5 The better the book the more room for the
   reader.
   Holbrook Jackson, *Maxims of Books and
   Reading* (1934)

6 Any book which is at all important should
   be reread immediately.
   Arthur Schopenhauer, *Parerga and
   Paralipomena* (1851)

7 Books must be read as deliberately and
   reservedly as they are written.
   Henry David Thoreau, 'Reading', *Walden*
   (1854)

8 In a sense, one can never read the book that
   the author originally wrote, and one can
   never read the same book twice.
   Edmund Wilson, *The Triple Thinkers*
   (1938)

9 No good Book, or good thing of any sort,
   shows its best face at first.
   Thomas Carlyle, 'Novalis', *Foreign Review*
   (1829)

10 It takes twenty years to get a good book
   read. For each reader is struck with a new
   passage and at first only with the striking
   and superficial ones, and by this very
   attention to these the rest are slighted. But
   with time the graver and deeper thoughts
   are observed and pondered. New readers
   come from time to time, — their attention
   whetted by frequent and varied allusions to
   the book; — until at last every passage has
   found its reader and commentator.
   Ralph Waldo Emerson, *Journals* (1913)

11 If I have not read a book before, it is, to all
   intents and purposes, new to me, whether it
   was printed yesterday or three hundred
   years ago.
   William Hazlitt, 'On Reading New Books',
   The Plain Speaker (1852)

12 One always tends to overpraise a long book
   because one has got through it.
   E.M. Forster, *Aspects of the Novel* (1927)

13 If I read a book that impresses me, I have to
   take myself firmly in hand before I mix with
   other people; otherwise they would think
   my mind rather queer.
   Anne Frank, *Diary* (1952)

14 Boys read one thing, men another, old men
   yet another.
   Latin proverb

15 Who often reads will sometimes wish to
   write.
   George Crabbe, 'Edward Shore', *Tales*
   (1819)

16 If you read books, you end up wanting to
   write literature.
   Quentin Crisp, in 'A Room of my Own' in
   The Observer (16 Jan. 1986)

17 But so many books thou readest,
   But so many schemes thou breedest,
   But so many wishes feedest,
   That thy poor head almost turns.
   Matthew Arnold, 'The Second Best' (1852)

18 I read books like mad, but I am careful not
   to let anything I read influence me.
   Michael Caine, interview in *Woman's Own*

19 The time to read is any time: no apparatus,
   no appointment of time and place, is
   necessary.
   John Aiken, *Letters from a Father to his Son*
   (1796)

20 There are favorable hours for reading a
   book, as for writing it.
   Henry Wadsworth Longfellow,
   'Table-Talk', *Driftwood* (1857)

21 What refuge is there for the victim who is
   oppressed with the feeling that there are a
   thousand new books he ought to read, while
   life is only long enough for him to attempt
   to read a hundred?
   Oliver Wendell Holmes, *Over the Teacups*
   (1891)

22 Read the best books first, or you may not
   have a chance to read them at all.
   Henry David Thoreau, *A Week on the
   Concord and Merrimack Rivers* (1849)

23   He is a worthy gentleman,
   Exceedingly well read, and profited
   In strange concealments.
   William Shakespeare, *Henry IV Part I*

24 Our high respect for a well-read man is
   praise enough of literature. If we encounter
   a man of rare intellect, we should ask him
   what books he reads.
   Ralph Waldo Emerson, 'Quotations and
   Originality', *Letters and Social Aims* (1875)

25 Read much, but not too many books.
   Benjamin Franklin, *Poor Richard's Almanac*
   (1738)

26   Who reads
Incessantly, and to his reading brings not
A spirit and judgment equal or superior,
(And what he brings what need he
          elsewhere seek?)
Uncertain and unsettled still remains,
Deep versed in books and shallow in himself
Crude or intoxicate, collecting toys
And trifles for choice matters, worth a
          sponge,
As children gathering pebbles on the shore.
John Milton, *Paradise Regained* (1671)

27 To read well, that is, to read true books in a
true spirit, is a noble exercise.
Henry David Thoreau, 'Reading', *Walden*
(1854)

28 I have confessed to you my utter inability to
remember in any comprehensive way what I
read. I can vehemently applaud, or
perversely stickle, at *parts*; but I cannot
grasp at a whole.
Charles Lamb, in a letter to William Godwin
(1803)

29 Serious reading is almost a lost art. Reading
under pressure is killing it. It is essential to
restore the activities of reflection, of
questioning, of appreciation to the reading
process. This takes time . . .
Joseph Tussman, *Experiment at Berkeley*
(1969)

30 Learn to read slow: all other graces
Will follow in their proper places.
William Walker, 'The Art of Reading'

31 Where do I find all the time for not reading
so many books?
Karl Kraus, *Aphorisms and More Aphorisms*
(1909)

32 As a general rule . . . those who lead the
busiest lives find the most time to read,
whereas those who read the least also have
little else except trifling things to occupy
their minds and energies.
Burton Rascoe, *The Joys of Reading* (1937)

33 I would sooner read a time-table or a
catalogue than nothing at all. They are
much more entertaining than half the novels
that are written.
Somerset Maugham, *The Summing Up* (1938)

34 Sometimes I read a book with pleasure, and
detest the author.
Jonathan Swift, *Thoughts on Various
Subjects* (1711)

35 I suggest that the only books that influence
us are those for which we are ready, and
which have gone a little farther down our
particular path than we have yet got
ourselves.
E.M. Forster, 'A Book That Influenced Me',
Two Cheers for Democracy (1951)

36 As you grow ready for it, somewhere or
other you will find what is needful for you in
a book.
George MacDonald, *The Marquis of Lossie*
(1877)

37 The value of a book in the changing world is
in its ability to hold things still long enough
for them to be understood, until fear and
confusion can be replaced by something less
paralyzing.
Frank G. Jennings, *This is Reading* (1964)

38 The more temptingly a writer lures the more
swiftly one should flee him — except,
always, for the poets, for the pure artists of
poetry or prose. Every writer, who has other
ends than to paint pictures and tell stories, is
plotting against the freedom of every reader:
the thing is to take from him not what he
wants to force on you, but what you
yourself need: if you don't cheat him he
cheats you.
Stephen McKenna, *Journal and Letters*
(1936)

39 No book, any more than helpful word, can
do anything decisive if the person concerned
is not already prepared through quite
invisible influences for a deeper receptivity
and absorption, if his hour of
self-communion has not come anyway.
Rainer Maria Rilke, in letter to Ilse
Blumenthal-Weiss (28 Dec. 1921)

40 I rejoice to concur with the common reader;
for by the common sense of readers,
uncorrupted with literary prejudices, after
all the refinements of subtility and the
dogmatism of learning, must be finally
decided all claim to poetical honours.
Samuel Johnson, 'Life of Gray', *Lives of the
English Poets* (1790)

41 The book-worm wraps himself up in his web
of verbal generalities, and sees only the
glimmering shadows of things reflected
from the minds of others.
William Hazlitt, *The Ignorance of the
Learned* (1821)

42 The more our acquaintance with good books increases, the smaller becomes the circle of people whose company is to our taste.
Ludwig Feuerbach, *Schriftsteller und Mensch* (1834)

43 Have you read any good books lately?
Peter Arno, caption to cartoon of lovers in a clinch, also used as catch-phrase by Richard Murdoch in *Much Binding in the Marsh* (BBC Radio, 1950s)

132 REALITY

1 Words, as is well known, are the great foes of reality.
Joseph Conrad, in prologue to Part 1, *Under Western Eyes* (1911)

2 Writing is everything but the reality.
Denton Welch, *The Denton Welch Journals* (25 Nov. 1945)

3 Reality is not an inspiration for literature. At its best, literature is an inspiration for reality.
Romain Gary, in *The New York Herald Tribune* (13 Jan. 1960)

4 The writer's very attempt to portray reality often leads him to a distorted view of it.
Gabriel García Márquez, in interview in *Writers at Work* (6th series, 1984)

5 Burdened with the complexity of the lives we lead, fretting over appearances, netted in with anxieties and apprehensions, half smothered in drifts of tepid thoughts and tepid feelings, we may refuse what poetry has to give; but under its influence serenity returns to the troubled mind, the world crumbles, loveliness shines like flowers after rain, and the further reality is once more charged with mystery.
Walter De La Mare, 'Dream and Imagination', *Behold This Dreamer* (1939)

6 A good poem is a contribution to reality. The world is never the same once a good poem has been added to it. A good poem helps to change the shape and significance of the universe, helps to extend everyone's knowledge of himself and the world around him.
Dylan Thomas, 'On Poetry', *Quite Early One Morning* (1960)

7 The fear of poetry is an indication that we are cut off from our own reality.
Muriel Rukeyser, *The Life of Poetry* (1949)

8 The great poet draws his creations only from out of his own reality.
Friedrich Nietzsche, *Ecce Homo* (1888)

9 Only writers know how they use the 'real' in their fictions. And no writer has yet been willing or able to explain how he does it.
Gore Vidal, in *Time* magazine (1978)

10 Good fiction is made of that which is real, and reality is difficult to come by.
Ralph Ellison, *Shadow & Act* (1964)

11 In very truth the realistic must not be true — but just so far removed from truth as to suit the erroneous idea of truth which the reader may be supposed to entertain.
Anthony Trollope, *Autobiography* (1883)

12 Chaos is the score upon which reality is written.
Henry Miller, *Tropic of Cancer* (1934)

133 RELIGION
See also GOD

1 Take up and read, take up and read.
Saint Augustine, *Confessions* (*c.* 400)

2 The Romans burnt the books of the Jews, of the Christians and of the Philosophers; the Jews burnt the books of the Christians and the Pagans; and the Christians burnt the books of the Pagans and the Jews.
Isaac D'Israeli, *Curiosities of Literature* (1791–1834)

3 After one has abandoned a belief in God, poetry is that essence which takes its place as life's redemption.
Wallace Stevens, *Opus Posthumous* (1957)

4 Poetry is a religion without hope.
Jean Cocteau, *Journal d'un inconnu* (1953)

5 The poet is the priest of the invisible.
Wallace Stevens, 'Adagia', *Opus Posthumous* (1957)

6 Popery almost destroys poetry. Englishmen who write good verse as Anglo-Catholics cease to write good verse as Roman Catholics. In our older literature there is no

good Papist poet: there is a weak rhymer
called Habington, a sort of Waller.
William Cory, in letter to Reginald,
Viscount Esher, *Ionicus* (1923)

7 Good religious poetry . . . is likely to be
most justly appreciated and most
discriminately relished by the undevout.
A.E. Housman, 'The Name and Nature of
Poetry' (1933)

8 Keith and I
Have terrific arguments
About Religion

My view is
Far too complicated
To explain in a
Poem.
E.J. Thribb, 'Lines on the Return to Britain
of Billy Graham'

REPUTATION
See FAME, POPULARITY

---

134 REVIEWS
See also CRITICISM, CRITICS

---

1 Writing reviews can be fun, but I don't think
the practice is very good for the character.
W.H. Auden, in interview in *Writers at
Work* (4th series, 1977)

2 On the whole, if an eminent reviewer feels
that he is losing his temper with an author,
he had better take the dog out for a walk; he
may be calmed by the time he comes back.
E.M. Forster, in *The Author* (Summer 1943)

3 Prolonged, indiscriminate reviewing of
books involves constantly inventing
reactions towards books about which one
has no spontaneous feelings whatever.
George Orwell, 'Confessions of a Book
Reviewer' (1946)

4 I looked out for what the metropolitan
reviewers would have to say. They seemed
to fall into two classes: those who had little
to say and those who had nothing.
Max Beerbohm, *Seven Men* (1919)

5 O, yes, I should like a good long review in
The Times.
Virginia Woolf, *Diary* (21 Oct. 1919)

6 No man can be criticised but by a greater
than he. Do not, then, read the reviews.
Ralph Waldo Emerson, *Journals* (1842)·

7 Some reviews give pain. That is regrettable,
but no author has any right to whine. He
was not obliged to be an author. He invited
publicity, and he must take the publicity
that comes along.
E.M. Forster, in *The Author* (Summer
1943)

8 One cannot review a bad book without
showing off.
W.H. Auden, 'Reading', *The Dyer's Hand*
(1962)

9 I certainly never wrote a review about a bad
book, unless it's an enormously fashionable
bad book.
John Gardner, in interview in *Writers at
Work* (6th series, 1984)

10 Reviewing dulls the palate.
Gavin Ewart, 'Diary of a Critic'

11 Reviewers are literary police officers; but
there are also police doctors. Therefore
there should be critical journals that provide
authors with sound medical and surgical
treatment, not just tracking down the illness
and gleefully exposing it. Hitherto most
cures have been barbaric.
Novalis, *Blütenstaub* (1797–8)

12 Beat him to death, the dog! He's a reviewer!
J.W. Goethe, 'Rezensent'

13 I could see by the way she sniffed that she
was about to become critical. There had
always been a strong strain of book-reviewer
blood in her.
P.G. Wodehouse, *Aunts aren't Gentlemen*
(1974)

14 Reviewers . . . actually newspaper persons
who chat about books in the press. They
have been with us from the beginning and
they will be with us at the end. They are
interested in writers, not writing. When they
like something of mine, I grow suspicious
and wonder.
Gore Vidal, in interview in *Writers at Work*
(5th series, 1981)

15 I'm pretty sure that no one, filling up a form,

ever puts down under 'Occupation' the
words *book reviewer*.
Paul Jennings, in *The Author* (Summer
1970)

16 Reviewers are forever telling authors they
can't understand them. The author might
often reply: Is that my fault?
**Julius Charles Hare and Augustus William
Hare**, *Guesses at Truth* (1827)

17 Some people don't read books at all — they
review them.
Kurt Tucholsky, *Gesammelte Werke* (1975)

18 I never read a book before reviewing it, it
prejudices a man so.
Sydney Smith, quoted in H. Pearson, *The
Smith of Smiths* (1934)

19 To review a book without having read it . . .
is not criticism. It is obtaining money under
false pretences.
Arthur Conan Doyle, quoted in *The Author*
(Jan. 1893)

20 Even reviewers read a preface.
Philip Guedalla, *The Missing Muse* (1929)

21 O you chorus of indolent reviewers,
Irresponsible, indolent reviewers.
Alfred, Lord Tennyson, 'Hendecasyllabics'

22 I regard reviews as a kind of infant's disease
to which newborn books are subject.
Georg Christoph Lichtenberg, *Notebooks*
(Jan. 1789–April 1793)

23 There are some books which cannot be
adequately reviewed for twenty or thirty
years after they come out.
John Morley, *Recollections* (1917)

24 I am sitting in the smallest room in my
house. I have your review in front of me.
Soon it will be behind me.
Max Reger, attr.

135 REVISION
See also SELF-CRITICISM

1 Often you must turn your stylus to erase, if
you hope to write something worth a second
reading.
Horace, *Satires*

2 The friends that have it I do wrong
When ever I remake a song,
Should know what issue is at stake:
It is myself that I remake.
W.B. Yeats, epigraph to *Collected Works in
Verse and Prose* (1908)

3 The Moving Finger writes; and, having writ
Moves on: nor all thy Piety nor Wit
Shall lure it back to cancel half a Line,
Nor all thy Tears wash out a Word of it.
Edward Fitzgerald, *Rubáiyát of Omar
Khayyám* (1859)

4 Whatever hath been written shall remain,
Nor be erased nor written o'er again,
The unwritten only still belongs to thee:
Take heed, and ponder well what that shall
be.
Henry Wadsworth Longfellow, 'Morituri
Salutamus'

5 Mastery in poetry consists largely in the
instinct for not ruining or smothering or
tinkering with moments of vision.
Edmund Blunden, *Leigh Hunt* (1930)

6 Blot out, correct, insert, refine,
Enlarge, diminish, interline;
Be mindful, when invention fails,
To scratch your head, and bite your nails.
Jonathan Swift, 'On Poetry: A Rhapsody'

7 If life had a second edition, how I would
correct the proofs!
John Clare, in letter to a friend

8 I cannot make a single note here, because I
am so terrifically pressed re-writing — yes,
typing out again at the rate, if possible, of
100 pages a week, this impossible eternal
book.
Virginia Woolf, *Diary* (16 Aug. 1925)

9 Thirty-seven. I once tried doing thirty-three,
but something was lacking, a certain — how
shall I say? — je ne sais quoi. On another
occasion, I tried forty-two versions, but the
final effect was too lapidary — you know
what I mean, Jack? What the hell are you
trying to extort — my trade secrets?
S.J. Perelman, on being asked how many
drafts of a story he usually made, in
interview in *Writers at Work* (2nd series,
1963)

10 My efforts to cut out 50,000 words may
sometimes result in my adding 75,000.
Thomas Wolfe, in letter to Maxwell
Perkins, his editor at Scribner's (1929)

11 I am inclined to think that as I grow older I

will come to be infatuated with the art of revision, and there may come a time when I will dread giving up a novel at all.
Joyce Carol Oates, in interview in *Writers at Work* (5th series, 1981)

12 First drafts are for learning what your novel or story is about. Revision is working with that knowledge to enlarge and enhance an idea, to re-form it . . . Revision is one of the true pleasures of writing.
Bernard Malamud, in interview in *Writers at Work* (6th series, 1984)

13 If you have one strong idea, you can't help repeating it and embroidering it. Sometimes I think that authors should write one novel and then be put in a gas chamber.
John P. Marquand, in *The New York Herald Tribune* (5 Oct. 1958)

14 Some writers 'rave' in a very precise manner. They produce a fair copy first, and then write it out in rough.
Kurt Tucholsky, *Gesammelte Werke* (1975)

15 I am not sure that there ought not to be a second version of every essay, in which the writer could say some of the things he intended to say when he sat down to write the first one.
Robert Lynd, *The Blithe Ones*

16 Every author's fairy godmother should provide him not only with a pen but also with a blue pencil.
F.L. Lucas, *Style* (1955)

17 I write I neither know how nor why, and always make worse when I try to amend.
Horace Walpole, in a letter to the Revd William Mason (11 May 1769)

18 An old tutor of a college said to one of his pupils: Read over your compositions, and wherever you meet with a passage which you think is particularly fine, strike it out.
Samuel Johnson, quoted in James Boswell, *Life of Samuel Johnson* (1791)

19 In composing, as a general rule, run your pen through every other word you have written; you have no idea what vigour it will give your style.
Sydney Smith, in Lady Holland's *Memoir* (1855)

136 RHYME

1 Rhymes are so scarce in this world of ours.
Charles Stuart Calverley, 'Lovers, and a Reflection'

2 Tell me not in joyous numbers
We can make our lives sublime
By — well, at least, not by
Dabbling much in rhyme.
Stephen Crane, 'Tell me not in joyous numbers'

3 Rhymes properly used are the good servants whose presence at the dinner-table gives the guests a sense of opulent security; never awkward or over-clever, they hand the dishes silently and professionally. You can trust them not to interrupt the conversation or allow their personal disagreements to come to the notice of the guests; but some of them are getting very old for their work.
Robert Graves, 'Rhyme', *Observations on Poetry* (1922–5)

4 With Donne, whose muse on dromedary trots,
Wreathe iron pokers into true-love knots;
Rhyme's sturdy cripple, fancy's maze and clue,
Wit's forge and fire-blast, meaning's press and screw.
Samuel Taylor Coleridge, 'On Donne's Poetry'

5 Abandoning rhyme and fixed rules in favour of other intuitive rules brings us back to fixed rules and to rhyme with renewed respect.
Jean Cocteau, *Professional Secrets* (1922)

6 The mighty master of unmeaning rhyme.
Lord Byron, of Erasmus Darwin, *English Bards and Scotch Reviewers* (1809)

7 The grand Napoleon of the realms of rhyme.
Lord Bryon, of himself, *Don Juan* (1819–24)

8 For rhyme the rudder is of verses,
With which like ships they steer their courses.
Samuel Butler, *Hudibras* (1662–80)

9   I rhyme
To see myself, to set the darkness echoing.
Seamus Heaney, 'Personal Helicon'

10 I rhyme for fun.
Robert Burns, 'Epistle to James Smith'

11 When you write in prose you say what you
mean. When you write in rhyme you say
what you must.
Oliver Wendell Holmes, *Over the Teacups*
(1891)

12 It is already sayde (and, I think, trulie sayde)
it is not ryming and versing that maketh
Poesie.
Sir Philip Sidney, *An Apologie for Poetrie*
(1595)

13 The troublesome and modern bondage of
Rhyming.
John Milton, *Paradise Lost* (1667)

14 Rhyme being no necessary adjunct or true
ornament of poem or good verse, in longer
works especially, but the invention of a
barbarous age, to set off wretched matter
and lame metre.
John Milton, preface to *Paradise Lost* (1668
edn)

15 Every good poem that I know I recalled by
its rhythm also. Rhyme is a pretty good
measure of the latitude and opulence of a
writer. If unskilled, he is at once detected by
the poverty of his chimes.
Ralph Waldo Emerson, 'Poetry and
Imagination', *Letters and Social Aims*
(1876)

137 RHYTHM

1 Rhythm is one of the principal translators
between dream and reality. Rhythm might
be described as, to the world of sound, what
light is to the world of sight.
Edith Sitwell, 'Some Notes on my Own
Poetry', in *Collected Poems* (1957)

2 Poetry, native and true poetry, is nothing
else than each poet's innermost feeling
issuing in rhythmic language.
John Keble, *Lectures on Poetry* (1912)

3 The poet presents his thoughts festively, on
the carriage of rhythm: usually because they
could not walk.
Friedrich Nietzsche, *Human, All Too
Human* (1878–80)

4 The witch-doctor hypnotizes his audience

with the monotonous rhythm of his drum;
the poet merely provides the audience with
the means to hypnotize itself.
Arthur Koestler, *The Act of Creation* (1964)

5 The rhythms of poetry rise from the
unconscious. This is not generally
understood, even by critics who write about
poetry. Before a poet writes a poem, he
hears it. He knows how the lines will move
before he knows what the words are.
Louis Simpson, *Air With Armed Men* (1972)

138 SATIRE

1 If an historian were to relate truthfully all
the crimes, weaknesses and disorders of
mankind, his readers would take his work
for satire rather than for history.
Pierre Bayle, *Dictionnaire historique et
critique* (1697)

2 One man's pointlessness is another's barbed
satire.
Franklin P. Adams, *Nods and Becks* (1944)

3   I'll publish, right or wrong:
Fools are my theme, let satire be my song.
Lord Byron, *English Bards and Scotch
Reviewers* (1809)

4 That is the grave omission of the usual
satirist, the omission of himself.
Frank Moore Colby, 'Satire and Teeth', *The
Colby Essays* (1926)

5 By rights, satire is a lonely and introspective
occupation, for nobody can describe a fool
to the life without much patient
self-inspection.
Frank Moore Colby, 'Simple Simon', *The
Colby Essays* (1926)

6 Satire is a sort of glass, wherein beholders
do generally discover everybody's face but
their own.
Jonathan Swift, preface to *The Battle of the
Books* (1704)

7 How shall we please this age? If in a song
We put above six lines, they count it long;
If we contract it to an epigram
As deep the dwarfish poetry they damn;
If we write plays, few see above an act,
And those lewd masks, or noisy fops
                         distract;
Let us write satire then, and at our ease

Vex th'ill-natured fools we cannot please.
Sir Charles Sedley, 'To Nysus'

8 Satire's my weapon, but I'm too discreet
To run amuck, and tilt at all I meet.
Alexander Pope, *Imitations of Horace*
(1733–8)

9 Satire should, like a polished razor keen,
Wound with a touch that's scarcely felt or
seen.
Lady Mary Wortley Montagu, 'To the
Imitator of the First Satire of Horace,
Book ii'

10 Satirists gain the applause of others through
fear, not through love.
William Hazlitt, *Characteristics* (1823)

11 Satire, being levelled at all, is never resented
for an offence by any.
Jonathan Swift, preface to *A Tale of a Tub*
(1704)

12 A satire which the censor is able to
understand deserves to be banned.
Karl Kraus, quoted in Werner Finck,
Finckenschläge (1976)

13 It's hard not to write satire.
Juvenal, *Satires*

139 SCIENCE

1 Full well I know 'tis difficult to chime
The laws of science with the rules of rhyme.
Solyman Brown, 'Dentologia: a Poem on
the Diseases of the Teeth, and their Proper
Remedies' (1833)

2 Books must follow sciences, and not
sciences books.
Francis Bacon, *Proposition touching
Amendment of Laws* (1605)

3 I consider poetry very subordinate to moral
and political science.
Percy Bysshe Shelley, in letter to Thomas
Love Peacock (1819)

4 Science is for those who learn; poetry for
those who know.
Joseph Roux, *Meditations of a Parish Priest*
(1886)

5 The term Science should not be given to
anything but the aggregate of the recipes
that are always successful. All the rest is
literature.
Paul Valéry, *Moralités* (1932)

6 Of all classes of writers, poets are the most
accurate in the use of ordinary words;
scientists the least, even those research
professors who are at pains to improvise a
supplementary vocabulary of extraordinary
ones.
Robert Graves, 'Scientific English',
Observations on Poetry (1922–5)

7 I don't think that literature, good literature,
has anything to fear from technology. The
very opposite. The more technology, the
more people will be interested in what the
human mind can produce *without* the help
of electronics.
Isaac Bashevis Singer, in interview in
Writers at Work (5th series, 1981)

8 Every good poem . . . is a bridge into the
unknown. Science, too, is always making
expeditions into the unknown. But this does
not mean that science can supersede poetry.
For poetry enlightens us in a different way
from science; it speaks directly to our
feelings or imagination. The findings of
poetry are no more and no less true that
science.
C. Day-Lewis, *Poetry for You* (1944)

9 A poet, like a scientist, is contributing
toward the organic development of culture:
it is just as absurd for him not to know the
work of his predecessors or of men writing
in other languages as it would be for a
biologist to be ignorant of Mendel or De
Vries.
T.S. Eliot, 'Contemporanea', in *The Egoist*
(June–July 1918)

10 When I find myself in the company of
scientists, I feel like a shabby curate who has
strayed by mistake into a drawing-room full
of dukes.
W.H. Auden, 'The Poet and the City', in
The Dyer's Hand (1962)

11 A touch of science, even bogus science, gives
an edge to the superstitious tale.
V.S. Pritchett, 'An Irish Ghost', *The Living
Novel & Later Appreciations* (1964)

140 SCIENCE FICTION

1 Don't read science fiction books. It'll look bad if you die in bed with one on the nightstand. Always read stuff that will make you look good if you die in the middle of it.
P.J. O'Rourke, *National Lampoon* (1979)

2 I love you sons of bitches. You're the only ones with guts enough to really care about the future, who really notice what machines do to us, what wars do to us, what cities do to us, what tremendous misunderstandings, mistakes, accidents, and catastrophes do to us. You're the only ones zany enough to agonize over time and distances without limit, over mysteries that will never die, over the fact that we are right now determining whether the space voyage for the next billion years or so is going to be Heaven or Hell.
Kurt Vonnegut, *God Bless You, Mr Rosewater* (1965)

3 Science-fiction is a kind of archaeology of the future.
Clifton Fadiman, *Selected Writings* (1955)

4 Science fiction, like Brazil, is where the nuts come from.
Thomas M. Disch, in *The Observer* (23 August 1987)

5 Science fiction is no more written for scientists than ghost stories are written for ghosts.
Brian W. Aldiss, in introduction to *Penguin Science Fiction* (1962)

6 Hubris clobbered by Nemesis.
Brian W. Aldiss, definition of science fiction, in introduction to *Science Fiction Art* (1975)

141 SCOTLAND AND THE SCOTS

1 O Caledonia! stern and wild,
Meet nurse for a poetic child!
Sir Walter Scott, *The Lay of the Last Minstrel* (1805)

2 Search Scotland over, from the Pentland to the Solway, and there is not a cottage-hut so poor and wretched as to be without its Bible; and hardly one that, on the same shelf, and next to it, does not treasure a Burns.
J.G. Lockhart, *Life of Burns* (1828)

3 The Scots are incapable of considering their literary geniuses purely as writers or artists. They must be either an excuse for a glass or a text for the next sermon.
George Malcolm Thomson, *Caledonia* (1927)

4 Och, I wish you hadn't come right now,
You've put me off my balance:
I was just translating my last wee poem
Into the dear auld Lallans.
Alan Jackson, 'A Scotch Poet Speaks'

5 A Scottish poet maun assume
The burden o' his people's doom,
And dee to brak' their livin' tomb.
Hugh MacDiarmid, *A Drunk Man Looks at the Thistle* (1926)

142 SELF-CRITICISM
See also REVISION

1 Our author by experience finds it true,
'Tis much more hard to please himself than
         you.
John Dryden, prologue to *Aureng-Zebe* (1675)

2 The same common sense which makes an author write good things, makes him dread they are not good enough to deserve reading.
La Bruyère, *Characters* (1688)

3 A mediocre mind thinks it writes divinely; a good mind thinks it writes reasonably.
La Bruyère, *Characters* (1688)

4 The writer who cannot sometimes throw away a thought about which another man would have written dissertations, without worrying whether or not the reader will find it, will never become a good writer.
Georg Christoph Lichtenberg, *Aphorisms* (1764–99)

5 The most essential gift for a good writer is a built-in, shock-proof, shit detector. This is the writer's radar and all great writers have it.
Ernest Hemingway, in interview in *Writers at Work* (2nd series, 1963)

6 He has written eight books. He would have done better to have planted eight trees, or begotten eight children.
Georg Christoph Lichtenburg, of himself, *Aphorisms* (1764–99)

7 My real judgement of my own work is that I have spoilt a number of jolly good ideas in my time.
G.K. Chesterton, *Autobiography* (1936)

8 The novelist must be his own most harsh critic and also his own most loving admirer — and about both he must say nothing.
Angus Wilson, in *Contemporary Novelists* (1976)

9 Autocriticism does honour to the writer, dishonour to the critic.
Eugène Ionesco, *Improvisation* (n.d.)

10 In a writer there must always be two people — the writer and the critic.
Leo Tolstoy, *Talks with Tolstoy* (ed. A.B. Goldenweizer, 1922)

11 A writer is unfair to himself when he is unable to be hard on himself.
Marianne Moore, in interview in *Writers at Work* (2nd series, 1963)

---

143 SELLING BOOKS

1 Blest be the hour wherein I bought this book;
His studies happy that composed the book,
And the man fortunate that sold the book.
Ben Jonson, *Every Man in his Humour* (1598)

2 People seldom read a book which is given to them. The way to spread a work is to sell it at a low price.
Samuel Johnson, quoted in James Boswell, *Life of Samuel Johnson* (1791)

3 The books that are sold most are the books one reads the least.
Edmond and Jules de Goncourt, *Journal* (1851)

4 The literary market is very bad. Shilling romances, and other books as cheap, and all good, for they are translations, many of them, from the best French writers, have quite knocked up the good old profession, which, established on a discreet foundation of puffing, permitted a fair profit to publisher and scribe.
Benjamin Disraeli, in letter to his sister (16 April 1857)

5 The truth is missed by people who say that good writing has no market. That is not the point. Good writing sometimes has a market, and very bad writing sometimes has a market. Useful writing sometimes has a market, and writing of no use whatsoever, even as recreation, sometimes has a market. Writing the most ridiculous errors and false judgements sometimes has a market. The point is that the market has nothing to do with the qualities attached to writing. It never had and it never will.
Hilaire Belloc, *The Cruise of the Nona* (1925)

6 There is no shortage of wonderful writers. What we lack is a dependable mass of readers . . . I propose that every person out of work be required to submit a book report before he or she gets his or her welfare check.
Kurt Vonnegut, in interview in *Writers at Work* (6th series, 1984)

7 Books have been published for the consolation of the distressed; for the guidance of the wandering; for the relief of the destitute; for the hope of the penitent; for uplifting the burdened soul above its sorrows and fears; for the general amelioration of the condition of all mankind; for the right against wrong; for the good against bad; for the truth. This book is published for two dollars per volume.
Robert J. Burdette, preface to *The Rise and Fall of the Moustache* (1877)

8 The worst thing that ever happened to writing is that it became a business. The purpose of business is to make money, and to achieve that end it is necessary to please as many people as possible, to amuse them, to entertain them — in short, to do everything that will help increase the volume of sales.
Dagobert Runes, *Treasury of Thought* (1966)

9 Literature, with a capital L, unless preserved by Time, has always been in a bad way, but books considered as merchandise have not.
Denys Val Baker, in *The Author* (Winter 1950)

10 A boy's gotta hustle his book.
Truman Capote, quoted in *Esquire* (1971)

11 If your publisher promises you a full-page ad
in the *New York Times*, get it in writing.
Bill Adler, *Inside Publishing* (1982)

12 Write what will sell! To this Golden Rule
every minor canon must be subordinate.
Edward Copleston, *Advice to a Young
Reviewer* (1807)

13 Religion and immorality are the only things
that sell books nowadays. I am going to
start a middle course and give them crime
and blood and three murders a chapter;
such is the insanity of the age that I do not
doubt for one moment the success of the
venture.
Edgar Wallace, in letter to his wife about
The Four Just Men (1905)

14 No wonder poets sometimes have to seem
So much more business-like than business
men.
Their wares are so much harder to get rid of.
Robert Frost, 'New Hampshire'

15 Gone today, here tomorrow.
Alfred Knopf, on book returns

16 May I suggest that we bombard each other
with unsold copies of our own books?
Lascelles Abercrombie, to Ezra Pound, on
being asked to choose weapons for a duel

17 When you are published be prepared for the
shock of not finding your book in every
bookstore.
Bill Adler, *Inside Publishing* (1982)

18 For nearly twenty years I have been a
published author . . . But I have never yet
seen a book of mine offered for sale in a
shop window.
George Bernard Shaw, in *The Author* (July
1903)

19 For, having to do with books, booksellers in
due time come to resemble their wares not
only in appearance but also in conversation.
Eugene Field, *The Love Affairs of a
Bibliomaniac* (1896)

20 Yon second-hand bookseller is second to
none in the worth of the treasures which he
dispenses.
James Henry Leigh Hunt, *On the
Beneficence of Bookstalls* (1899)

21 One is led to fear that a second-hand
bookseller may belong to that unhappy class

of men who have no belief in the good of
what they get their living by, yet keep
conscience enough to be morose rather than
unctuous in their vocation.
George Eliot, *Daniel Deronda* (1876)

22 Shelley-Prometheus Unbound 4/9d, Bound
7/6d.
From a bookseller's list

23 The booksellers are generous liberal-minded
men.
Samuel Johnson, quoted in James Boswell,
Life of Samuel Johnson (1791)

24 For book-sellers are various, good and bad,
sly and frank, straight and crooked, wise,
wayward, mean, generous, greedy,
open-handed, proud, humble, quiet, noisy,
well read and ill read, as other tradesmen
are; but there is, I find, a numerous
company of the best of them.
Holbrook Jackson, *The Anatomy of
Bibliomania* (1950)

25 Booksellers are a dedicated breed, sober,
cautious and impossible to excite (their
assistants tend to be mousy and underpaid):
a few are rude and interesting.
Anthony Blond, *The Book Book* (1985)

26 Bookshops are the first and foremost of fine
sights in all the fair cities of the world, and
the surest retreats of delectable temptation.
Holbrook Jackson, *The Anatomy of
Bibliomania* (1950)

27 What we want above all things is not more
books, not more publishers, not more
education, not more literary genius, but
simply and prosaically more shops.
George Bernard Shaw, in *The Author*
(1903)

28 You must put books alongside the subject
they relate to if you want to attract a wider
audience. If someone is in a supermarket
buying food then it makes sense to sell
cookery books there too.
Terence Conran, in *The Times* (18 Sept.
1985)

29 Our bookselling is becoming all too much
like selling national brands of cars and
breakfast cereals — which is great for cars
and cereals, but terrible for books.
Mary Ann Lash, in *Publishers Weekly* (6
June 1985)

30 The contents of a successful book can sell
well repackaged on record, audio or video

cassette and as computer software.
Editorial in *The Economist* (27 April 1985)

31 If booksellers wanted to be millionaires
they'd be in another line of business.
Godfrey Smith, in *The Sunday Times* (4
May 1986)

144 SENTENCE

1 A sentence is not easy to define.
Ernest Gowers, *The Complete Plain Words*
(1954)

2 A sentence is a sound in itself on which
other sounds called words may be strung.
Robert Frost, in letter to John T. Bartlett

3 By being so long in the lowest form [at
Harrow] I gained an immense advantage
over the cleverer boys . . . I got into my
bones the essential structure of the normal
British sentence.
Winston Churchill, *My Early Life* (1930)

4 Words have weight, sound and appearance;
it is only by considering these that you can
write a sentence that is good to look at and
good to listen to.
Somerset Maugham, *The Summing Up*
(1938)

5 A sentence should read as if its author, had
he held a plough instead of a pen, could
have drawn a furrow deep and straight to
the end.
Henry David Thoreau, 'Sunday', *A Week
on the Concord and Merrimack Rivers* (1849)

6 No complete son of a bitch ever wrote a
good sentence.
Malcolm Cowley, in *Esquire* (1977)

7 One's astonishment, half tragic, half comic,
at coming across a good sentence that one
has completely forgotten having written.
Poverty and wealth!
Theodor Haecker, *Nachtbücher* (1959)

8 A perfectly healthy sentence is extremely
rare.
Henry David Thoreau, *Journal* (1906)

9 One's complete sentences are attempts, as
often as not, to complete an incomplete self
with words.
William Gass, in interview in *Writers at
Work* (5th series, 1981)

10 The maker of a sentence launches out into
the infinite and builds a road into Chaos and
old Night, and is followed by those who
hear him with something of wild, creative
delight.
Ralph Waldo Emerson, *Journals* (1834)

11 Whenever the literary German dives into a
sentence, that is the last you are going to see
of him till he emerges on the other side of
his Atlantic with his verb in his mouth.
Mark Twain, *A Connecticut Yankee in King
Arthur's Court* (1889)

12 With sixty staring me in the face, I have
developed inflammation of the sentence
structure and a definite hardening of the
paragraphs.
James Thurber, remark at age 59

145 SEX
See also PORNOGRAPHY

1 As a book-worm I have got so used to lewd
and lascivious books that I no longer notice
them. The most virtuous lady novelists write
things that would have made a bartender
blush two decades ago . . . When I began
reviewing I used to send my review copies,
after I had sweated through them, to the
YMCA. By 1920 I was sending all discarded
novels to a medical college.
H.L. Mencken, *Prejudices* (1926)

2 It is the sexless novel that should be
distinguished: the sex novel is now normal.
George Bernard Shaw, *Table-Talk* (1925)

3 Sex? No time for it. Gets in the way of the
action.
Alistair Maclean, attr.

4 We romantic writers are there to make
people feel and not think. A historical
romance is the only kind of book where
chastity really counts.
Barbara Cartland, attr.

5 We have long passed the Victorian Era when
asterisks were followed after a certain
interval by a baby.
Somerset Maugham, *The Constant Wife*
(1926)

6 Madame Bovary is the sexiest book
imaginable. The woman's virtually a

nymphomaniac but you won't find a vulgar word in the entire thing.
Noël Coward, attr.

7 'It's one of these knee-stroking novels,' said Oliver. 'What are they?' asked Treece. 'Oh you know, all pale young working-class men reading Shelley to one another and saying, "Art thou pale for weariness?" and girls who softly stroke their own knees and say, "You know, you're a very strange person."'
Malcolm Bradbury, *Eating People is Wrong* (1959)

8 I placed
my hand
upon
her thigh.

By the way
she moved
away
I could see
her devotion
to literature
was not
perfect.
Irving Layton, 'Misunderstanding'

9 Everyone should study at least enough philosophy and *belles lettres* to make his sexual experience more delectable.
Georg Christoph Lichtenberg, *The Lichtenberg Reader* (1959)

10 A lady's husband seeks compensation by reading the lessons in church with great gusto, particularly such passages as deal with fornication.
Douglas Sutherland, *The English Gentleman's Wife* (1979)

11 I have never heard of a girl being seduced by a book.
James A. Walker, Mayor of New York, quoted in J.K. Galbraith, *The Age of Uncertainty* (1977)

12 In a torn grey robe and old beret,
I sit in the cold writing poems,
Drawing nudes on the crooked margins,
Copulating with sixteen year old
Nymphomaniacs of my imagination.
Kenneth Rexroth, 'The Advantages of Learning'

13 Thinking barbed thoughts in stanza form
after shafting's right sweat. Time for a
nap.
Edward Pygge, 'What about You?', parody of a poem by Kingsley Amis

14 Depending upon shock tactics is easy, whereas writing a good play is difficult. Pubic hair is no substitute for wit.
J.B. Priestley, *Outcries and Asides* (1974)

15 I wrote the first serious novels in English. I invented adultery, which didn't exist in the English novel till I began writing.
George Moore, *Life* (1936)

16 Literature is mostly about having sex and not much about having children; life is the other way round.
David Lodge, *The British Museum is Falling Down* (1965)

17 I will endeavour to put the word sex in capital letters on the cover of every issue of the *Literary Review* under my editorship, regardless of its actual contents . . . My purpose is simply to embolden booksellers.
Auberon Waugh, quoted in *The Daily Telegraph* (9 May 1986)

18 Western man, especially the Western critic, still finds it very hard to go into print and say: 'I recommend you to go and see this because it gave me an erection.'
Kenneth Tynan, in *Playboy* (1977)

19 The truth is that the general public is indifferent to sex novels. This fuss about them is childish. The public for unwholesome fiction — ask any reputable publisher — is negligible.
Michael Joseph, in *The Daily Mail* (7 Nov. 1927)

20 *Mother*: Any road, you seem to know a lot about it.
Son: Lesbianism? Yes, well I came across it in literature.
Mother: Well, I hope it *is* in literature and not in Halifax.
Alan Bennett, *Me! I'm Afraid of Virginia Woolf* (London Weekend Television, 1978)

21 This fictional account of the day-by-day life of an English gamekeeper is still of considerable interest to outdoor-minded readers, as it contains many passages on pheasant raising, the apprehending of poachers, ways to control vermin, and other chores and duties of the professional gamekeeper. Unfortunately one is obliged to wade through many pages of extraneous material in order to discover and savour these sidelights on the management of a Midlands shooting estate, and in this reviewer's opinion this book cannot take the

place of J.R. Miller's *Practical
Gamekeeping*.
Anonymous, in review of D.H. Lawrence,
Lady Chatterley's Lover in *Field and Stream*

22 It is not good enough to spend time and ink
in describing the penultimate sensations and
physical movements of people getting into a
state of rut, we all know them too well.
John Galsworthy, of D.H. Lawrence's *Sons
and Lovers*, in a letter to Edward Garnett
(13 Apr. 1914)

23 Its avowed purpose is to excite sexual
desire, which, I should have thought, is
unnecessary in the case of the young,
inconvenient in the case of the of the middle
aged, and unseemly in the old.
Malcolm Muggeridge, *Tread Softly for you
Tread on my Jokes* (1966)

24 I think good taste is coming back. People are
fed up with what I call 'flasher fiction'. They
don't want all the ins-and-outs and the
physical minutiae.
Mandy Rice Davies, quoted in *The London
Standard* (13 Aug. 1986)

25 With sex so much harder to write about
maybe we'll have more novels about work
from now on.
David Lodge, quoted in *The Guardian* (7
March 1987)

26 It will do us no harm to retool our
imaginations. Aids is a major revolution in
how writers write . . . we're practically back
to a literature of dot dot dot. Our heroes
and heroines will have to change. The only
thing Aids is good for is fiction. Writers will
have to think differently . . . I think you'll
see a new seriousness in the novel.
Fay Weldon, quoted in *The Guardian* (7
March 1987)

SIMILE
See FIGURES OF SPEECH

SKIPPING
See BROWSING

146 SLANG

1 Slang is a poor man's poetry.
John Moore, *You English Words* (1962)

2 All slang is metaphor, and all metaphor is
poetry.
G.K. Chesterton, 'A Defence of Slang'

3 The one stream of poetry which is
continually flowing is slang.
G.K. Chesterton, *The Defendant* (1901)

4 Slang is nothing more nor less than a
wardrobe in which language, having some
bad deed to do, disguises itself. It puts on
word-masks and metaphoric rags.
Victor Hugo, *Les Misérables* (1862)

5 Slang is vigorous and apt. Probably most of
our vital words were once slang.
John Galsworthy, *Castles in Spain and
Other Screeds* (1927)

6 Slang is a language that rolls up its sleeves,
spits on its hands and goes to work.
Carl Sandburg, in *The New York Times* (13
Feb. 1959)

7 Dialect words — those terrible marks of the
beast to the truly genteel.
Thomas Hardy, *The Mayor of Casterbridge*
(1886)

8 Correct English is the slang of prigs who
write history and essays. And the strongest
slang of all is the slang of poets.
George Eliot, *Middlemarch* (1871–2)

147 SOLACE OF BOOKS
See also JOYS OF READING, USES OF BOOKS

1 Give me books, fruit, French wine and fine
weather and a little music out of doors,
played by somebody I do not know.
John Keats, in letter to Fanny Keats (29
Aug. 1819)

2 Here with a Loaf of Bread beneath the
        bough,
A Flask of Wine, a Book of Verse — and
        Thou
        Beside me singing in the Wilderness —
And Wilderness is Paradise enow.
Edward Fitzgerald, *The Rubáiyát of Omar
Khayyám* (1859)

3 A book is good company. It is full of conversation without loquacity. It comes to your longing with full instruction, but pursues you never.
Henry Ward Beecher, *Proverbs From Plymouth Pulpit* (1887)

4 Books are the most mannerly of companions, accessible at all times, in all moods, frankly declaring the author's mind, without offence.
Bronson Alcott, *Concord Days* (1872)

5 That I can read and be happy while I am reading, is a great blessing. Could I remember, as some men do, what I read, I should have been able to call myself an educated man. But that power I never possessed. Something is always left, — something dim and inaccurate, — but still something sufficient to preserve the taste for more.
Anthony Trollope, *Autobiography* (1883)

6 Good books, like good friends, are few and chosen; the more select the more enjoyable; and like these are approached with diffidence, nor sought too familiarly nor too often, having the precedence only when friends tire.
Bronson Alcott, 'Books', *Laurel Leaves* (1876)

7 The best companions are the best books.
Lord Chesterfield, in letter to Lord Huntingdon (*c.* 1760)

8 I never read any novels except my own. When I feel worried, agitated or upset, I read one and find the last pages soothe me and leave me happy. I quite understand why I am popular in hospitals.
Barbara Cartland, 'Six of the Best', quoted in Nicholas Parsons, *The Book of Literary Lists* (1985)

9 The action scenes are over at my age. I indulge, with all the art I can, my taste for reading. If I would confine it to valuable books, they are almost as rare as valuable men. I must be content with what I can find . . . I am reading an idle tale, not expecting wit or truth in it, and am very glad it is not metaphysics to puzzle my judgment, or history to mislead my opinion.
Lady Mary Wortley Montagu, in letter to her daughter the Countess of Bute (20 Sept. 1757)

10 My books are friends that never fail me.
Thomas Carlyle, in letter to his mother (1817)

11 I know every book of mine by its scent, and I have but to put my nose between the pages to be reminded of all sorts of things.
George Gissing, 'Spring', *The Private Papers of Henry Ryecroft* (1903)

12 'T has ever been the top of my desires,
The utmost height to which my wish
    aspires,
That Heav'n would bless me with a small
    estate,
Where I might find a close obscure retreat;
There, free from noise, and all ambitious
    ends,
Enjoy a few choice books, and fewer friends.
John Oldham, 'A Satire Addressed to a Friend'

13 An elegant sufficiency, content,
Retirement, rural quiet, friendship, books,
Ease and alternate labour, useful life,
Progressive virtue, and approving Heaven!
James Thomson, 'Spring', *The Seasons* (1728)

14 Books are the quietest and most constant of friends; they are the most accessible and wisest of counsellors, and the most patient of teachers.
Charles William Eliot, *The Happy Life* (1896)

15 Everywhere I have sought rest and found it not, except sitting apart in a corner with a little book.
Thomas à Kempis, attr.

16 Who is he . . . that will not be much lightened in his mind by reading of some enticing story, true or feigned?
Robert Burton, *Anatomy of Melancholy* (1621)

17 I have never known any distress that an hour's reading did not relieve.
Baron de Montesquieu, *Pensées diverses* (1899)

18 The scholar only knows how dear these silent, yet eloquent, companions of pure thoughts and innocent hours become in the season of adversity. When all that is worldly turns to dross around us, these only retain their steady value. When friends grow cold, and the converse of intimates languishes into vapid civility and common-place, these

only continue the unaltered countenance of
happier days, and cheer us with that true
friendship which never deceived hope nor
deserted sorrow.
Washington Irving, *Sketch Book* (1820)

19 Better than men and women, friend,
   That are dust, though dear in our joy and
      pain,
   Are the books their cunning hands have
      penned,
   For they depart, but the books remain;
   Through these they speak to us what was
      best
   In the loving heart and the noble mind;
   All their royal souls possessed
   Belongs forever to all mankind!
   When others fail him, the wise man looks
   To the sure companionship of books.
   Eugene Field, *The Love Affairs of a
   Bibliomaniac* (1896)

20 Books are a guide in youth, and an
   entertainment for age. They support us
   under solitude, and keep us from becoming
   a burthen to ourselves. They help us to
   forget the crossness of men and things,
   compose our cares and our passions, and lay
   our disappointments asleep. When we are
   weary of the living, we may repair to the
   dead, who have nothing of peevishness,
   pride, or design in their conversation.
   Jeremy Collier, *Essays upon Several Moral
   Subjects* (1697)

21 To gain distraction from troublesome
   thoughts, I have only to take refuge in
   books; . . . They always receive me with the
   same countenance . . . The sick man is not
   to be pitied who has his cure in his sleeve. In
   the experience and practice of this maxim,
   which is a very true one, consists all the fruit
   which I reap from books . . . It is the best
   provision I have found for this human
   voyage . . .
   Michel de Montaigne, 'On Three Kinds of
   Society', *Essays* (1580–8)

22 O books, ye monuments of mind, concrete
      wisdom of the wisest;
   Sweet solaces of daily life, proofs and results
      of immortality;
   Trees yielding all fruits, whose leaves are for
      the healing of the nations;
   Groves of knowledge, where all may eat,
      nor fear a flaming sword;
   Gentle comrades, kind advisers; friends,
      comforts, treasures,

Helps, governments, diversities of tongues;
      who can weigh your worth?
Martin Tupper, 'Of Reading', *Proverbial
Philosophy* (1838)

23 To divert at any time a troublesome fancy,
   run to thy books; they always receive thee
   with the same kindness.
   Thomas Fuller, 'Of Books', *The Holy and
   the Profane State* (1642)

24 Books are the true levellers. They give to all,
   who will faithfully use them, the society, the
   spiritual presence, of the best and greatest of
   our race. No matter how poor I am, no
   matter though the prosperous of my own
   time will not enter my obscure dwelling, if
   the Sacred Writers will enter and take up
   their abode under my roof . . . I shall not
   pine for want of intellectual companionship,
   and I may become a cultivated man, though
   excluded from what is called the best society
   in the place where I live.
   William Ellery Channing, *Self-Culture*
   (1838)

25 Books are for me a solace and a joy. We are
   told that of the making of them there is no
   end. Be it so. Let us rejoice that, whatever
   comes, books will continue to be, books that
   suit our every mood and fancy. If all is
   vanity, as 'The Preacher' says, how can we
   better employ our time than by reading
   books and writing about them?
   A. Edward Newton, *A Magnificent Farce*
   (1922)

26   The great end
   Of poesy, that it should be a friend
   To sooth the cares, and lift the thoughts of
      man.
   John Keats, 'Sleep and Poetry'

148 SOLITUDE

1 The writer's greed is appalling. He wants, or
  seems to want, everything and practically
  everybody; in another sense, and at the
  same time, he needs no one at all.
  James Baldwin, 'Alas, Poor Richard',
  Nobody Knows My Name (1961)

2 Writing is the loneliest job in the world.
  Bill Adler, *Inside Publishing* (1982)

3   A writer is essentially a man who does not
    resign himself to loneliness.
    François Mauriac, *God and Mammon* (1929)

4   The poet is both the loneliest and the least
    lonely of men.
    C.F. Ramuz, *Remarques*

5   The man of letters loves not only to be read
    but to be seen. Happy to be by himself, he
    would be happier still if people knew that he
    was happy to be by himself, working in
    solitude at night under his lamp.
    Rémy de Gourmont, *Epigrams* (1905)

6   Writing, at its best, is a lonely life.
    Organizations for writers palliate the
    writer's loneliness, but I doubt if they
    improve his writing.
    Ernest Hemingway, acceptance speech for
    the Nobel Prize (10 Dec. 1954)

7   Writing is a solitary occupation. Family,
    friends, and society are the natural enemies
    of the writer. He must be alone,
    uninterrupted, and slightly savage if he is to
    sustain and complete an undertaking.
    Lawrence Clark Powell, quoted in Jessamyn
    West, *Hide and Seek* (1973)

8   A writer and nothing else: a man alone in a
    room with the English language, trying to
    get human feelings right.
    John K. Hutchens, in *The New York Herald
    Tribune* (10 Sept. 1961)

9   Works of art are of an infinite loneliness and
    with nothing so little to be reached as with
    criticism.
    Rainer Maria Rilke, *Letters to a Young Poet*
    (1903)

10 No one in the modern world is more lonely
    than the writer with a literary conscience.
    Ellen Glasgow, *Letters of Ellen Glasgow*
    (1958)

11 Again and again he must stand back from
    the press of habit and convention. He must
    keep on recapturing solitude.
    Walter De La Mare, *Private View* (1953)

12 A poet is a nightingale, who sits in darkness
    and sings to cheer its own solitude with
    sweet sounds.
    Percy Bysshe Shelley, *A Defence of Poetry*
    (1821)

13 You may sing to yourself alone, but you
    cannot sing for yourself alone. The poet is
    the only child of solitude. He should guard

and cultivate his solitude. But, as he goes
about his business there, he must not forget
his other obligation: as he explores the
labyrinth he must not lose hold of the clue.
C. Day-Lewis, *The Poetic Image* (1947)

14 I don't think it does any harm to the artist to
    be lonely as an artist. Let's all 'get together',
    if we must, and go to the pictures. If the
    artist feels personally unimportant, it may
    be that he is. I'm selfish enough not to feel
    worried very much about the writer in his
    miserable artistic loneliness, whether it's in
    Wales or Paris or London.
    Dylan Thomas, in letter to Pennar Davies
    (1939)

15 I've always felt strongly that a writer
    shouldn't be engaged with other writers, or
    with people who make books, or even with
    people who read them. I think the farther
    you get away from the literary traffic, the
    closer you are to sources. I mean, a writer
    doesn't really *live*, he observes.
    Nelson Algren, in interview in *Writers at
    Work* (1st series, 1958)

16 What is needed is, in the end, simply this:
    solitude, great inner solitude. Going into
    yourself and meeting no one for hours on
    end — that is what you must be able to
    attain. To be alone, as you were alone in
    childhood, when the grown-ups were going
    about, involved with things which seemed
    important and great, because the great ones
    looked so busy and because you grasped
    nothing of their business.
    Rainer Maria Rilke, *Letters to a Young Poet*
    (1903)

17 Go, little book! From this my solitude
            I cast thee on the Waters, — go thy
                    ways:
    And if, as I believe, thy vein be good,
            The World will find thee after many
                    days.
    Be it with thee according to thy worth:
            Go, little Book; in faith I send thee
                    forth.
    Robert Southey, 'L'Envoy', *The Lay of the
    Laureate* (1816)

---

149 SONNET

---

1   I intended an Ode,
            And it turned to a Sonnet,

It began *à la mode*,
I intended an Ode;
But Rose crossed the road
      In her latest new bonnet;
I intended an Ode;
      And it turned to a Sonnet.
Henry Austin Dobson, 'Rose-Leaves'

2 I never wrote but one sonnet before, and
   that was not in earnest, and many years ago,
   as an excuse — and I will never write
   another. They are the most puling,
   petrifying, stupidly platonic composition.
   Lord Byron, *Journal* (18 Dec. 1813)

3 Scorn not the Sonnet: Critic, you have
               frowned,
   Mindless of its just honours; with this key
   Shakespeare unlocked his heart.
   William Wordsworth, 'Scorn not the
   Sonnet'

4 A sonnet is a moment's monument, —
   Memorial from the Soul's eternity
   To one dead deathless hour.
   Dante Gabriel Rossetti, *The House of Life*
   (1881)

5 The sonnet is a sort of poetic fugue of which
   the theme should pass and repass until it is
   resolved according to its determined form.
   Théophile Gautier, in preface to Charles
   Baudelaire's *Les Fleurs du mal* (1857)

6 The sonnet form is like the armour of
   knights of old — protection for the weak
   and an encumbrance to the strong.
   R. Williams Parry, remark as adjudicator at
   National Eisteddfod (1921)

7 A true sonnet goes eight lines and then takes
   a turn for better or worse and goes six or
   eight lines more.
   Robert Frost, remark on television (29
   March 1954)

150 SPELLING

1 English orthography satisfies all the
   requirements of respectability under the law
   of conspicuous waste. It is archaic,
   cumbrous, and ineffective; its acquisition
   consumes much time and effort; failure to
   acquire it is easy of detection. Therefore it is
   the first and readiest test of reputability in
   learning, and conformity to its ritual is
   indispensable to a blameless scholastic life.
   Thorstein Veblen, *The Theory of the Leisure
   Class* (1899)

2 My spelling is Wobbly. It's good spelling but
   it Wobbles, and letters get in the wrong
   place.
   A.A. Milne, *Winnie-the-Pooh* (1926)

3 As our alphabet now stands, the bad
   spelling, or what is called so, is generally the
   best, as conforming to the sound of the
   letters and of the words.
   Benjamin Franklin, in letter to Mrs Jane
   Mecom (4 July 1786)

4 In language there is a spice of spelling.
   Geoffrey Grigson, *The Private Art* (1982)

151 STORY

1 Sey forth thy tale, and tarry not the time.
   Geoffrey Chaucer, 'The Reve's Prologue'
   The Canterbury Tales (*c.* 1387)

2 Yes — oh dear yes — the novel tells a story.
   E.M. Forster, *Aspects of the Novel* (1927)

3 A story must be exceptional enough to
   justify its telling.
   Thomas Hardy, entry in notebook (23 Feb.
   1893)

4 There are only two or three human stories,
   and they go on repeating themselves as
   fiercely as if they had never happened
   before.
   Willa Cather, *O Pioneers!* (1913)

5 Religion, aristocracy, sex and mystery . . .
   Christ, said the Duchess, I'm pregnant.
   Whodunnit?
   Somerset Maugham, on the recipe for a
   good story, attr.

6 History tells how it was. A story — how it
   might have been.
   Alfred Andersch, *Winterspelt* (1974)

7 The first thing that you have to consider
   when writing a novel is your story, and then
   your story — and then your story!
   Ford Madox Ford, *It Was the Nightingale*
   (1934)

8 Stories, like whiskey, must be allowed to mature in the cask.
Sean O'Faolain, in *The Atlantic Monthly* (Dec. 1956)

9 With a tale forsooth he cometh unto you, with a tale which holdeth children from play, and old men from the chimney corner.
Sir Philip Sidney, *The Defence of Poesy* (1595)

10 I have often thought that a story-teller is born, as well as a poet.
Sir Richard Steele, in *The Guardian* (no. 42, 1713)

11 I think you must remember that a writer is a simple-minded person to begin with and go on that basis. He's not a great mind, he's not a great thinker, he's not a great philosopher, he's a story-teller.
Erskine Caldwell, in *The Atlantic Monthly* (July 1958)

12 I am always at a loss to know how much to believe of my own stories.
Washington Irving, 'To the Reader', *Tales of a Traveller* (1824)

13 A short story is a way of indicating the complexity of life in a few pages, producing the surprise and effect of a profound knowledge in a short time.
Bernard Malamud, in interview in *Writers at Work* (6th series, 1984)

14 You have never seen a short story in your life. The events of life have never fallen into the form of the short story or the form of a poem, or into any other form. Your own consciousness is the only form you need.
William Saroyan, 'A Cold Day', *The Daring Young Man on the Flying Trapeze* (1958)

15 We who with songs beguile your pilgrimage
And swear that Beauty lives though lilies die,
We Poets of the proud old lineage
Who sing to find your hearts, we know not why, —
What shall we tell you? Tales, marvellous tales
Of ships and stars and isles where good men rest.
James Elroy Flecker, prologue to *The Golden Journey to Samarkand* (1913)

16 Every fine story must leave in the mind of the sensitive reader an intangible residuum of pleasure, a cademe, a quality of voice that is exclusively the writer's own, individual, unique.
Willa Cather, 'Miss Jewett', *Not Under Forty* (1936)

17 A short story is always a disclosure, frequently an evocation . . . frequently a celebration of a character at bursting point.
V.S. Pritchett, in preface to *The Oxford Book of Short Stories* (1981)

18 I think a short story should be either a poem or a novel. Unless it's just an anecdote.
Philip Larkin, in interview in *The Paris Review* (1982)

19 Not that the story need be long, but it will take a long while to make it short.
Henry David Thoreau, letter (16 Nov. 1857)

20 From a mere nothing springs a mighty tale.
Propertius, *Elegies*

21 An honest tale speeds best being plainly told.
William Shakespeare, *Richard III*

22 There is much good sleep in an old story.
German proverb

23 A story has been thought to its conclusion when it has taken its worst possible turn.
Friedrich Dürrenmatt, '21 Points', *The Physicists* (1962)

24 He always hurries into the midst of the story as if they knew it already.
Horace, *Ars Poetica*

---

152 STYLE

1 Learn to write well, or not to write at all.
John Sheffield, Duke of Buckingham and Normanby, *An Essay upon Satire* (c. 1680)

2 Correct idiom is the foundation of good style.
Aristotle, *Rhetoric*

3 Those who write as they speak, although they speak very well, write badly.
Comte de Buffon, *Discours sur le style,* delivered to the French Academy (25 Aug. 1753)

4 Style has no fixed laws; it is changed by the

usage of the people, never the same for any length of time.
Seneca, *Ad Lucilium*

5 If an academy should be established for the cultivation of our style, I . . . hope the spirit of English liberty will hinder or destroy (it).
Samuel Johnson, in preface to his *Dictionary of the English Language* (1755)

6 Style! style! why, all writers will tell you that it is the very thing which can least of all be changed. A man's style is nearly as much a part of him as his physiognomy, his figure, the throbbing of his pulse.
François de Salignac Fénelon, *Dialogues sur l'éloquence* (1718)

7 Style is the physiognomy of the mind and is more unerring than that of the body. Imitating another's style is like wearing a mask.
Arthur Schopenhauer, *Parerga and Paralipomena* (1851)

8 A man's style is intrinsic and private with him like his voice or his gesture, partly a matter of inheritance, partly of cultivation. It is more than a pattern of expression. It is the pattern of the soul.
Maurice Valency, introduction to *Jean Giraudoux: Four Plays* (1958)

9 The great writer finds style as the mystic finds God, in his own soul.
Havelock Ellis, *The Dance of Life* (1923)

10 And, after all, it is style alone by which posterity will judge of a great work, for an author can have nothing truly his own but his style.
Isaac D'Israeli, 'Style', *Literary Miscellanies* (1840)

11 A really good style comes only when a man has become as good as he can be. Style is character.
Norman Mailer, in interview in *Writers at Work* (3rd series, 1967)

12 Style is the hallmark of a temperament stamped upon the material at hand.
André Maurois, *The Art of Writing* (1960)

13 Style is a magic wand, and turns everything to gold that it touches.
Logan Pearsall Smith, *Afterthoughts* (1931)

14 Style is nothing, but nothing is without its style.
Antoine de Rivarol, *Notes, pensées et maximes* (late 18th century)

15 He's always been successful in hiding his lack of brains behind a graceful writing style.
Kurt Tucholsky, on himself, *Gesammelte Werke* (1960–2)

16 When we see a natural style, we are quite surprised and delighted, for we expected to see an author and we find a man.
Blaise Pascal, *Pensées* (1670)

17 These things [subject matter] are external to the man; style is the man.
Comte de Buffon, in address given to the Académie Française (25 Aug. 1753)

18 Don't bother me with politics, the only thing that interests me is style.
Jack Kerouac, in interview in *Writers at Work* (4th series, 1977)

19 In matters of grave importance, style, not sincerity, is the vital thing.
Oscar Wilde, *The Importance of Being Earnest* (1895)

20 Style and structure are the essence of a book; great ideas are hogwash.
Vladimir Nabokov, in interview in *Writers at Work* (4th series, 1977)

21 Manner is all in all, whate'er is writ,
The substitute for genius, sense, and wit.
William Cowper, 'Table Talk' (1782)

22 If any man wish to write a clear style let him be first clear in his thoughts; and if any would write in a noble style, let him first possess a noble soul.
J.W. Goethe, quoted in Johann Peter Eckermann, *Conversations with Goethe* (14 April 1824)

23 Style is the dress of thoughts; and let them be ever so just, if your style is homely, coarse, and vulgar, they will appear to as much disadvantage.
Lord Chesterfield, in letter to his son (24 Nov. 1749)

24 My style may be worthless but my intentions are kindly.
Gildas, *De Excidio Britanniae* (*c.* 547)

25 A bad style is as bad as bad manners.
Arthur Hugh Clough, *Letters and Remains* (1865)

26 No style is good that is not fit to be spoken or read aloud with effect.
William Hazlitt, 'The Conversation of Authors'

27 Style is the dress of thought; a modest dress,
Neat, but not gaudy, will true critics please.
Revd Samuel Wesley, 'An Epistle to a
Friend concerning Poetry' (1700)

28 I might say that what amateurs call a style is
usually only the unavoidable awkwardness
in first trying to make something that has
not heretofore been made.
Ernest Hemingway, in interview in *Writers
at Work* (2nd series, 1963)

29 Often a purple patch or two is stuck on a
serious work to give it a touch of colour.
Horace, *Ars Poetica*

30 To write well one must have a natural
facility and an acquired difficulty.
Joseph Joubert, *Pensées* (1842)

31 Our admiration of fine writing will always
be in proportion to its real difficulty and its
apparent ease.
Charles Caleb Colton, *Lacon* (1825)

32 A good style should show no sign of effort.
What is written should seem a happy
accident.
Somerset Maugham, *The Summing Up*
(1938)

33 What is style? For many people, a very
complicated way of saying very simple
things. According to us, a very simple way
of saying very complicated things.
Jean Cocteau, *Le Rappel à l'ordre* (1926)

34 Master alike in speech and song
        Of fame's great antiseptic — Style,
You with the classic few belong
        Who tempered wisdom with a smile.
James Russell Lowell, 'To Oliver Wendell
Holmes on his 75th Birthday'

35 People think that I can teach them style.
What stuff it all is! Have something to say,
and say it as clearly as you can. That is the
only secret of style.
Matthew Arnold, quoted in G.W.E. Russell,
Collections and Recollections (1898)

36 An author arrives at a good style when his
language performs what is required of it
without shyness.
Cyril Connolly, *Enemies of Promise* (1938)

37 The whole secret of a living style and the
difference between it and a dead style, lies in
not having too much style — being in fact a
little careless, or rather seeming to be here
and there . . . Otherwise your style is like

worn half-pence — all the fresh images
rounded off by rubbing, and no crispness at
all.
Thomas Hardy, in entry in notebook
(March 1875)

38 Write with your spade, and garden with
your pen.
Roy Campbell, *The Georgiad* (1931)

39 A style resembling either early architecture
or utter dilapidation, so loose and rough it
seemed; a wind-in-the-orchard style, that
tumbled down here and there an appreciable
fruit with uncouth bluster; sentences
without commencements running to abrupt
endings and smoke, like waves against a
sea-wall, learned dictionary words giving a
hand to street-slang, and accents falling on
them haphazard, like slant rays from driving
clouds; all the pages in a breeze, the whole
book producing a kind of electrical agitation
in the mind and the joints.
George Meredith, on Carlyle's style,
Beauchamp's Career (1876)

40 Whoever wishes to attain an English style,
familiar but not coarse, and elegant but not
ostentatious, must give his days and nights
to the volumes of Addison.
Samuel Johnson, *Lives of the English Poets*
(1779–81)

41 The grand style arises in poetry when a
noble nature, poetically gifted, treats with
simplicity or with severity a serious subject.
Matthew Arnold, 'The Study of Poetry',
Essays in Criticism (2nd series, 1888)

42 He could not think up to the height of his
own towering style.
G.K. Chesterton, of Tennyson, *The
Victorian Age in Literature* (1913)

43 I am well aware that an addiction to silk
underwear does not necessarily imply that
one's feet are dirty. None the less, style, like
sheer silk, too often hides eczema.
Albert Camus, *The Fall* (1956)

44 Elegance in prose composition is mainly
this: A just admission of topics and of
words; neither too many nor too few of
either; enough of sweetness in the sound to
induce us to enter and sit still; enough of
illustration and reflection to change the
posture of our minds when they would tire;

and enough of sound matter in the complex to repay us for our attendance.
Walter Savage Landor, 'Chesterfield and Chatham', *Imaginary Conversations* (1824–9)

45 I am grateful for the gift of the little book (*The Spirit of Place*). I knew the contents, and I read them again with the first freshness, the delight in the delicacy of the touch that can be so firm. It is the style of a queenly lady walking without her robes.
George Meredith, in a letter to Alice Meynell (20 Jan. 1899)

46 The Mandarin style . . . is beloved by literary pundits, by those who would make the written word as unlike as possible to the spoken one. It is the title of those writers whose tendency is to make their language convey more than they mean or more than they feel.
Cyril Connolly, *Enemies of Promise* (1938)

47 The inflated style is itself a kind of euphemism. A mass of Latin words falls upon the facts like soft snow, blurring the outlines and covering up the details. The great enemy of clear language is insincerity. When there is a gap between one's real and one's declared aims, one turns as it were instinctively to long words and exhausted idioms like a cuttlefish, squirting out ink.
George Orwell, 'Politics and the English Language', *Shooting an Elephant* (1950)

48 He most honors my style who learns under it to destroy the teacher.
Walt Whitman, 'Song of Myself'

49 All progress in literary style lies in the heroic resolve to cast aside accretions and exuberances, all the conventions of a past age that were once beautiful because alive and are now false because dead.
Havelock Ellis, *The Dance of Life* (1923)

50 Effectiveness of assertion is the alpha and omega of style.
George Bernard Shaw, *Man and Superman* (1903)

51 Proper words in proper places, make the true definition of a style.
Jonathan Swift, letter to a young clergyman (9 Jan. 1720)

52 A strict and succinct style is that, where you can take away nothing without loss, and that loss be manifest.
Ben Jonson, *Explorata, Consuetudo*

53 The infallible test of a blameless style: namely, its untranslatableness in words of the same language, without injury to the meaning.
Samuel Taylor Coleridge, *Biographia Literaria* (1817)

54 Style is as much under the words as in the words.
Gustave Flaubert, in a letter to Ernest Feydeau (1860)

55 Which, of all defects, has been the one most fatal to a good style? The not knowing when to come to an end.
Sir Arthur Helps, *Companions of My Solitude* (1851)

56 Write as you will
In whatever style you like
Too much blood has run under the bridge
To go on believing
That only one road is right.

In poetry everything is permitted.

With only this condition, of course:
You have to improve on the blank page.
Nicanor Parra, 'Young Poets'

57 All styles are good, except the tiresome.
Voltaire, in preface to *L'Enfant Prodigue* (1736)

153 SUBJECT-MATTER

1 As to the pure mind all things are pure, so to the poetic mind all things are poetical.
Henry Wadsworth Longfellow, 'Twice-Told Tales', *Driftwood* (1857)

2 It is the honourable characteristic of poetry that its materials are to be found in every subject which can interest the human mind.
William Wordsworth, 'Advertisement' to *Lyrical Ballads* (1798)

3 A poem on a flea may be a very good poem, and a poem on the immortality of the soul may be a very bad poem.
Elizabeth Drew, *Discovering Poetry* (1933)

4 I can write about anything, from gee-gees to Jesus.
Horatio Bottomley, quoted in Alan Hyman, *The Rise and Fall of Horatio Bottomley* (1972)

5 No: we are not to dictate to an artist either subject or treatment, nor are we to deny to him any subject or any treatment. We are not schoolmistresses. We are not censors. All that matters is that the subject be one that awakens the artist's aesthetic passion, and that the harmony between subject and treatment be such that it casts a spell upon him, enabling him to be visited by his god, and so casts a spell upon us, enabling us to be visited by ours.
Charles Morgan, 'The Artist and the Community', *Liberties of the Mind* (1951)

6 A poet cannot choose his time or his subject-matter, any more than we can choose the parents who give birth to us. But in accepting the limitations of his time, and using them as the harness of his genius, the great poet transcends it.
C. Day-Lewis, *The Poet's Task* (1951)

7 When a poet's mind is perfectly equipped for its work, it is constantly amalgamating disparate experience; the ordinary man's experience is chaotic, irregular, fragmentary. The latter falls in love, or reads Spinoza, and these two experiences have nothing to do with each other, or with the noise of the typewriter or the smell of cooking; in the mind of the poet these experiences are always forming new wholes.
T.S. Eliot, 'The Metaphysical Poets' (1921)

8 Rightly thought of there is poetry in peaches . . . even when they are canned.
H. Granville-Barker, *The Madras House* (1910)

9 At bottom, no real object is unpoetical, if the poet knows how to use it properly.
J.W. Goethe, quoted in Johann Peter Eckermann, *Conversations with Goethe* (5 July 1827)

10 The thing to avoid, in whatever the day's version of poeticality, is being too poetical. The poetic has to be made of the unpoetic, of ordinary materials. There are no other materials.
Geoffrey Grigson, *The Private Art* (1982)

11 Seek what to write, rather than how to write it.
Seneca, *Ad Lucilium*

12 Writing comes more easily if you have something to say.
Sholem Asch, in *The New York Herald Tribune* (6 Nov. 1955)

13 Dear authors! suit your topics to your
          strength,
And ponder well your subject and its length.
Lord Byron, 'Hints from Horace'

14 'Give me a theme,' the little poet cried,
'And I will do my part.'
' 'Tis not a theme you need,' the world
          replied;
'You need a heart.'
Richard Watson Gilder, 'Wanted, a Theme'

154 SUFFERING
See also DESPAIR

1 A poet writes always of his personal life, in his finest work out of its tragedy, whatever it be, remorse, lost love, or mere loneliness; he never speaks directly as to someone at the breakfast table, there is always a phantasmagoria.
W.B. Yeats, *Essays and Introductions* (1961)

2 Grief brought to numbers cannot be so
          fierce
For, he tames it, that fetters it in verse.
John Donne, 'The Triple Fool'

3 To whom it may concern:
No one knows how a poet suffers.
These are some of my poems.
They are about suffering.
I have collected nearly 2,000
rejection slips in the last 5 years.
Please send me one of yours.
Mark Vinz, *Letters to the Poetry Editor* (1975)

4 I doubt whether funny poetry is poetry at all. Tears are at the root of the human heart, like the molten metal in the bowels of the earth.
R. Williams Parry, in *Y Brython* (3 Feb. 1921)

5 Most wretched men
Are cradled into poetry by wrong.
They learn in suffering what they teach in
          song.
Percy Bysshe Shelley, 'Julian and Maddalo' (1818–19)

6 My sorrows are not literary ones, but those of daily life.
James Russell Lowell, in letter to C.F. Briggs (21 Aug. 1845)

7 Deprivation is for me what daffodils were
   for Wordsworth.
   Philip Larkin, in interview in *The Observer*
   (1979)

8 The good writing of any age has always
   been the product of someone's neurosis, and
   we'd have a mightly dull literature if all the
   writers that came along were a bunch of
   happy chuckleheads.
   William Styron, in interview in *Writers at
   Work* (1st series, 1958)

9 Never make excuses, never let them see you
   bleed, and never get separated from your
   baggage.
   Wesley Price, 'Three Rules of Professional
   Comportment for Writers'

10 I know not, madam, that you have a right,
   upon moral principles, to make your readers
   suffer so much.
   Samuel Johnson, remark to Mrs Sheridan,
   after the publication of her novel *Memoirs
   of Miss Sydney Biddulph* (1763)

11 For the modern consciousness, the artist
   (replacing the saint) is the exemplary
   sufferer. And among artists, the writer, the
   man of words, is the person to whom we
   look to be able best to express his suffering.
   Susan Sontag, 'The Artist as Exemplary
   Sufferer', *Against Interpretation* (1961)

12 The Poet is like the prince of the clouds . . .
   His giant wings prevent him from walking.
   Charles Baudelaire, 'L'Albatros'

13 When a man can observe himself suffering
   and is able, later, to describe what he's gone
   through, it means he was born for literature.
   Edouard Bourdet, *Vient de paraître* (1927)

14 Discouraged, scorn'd, his writings vilified,
   Poorly — poor man — he liv'd; poorly —
        poor man — he died.
   Phineas Fletcher, *The Purple Island* (1633)

TALENT
See GENIUS

---

155 TALK

---

1 O! let my books be then the eloquence
   And dumb presagers of my speaking breast.
   William Shakespeare, Sonnet 23

2 Books will speak plain when counselors
   blanch.
   Francis Bacon, 'Of Counsel', *Essays* (1597)

3 The pen is the tongue of the hand — a silent
   utterer of words for the eye.
   Henry Ward Beecher, *Proverbs from
   Plymouth Pulpit* (1887)

4 Writing, when properly managed (as you
   may be sure I think mine is), is but a
   different name for conversation.
   Laurence Sterne, *Tristram Shandy*
   (1759–67)

5 What is reading but silent conversation?
   Walter Savage Landor, 'Aristoteles and
   Callisthenes', *Imaginary Conversations*
   (1853)

6 The reading of all good books is like
   conversation with the finest men of past
   centuries.
   René Descartes, *Discourse on Method*
   (1639)

7 Literature in many of its branches is no
   other than the shadow of good talk.
   Robert Louis Stevenson, 'Talk and Talkers',
   Memories and Portraits (1887)

8 Resistance to a mechanical way of living can
   be sustained better by excellent writing than
   by excellent conversation.
   Vernon Watkins, in letter to Pennar Davies
   (1939)

9 Nothing a man writes can please him as
   profoundly as something he does with his
   back, shoulders and hands. For writing is an
   artificial activity. It is a lonely and private
   substitute for conversation.
   Brooks Atkinson, 'June 13', *Once Around
   the Sun* (1951)

10 If we may be excused the antithesis, we
   should say that eloquence is heard, poetry is
   overheard.
   John Stuart Mill, *Thoughts on Poetry and its
   Varieties* (1859)

11 Let your reading aloud be good talk, and
   shun elocution and histrionics as you would
   the plague.
   Holbrook Jackson, *The Anatomy of
   Bibliomania* (1950)

12 The author must keep his mouth shut when
   his work starts to speak.
   Friedrich Nietzsche, *Human, All Too
   Human* (vol. 2, 1880)

13 A conversation among literary men is
    muddy.
    Ralph Waldo Emerson, *Journals* (1913)

14 I never desire to converse with a man who
    has written more than he has read.
    Samuel Johnson, *Johnsonian Miscellanies*
    (vol. 2, 1897)

15 They're fancy talkers about themselves,
    writers. If I had to give young writers advice,
    I would say don't listen to writers talking
    about writing or themselves.
    Lillian Hellman, in *The New York Times*
    (21 Feb. 1960)

16 I have always rather tried to escape the
    acquaintance and conversation of authors.
    An author talking of his own works, or
    censuring those of others, is to me a dose of
    ipecacuana.
    Horace Walpole, *Walpoliana* (1800)

17 An author who speaks about his own books
    is almost as bad as a mother who talks
    about her own children.
    Benjamin Disraeli, in speech at Glasgow
    (1873)

18 I just think it's bad to talk about one's
    present work, for it spoils something at the
    root of the creative act. It discharges the
    tension.
    Norman Mailer, in interview in *Writers at
    Work* (3rd series, 1967)

19 A writer's true calling is not about speaking,
    but about being 'mute', about writing.
    Jerzy Kosinski, in interview in *Writers at
    Work* (5th series, 1981)

20 I would never read a book if it were possible
    to talk for half an hour with the man who
    wrote it.
    Woodrow Wilson, in a speech to students at
    Princeton University (1910)

21 More difficult to do a thing than to talk
    about it? Not at all. That is a gross popular
    error. It is very much more difficult to talk
    about a thing than to do it. In the sphere of
    actual life that is of course obvious. Anyone
    can make history. Only a great man can
    write it.
    Oscar Wilde, 'The Critic as Artist',
    Intentions (1891)

22 I wish you would read a little poetry
    sometimes. Your ignorance cramps my
    conversation.
    Anthony Hope, *The Dolly Dialogues* (1894)

23 Remarks are not literature.
    Gertrude Stein, *The Autobiography of Alice
    B. Toklas* (1933)

156 TELEVISION AND RADIO

1 Broadcasting is in no sense to be regarded as
   a substitute for the reading of good books or
   the study of good music.
   John Reith, *Broadcast Over Britain* (1924)

2 When you are interviewed by a talk-show
   host, don't expect the host to have read your
   book.
   Bill Adler, *Inside Publishing* (1982)

3 Like gas, electricity and water, television
   provides story-telling on tap, instant fiction
   at the turn of a switch.
   Emyr Humphreys, 'Fickle Fact and Sober
   Fiction' (1986)

4 Literature has taken a back seat to the
   television, don't you think? It really has. We
   don't have a culture anymore that favors the
   creation of writers, or supports them very
   well.
   Tennessee Williams, in interview in *Writers
   at Work* (6th series, 1984)

5 For some, television is destroying if it hasn't
   already destroyed most people's reading.
   For others, it is the gateway to more and
   better reading, through the dramatisations
   of fine novels, for instance. But the vast
   majority of us have not, in this century, read
   other than the ephemeral. Would that it
   were otherwise, given the amounts spent on
   universal education. But that is the nature of
   society, not the result of television. And it
   can be argued that some of what people
   now see on television is better nourishment
   that most of the reading they are presumed
   to have discarded.
   Richard Hoggart, in *The Daily Telegraph* (1
   Nov. 1986)

6 It does not require nationwide opinion polls
   to discover that a person cannot look at
   television and at the same time read a book.
   Kenneth Baker, in *The Daily Telegraph* (8
   Nov. 1986)

7 While television has not struck the body
   blow at books which was at one time feared,
   it has secured the vast new growth market

for sheer communication in a way which books have not done.
Philip Unwin, in epilogue to Stanley Unwin, *The Truth about Publishing* (8th edn, 1976)

8 Books are on their way out, nowadays, didn't you know that? Words are on their last legs. Words, print and also thought. That's also for the high jump. The sentence, that dignified entity with subject and predicate, is shortly to be made illegal. Wherever two or three words are gathered together, you see, there is a grave danger that thought might be present. All assemblies of words will be forbidden, in favour of patterns of light, videotape, every man his own telecine.
Alan Bennett, *Getting On* (1971)

9 I started *Origin of Species* today, but it's not as good as the television series.
Sue Townsend, *The Secret Diary of Adrian Mole* (1982)

157 THEATRE

1 The stage but echoes back the public voice.
The drama's laws the drama's patrons give.
For we that live to please, must please to
        live.
Samuel Johnson, Prologue at the opening of the Drury Lane Theatre (1747)

2 Authors are actors, books are theatres.
Wallace Stevens, *Opus Posthumous* (1957)

3 A dramatist is one who from his earliest years has found that sheer gazing at the shocks and countershocks among people is quite sufficiently engrossing without having to encase it in comment.
Thornton Wilder, in interview in *Writers at Work* (1st series, 1958)

4 I see the playwright as a lay preacher peddling the ideas of his time in popular form.
August Strindberg, preface to *Miss Julie* (1888)

5 Everything influences playwrights. A playwright who isn't influenced is never of any use. He's the litmus paper of the arts.
Arthur Miller, in interview in *Writers at Work* (3rd series, 1967)

6 Great drama is the souvenir of the adventure of a master among the pieces of his own soul.
George Jean Nathan, 'Great Drama', *The World in Falseface* (1923)

7 Show me a congenital eavesdropper with the instincts of a Peeping Tom and I will show you the makings of a dramatist.
Kenneth Tynan, *Pausing on the Stairs* (1957)

8 To make sure of success as a dramatist in Berlin you'd have to be either dead, a pervert or a foreigner; the most certain way of catching on is being a dead foreign pervert.
Ludwig Fulda, quoted in Wolfgang Drews, *Theater* (1961)

9 Plays, gentlemen, are to their authors what children are to women: they cost more pain than they give pleasure.
Pierre-Augustin Caron de Beaumarchais, preface to *The Barber of Seville* (1775)

10 Writing a play is the most difficult thing a writer can do with a pen.
Kenneth Tynan, in *Time and Tide* (1964)

11 My dear Sir, I have read your play. Oh, my dear Sir. Yours faithfully.
Herbert Beerbohm Tree, to an aspiring dramatist

12 Drama — what literature does at night.
George Jean Nathan, *Testament of a Critic* (1931)

13 A play isn't a text. It's an event.
Tom Stoppard, quoted by Pendennis in *The Observer* (20 Aug. 1981)

14 What is the stage? It's a place, baby, you know, where people play at being serious, a place where they act comedies.
Luigi Pirandello, *Six Characters in Search of an Author* (1921)

15 In London, theatregoers expect to laugh; in Paris, they wait grimly for proof that they should.
Robert Dhéry, in *Look* (4 March 1958)

16 In the theatre, a hero is one who believes that all women are ladies, a villain one who believes that all ladies are women.
George Jean Nathan, in *The New York Times* (5 Nov. 1950)

17 The drama is make-believe. It does not deal with truth but with effect.
Somerset Maugham, *The Summing Up* (1938)

18 Theatre takes place in all the time wherever one is and art simply facilitates persuading one this is the case.
John Cage, '45 Minutes for a Speaker', *Silence* (1961)

19 The structure of a play is always the story of how the birds came home to roost.
Arthur Miller, 'The Shadows of the Gods: A Critical View of the American Theatre', in *Harper's Magazine* (Aug. 1958)

20 Some mystery should be left in the revelation of character in a play, just as a great deal of mystery is always left in the revelation of character in life, even in one's own character to himself.
Tennessee Williams, stage directions, *Cat on a Hot Tin Roof* (1955)

21 A talent for drama is not a talent for writing, but is an ability to articulate human relationships.
Gore Vidal, in *The New York Times* (17 June 1956)

22 A play should give you something to think about. When I see a play and understand it the first time, then I know it can't be much good.
T.S. Eliot, in *The New York Post* (22 Sept. 1963)

23 In most schools drama is taught as a suspiciously amusing branch of literature: we would gain much if it were taught as an offshoot of sociology.
Kenneth Tynan, *Tynan on Theatre* (1964)

24 Drama is a synthetic and not an analytical art. Very few novelists grasp the fact that a tone of voice and a slight change of facial expression may suggest more than pages of analysis and description.
E.A. Baughan, in *John o'London's Weekly* (8 Dec. 1928)

25 Drama is action, sir, action and not confounded philosophy.
Luigi Pirandello, *Six Characters in Search of an Author* (1921)

26 The inclination to digress is human. But the dramatist must avoid it even more strenuously than the saint must avoid sin,

for while sin may be venial, digression is mortal.
Somerset Maugham, *The Summing Up* (1938)

27 A novelist may lose his readers for a few pages; a playwright never dares lose his audience for a minute.
Terence Rattigan, in *The New York Journal-American* (29 Oct. 1956)

28 One of the best tips for writing a play is 'Never let them sit down'. Keep the characters buzzing about without a pause.
P.G. Wodehouse, *Performing Flea* (1953)

29 The unencumbered stage encourages the truth operative in everyone. The less seen, the more heard. The eye is the enemy of the ear in real drama.
Thornton Wilder, in *The New York Times* (6 Nov. 1961)

30 The reason why Absurdist plays take place in No Man's Land with only two characters is mainly financial.
Arthur Adamov, in speech at Edinburgh (13 Sept. 1962)

31 How can you write a play of which the ideas are so significant that they will make the critic of *The Times* get up in his stall and at the same time induce the shop girl in the gallery to forget the young man who is holding her hand?
Somerset Maugham, *Cakes and Ale* (1930)

32 I go to the theatre to be entertained. I don't want to see plays about rape, sodomy and drug addiction — I can get all that at home.
Cartoon caption in *The Observer* (8 July 1962)

33 The theatre, so called, can flourish on barbarism, but any drama worth speaking of can develop but in the air of civilisation.
Henry James, in letter to C.E. Wheeler (2 April 1911)

34 We live in what is, but we find a thousand ways not to face it. Great theater strengthens our faculty to face it.
Thornton Wilder, in interview in *Writers at Work* (1st series, 1958)

35 The theater, when all is said and done, is not life in miniature, but life enormously magnified, life hideously exaggerated.
H.L. Mencken, *Prejudices* (1919)

36 You need three things in the theatre — the play, the actors and the audience, and each must give something.
Kenneth Haigh, in *Theatre Arts* (July 1958)

37 Men go to the theatre to forget; women, to remember.
George Jean Nathan, 'The Theatre', in *American Mercury* (July 1926)

38 The play left a taste of lukewarm parsnip juice.
Alexander Woollcott, quoted by Howard Techmann, *Smart Alex* (1976)

---

158 THOUGHT

---

1 Let him who reads, reflect.
Ellis Wynne, *Gweledigaetheu y Bardd Cwsc* (1703)

2 Thought flies and words go on foot. Therein lies all the drama of a writer.
Julien Green, *Journal* (4 May 1943)

3 There are a thousand thoughts lying within a man that he does not know till he takes up the pen to write.
William Makepeace Thackeray, *The History of Henry Esmond* (1852)

4 A single word even may be a spark of inextinguishable thought.
Percy Bysshe Shelley, *A Defence of Poetry* (1821)

5 So before writing, learn to think.
Nicolas Boileau-Despréaux, *L'Art Poétique* (1674)

6 Books are . . . funny little portable pieces of thought.
Susan Sontag, in *Time* magazine (1978)

7 Books are sepulchres of thought.
Henry Wadsworth Longfellow, 'The Wind over the Chimney'

8 Many books require no thought from those who read them, and for a very simple reason — they made no such demand upon those who wrote them.
Charles Caleb Colton, *Lacon* (1825)

9 Few books have more than one thought: the generality indeed have not quite so many.
Julius Charles Hare and Augustus William Hare, *Guesses at Truth* (1827)

10 i never think at all when i write nobody can do two things at the same time and do them both well.
Don Marquis, 'archy on the radio', *Archy's Life of Mehitabel* (1933)

11 Experience is the child of Thought, and Thought is the child of Action. We cannot learn men from books.
Benjamin Disraeli, *Vivian Grey* (1826–7)

12 There is no less wit nor invention in applying rightly a thought one finds in a book, than in being the first author of that thought.
Pierre Bayle, *Dictionnaire historique et critique* (1702)

13 Thought itself needs words. It runs on them like a long wire. And if it loses the habit of words, little by little it becomes shapeless, sombre.
Ugo Betti, *Goat Island* (1946)

14 The immense profundity of thought contained in commonplace turns of phrase — holes burrowed by generations of ants.
Charles Baudelaire, *Fusées* (1862)

15 A moment's thinking is an hour in words.
Thomas Hood, *Hero and Leander* (1827)

16 The ablest writer is a gardener first, and then a cook. His tasks are, carefully to select and cultivate his strongest and most nutritive thoughts, and, when they are ripe, to dress them wholesomely, and so that they may have a relish.
Julius Charles Hare and Augustus William Hare, *Guesses at Truth* (1827)

17 Poetry, whose material is language, is perhaps the most human and least worldly of the arts, the one in which the end product remains closest to the thought that inspired it.
Hannah Arendt, *The Human Condition* (1958)

18 A fine thought, to become poetry, must be seasoned in the upper warm garrets of the mind for long and long, then it must be brought down and slowly carved into words, shaped with emotion, polished with love.
David Grayson, *Adventures in Contentment* (1907)

19 No man was ever yet a great poet, without
being at the same time a profound
philosopher.
Samuel Taylor Coleridge, *Biographia
Literaria* (1817)

20 A poem does not admit argumentation,
though it does admit development of
thought.
Samuel Taylor Coleridge, *Table Talk* (21
July 1832)

21 Poetry does not move us to be just or unjust,
in itself. It moves us to thoughts in whose
light justice and injustice are seen in fearful
sharpness of outline.
Jacob I. Bronowski, *The Poet's Defence*
(1939)

22 A poem is made up of thoughts, each of
which filled the whole sky of the poet in its
turn.
Ralph Waldo Emerson, *Journals* (1834)

23 Like a Poet hidden
        In the light of thought,
Singing hymns unbidden,
        Till the world is wrought
To sympathy with hopes and fears it heeded
        not.
Percy Bysshe Shelley, 'To a Skylark'

24 A poet should express the emotion of all the
ages and the thought of his own.
Thomas Hardy, *Notebooks* (1955)

25 A certain pragmatical, senseless companion
would make a visit to a philosopher. He
found him alone in his study, and fell a
wondering how he should endure to lead so
solitary a Life. The Learned Man told him:
Sir, says he, you are exceedingly mistaken,
for I was in very good company till you
came in. The moral: Good thoughts and
good books are very good company.
Sir Roger L'Estrange, *Abstemius's Fables*
(1692)

159 TIME

1 The thieves of time are greater enemies of a
writer than even plagiarists or pirates. For
they are stealing his irreplaceable and most
precious possession, his very life.
Paul Tabori, in *The Author* (Autumn 1969)

2 In the dramatis personae of the realistic
novel, time is the leading character.
Emyr Humphreys, 'Fickle Fact and Sober
Fiction' (1986)

3 The literary sensibility is geared to the
timeless, that is, to the now only as an
avenue by which all time can be reached.
John Simon, 'Should Albee Have Said "No
Thanks"?', in *The New York Times* (20 Aug.
1967)

4 Time is the only critic without ambition.
John Steinbeck, in interview in *Writers at
Work* (4th series, 1977)

5 We call books immortal: do they live?
If so, believe me, Time has made them pure;
In books, the veriest wicked rest in peace.
E.G. Bulwer-Lytton, 'The Soul of Books'

6 . . . the tree of poetry
that is eternity wearing
the green leaves of time.
R.S. Thomas, 'A Prayer'

7 Time that is intolerant
Of the brave and innocent,
And indifferent in a week
To a beautiful physique,
Worships language and forgives
Everyone by whom it lives.
W.H. Auden, 'In Memory of W.B. Yeats'

8 Endless volumes, larger, fatter,
Prove man's intellectual climb,
But in essence it's a matter
Just of having lots of time.
Editorial in *The Times Literary Supplement*
(28 Dec. 1967)

9 You have so much mental time on your
hands when you are a bureaucrat: you have
time to think and to learn how to write in
your head.
Carlos Fuentes, in interview in *Writers at
Work* (6th series, 1984)

160 TITLE

1 Suit your title to your Book; and through
        past centuries take a look.
For wherever there are quotations, titles
        abound.
Anonymous

2 Were it inquired of an ingenious writer what

page of his work had occasioned his most perplexity, he would often point to the title-page. The curiosity which we there would excite is, however, most fastidious to gratify.
Isaac D'Israeli, *Curiosities of Literature* (1791–1834)

3   You might think the least important thing about a book is its title. Surely what matters is the content. And yet one fusses over the title for hours, as if, like the figurehead of some romantic merchantman, it conferred magic properties on the ship and all who sailed in her.
Gerald Priestland, *Priestland's Progress* (1982)

4   The Ancient Mariner would not have taken so well if it had been called The Old Sailor.
Samuel Butler, 'Titles and Subjects', *Note Books* (ed. H. Festing-Jones, 1912)

5   I think I am the first writer to use 'fuck' in a title.
Kurt Vonnegut, in interview in *Writers at Work* (6th series, 1984)

161 TOOLS OF THE TRADE

1   If all the trees in all the woods were men,
And each and every blade of grass a pen;
If every leaf of every shrub and tree
Turned to a sheet of foolscap; every sea
Were changed to ink, and all the earth's
          living tribes
Had nothing else to do but act as scribes,
And for ten thousand ages, day and night,
The human race should write, and write,
          and write,
Till all the pens and paper were used up,
And the huge inkstand was an empty cup,
Still would the scribblers clustered round its
          brink
Call for more pens, more paper, and more
          ink.
Oliver Wendell Holmes, 'Cacoëthes Scribendi'

2   A book calls for pen, ink, and a writing desk; today the rule is that pen, ink, and a writing desk call for a book.
Friedrich Nietzsche, *Human, All Too Human* (vol. 2, 1880)

3   I hope this pen works. Yes, it does.
Virginia Woolf, *Diary* (30 Sept. 1918)

4   The pen is the tongue of the mind.
Miguel de Cervantes, *Don Quixote* (1605–15)

5   There is no lighter burden, nor more agreeable, than a pen.
Petrarch, *Letter to Posterity* (1367–72)

6   This pen's all I have of magic wand.
Tony Harrison, 'V'

7   Between my finger and my thumb
The squat pen rests.
I'll dig with it.
Seamus Heaney, 'Digging'

8   The pen is a formidable weapon, but a man can kill himself with it a great deal more easily than he can other people.
George Dennison Prentice, *Prenticeana* (1860)

9   Oh! nature's noblest gift — my grey goose
          quill:
Slave of my thoughts, obedient to my will.
Torn from thy parent bird to form a pen.
That mighty instrument of little men!
Lord Byron, *English Bards and Scotch Reviewers* (1809)

10 I like writing with a Peacock's Quill; because its Feathers are all Eyes.
Thomas Fuller, *Gnomologia* (1732)

11 Let there be gall enough in thy ink, though thou wrote with a goose-pen, no matter.
William Shakespeare, *Twelfth Night*

12 The fairer the paper, the fouler the blot.
Thomas Fuller, *Gnomologia* (1732)

13 Ink, n. A villainous compound of taumogallate of iron, gum-arabic and water, chiefly used to facilitate the infection of idiocy and promote intellectual crime.
Ambrose Bierce, *The Devil's Dictionary* (1911)

14 The palest ink is better than the best memory.
Chinese proverb

15 The machine has several virtues . . . One may lean back in his chair and work it. It piles an awful stack of words on one page. It don't muss things or scatter ink blots around.
Mark Twain, from his first letter written on a typewriter

16 Typewriters quotha! They are as bad as postal cards. Both of them are unclean

things I have never touched . . . I could never say what I would if I had to pick out my letters like a learned pig.
James Russell Lowell, in letter to Mrs W.K. Clifford (11 June 1889)

17 I sit at my typewriter looking serene,
Tapping like Catullus at my love and hate.
John Pook, 'Weekend at Home'

18 The typewriter separated me from a deeper intimacy with poetry, and my hand brought me closer to that intimacy again.
Pablo Neruda, in interview in *Writers at Work* (5th series, 1981)

19 On the hottest day of the year I saw two nuns buying a typewriter in Selfridges. Oh, what were they going to do with it?
Barbara Pym, *A Very Private Eye* (1984)

20 Electric typewriters are intelligent, warm, sexy and they hum soothingly, unlike wives.
Charles Wood, 'The Unkindest Cut' in *The Anti-Book List* (ed. Brian Redhead and Kenneth McLeish, 1981)

21 When IBM invented the electronic typewriter everybody thought the company was made up of idiots because nobody had complained about the typewriter as it was.
Kurt Vonnegut, in *The Economist* (9 Nov. 1985)

22 Customers are invited to punch in prosaic personal details of the loved, missed or humbly admired one to whom the greeting is bound. The muse then descends on the Apple-Macintosh 512K and, after a couple of seconds, it spits out a choice of creaking rhymes. 'We are not trying to compete with Keats or anyone like that', Robert Sharpe, the managing director of Computer Poets Ltd, explained, a shade unnecessarily, yesterday.
News item in *The Guardian* (8 July 1987)

23 Dr Louis T. Milic of the Columbia University Department of English expressed a note of caution about computers. He said that attention might be diverted to secondary work and that the nature of literature might be distorted if computers changed matters that were essentially qualitative into a quantitative form. But Professor Milic admitted that computers are improving — perhaps even to the point of writing poetry as good as that composed by a drunken poet. He cited a sentence generated by a group from the Massachusetts Institute of Technology working with a computer, and contained in a study called 'Random Generation of English Sentences'. The sentence is 'What does she put four whistles beside heated rugs for?'
News item in *The New York Times* (10 Sept. 1964)

24 The two great pressures of our day: the photocopier at home and piracy abroad.
Peter Mayer, in *The Financial Times* (10 April 1985)

---

162 TRADE
See also CRAFT

---

1 Writing is a trade . . . which is learned by writing.
Simone de Beauvoir, *La Force de l'age* (1960)

2 It's no good starting out by thinking one is a heaven-born genius — some people are, but very few. No, one is a tradesman — a tradesman in a good honest trade. You must learn the technical skills, and then, within that trade, you can apply your own creative ideas; but you must submit to the discipline of form.
Agatha Christie, *An Autobiography* (1977)

3 To make a book is as much a trade as to make a clock; something more than intelligence is required to become an author.
La Bruyère, *Characters* (1688)

4 A losing trade, I assure you, sir: literature is a drug.
George Borrow, *Lavengro* (1851)

5 Literature was formerly an art and finance a trade: today it is the reverse.
Joseph Roux, *Meditations of a Parish Priest* (1886)

6 So poetry, which is in Oxford made
An art, in London only is a trade.
John Dryden, *Prologue to the University of Oxford* (1684)

7 Literature flourishes best when it is half a trade and half an art.
W.R. Inge, 'The Victorian Age', *Outspoken Essays: Second Series* (1922)

8 The book-trade is a spiritual barometer of a
nation's well-being.
John Buchan, remark (1928)

9 Literature is a thriving trade. Moxon has
just brought me the account of my fifth
(popular) edition of *Faust*, of which he has
sold 1,500 copies. I find myself £6. 2. 7 out
of pocket.
Abraham Hayward, in letter to Sir George
Cornewall Lewis (8 Feb. 1840)

10 If nature prompts you, or if friends
               persuade,
Why, write; but ne'er pursue it as a trade.
William Whitehead, 'A Charge to the Poets'

11 To be a poet and not know the trade,
To be a lover and repel all women;
Twin ironies by which great saints are made,
The agonizing pincer-jaws of Heaven.
Patrick Kavanagh, 'Sanctity'

---

163 TRADITION

1 The poets of each generation seldom sing a
new song. They turn themes men always
have loved, and sing them in the mode of
their times.
Clarence Day, 'Humpty-Dumpty and
Adam', *The Crow's Nest* (1921)

2 In English writing we seldom speak of
tradition, though we occasionally apply its
name in deploring its absence.
T.S. Eliot, 'Tradition and the Individual
Talent', *Selected Essays* (1932)

3 It is part of the business of the critic to
preserve tradition — where a good tradition
exists. It is part of his business to see
literature steadily and to see it whole; and
this is eminently to see it not as consecrated
by time, but to see it beyond time; to see the
best work of our time and the best work of
twenty-five hundred years ago with the
same eyes.
T.S. Eliot, in introduction to *The Sacred
Wood* (1920)

---

164 TRAGEDY

1 A tragedy, then, is the imitation of an action
that is serious and also, as having
magnitude, complete in itself; in language

with pleasurable accessories, each kind
brought in separately in the parts of the
work; in a dramatic, not in a narrative form;
with incidents arousing pity and fear,
wherewith to accomplish its catharsis of
such emotion.
Aristotle, *Poetics*

2 Only a great mind overthrown yields
tragedy.
Jacques Barzun, *The House of Intellect*
(1959)

3 Tragedie is to seyn a certeyn storie,
As olde bookes maken us memorie,
Of hym that stood in greet prosperitee
And is yfallen out of heigh degree
Into myserie, and endeth wrecchedly.
Geoffrey Chaucer, 'The Monk's Tale', *The
Canterbury Tales* (*c*. 1387)

4 A tragedy means always a man's struggle
with that which is stronger than man.
G.K. Chesterton, 'The Bluff of the Big
Shops', *Outline of Sanity* (1926)

5 In tragedy great men are more truly great
than in history. We see them only in the
crises which unfold them.
Napoleon I, *Maxims* (1804–15)

6 In nature, the most violent passions are
silent; in Tragedy they must speak, and
speak with dignity too.
Lord Chesterfield, in letter to his son (23
Jan. 1752)

7 A tragic writer does not have to believe in
God, but he must believe in man.
Joseph Wood Krutch, 'The Tragic Fallacy',
The Modern Temper (1929)

8 One cannot balance tragedy in the scales
Unless one weighs it with the tragic heart.
Stephen Vincent Benét, *John Brown's Body*
(1928)

9 Tragedy is restful; and the reason is that
hope, that foul, deceitful thing, has no part
in it.
Jean Anouilh, *Antigone* (1942)

10 Farce is nearer tragedy in its essence than
comedy is.
Samuel Taylor Coleridge, *Table Talk* (1833)

11 Writers of comedy have outlook, whereas
writers of tragedy have, according to them,
insight.
James Thurber, 'The Case for Comedy',
Lanterns and Lances (1961)

12 Tragedy and comedy are simply questions of value; a little misfit in life makes us laugh; a great one is tragedy and cause for expression of grief.
Elbert Hubbard, *The Note Book* (1927)

---

165 TRANSLATION

1 Translators, traitors.
Italian proverb

2 Not a translation — only taken from the French.
Richard Brinsley Sheridan, *The Critic* (1779)

3 Translations, like wives, are seldom faithful if they are in the least attractive.
Roy Campbell, in *The Poetry Review* (June/July 1949)

4 What is most difficult to render from one language into another is the tempo of its style.
Friedrich Nietzsche, *Beyond Good and Evil* (1886)

5 It were as wise to cast a violet into a crucible that you might discover the formal principle of its colour and odour, as seek to transfuse from one language into another the creations of a poet.
Percy Bysshe Shelley, *A Defence of Poetry* (1821)

6 It is indeed impossible to translate poetry, in the sense of finding a precise equivalent to poetical language. But it is none the less possible to be inspired to write fine native verse by the inspiration of fine foreign verse.
G.K. Chesterton, *Chaucer* (1932)

7 The art of translation lies less in knowing the other language than in knowing your own.
Ned Rorem, 'Random Notes from a Diary', *Music from Inside Out* (1967)

8 Some hold translations not unlike to be
The wrong side of a Turkey tapestry.
James Howell, *Familiar Letters* (1645–55)

9 A translation is no translation unless it will give you the music of a poem along with the words of it.
J.M. Synge, *The Aran Islands* (1902)

10 Poetry is what gets lost in translation.
Robert Frost, attr.

11 Such is our pride, our folly, or our fate,
That few, but such as cannot write,
        translate.
Sir John Denham, 'To Richard Fanshaw' (1648)

12 He is Translation's thief that addeth more,
As much as he that taketh from the store
Of the first author.
Andrew Marvell, 'To . . . Dr Witty'

13 We all learned our literature through translation. More people have studied the Bible only in translation, have read Homer in translation, and all the classics.
Isaac Bashevis Singer, in interview in *Writers at Work* (5th series, 1981)

14 Poesy is of so subtle a spirit, that in pouring out of one language into another, it will all explode.
Sir John Denham, in preface to *The Destruction of Troy* (1636)

---

166 TRUTH

1 We must think things not words, or at least we must constantly translate our words into the facts for which they stand, if we are to keep the real and the true.
Oliver Wendell Holmes, address to New York State Bar Association (17 Jan. 1889)

2 Poetry is not magic. In so far as poetry, or any other of the arts, can be said to have an ulterior purpose, it is, by telling the truth, to disenchant and disintoxicate.
W.H. Auden, *The Dyer's Hand* (1963)

3 Poetry . . . has nothing to do with facts, though everything to do with truth.
Gerald Bullett, *Readings in English Literature* (1946)

4 The truest poetry is the most feigning.
William Shakespeare, *As You Like It*

5 Poetry is truth in its Sunday clothes.
Joseph Roux, *Meditations of a Parish Priest* (1886)

6 Too true, too sincere. The Muse prefers the liars, the gay and warty lads.
W.B. Yeats, on the poetry of James Reed, quoted by Robert Graves and Alan Hodge, *The Long Weekend* (1940)

7 The truth, which is a standard for the
naturalist, for the poet is only a stimulus.
George Santayana, 'Ideas', *Soliloquies in
England* (1922)

8 Wise poets that wrapt Truth in tales,
Knew her themselves through all her veils.
Thomas Carew, 'Ingrateful Beauty
Threatened'

9 Poetry should aim at practical truth.
Comte de Lautréamont, *Poésies* (1870)

10 Each poet's truth — that's the important
thing, but it is neither everybody's truth nor
the truth of another poet.
Geoffrey Grigson, *The Private Art* (1982)

11 Any fool may write a most valuable book by
chance, if he will only tell us what he heard
and saw with veracity.
Thomas Gray, in letter to Horace Walpole
(25 Feb. 1768)

12 Thank God for books! And yet thank God
that the great realm of truth lies yet outside
of books, too vast to be mastered by types or
imprisoned in libraries.
Henry Ward Beecher, *Proverbs from
Plymouth Pulpit* (1887)

13 And Truth severe, by fairy Fiction drest.
Thomas Gray, *The Bard* (1757)

14 Truth is always duller than fiction.
Piers Paul Read, in *The Observer* (1981)

15 My task which I am trying to achieve is by
the power of the written word to make you
touch, to make you feel — it is, before all, to
make you see! That — and no more; and it
is everything! If I succeed you shall find
there, according to your deserts,
encouragement, consolation, fear, charm —
all you demand and perhaps also that
glimpse of truth for which you have
forgotten to ask.
Joseph Conrad, preface to *The Nigger of the
Narcissus* (1897)

16 'Tis strange — but true; for truth is always
strange;
Stranger than fiction: if it could be told,
How much would novels gain by the
exchange.
Lord Byron, *Don Juan* (1819–24)

17 Some books are lies from end to end.
Robert Burns, 'Death and Dr Hornbook'

18 We get no good
By being ungenerous, even to a book,
And calculating profits, — so much help
By so much reading. It is rather when
We gloriously forget ourselves and plunge
Soul-forward, headlong, into a book's
profound,
Impassioned for its beauty and salt of
truth
'Tis then we get the right good from a book.
Elizabeth Barrett Browning, *Aurora Leigh*
(1857)

19 It perpetually happens that one writer tells
less truth than another, merely because he
tells more truths.
Thomas Babington Macaulay, 'History', in
The Edinburgh Review (1828)

20 Things evidently false are not only printed,
but many things of truth most falsely set
forth.
Sir Thomas Browne, 'To the Reader',
Religio Medici (1642)

21 Ideology wants to convince you that its
truth is absolute. A novel shows you that
everything is relative.
Milan Kundera, *Comedy is Everywhere*
(1969)

22 Poetry implies the whole truth, philosophy
expresses a part of it.
Henry David Thoreau, *Journal* (26 June
1852)

23 All the poet can do today is to warn.
That is why the true Poets must be truthful.
Wilfred Owen, quoted in preface to his
Collected Poems (1931)

167 UNIVERSAL AND PARTICULAR

1 The poet should seize the Particular; and he
should, if there be anything in it, thus
represent the Universal.
J.W. Goethe, quoted in Johann Peter
Eckermann, *Conversations with Goethe* (11
June 1825)

2 Poetry, I take it, is as universally contagious
as the small-pox; everyone catches it once in
their life at least, and the sooner the better;
for methinks an old rhymster makes as
ridiculous a figure as Socrates at fourscore.
Richard West, in letter to Horace Walpole
(12 Jan. 1736)

3 The poems to come are for you and me and are not for most people.
e e cummings, in introduction to *Poems 1923–1954*

4 He was a poet and hated the approximate.
Rainer Maria Rilke, *The Notebook of Malte Laurids Brigge* (1910)

---

168 URGE TO WRITE
See also ITCH TO WRITE

---

1 A man starts upon a sudden, takes Pen, Ink and Paper, and without ever having had a thought of it before, resolves within himself he will write a Book; he has no Talent at Writing, but he wants fifty Guineas.
La Bruyère, *Characters* (1688)

2 There is no measure or limit to this fever for writing; every one must be an author; some out of vanity to acquire celebrity and raise up a name, others for the sake of lucre and gain.
Martin Luther, *Table Talk* (1569)

3 Keep going. Writing is finally play, and there's no reason why you should get paid for playing. If you're a real writer, you write no matter what. No writer need feel sorry for himself if he writes and enjoys the writing, even if he doesn't get paid for it.
Irwin Shaw, advice for young writers, in interview in *Writers at Work* (5th series, 1981)

4 I write for no other purpose than to add to the beauty that now belongs to me. I write a book for no other reason than to add three or four hundred acres to my magnificent estate.
Jack London, quoted by Charles Child Walcutt, *Jack London* (1966)

5 There are three reasons for becoming a writer: the first is that you need the money; the second, that you have something to say that you think the world should know; the third is that you can't think what to do with the long evenings.
Quentin Crisp, *The Naked Civil Servant* (1968)

6 I'll call for pen and ink, and write my mind.
William Shakespeare, *Henry VI*

7 You don't write because you want to say something, you write because you've got something to say.
F. Scott Fitzgerald, 'The Note-Books', *The Crack-Up* (1945)

8 If I want to write I write — and if I don't want to, I won't.
D.H. Lawrence, in a letter to Ernest Collings (24 Dec. 1912)

Oh that my words were now written! oh that they were printed in a book!
Job 19:23

10 To write is to put one's obsessions in order.
Jean Grenier, *Albert Camus*

11 Of the contemporary scene I can say only that there are not enough peoms written according to my ideas, but then if there were I should have less incentive to write myself.
Philip Larkin, *Poets of the 1950s* (ed. D.J. Enright, 1955)

12 As for my next book, I am going to hold myself from writing till I have it impending in me: grown heavy in my mind like a ripe pear; pendant, gravid, asking to be cut or it will fall.
Virginia Woolf, *A Writer's Diary* (1953)

13 I am convinced more and more every day that fine writing is, next to fine doing, the top thing in the world.
John Keats, in letter to J.H. Reynolds (1819)

14 A writer lives, at best, in a state of astonishment. Beneath any feelings he has of the good or evil of the world lies a deeper one of wonder at it all. To transmit that feeling, he writes.
William Sansom, *Blue Skies, Brown Studies* (1961)

15 In a very real sense, the writer writes in order to teach himself, to understand himself, to satisfy himself; the publishing of his ideas, though it brings gratifications, is a curious anti-climax.
Alfred Kazin, in *Think* (Feb. 1963)

16 Even if nature says no, indignation makes me write verse.
Juvenal, *Satires*

169 USES OF BOOKS
See also JOYS OF READING, SOLACE OF
BOOKS

1 Books are not seldom talismans and spells.
William Cowper, 'The Winter Walk at
Noon', *The Task* (1785)

2 You don't learn anything when you read
him, but you become something.
J.W. Goethe, comment on J.J. Winckelmann

3 Of all the needs a book has the chief need is
that it be readable.
Anthony Trollope, *Autobiography* (1883)

4 No man can read with profit that which he
can not learn to read with pleasure.
Noah Porter, *Books and Reading* (1871)

5 Books are the best of things, well used;
abused, among the worst.
Ralph Waldo Emerson, 'Nature', *Addresses
and Lectures* (1837)

6 Books are to be called for and supplied on
the assumption that the process of reading is
not half-sleep, but in the highest sense an
exercise, a gymnastic struggle; that the
reader is doing something for himself.
Walt Whitman, *Democratic Vistas* (1871)

7 Reading is not a duty, and has consequently
no business to be made disagreeable.
Augustine Birrell, 'The Office of Literature',
Obiter Dicta (1884)

8 One reads not to retain what one has read,
but to forget what one has experienced.
Walter Benjamin, quoted from *Stultifera
Navis* (1957)

9 Reading, to most people, means an ashamed
way of killing time disguised under a
dignified name.
Ernest Dimnet, *The Art of Thinking* (1928)

10 Reading is not idleness — any more than
listening to music or looking at pictures — it
is the passive, receptive state of civilisation
without which the active and creative would
be meaningless.It is the immortal spirit of
the dead realised within the bodies of the
living.
Stephen Spender, *Journal* (1980–82)

11 Reading is to the mind, what exercise is to
the body. As by the one, health is preserved,
strengthened, and invigorated; by the other,
virtue (which is the health of the mind) is
kept alive, cherished and confirmed. But as
exercise becomes tedious and painful, when
we make use of it only as the means of
health, so reading is apt to grow uneasy and
burdensome when we apply ourselves to it
for our improvement in virtue. For this
reason, the virtue which we gather from a
fable or an allegory, is like the health we get
by hunting; as we are engaged in an
agreeable pursuit that draws us on with
pleasure, and makes us insensible of the
fatigues that accompany it.
Richard Steele, in *The Tatler* (17 March
1709)

12 The man who reads only for improvement is
beyond the hope of much improvement
before he begins.
Jonathan Daniels, *Three Presidents and
Their Books* (1956)

13 Good literature continually read for pleasure
must, let us hope, do some good to the
reader.
A.E. Housman, 'The Name and Nature of
Poetry' (1933)

14 Some read to think — these are rare; some
to write, these are common; and some read
to talk, and these form the great majority.
Charles Caleb Colton, *Lacon* (1825)

15 Reading maketh a full man, conference a
ready man, and writing an exact man.
Francis Bacon, 'Of Studies', *Essays* (1597)

16 A truly good book teaches me better than to
read it. I must soon lay it down, and
commence living on its hint . . . What I
began by reading, I must finish by acting.
Henry David Thoreau, *Journal* (1884)

17 Some books leave us free and some books
make us free.
Ralph Waldo Emerson, *Journals* (1913)

18 This books can do — nor this alone: they
        give
New views to life, and teach us how to live;
They soothe the grieved, the stubborn they
        chastise;
Fools they admonish, and confirm the wise,
Their aid they yield to all: they never shun
The man of sorrow, nor the wretch undone;
Unlike the hard, the selfish, and the proud,
They fly not from the suppliant crowd,
Nor tell to various people various things,

But show to subjects, what they show to
    Kings.
George Crabbe, *The Library* (1781)

19 Books are necessary to correct the vices of
the polite.
Oliver Goldsmith, *The Citizen of the World*
(1762)

20 Books that you may carry to the fire, and
hold readily in your hand, are the most
useful after all.
Samuel Johnson, quoted by John Hawkins,
Life of Samuel Johnson (1787)

21 To desire to have many books, and never to
use them, is like a child that will have a
candle burning by him, all the while he is
sleeping.
Henry Peacham, *The Compleat Gentleman*
(1622)

22 Books of poems lying around are handy
For killing persistent irritating flies.
Geoffrey Grigson, *History of Him* (1951)

170 VANITY

1   Master of nuance and scruple,
Pray for me and for all writers, living or
                            dead:
            Because there are many whose works
Are in better taste than their lives, because
                    there is no end
To the vanity of our calling, make
                    intercession
        For the treason of all clerks.
W.H. Auden, 'At the Grave of Henry James'

2   Good writers are often excellent at a
hundred other things, but writing promises
a greater latitude for the ego.
John Cheever, in interview in *Writers at
Work* (5th series, 1981)

3   Most people enjoy the sight of their own
handwriting as they enjoy the smell of their
own farts.
W.H. Auden, 'Writing', *The Dyer's Hand*
(1962)

4   'Tis pleasant, sure, to see one's name in
                    print;
A Book's a Book, altho' there's nothing in't.
Lord Byron, *English Bards and Scotch
Reviewers* (1809)

5   On the day when a young writer corrects his
first proof-sheet he is as proud as a
schoolboy who has just got his first dose
of the pox.
Charles Baudelaire, *Intimate Journals* (1887)

6   For several days after my first book was
published I carried it about in my pocket,
and took surreptitious peeps at it to make
sure that the ink had not faded.
J.M. Barrie, in speech at the Critics' Circle,
London (1922)

7   I am never indifferent, and never pretend to
be, to what people say or think of my books.
They are my children, and I like to have
them liked.
Henry Wadsworth Longfellow, in letter to
Richard Henry Stoddard (1878)

8   I am very foolish over my own book. I have
a copy which I constantly read and find very
illuminating. Swift confesses to something
of the sort with his own compositions.
J.B. Yeats, in a letter to his son, W.B. Yeats

9   I seldom read my own work. It seems to be a
particularly offensive form of narcissism. It's
like playing back tapes of your own
conversation.
John Cheever, in interview in *Writers at
Work* (5th series, 1981)

10 Most authors' talents are not equal to their
egos.
Bill Adler, *Inside Publishing* (1982)

11 There are two literary maladies — writer's
cramp and swelled head. The worst of
writer's cramp is that it is never cured: the
worst of swelled head is that it never kills.
Coulson Kernahan, in lecture

12 Of all the maggots that can make their way
into the brains through the ears, there is
none so disastrous as the persuasion that
you are a great poet. There is surely
something in the construction of the ears of
small authors which lays them specially
open to the inroads of this pest.
James Russell Lowell, 'The Life and Letters
of James Gates Percival', *My Study Window*
(1871)

13 No writer goes the whole length with any
other. Each of them shivers at the lapses of
the rest, and is blind to his own. And the
youngest shiver the most. And the greatest
writers have them.
Ivy Compton-Burnett, *A God and His Gifts*
(1963)

14 There was never yet a true orator or poet who thought anyone better than himself.
Cicero, *Epistolae ad Atticum*

15 No poet or novelist wishes he was the only one who ever lived, but most of them wish they were the only one alive, and quite a number fondly believe their wish has been granted.
W.H. Auden, *The Dyer's Hand* (1962)

16 It is taken for granted that, on every publication, there is at least a seeming violation of modesty; a presumption, on the writer's side, that he is able to entertain or instruct the world; which implies a supposition that he can communicate, what they cannot draw from their own reflections.
William Shenstone, *Essays on Men and Manners* (1764)

17 An author, like any other so-called artist, is a man in whom the normal vanity of all men is so vastly exaggerated that he finds it a sheer impossibility to hold it in. His overpowering impulse is to gyrate before his fellow men, flapping his wings and emitting defiant yells. This being forbidden by the police of all civilized nations, he takes it out by putting his yells on paper. Such is the thing called self-expression.
H.L. Mencken, *Prejudices* (1926)

18 Here's my small book out, nice and new, Fresh-bound — whom shall I give it to?
Catullus, *Carmina*

19 A presentation copy . . . is a copy of a book which does not sell, sent you by the author, with his foolish autograph at the beginning of it; for which, if a stranger, he only demands your friendship; if a brother author, he expects from you a book of yours, which does not sell, in return.
Charles Lamb, 'Popular Fallacies', *Last Essays of Elia* (1833)

20 I have never met an author who admitted that people did not buy his book because it was dull.
Somerset Maugham, *The Summing Up* (1938)

21 'Tis a vanity common to all writers, to over-value their own productions.
John Dryden, dedication to *Examen Poeticum* (1693)

22 Every author, however modest, keeps a most outrageous vanity chained like a madman in the padded cell of his breast.
Logan Pearsall Smith, *Afterthoughts* (1931)

23 I would give up half my books for a new profile.
John Ruskin, *Hortus Inclusus* (1887)

24 I never saw an author in my life, saving perhaps one, that did not purr as audibly as a full-grown domestic cat on having his fur smoothed the right way by a skilful hand.
Oliver Wendell Holmes, *The Autocrat of the Breakfast Table* (1857–8)

25 There is no amount of praise which a man and an author cannot bear with equanimity. Some authors can even stand flattery.
Maurice Baring, *Dead Letters* (1910)

26   Ne'er
Was flattery lost on poet's ear;
A simple race! they waste their toil
For the vain tribute of a smile.
Sir Walter Scott, *The Lay of the Last Minstrel* (1805)

27 In some ways a poet is a strange mixture of humility and of a self-confidence which borders on self-esteem. Without the latter how could he dare produce work in the face of what all the great poets have written?
John Ormond, autobiographical essay in *Artists in Wales* (ed. Meic Stephens, 1973)

28 Modesty is a virtue not often found among poets, for almost every one of them thinks himself the greatest in the world.
Miguel de Cervantes, *Don Quixote* (1605–15)

29 The vain poet is of the opinion that nothing of his can be too much: he sends to you basketful after basketful of juiceless fruit, covered with scentless flowers.
Walter Savage Landor, 'Archdeacon Hare and Walter Landor', *Imaginary Conversations* (1824–9)

30 The arrogance of poets is only a defense; doubt gnaws the greatest among them; they need our testimony to escape despair.
François Mauriac, 'L'Orgueil des poètes', *Journal* (1936–53)

31 I think I may boast myself to be, with all possible vanity, the most unlearned and uninformed female who ever dared to be an authoress.
Jane Austen, letter to the Revd James Clarke (1815)

32 It does no harm to repeat, as often as you
can, 'Without me the literary industry would
not exist'.
Doris Lessing, in *The Author* (Spring 1980)

171 VERS LIBRE

1 Writing free verse is like playing tennis with
the net down.
Robert Frost, in address at Milton
Academy, Milton, Mass. (17 May 1935)

2 As regards his free verse, I — plus some
chianti — once put forward the old notion
that free verse was like fishing with barbless
hooks. Henley replied volcanically. It was,
said he, 'the cadences that did it'.
Rudyard Kipling, *Something of Myself*
(1937)

3 Verse libre; a device for making poetry
easier to read and harder to write.
H.L. Mencken, *A Book of Burlesques*
(1916)

4 No *vers* is *libre* for the man who wants to do
a good job.
T.S. Eliot, introduction to Ezra Pound's
Poems (1940)

172 WALES AND THE WELSH

1 If we lose our native literary tradition
extending over fourteen centuries, all will be
lost, and there will be no such thing as
Welsh culture.
Tom Ellis, in speech at Welsh Arts Council
reception, Cardiff (April 1977)

2 In a culture like that of Wales in the
Middle Ages, which regarded poets as
socially important, a would-be poet, like a
would-be dentist in our own culture, was
systematically trained and admitted to the
rank of poet only after meeting high
professional standards.
W.H. Auden, 'The Poet and the City', *The
Dyer's Hand* (1962)

3 Clear Cymric voices carry well this Autumn
night,
Aneurin and Taliesin, cruel owls
for whom it is never altogether dark, crying

before the rules made poetry a pedant's
game.
Basil Bunting, *Briggflatts* (1966)

4 However grim their life, and hard,
One thing they dearly love, a bard.
Even the meanest hand at lays
Is plied with ale and crowned with bays,
And set with honor in their books
Above even liars, thieves, and crooks.
This is the one redeeming grace.
That saves them for the human race.
Rolfe Humphries, 'For my Ancestors'

5 Poets of Wales, like trees on fire,
Light the black twentieth century.
Adrian Mitchell, 'Lament for the Welsh
Makers'

6 Sing for Wales or shut your trap
All the rest's a load of crap.
Harri Webb, 'Advice to a Young Poet'

7 To live in Wales,

Is to be mumbled at
by re-incarnations of Dylan Thomas
in numerous diverse disguises.
Peter Finch, 'A Welsh Wordscape'

8 And when the firemen turned off the hose
and were standing in the wet and smoky
room, Jim's aunt, Miss Prothero, came
downstairs and peered in at them. She said
the right thing, always. She looked at the
three tall firemen in their shining helmets,
standing among the smoke and cinders and
dissolving snowballs, and she said: 'Would
you like something to read?'
Dylan Thomas, 'Memories of Christmas',
Quite Early One Morning (1954)

173 WAR

1 Above all I am not concerned with Poetry.
My subject is War, and the pity of War.
The Poetry is in the pity.
Wilfred Owen, in draft preface to a volume
of poems (1920)

2 I am the man who looked for peace and
found
My own eyes barbed.
I am the man who groped for words and
found
An arrow in my hand.
Sidney Keyes, 'War Poet'

3 My argument is that War makes rattling
good history, but Peace is poor reading.
Thomas Hardy, *The Dynasts* (1903)

4 In literature the lower ranks are as necessary
as in the army.
Anton Chekhov, quoted by Richmal
Crompton in *The Daily Telegraph* (20 Nov.
1936)

5 In a war or a revolution, a poet may do very
well as a guerilla fighter or a spy, but it is
unlikely that he will make a good regular
soldier, or, in peace time, a conscientious
member of a parliamentary committee.
W.H. Auden, 'The Poet and the City', in
The Dyer's Hand (1962)

6 It is absolutely impossible to slaughter a
man in this position without making him a
martyr and a hero, even though the day
before the rising he may have been only a
minor poet.
George Bernard Shaw, referring to some of
the leaders of the Easter Rising, Dublin,
1916, in letter to the *Daily News* (10 May
1916)

7 Total war is not won by a brigade of
authors.
Margaret Kennedy, in *The Author* (1940)

8 Beneath the rule of men entirely great,
The pen is mightier than the sword.
E.G. Bulwer-Lytton, *Richelieu* (1839)

9 Caesar had perished from the world of men,
Had not his sword been rescued by his pen.
Henry Vaughan, 'On Sir Thomas Bodley's
Library'

10 In 1941 I walked into the Air Ministry and
asked with great scepticism if they could use
a writer and was staggered and delighted to
be told Yes.
H.E. Bates, in *The Author* (Autumn 1944)

174 WISDOM

1 If all the sky were paper, and all the trees
pens, and all the waters of the earth ink,
they would not suffice to record my
wisdom.
Saccai, attr. (*c.* 1350)

2 Books should to one of these four ends
conduce,
For wisdom, piety, delight, or use.
Sir John Denham, 'Of Prudence'

3 The earliest poets and authors made fools
wise. Modern authors try to make wise men
fools.
Joseph Joubert, *Pensées* (1842)

4 The foolishest book is a kind of leaky boat
on a sea of wisdom; some of the wisdom
will get in somehow.
Oliver Wendell Holmes, *The Poet at the
Breakfast Table* (1872)

175 WOMEN

1 Except some professional scholars, I have
often observed that women in general read
much more than men; but, for want of a
plan, a method, a fixed object, their reading
is of little benefit to themselves, or others.
Edward Gibbon, *Autobiography* (1827)

2 I have met with women whom I really think
would like to be married to a poem, and to
be given away by a novel.
John Keats, in letter to Fanny Brawne (8
July 1819)

3 Should poets bicycle-pump the heart
Or squash it flat?
Man's love is of man's life a thing apart;
Girls aren't like that.
Kingsley Amis, 'Something Nasty in the
Book-shop'

4 Thro' all the drama — whether damned or
not —
Love gilds the scene, and women guide the
plot.
Richard Brinsley Sheridan, *The Rivals*
(1775)

5 Beware, madam, of the witty devil,
The arch intriguer who walks disguised
In a poet's cloak, his gay tongue oozing evil.
Robert Graves, 'Beware, Madam!'

6 For these fellows of infinite tongue, that can
rhyme themselves into ladies' favours, they
do always reason themselves out again.
William Shakespeare, *Henry V*

7   Let her not know extravagant despair
    Because no poet finds her wholly fair.
    T.H. Jones, 'A Wish For my Eldest
    Daughter'

8   She that with poetry is won
    Is but a desk to write upon.
    Samuel Butler, *Hudibras* (1674–80)

9   From women's eyes this doctrine I derive:
    They are the ground, the books, the
              academes,
    From whence doth spring the true
              Promethean fire.
    William Shakespeare, *Love's Labour's Lost*

10 Unfortunately, thrashing your young
    woman doesn't make her admire you more
    as a novelist.
    William Cooper, *Scenes from Provincial Life*
    (1950)

11 There's a lady for my humour!
    A pretty book of flesh and blood, and well
    Bound up, in a fair letter, too. Would I
    Had her, with all the Errata.
    James Shirley, *The Cardinal* (1641)

12 When I had curls
    I knew more girls.
    I do more reading
    now my hair is receding.
    James Simmons, 'Epigrams'

13 One would imagine that books were, like
    women, the worse for being old; that they
    have a pleasure in being read for the first
    time; that they open their leaves more
    cordially; that the spirit of enjoyment wears
    out with the spirit of novelty; and that, after
    a certain age, it is high time to put them on
    the shelf.
    William Hazlitt, 'On Reading New Books'

14 It is with books as with young girls. It is
    often the best, the worthiest that are left the
    longest on the shelf. Yet eventually someone
    comes who recognizes them and draws them
    from the darkness of seclusion into the light
    of a fine sphere of activity.
    Ludwig Feuerbach, *Schrifsteller und Mensch*
    (1834)

15 There are no books like a dame.
    Oscar Hammerstein II, 'There is Nothing
    Like a Dame', song from *South Pacific*
    (1949)

16 Romances paint at full length people's
              wooings,

    But only give a bust of marriages:
    For no one cares for matrimonial cooings,
              There's nothing wrong in a connubial
                 kiss:
    Think you, if Laura had been Petrarch's
                 wife,
    He would have written sonnets all his life?
    Lord Byron, *Don Juan* (1819–24)

17 If, as Dr Johnson said, a man who is not
    married is only half a man, so a man who is
    very much married is only half a writer.
    Cyril Connolly, *Enemies of Promise* (1938)

18 All poet's wives have rotten lives
    Their husbands look at them like knives.
    Delmore Schwartz, attr.

19 A poet looks at the world as a man looks at
    a woman.
    Wallace Stevens, *Opus Posthumous* (1957)

20 The main theme of poetry is, properly, the
    relations of man and woman, rather than
    those of man and man.
    Robert Graves, *The White Goddess* (1948)

21 'Why', someone said to me, 'do you always
    dedicate your novels to your wife?' And I
    said it was because it's my wife, more than
    my children or my friends, who has to put
    up with it all.
    William Trevor, in *The Author* (Autumn
    1973)

22 Men have had every advantage of us in
    telling their own story. Education has been
    theirs in so much higher a degree; the pen
    has been in their hands. I will not allow
    books to prove anything.
    Jane Austen, Anne Elliot in *Persuasion*
    (1818)

23 Literature cannot be the business of a
    woman's life, and it ought not to be.
    Robert Southey, in letter to Charlotte
    Brontë (1836)

24 Girls, do you know Charlotte has been
    writing a book, and it is much better than
    likely?
    Patrick Brontë, father of Charlotte Brontë,
    on *Jane Eyre* (1847)

25 I wish critics would judge me as an *author*,
    not as a woman.
    Charlotte Brontë, to George Henry Lewes
    (19 Jan. 1850)

26 A woman writer is first a writer who

consecrates her life to writing and has no
other occupation.
Simone de Beauvoir, in documentary film
(1978)

27 Helen discovered that she was almost alone,
among all her other friends, in never having
been married or never having written a
book. She decided that the second choice
would probably have less permanent
consequences.
Eric Linklater, *Magnus Merriman*
(1934)

28 'She writes because she *must*,
   My gifted daughter Ann'.
How nice! We won't pretend
   She writes because she can.
William Plomer, 'Gifted Daughter'

29 But of all plagues, the greatest is untold,
The book-learned wife in Greek and Latin
   bold,
The critic-dame, who at her table sits,
Homer and Virgil quotes, and wrights their
   wits.
John Dryden, *Juvenal's Sixth Satire* (1693)

30 The romantic novel brigade are a formidable
band — mostly women, often wealthy,
occasionally heads of Oxford women's
colleges.
Anthony Blond, *The Book Book* (1985)

31 Far from the vulgar haunts of men
Each sits in her 'successful room',
Housekeeping with her fountain pen
And writing novels with her broom.
Roy Campbell, 'On Some South African
Novelists'

32 Today the women come and go
Talking of T.S. Eliot.
Peter Viereck, '1912–1952, Full Cycle'

33 T.S. Eliot is quite at a loss
When clubwomen bustle across
At literary teas
Crying, 'What, if you please,
Did you mean by *The Mill on the Floss?*'
W.H. Auden, 'T.S. Eliot'

34 There are some things (like first love and
one's reviews) at which a woman in her
middle years does not care to look too
closely.
Stella Gibbons, in Foreword to *Cold
Comfort Farm* (1932)

35 There are many women like me, who have

spent sleepless nights reciting the words of
their dead husbands over and over again.
Nadezhda Mandelstam, *Hope Against
Hope* (1971)

176 WORDS

1 The word itself, of which our works of art
are fashioned, is the first art-form, older
than the roughest shaping of clay or stone.
A word is the carving and colouring of a
thought, and gives to it permanence.
Osbert Sitwell, *Laughter in the Next Room*
(1949)

2 The feeling for words comes at an early age
— or rather it is lost in most cases at an early
age, leaving the rest poets.
Peter de Vries, *Reuben, Reuben* (1964)

3 In a world full of audio visual marvels, may
words matter to you and be full of magic.
Godfrey Smith, in letter to a new
grandchild, in *The Observer* (5 July 1987)

4 You don't make a poem with thoughts: you
must make it with words.
Jean Cocteau, in interview in *The Sunday
Times* (20 Oct. 1933)

5 The poet, from the start, is a man playing
with words, fascinated, obsessed by them.
As he gains mastery over them, he makes
the game increasingly more difficult for
himself, partly by inventing new rules,
breaking away from the traditional
techniques in which his juvenilia were
written, attempting more subtle or daring
combinations of words: partly because his
experience has become richer and more
complex, thus demanding of him greater
verbal efforts to get at the truth of it.
C. Day-Lewis, *The Poet's Task* (1951)

6   Words strain,
Crack and sometimes break, under the
                burden,
Under the tension, slip, slide, perish,
Decay with imprecision, will not stay in
                place,
Will not stay still.
T.S. Eliot, *Four Quartets* (1943)

7 We all write poems; it is simply that poets
are the ones who write in words.
John Fowles, *The French Lieutenant's
Woman* (1969)

8 'Why do you want to write poetry?' If the
   young man answers: 'I have important
   things I want to say,' then he is not a poet. If
   he answers: 'I like hanging around words
   listening to what they say,' then maybe he is
   going to be a poet.
   W.H. Auden, 'Squares and Oblongs', *Poets
   at Work* (1948)

9 I fell in love — that is the only expression I
   can think of — at once, and am still at the
   mercy of words, though sometimes now,
   knowing a little of their behaviour very well,
   I think I can influence them slightly and
   have even learned to beat them now and
   then, which they appear to enjoy.
   Dylan Thomas, letter to student of his
   poetry (1951)

10 Words should be an intense pleasure just as
   leather should be to a shoemaker.
   Evelyn Waugh in *The New York Times* (19
   Nov. 1950)

11 For words, like Nature, half reveal
   And half conceal the Soul within.
   Alfred, Lord Tennyson, prologue to *In
   Memoriam* (1850)

12 I have only tried to make a shape in words.
   David Jones, preface to *In Parenthesis*
   (1937)

13 A word is not the same with one writer as
   with another. One tears it from his guts. The
   other pulls it out of his overcoat pocket.
   Charles Péguy, 'The Honest People', *Basic
   Verities* (1943)

14 . . . Trying to learn to use words, and every
                   attempt
   Is a wholly new start, and a different kind of
                   failure,
   Because one has only learnt to get the better
                   of words
   For the thing one no longer has to say, or
                   the way in which
   One is no longer disposed to say it. And so
                   each venture
   Is a new beginning, a raid on the inarticulate
   With shabby equipment always
                   deteriorating
   In the general mess of imprecision of feeling,
   Undisciplined squads of emotion.
   T.S. Eliot, *Four Quartets* (1943)

15 It's strange that words are so inadequate
   Yet, like the asthmatic struggling for breath,
   So the lover must struggle for words.
   T.S. Eliot, *The Elder Statesman* (1958)

16 A poem should be wordless
   As the flight of birds.
   Archibald MacLeish, 'Ars Poetica'

17 Words make love with one another.
   André Breton, *Surrealist Manifesto* (1924)

18 One of the marks of a great poet is that he
   creates his own family of words and teaches
   them to live together in harmony and to
   help one another.
   Gerald Brenan, *Thoughts in a Dry Season*
   (1978)

19 The bad poet dwells partly in a world of
   objects and partly in a world of words, and
   he never can get them to fit.
   T.S. Eliot, 'Swinburne as a Poet', *The Sacred
   Wood* (1920)

20 Words, words, nothing but words.
   Anonymous old lady, complaining of Edith
   Sitwell's poetry, quoted in her *A Poet's
   Notebook* (1943)

21 *Polonius*: What do you read, my lord?
   Hamlet: Words, words, words.
   William Shakespeare, *Hamlet*

22   And every phrase
   And sentence that is right (where every
                   word is at home,
   Taking its place to support the others,
   The word neither diffident nor ostentatious,
   An easy commerce of the old and the new,
   The common word exact without vulgarity,
   The formal word precise but not pedantic,
   The complete consort dancing together)
   Every phrase and every sentence is an end
                   and a beginning,
   Every poem an epitaph.
   T.S. Eliot, *Four Quartets* (1943)

23 A word carries far — very far — deals
   destruction through time as the bullets go
   flying through space.
   Joseph Conrad, *Lord Jim* (1900)

24 But words are things, and a small drop of
                   ink,
   Falling like dew, upon a thought, produces
   That which makes thousands, perhaps
                   millions think;
   'Tis strange, the shortest letter which man
                   uses
   Instead of speech, may form a lasting ink
   Of ages.
   Lord Byron, *Don Juan* (1819–24)

25 All words are pegs to hang ideas on.
   Henry Ward Beecher, *Proverbs from
   Plymouth Pulpit* (1887)

26 Words are, of course, the most powerful drug used by mankind.
Rudyard Kipling, in speech (14 Feb, 1923)

27 Words may be deeds.
Aesop, *Fables*

28 Out of the slimy mud of words, out of the
    sleet and hail of verbal imprecisions,
Approximate thoughts and feelings, words
    that have taken the place of
    thoughts and feelings,
There spring the perfect order of speech, and
    the beauty of incantation.
T.S. Eliot, *Four Quartets* (1943)

29 Words build bridges into unexplored regions.
Adolf Hitler, quoted in Alan Bullock, *Hitler, A Study of Tyranny* (1952)

30 Words are really a mask. They rarely express the true meaning; in fact they tend to hide it.
Hermann Hesse, quoted in Miguel Serrano, *C.G. Jung and Hermann Hesse* (1966)

31 I hate false words, and seek with care, difficulty, and moroseness, those that fit the thing.
Walter Savage Landor, 'Bishop Burnet and Humphrey Hardcastle', *Imaginary Conversations* (1824–9)

32 You can stroke people with words.
F. Scott Fitzgerald, *The Crack-Up* (1945)

33 For just when ideas fail, a word comes in to save the situation.
J.W. Goethe, *Faust, Studierzimmer* (1808)

34 We should have a great many fewer disputes in the world if words were taken for what they are, the signs of our ideas only, and not for things themselves.
John Locke, *An Essay Concerning Human Understanding* (1690)

35 Woe to us who know the words without knowing the Word.
D. Gwenallt Jones, 'Ar Gyfeiliorn'

36 In good writing, words become one with things.
Ralph Waldo Emerson, *Journals* (1831)

37 A world of facts lies outside the world of words.
T.H. Huxley, *Lay Sermons* (1870)

38 I would rather be Charles Lamb than Charles XII. I would rather be remembered by a song than by a victory. I would rather build a fine sonnet than have built St Paul's . . . Fine phrases I value more than bank-notes. I have ear for no other harmony than the harmony of words.
Alexander Smith, 'Men of Letters', *Dreamthorp* (1863)

39 Good words are worth much and cost little.
George Herbert, *Jacula Prudentum* (1651)

40 Words are wise men's counters, they do but reckon by them; but they are money of fools.
Thomas Hobbes, *Leviathan* (1651)

41 Words are the small change of thought.
Jules Renard, *Journal* (Nov. 1888)

42 Words should be weighed and not counted.
Yiddish proverb

43 A glotoun of words.
William Langland, *The Vision of William concerning Piers the Plowman* (c. 1370)

44 Some men have a peculiar taste for bad words. They will pick you out of a thousand the still-born words, the falsettos, the wing-clipped and lame words, as if only the false notes caught their ears.
Henry David Thoreau, *Journal* (1858)

45 How strangely do we diminish a thing as soon as we try to express it in words.
Maurice Maeterlinck, 'Mystic Morality', *The Treasure of the Humble* (1896)

46 It is extremely natural for us to desire to see such our thoughts put into the dress of words, without which indeed we can scarce have a clear and distinct idea of them our selves.
Eustace Budgell, in *The Spectator* (no. 379, 1711–12)

47 Words form the thread on which we string our experiences.
Aldous Huxley, *The Olive Tree* (1937)

48 Thanks to words, we have been able to rise above the brutes; and thanks to words, we have often sunk to the level of the demons.
Aldous Huxley, *Adonis and the Alphabet* (1956)

49 Isn't everyone consoled when faced with a trouble or fact he doesn't understand, by a word, some simple word, which tells us nothing and yet calms us?
Luigi Pirandello, *Six Characters in Search of an Author* (1921)

50 Those things for which we find words, are things we have already overcome.
Friedrich Nietzsche, 'Skirmishes in a War with the Age', *Twilight of the Idols* (1888)

51 The words not only affect us temporarily; they change us, they socialize or unsocialize us.
David Riesman, 'Storytellers as Tutors', *The Lonely Crowd* (1950)

52 Words are the only things that last forever.
William Hazlitt, 'On Thought and Action', *Table Talk* (1821–2)

53 Once a word has been allowed to escape, it cannot be recalled.
Horace, *Epistles*

54 Look out how you use proud words,
When you let proud words go, it is not easy
            to call them back,
They wear long boots, hard boots; they
            walk off proud; they can't hear
            you calling —
Look out how you use proud words.
Carl Sandberg, 'Primer Lesson', *Slabs of the Sunburnt West* (1922)

55 Here are a few of the unpleasant'st words
That ever blotted paper.
William Shakespeare, *The Merchant of Venice*

56 How describe the delicate thing that happens when a brilliant insect alights on a flower? Words, with their weight, fall upon the picture like birds of prey.
Jules Renard, *Journal* (Sept. 1893)

57 All our life is crushed by the weight of words: the weight of the dead.
Luigi Pirandello, *Henry IV* (1922)

58 One forgets words as one forgets names. One's vocabulary needs constant fertilisation or it will die.
Evelyn Waugh, *Diaries* (1976)

59 A word never — well, hardly ever — shakes off its etymology and its formation. In spite of all changes in and extensions of and additions to its meanings, and indeed rather pervading and governing them, there will persist the old idea.
J.L. Austin, 'A Plea for Excuses', *Philosophical Papers* (1961)

60 The smashers of language are looking for a new justice among words. It does not exist. Words are unequal and unjust.
Elias Canetti, *The Human Province* (1978)

61 Men ever had, and ever will have, leave
To coin new words well suited to the age.
Words are like leaves, some wither ev'ry
            year,
And ev'ry year a younger race succeeds.
Horace, *Ars Poetica*

62 Words are like leaves; and where they most
            abound,
Much fruit of sense beneath is rarely found.
Alexander Pope, *An Essay On Criticism* (1711)

63 'Well,' said the Owl, 'the customary procedure in such cases is as follows.' 'What does Crustimoney Proseedcake mean?' said Pooh. 'For I am a bear of Very Little Brain, and long words bother me.'
A.A. Milne, *Winnie-the-Pooh* (1927)

---

177 WRITERS

1 A man may be a very good author with some faults, but not with many faults.
Voltaire, *Letters on the English*

2 I shall be but a shrimp of an author.
Thomas Gray, in letter to Horace Walpole (1768)

3 It is with books as with men — a very small number play a great part; the rest are lost in the multitude.
Voltaire, 'Books', *Philosophical Dictionary* (1764)

4 No one will ever get at my verses who insists upon viewing them as a literary performance.
Walt Whitman, *A Backward Glance O'er Travel'd Roads* (1947)

5 You see, the author's standpoint is only one of many, and his idea of the significance of his own work is lost in the welter of other voices. Does he know his own work as well as he imagines? I rather think not. I rather think he's like a medium who, when he comes out of his trance, is amazed at what he's said and done.
Henry Miller, in interview in *Writers at Work* (2nd series, 1963)

6 What I like in a good author is not what he says, but what he whispers.
Logan Pearsall Smith, *Afterthoughts* (1931)

7 I have never been one to write by rule, not even by my own rules.
William Carlos Williams, in letter to Richard Eberhart (23 May 1954)

8 The world, in its sheer exuberance of kindness, will try to bury the poet with warm and lovely human trivialities. It will even ask him to autograph books.
Christopher Morley, *Inward Ho!* (1923)

9 It becomes not me to draw my pen in defence of a bad cause, when I have so often drawn it for a good one.
John Dryden, in preface to *Fables* (1700)

10 Sin is the writer's element.
François Mauriac, 'Literature and Sin', *Second Thoughts* (1961)

11 The health of a writer should not be too good, and perfect only in those periods of convalescence when he is not writing.
Cyril Connolly, *Enemies of Promise* (1938)

12 A work that aspires, however humbly, to the condition of art should carry its justification in every line.
Joseph Conrad, preface to *The Nigger of the Narcissus* (1897)

13 So have I loitered my life away, reading books, looking at pictures, going to plays, hearing, thinking, writing on what pleased me best. I have wanted only one thing to make me happy, but wanting that have wanted everything.
William Hazlitt, 'My First Acquaintance with Poets'

14 Some men have only one book in them; others, a library.
Sydney Smith, in Lady Holland's *Memoir* (1855)

15 Beware the man of one book.
Isaac D'Israeli, *Curiosities of Literature* (1791–1834)

16 There is nothing more dreadful to an author than neglect, compared with which, reproach, hatred and opposition are names of happiness.
Samuel Johnson, in *The Rambler* (1750–2)

17 Even monarchs have need of authors, and fear their pens more than ugly women the painter's pencil.
Baltasar Gracián, *The Art of Worldly Wisdom* (1647)

18 Great authors are admirable in this respect: in every generation they make for disagreement. Through them we become aware of our differences.
André Gide, 'Third Imaginary Interview', *Pretexts* (1903)

19 There is plenty of room in the world for horses and poets of all the colours of the rainbow.
Pablo Neruda, *Memoirs* (1977)

20 There was a period of the cult of Pure Sound when infants were read passages from Homer, and then questioned as to their impressions — not unlike Darwin playing the trombone to his french beans.
William Empson, *Seven Types of Ambiguity* (1947)

21 With pen and pencil we're learning to say Nothing, more cleverly every day.
William Allingham, 'Blackberries'

22 A writer needs three things, experience, observation, and imagination, any two of which, at times any one of which, can supply the lack of the others.
William Faulkner, in interview in *Writers at Work* (1st series, 1958)

23 He who would not be frustrate of his hope to write well hereafter in laudable things ought himself to be a true poem.
John Milton, *Apology for Smectymnuus* (1642)

24 The essential is not to think of one's self as a writer and to do nothing which will put one's self in that popinjay attitude. You don't write as a writer, you write as a man.
Archibald MacLeish, in interview in *Writers at Work* (5th series, 1981)

25 The writer cannot afford to question his own essential nature.
Randall Jarrell, *A Sad Heart at the Supermarket* (1965)

26 One man is as good as another until he has written a book.
Benjamin Jowett, *Letters* (1899)

27 Authors and uncaptured criminals are the only people free from routine.
Eric Linklater, *Poet's Pub* (1925)

28 I hold a beast, an angel and a madman in
me, and my enquiry is as to their working,
and my problem is their subjugation and
victory, downthrow and upheaval, and my
effort is their self expression.
Dylan Thomas, in letter to Henry Treece

29 Every writer creates his own precursors.
Jorge Luis Borges, *Other Inquisitions*
(1952)

30 Creative writers are always greater than the
causes that they represent.
E.M. Forster, 'Gide and George', *Two
Cheers for Democracy* (1951)

31 The only impeccable writers are those who
never wrote.
William Hazlitt, 'On the Aristocracy of
Letters', *Table Talk* (1821–2)

32 Dear Madame, you make an absurd, though
common mistake in supposing that any
human creature can help you to be an
authoress, if you cannot become one in
virtue of your own prowess . . .
Charles Dickens, to an inquiring reader

33 The fact that many people should be
shocked by what he writes practically
imposes it as a duty upon the writer to go on
shocking them.
Aldous Huxley, 'Vulgarity in Literature',
Music at Night (1931)

34 Real men do things. They don't just write
about them.
Frederic Raphael, in *The Sunday Times* (8
Oct. 1978)

---

178 WRITER'S BLOCK

1 All things can tempt me from this craft of
verse.
W.B. Yeats, 'All Things Can Tempt Me'

2 When a man does not write his poetry, it
escapes by other vents through him.
Ralph Waldo Emerson, 'Behaviour', *The
Conduct of Life* (1860)

3 At words poetic, I'm so pathetic
That I always have found it best,
Instead of getting 'em off my chest,
To let 'em rest
Unexpressed.
Cole Porter, 'You're the Top'

4 The poet is he that hath fat enough, like
bears and marmots, to suck his claws all
winter.
Henry David Thoreau, 'Sunday', *A Week
on the Concord and Merrimack Rivers*
(1849)

5 My pulse is weak, my spirits low;
    I cannot think, I cannot write.
I strive to spin a verse — but lo!
    My rhymes are very rarely right.
Henry S. Leigh, 'Rhymes (?)'

6 Poetry is a distinct faculty — it won't come
when called — you may as well whistle for a
wind.
Lord Byron, quoted by E.J. Trelawny, in
Records of Shelley, Byron and the Author
(1878)

7 If one waits for the right time to come before
writing, the right time never comes.
James Russell Lowell, in a letter to Charles
Eliot Norton (22 April 1883)

8 Any memory of pain is deeply buried, and
there is nothing more painful for a writer
than an inability to work.
John Cheever, in interview in *Writers at
Work* (5th series, 1981)

9 This happens to writers when there are dead
spells. We die sometimes. And it's as though
we're in a tomb; it's a death. That's what we
all fear, and that's why so many of us
become alcoholics or suicides or insane —
or just no-good philanderers.
William Goyen, in interview in *Writers at
Work* (6th series, 1984)

10 Yes, for the last two weeks I have written
scarcely anything. I have been idle; I have
failed.
Katherine Mansfield, *Diary* (13 Nov. 1921)

11 I sought a theme and sought for it in vain,
I sought it daily for six weeks or so.
W.B. Yeats, 'The Circus Animals'
Desertion'

12 I am dizzy with boredom, with
discouragement, with fatigue! I have spent
four hours without being able to write one
sentence. I haven't yet written a line today,
or rather I have scribbled a hundred. What
an atrocious job! Oh, art! art! What is this
mad chimaera which eats up one's heart,
and why?
Gustave Flaubert, in letter to Louise Colet

13 God lets you write, he also lets you not write.
Kurt Vonnegut, attr.

14 Biting my truant pen, beating myself for spite:
'Fool!' said my Muse to me, 'look in thy heart, and write'.
Sir Philip Sidney, *Astrophel and Stella*, Sonnet 1 (*c*. 1582)

15 Better to write twaddle, anything, than nothing at all.
Katherine Mansfield, attr.

179 WRITING

1 Ready writing makes not good writing; but good writing brings on ready writing.
Ben Jonson, *Explorata*

2 It is the glory and the merit of some men to write well, and of others not to write at all.
La Bruyère, *Characters* (1688)

3 All good writing is swimming under water and holding your breath.
F. Scott Fitzgerald, in letter to Frances Scott Fitzgerald

4 Good writing is a kind of skating which carries off the performer where he would not go.
Ralph Waldo Emerson, *Journals* (vol. 7, 1913)

5 The secret of all good writing is sound judgment.
Horace, *Ars Poetica*

6 Certainly the Art of Writing is the most miraculous of all things man has devised.
Thomas Carlyle, on *Heroes, Hero-Worship and the Heroic in History* (1840)

7 If it were not for a rainy day, a drunken vigil, a fit of the spleen, a course of physic, a sleepy Sunday, an ill run at dice, a long tailor's bill, a beggar's purse, a factious head, a hot sun, costive diet, want of books, and a just contempt for learning — but for these . . . the number of authors and of writing would dwindle away to a degree most woeful to behold.
Jonathan Swift, *A Tale of a Tub* (1704)

8 Nothing goes by luck in composition. It allows of no tricks. The best you can write will be the best you are.
Henry David Thoreau, *Journal* (28 Feb. 1841)

9 Your business as a writer is not to illustrate virtue but to show how a fellow may move toward it or away from it.
Robert Penn Warren, in *Paris Review* (Spring-Summer 1957)

10 To write is to become disinterested. There is a certain renunciation in art.
Albert Camus, *Notebooks 1935–1942* (1962)

11 It's dangerous for an artist to know too much of what he's about. If there are poems in the pool and a poacher finds he can tickle them out, that's all he needs to know. Let others work at watching him, if the light's good enough. And if he's worth watching. And if they are really fish.
John Ormond, autobiographical essay in *Artists in Wales* (vol. 2, ed. Meic Stephens, 1973)

12 Writing is the gradual revelation of a wholeness already felt when we had the idea for the poem.
Stephen Spender, in interview in *Writers at Work* (6th series, 1984)

13 The writer's intention hasn't anything to do with what he achieves. The intent to earn money or the intent to be famous or the intent to be great doesn't matter in the end. Just what comes out.
Lillian Hellman, in interview in *Writers at Work* (3rd series, 1967)

14 'It satisfies my ear', you say. Well, I don't write for your ear.
D.H. Lawrence, in letter to Edward Marsh (19 Nov. 1913)

15 Topographical writers are those who are interested in other places; travel writers are those who are only interested in themselves.
Miles Kington, in *The Times* (4 July 1985)

180 YOUTH

1 Every poet was born yesterday.
R. Williams Parry, 'Barddoniaeth Dau Dramp'

2 Most of the basic material a writer works
   with is acquired before the age of fifteen.
   Willa Cather, quoted in René Rapin, *Willa
   Cather* (1930)

3 No one can ever write about anything that
   happened to him after he was twelve years
   old.
   Ignazio Silone, quoted in Murray Kempton,
   America Comes of Middle Age (1963)

4 Nine-tenths of the best poetry of the world
   has been written by poets less than thirty
   years old; a great deal more than half of it
   has been written by poets under twenty-five.
   H.L. Mencken, *Prejudices* (1919)

5 The poet is one who carries the simplicity of
   childhood into the powers of manhood;
   who, with a soul unsubdued by habit,
   unshackled by custom, contemplates all
   things with the freshness and the wonder of
   a child.
   Samuel Taylor Coleridge, *Lectures on
   Shakespeare*, 8 (1811–12)

6 For the first twenty years you are still
                   growing,
   Bodily that is; as a poet, of course,
   You are not born yet. It's the next ten
   You cut your teeth on to emerge smirking
   For your brash courtship of the muse.
   R.S. Thomas, 'To a Young Poet'

7 Blessed is the poet who did not give up, on
   becoming a man, speaking and
   understanding and thinking as a boy.
   R. Williams Parry, 'Angerdd Beirdd Cymru'

8 Most poets are dead by their late twenties.
   Robert Graves, quoted in *The Observer* (11
   Nov. 1962)

9 In literature young men usually begin their
   careers by being judges, and as wisdom and
   old experience arrive they reach the dignity
   of standing as culprits at the bar before new
   young bloods who have in their turn sprung
   up in the judgment-seat.
   Thomas Hardy, quoted in F.E. Hardy, *The
   Early Life of Thomas Hardy* (1928)

10 The best that can happen for a writer is to be
    taken up very late or very early, when either
    old enough to take its measure, or so young
    that when dropped by society he has all life
    before him.
    Cyril Connolly, *Enemies of Promise* (1938)

11 I was never an Angry Young Man. I am
    angry only when I hit my thumb with a
    hammer.
    Kingsley Amis, in *The Eton College
    Chronicle* (June 1979)

12 Young writers. If they're meant to be
    writers, they will write. There's nothing that
    can stop them. It may kill them. They may
    not be able to stand the terrible indignities,
    humiliation, privations, shocks that attend
    the life of an American writer. They may
    not. Yet they may have some sense of humor
    about it, and manage to survive.
    Tennessee Williams, in interview in *Writers
    at Work* (6th series, 1984)

13 There are no young writers worth a damn.
    William Faulkner, in letter to Bennett Cerf

14 The trouble with our younger authors is that
    they are all in their sixties.
    Somerset Maugham, quoted in 'Sayings of
    the Week' in *The Observer* (14 Oct. 1951)

15 A young man is afraid of his demon and
    puts his hand over the demon's mouth
    sometimes and speaks for him. And the
    things the young man says are very rarely
    poetry.
    D.H. Lawrence, note to *Collected Poems*
    (1928)

16 O friend unseen, unborn, unknown,
              Student of our sweet English tongue,
    Read out my words at night, alone:
              I was a poet, I was young.
    James Elroy Flecker, 'To a Poet a Thousand
    Years Hence'

17 Superficial the reading of grown men in
    some sort must ever be; it is only once in a
    lifetime that we can know the passionate
    reading of youth.
    Walter Bagehot, *Literary Studies* (1879)

18 Of all the compliments that can be paid to a
    writer, there is one especially that will make
    him glow with pleasure, namely: 'You are
    admired so much among the younger
    generation'.
    François Mauriac, *God and Mammon*
    (1936)

19 There is usually something wrong with
    writers the young like.
    Anthony Burgess, in *Playboy* (1974)

20 People have wanted to make novel-reading

useful to the young; I can't think of anything more senseless: it's like setting fire to the house so that the fire-brigade can be called out.
Jean-Jacques Rousseau, preface to *La Nouvelle Héloise* (1760)

21 There is no reason why the same man should like the same books at eighteen and forty-eight.
Ezra Pound, *The ABC of Reading* (1934)

AUTHOR INDEX

References are to sections and quotation numbers
within sections.

Abercrombie, Lascelles 57:2,
115:64, 143:16
Abse, Dannie 35:6, 116:7, 117:3
Adamov, Arthur 157:30
Adams, Franklin P. 25:11, 69:9,
138:2
Adams, John 50:1
Adams, Robert Martin 33:42, 84:7
Adam Smith Institute 80:42
Addison, Joseph 22:5, 33:43, 50:3,
67:1, 73:3, 120:6, 122:6
Ade, George 121:34
Adler, Bill 44:4, 54:6, 143:11, 17,
148:2, 156:2, 170:10
Adorno, T.W. 35:19
Aesop 176:27
Aiken, John 131:19
Alain (E.A. Chartier) 52:11
Alcott, Bronson 147:4, 6
Aldiss, Brian W. 140:5, 6
Aldrich, Thomas Bailey 29:3, 50:13,
120:8
Algren, Nelson 1:44, 148:15
Allingham, William 177:21
Amis, Kingsley 14:9, 42:20, 77:27,
175:3, 180:11
Andersch, Alfred 151:6
Anderson, Sherwood 94:11
Anderson, Shirley 80:44
Aneirin 109:2
Anouilh, Jean 121:1, 163:9
Anthony, Katherine 18:4
Appleyard, Brian 80:41
Aragon, Louis 115:34
Archer, Jeffrey 73:18
Arendt, Hannah 158:17
Aretino, Pietro 87:5
Aristotle 34:21, 53:2, 13, 66:18,
152:2, 164:1
Armstrong, Benjamin 39:19
Arno, Peter 131:43
Arnold, Matthew 16:4, 33:6, 91:3,
95:13, 97:4, 113:29, 115:14,
20, 131:17, 152:35, 41
Artaud, Antonin 89:9
Asch, Sholem 153:12
Ascherson, Neal 100:26
Atkinson, Brooks 34:5, 155:9
Attila the Stockbroker 124:6
Auden, W.H. 4:4, 5:7, 9:9, 20,
12:18, 23, 27:5, 35:5, 43:9,
58:14, 59:5, 69:8, 71:3, 76:24,
78:2, 5, 13, 85:13, 88:3, 91:2,
94:16, 95:12, 98:1, 99:10,
100:33, 106:13, 113:49, 52,
115:48, 82, 117:2, 5, 14, 124:4,
125:4, 134:1, 8, 139:10, 159:8,
166:2, 170:1, 3, 15, 172:2,
173:5, 175:33, 176:8
Augustine, Saint 133:1
Austen, Jane 79:4, 100:18, 170:31,
175:22
Austin, J.L. 176:59
Aymé, Marcel 40:2
Aytoun, William 114:1

Bacon, Francis 23:12, 34:15, 39:4,
5, 43:3, 76:2, 79:17, 139:2,
155:2, 169:15
Bagehot, Walter 76:15, 83:1, 84:26,
104:9, 180:17
Bagley, Desmond 1:25
Bailey, Hilary 54:4
Bainbridge, Beryl 61:2
Baker, Denys Val 143:9
Baker, Kenneth 156:6
Bakewell, Joan 80:43
Baldwin, James 148:1
Balfour, A.J. 18:3, 66:13, 75:26,
80:26
Balzac, Honoré de 41:7, 50:29
Bankhead, Tallulah 39:6
Banner, Simon 123:15
Banning, Margaret Culkin 52:4
Banville, Théodore de 96:1, 115:38
Baring, Maurice 170:25
Barrès, Maurice 110:3
Barrie, J.M. 50:38, 122:11, 170:6
Barrington, Viscount 124:7
Barth, John 42:5
Barthes, Roland 84:24
Bartlett, Elizabeth 44:1
Bartholin, Thomas 76:4
Barzun, Jacques 21:5, 164:2
Bateman, Michael 40:17
Bates, H.E. 173:10
Baudelaire, Charles 34:20, 110:1,
113:1, 154:12, 158:14, 170:5
Baughan, E.A. 157:24
Bayle, Pierre 138:1, 158:12
Beaslai, Piaras 71:5
Beaumarchais, Pierre-Augustin
Caron de 48:7, 157:9
Beauvoir, Simone de 103:9, 162:1,
175:26
Beaverbrook, Lord 121:10, 125:8
Beckett, Samuel 34:66
Beecher, Henry Ward 80:28, 121:24,
147:3, 155:3, 166:12, 176:25
Beerbohm, Max 34:63, 48:4, 98:5,
130:2, 134:4
Behan, Brendan 34:28, 107:6
Bell, Clive 34:3
Bell, Vicars 115:76
Belloc, Hilaire 10:9, 26:1, 83:17,
94:12, 120:17, 128:10, 143:5
Bellow, Saul 84:9, 100:7
Beloff, Max 66:5
Benchley, Robert 50:7
Benét, Stephen Vincent 164:8
Benjamin, Walter 26:8, 169:8
Bennett, Alan 53:15, 145:20, 156:8
Bennett, Arnold 23:7, 9, 32:8,
94:25, 100:39
Bennoch, Francis 42:4
Benson, A.C. 10:3
Bentham, Jeremy 115:58, 75
Bentley, Edmund Clerihew 18:1
Berkeley, William 122:9
Bernanos, Georges 10:14
Berryman, John 50:27

Betjeman, John 50:28, 55:5, 66:21
Betti, Ugo 158:13
Bevan, Aneurin 121:27
Bierce, Ambrose 39:1, 40:1, 48:2,
50:25, 66:15, 76:17, 106:14,
114:7, 130:32, 161:13
Billington, Rachel 124:1
Binney, Horace 70:4
Birrell, Augustine 51:1, 62:6, 80:5,
84:11, 169:7
Bishop, Jim 34:31, 66:14
Bishop, John Peale 89:15
Bishop, Morris 106:9
Blackmur, R.P. 33:9
Blake, William 16:9, 50:24, 59:2,
64:2, 69:4, 123:2
Blond, Anthony 47:6, 82:2, 143:25,
175:30
Blunden, Edmund 135:5
Blunt, David 128:18
Bodenheim, Maxwell 104:4
Boileau-Despréaux, Nicolas 7:5,
22:4, 101:6, 108:1, 158:5
Book Trade Year Book, The 43:5
Boon, John 128:8
Boorstin, Daniel 15:1, 2
Borges, Jorge Luis 75:16, 80:14,
120:14, 177:29
Borrow, George 162:4
Bottome, Phyllis 112:3
Bottomley, Horatio 153:4
Bourdet, Edouard 154:13
Bowen, Catherine Drinker 18:22
Bowen, John 33:24
Bowra, Maurice 57:1
Boyle, Roger 73:11
Bradbury, Malcolm 145:7
Bradley, A.C. 92:3, 4, 95:11
Bradley, F.H. 8:3
Braley, Berton 61:5
Brant, Sebastian 17:13, 14
Brecht, Bertolt 84:1
Brenan, Gerald 120:4, 176:18
Breton, André 115:27, 176:17
Brett, Simon 37:8
Bridges, Robert 85:12
Brien, Alan 82:10
Bronowski, Jacob I. 158:21
Brontë, Charlotte 79:6, 100:30,
175:25
Brontë, Patrick 175:24
Brooks, Gwendolyn 115:56
Brooks, Mel 44:7
Brooks, Van Wyck 44:5
Brown, Heyward, 119:9, 120:5
Brown, Solyman 139:1
Browne, Sir Thomas 103:10, 166:20
Browning, Elizabeth Barrett 12:19,
31:5, 39:7, 81:25, 124:2,
166:18
Browning, Robert 34:44, 59:11,
92:14, 102:8, 104:2, 119:1
Brunet, Gustave 51:3
Buchan, John 162:8
Budgell, Eustace 176:46

175

Note that **emboldened** references are to entire topic
sections.
Other references are to sections and quotation
numbers within sections.

COLLINS DICTIONARY OF BUSINESS QUOTATIONS

Simon James and Robert Parker

Pan Am takes good care of you. Marks and Spencer loves you. Securicor cares . . . At Amstrad: 'We want your money' — Alan Sugar.

If only Groucho had writen Das Kapital — Anonymous.

The *Collins Dictionary of Business Quotations* is a compilation of over 2500 entertaining and illuminating quotations from the world of commerce, from *Accounts* and *Bargains* to *Personnel Management* and *Trade Unions*, giving proof at last that money really does talk!

The literature of the commercial world has been a much neglected source of information, advice and amusement for the businessman and woman of today, a situation at last rectified by this unique collection. Here are the thoughts of tycoons, politicians, economists, managing directors, shop stewards and typists on all aspects of business, from the earliest barter to the consumer society of the modern era.

Ideal for that telling phrase or aside in speech-making or reporting, the *Collins Dictionary of Business Quotations* proves that even accountancy can be fun, and that, as Lord Beaverbrook put it, 'Business is more exciting than any game'.

Simon James has compiled several dictionaries of quotations, including a *Dictionary of Economic Quotations,* and is the author of a number of books on fiscal and financial management. Robin Parker is Professor of Accountancy at the University of Exeter and has written over a dozen books, including the *Macmillan Dictionary of Accounting.*

ISBN 0 00 434379 4

COLLINS CONCISE DICTIONARY OF QUOTATIONS

Donald Fraser

'*I might repeat to myself, slowly and soothingly, a list of quotations beautiful from minds profound; if I can remember any of the damn things.*' — Dorothy Parker.

Very much a book for the modern era, the coverage of the *Collins Concise Dictionary of Quotations* ranges from Thucydides to Thatcher, from William Shakespeare to Woody Allen, taking in all the classics as well as the colourful and witty sayings of the 20th century. The wit and wisdom, pithiness and poetry of over 1300 authors provide a total of over 8000 quotations, all arranged alphabetically by author. The extensive index, a vitally important part of any dictionary of quotations, comprises one third of the book, and features both keywords and the phrases in which they occur.

As a reference work the Dictionary can be used to verify half-remembered quotations, or to give the source of common phrases or sayings whose origin has been forgotten. It can also be used — with the aid of the index — to suggest apposite quotations on particular subjects or simply to provide hours of entertaining browsing.

Donald Fraser is a lecturer in English at the University of Strathclyde. He is also the co-author of *A Dictionary of Musical Quotations*.

'The dictionary is clear and comprehensive.' — *Sunday Times*.

ISBN 0 00 434376 X

COLLINS DICTIONARY OF MILITARY QUOTATIONS

Trevor Royle

There's many a boy here today who looks on war as all glory; but boys, it is all hell — General Sherman.

Retreat, hell! We're just fighting in another direction — Major-General Smith.

The *Collins Dictionary of Military Quotations* is a compilation of over 3500 enthralling quotations on the world of war, from Biblical battles and skirmishes beneath the walls of Troy, to the modern era of long-distance weapons of destruction and the nuclear deterrent.

The quotations cover the whole field of war and its consequences, through the words not only of the great leaders and their campaigns — such as Alexander at the Issus, Wellington at Waterloo, Sitting Bull at the Little Big Horn and Montgomery at Alamein — but also of the common man in arms, whether on sick parade or watching the sky line in trepidation.

The book is divided into four main areas: *Captains and Kings, Battles and Wars, Armies and Soldiers* and *War and Peace*, with a final short section, *Last Post*, describing the tragic aftermath of conflict.

The author, Trevor Royle, is a well-known writer and broadcaster on military history. His other books include a highly praised biography of Lord Kitchener, *The Kitchener Enigma*.

ISBN 0 00 434377 8